CHRONICLE
— OF —
20TH CENTURY
MURDER

TRUE CRIME

CHRONICLE

OF

20TH CENTURY

MURDER

BRIAN LANE

First published in Great Britain in 1993 by
True Crime
an imprint of Virgin Publishing Ltd
332 Ladbroke Grove
London W10 5AH

A catalogue record for this title is available from the British Library

Typeset by Intype, London

Printed and bound in Great Britain by
Butler & Tanner Ltd, Frome, Somerset

Chronological Index

1

Introduction

This book began its existence as an innocent attempt to answer a deceptively simple question. As a crime historian with a weakness for showing off, I have often engaged – wisely or not – in public discussion on the nature of Crime; and in particular its inter-reaction with the society that it feeds off. In other words, the debate as to whether Crime reflects its own time. Like many simple questions, the answer to it is as complex as can be – or, rather, there are several answers: 'No, 'Maybe' and 'Yes'.

Take the 'No' answer first: the proposition that there is nothing, philosophically at least, to distinguish the crime of one age from that of another.

A QUESTION OF MOTIVE

Fundamental to all crime – though in the course of this book we are mainly concerned with homicide – is *motive*. Let nobody tell you there is any such thing as a motiveless murder.

The misconception has arisen because it is customary to classify murder according to the relationship between the killer and the victim – that the victim owned something coveted by the killer, perhaps; or had come into conflict with him; or had proved an unfaithful spouse; and so on. However, with certain types of murder – particularly those categorised as 'serial' murders – the crime is *apparently* random and without purpose. In fact what has happened is that the motive is so deeply locked into the killer's inner psyche that the victim need only be one of a *type* – an elderly woman, a child, a priest . . . The American multicide Joseph Medley, for example, killed only women with red hair; and Ramiro Artieda slew only girls who 'looked like' the fiancée who had jilted him.

Further complications arise when a killer's impaired logic fails to *correctly* identify members of his target group, resulting in a quasi-random selection. Take the case of the Yorkshire Ripper. Although he laid claim to the benevolent motive of clearing the streets of prostitutes, Peter Sutcliffe fell into the error of equating prostitutes with any woman walking along the street alone after dark. Yes, Sutcliffe was a psychotic; yes, he often failed to identify his target correctly. He was nevertheless driven by a powerful *motive* – 'I were just cleaning up streets, our kid. Just cleaning up streets,' he explained to his brother Carl.

It follows that if all murderers have a motive, then there must be a way of categorising those motives; and there is. The remarkable fact is that all murders fall into one or another of only six categories of motive. I should add here that the present author lays no claim to this revelation. It was first proposed in print by that doyenne of true-crime writers, Miss F. Tennyson Jesse, in her *Murder and its Motives* (1924). According to Miss Tennyson Jesse the six classes are Gain, Jealousy, Revenge, Elimination, Lust and Conviction.

It will become evident as readers peruse the entries in this chronology that there are many clear examples of each of these motives – the cynical greed of George Joseph Smith (1914), who courted, married and sometimes murdered his bigamous wives simply in order to Gain their modest possessions; insane Jealousy drove Dr Geza de Kaplany to destroy his wife with acid in 1962, and in 1907 Horace Rayner exacted a terrible Revenge on a father who had denied his existence. For sheer savage Lust there is little to rival the sexual sadism of Neville Heath; except perhaps the cannibalism of Japanese student Issei Sagawa who consumed his victim in what he described as the ultimate act of love. Elimination is one of the most frequently encountered motives – it was why Harry Dobkin used the Blitz of London to dispose of a waspish and grasping ex-wife. As for Conviction, take Denise Labbé, whose ritual sacrifice of her baby seemed worthwhile to seal her love for the dashing, if mad, Lieutenant Jacques Algarron.

But such single-word concepts are at best only a convenience, because many crimes will traverse categories, or be motivated by more than one emotion. An advanced understanding of the criminal mind made possible by the rapid development of psychology has enabled us to embroider this list of motives with silks of richer colours and deeper shades. 'Elimination', for example, may be no more complex or difficult to understand than the removal of an unwanted spouse – after all, that's what turned Crippen into a household name. But at the periphery of Elimination there are some very bizarre crimes indeed. Take the burning alive of James and Marjorie Etherington on St Lucia in 1971. Their killers, a criminous trio named Florius, Faucher and Charles, were convinced that unless they totally destroyed the these two witnesses to their burglary the police would be able to retrieve electronic records of the crime from the thoughts still in their heads.

The world has lost count of its psychopaths and psychotics, those madmen throughout history who have slaughtered with no discernible reason – no gain, no lust; cold, calculating killers. Killers like the fanatical Nazi sympathiser Joseph Franklin who shot dead mixed-race couples; like Harvey Carignan who was acting as an 'instrument of God', killing to rid the world of sin, and Herbert Mullin, whose 'voices' told him that only through bloodshed could he avert a cataclysmic earthquake which would destroy California.

But all these 'visionaries', these 'missionaries' who accept a self-imposed responsibility for improving the quality of life and ridding society of its 'undesirable' elements, have one, basic, all-encompassing *motive* – that of Conviction. A deep and abiding belief in their own rightness that transcends socially acceptable behaviour and even the law.

I would like to propose just one small change to the existing sextet of universal motives and add a seventh. As the result of a need to discover some means of combating the seemingly unrestrained escalation of serial murder – particularly in the United States – criminologists and forensic psychiatrists have been exploring methods of identifying individuals who may be predisposed to deviant behaviour. One section of this programme has been concerned with compiling lists of behaviour patterns common to known serial killers, another part with categorising their specific motivations. Although the vast majority fit comfortably into the traditional six (with Lust being predominant), a small minority exhibit a newly identified motive. Labelled Thrill killers, they display many of the characteristics of Lust killers, but what distinguishes thrill killing is that although sexual abuse *may* take place, the motive is not sexual gratification but the desire for an experience, or 'thrill'. Quite simply, the *act* of killing is its own reward.

This is a useful addition, because it also helps to absorb those rare murders which prove to be the exceptions to the 'rule of six' – cases such as Frederick Field, who strangled prostitute Beatrice Sutton because, he claimed, he was 'browned off'. He later confessed that he had also been browned off a couple of years earlier when he murdered Norah Upchurch.

And so, to return to the original question armed with our seven motives, it can be seen that the *roots* of murder have remained unchanged throughout times, culture and geography, from the 'first' murder by Cain of his brother Abel (a classic case of Jealousy) to, say, the depredations of Jeffrey Dahmer, the serial cannibal whose killing pattern was determined by sexual lust. Thus, in one sense – that of the persistence of motive – crimes are not a product of their time so much as a result of unchangeable aspects of human nature.

MAKING THE WORLD A SMALLER PLACE

Despite the clear truth of the 'No' answer in purely academic terms, it tends to lack colour and fails to take account of seminal events and discoveries in human history which have inevitably imposed themselves on the progress and pattern of crime, law and law enforcement.

This is the area in which we find the 'Maybe' answer, because there is no denying that the development of stable agricultural societies out of small nomadic hunting groups led to the acquisition of land and possessions which might prove attractive to less scrupulous and less hard-working neighbours.

And with the increased vulnerability the first 'policeman' would have been mobilised – members of the group who would take turns as watchmen to fend off or warn of the approach of danger. Means also became established by custom of dealing with crimes and indiscretions committed *within* the group or tribe, with the effect of rationalising the relationship between crime and punishment. The system of English law (and that adopted by other parts of the world which fell under English colonisation, including America) derived from Anglo-Saxon tribal customs which, with some systematisation in 1250, still provide the basis for the Common Law. It might be added that as the result of the spread of the Holy Roman Empire, and in particular the Church of Rome, Continental Europe and many French and Dutch colonies adopted the system of Roman law formalised under the Emperor Justinian.

Another far-reaching influence on the pattern of international crime was the availability of firearms made general by the American gun manufacturer Samuel Colt with the introduction of a range of revolvers, from the 'Walker' in 1847 to the ironically named 'Peacemaker' around 1873 (and still in production today). Lethal, accurate over far greater distances than any previous weapons, guns enabled killings to be carried out with less chance of observation. Guns also introduced the possibility of multiple killing – after all, a spear could kill only one person at a time, a Colt 'equaliser' six!

The use of gaslight to illuminate city streets was introduced to Britain in the early decades of the nineteenth century, with a consequent reduction in the activities of footpads, who until then had infested every dark corner like vermin. The organisation of a regular police force resulted, if not in fewer crimes, then at least in a greater likelihood of a felon being brought to book – or in most cases brought to the gallows. In England the task of thief-taking had been in the hands of what scant team of watchmen could be mustered by the parish – and a rag-bag lot they generally were; senile, simple, or downright criminous, the watchmen were often little better than the villains they were paid to catch. The legendary Bow Street Runners were formed by magistrate and novelist Henry Fielding in 1749, and they gave way to the permanent police force established by Robert Peel's government – in 1829 in London, and throughout the country by 1956. In the United States the first state police force – the Texas Rangers – came into being in 1835, though it was not until 1907 that a proposal was adopted for a detective agency with federal powers; in July of the following year the Federal Bureau of Investigation was founded.

Latterly, the advent of mass communication such as the telegraph and telephone, and rapid transport by railway and motor car added their own spicing to the melting pot of society's crime and crime detection.

What is most notable is an overview of criminal history, then, is that while minor changes in the *method* of committing acts of homicide have resulted from scientific and technological developments – the gun, for example, or modern poisons – the crimes themselves remain a fairly stable result of *motive*. To give emphasis to this, it is tempting to think of such activities as terrorism and political assassination as 'modern' murders; however, the briefest glimpse back through political history reveals more than a sprinkling of disposable diplomats – and poor Julius Caesar was no less a victim of political intrigue than President John F. Kennedy. Of course murder aboard railway trains was impossible before the invention of the steam engine – but in *essence* it was no different from murder on horse-drawn coaches. Where the greatest changes have resulted from the development of society over the centuries is in the *detection* of crime and in the treatment of offenders. The law-enforcement agencies now have an unprecedented range of sophisticated scientific wizardry to add to their arsenal of weapons against the criminal; and if the crook has increased his mobility with motor vehicles, then the police are increasingly taking to the air in helicopters. As police forces internationally are making the criminal's world a smaller place, powerful computers are brought in to manipulate information with a speed and accuracy never dreamed of when Scotland Yard formed its first Murder Squad in 1907.

However, this is the point at which the debate either stops – with the possibility that broad changes in the pattern of crime *may* have resulted from social progress – or moves on to a consideration of the 'Yes' answer.

MURDER IN THE TWENTIETH CENTURY

Colin Wilson, in his estimable work *Casebook of Crime*, suggests that 'murder has not really come into its own until the twentieth century. Our age could be called the age of murder . . .' A study of Crime, and particularly the crime of homicide, reveals that as at no time before, murder in this present century has become immensely varied, and murderers increasingly idiosyncratic. We begin to see the question 'Does Crime reflect the society in which it occurs?' in a different light. In the twentieth century at least, the answer is 'yes'.

Although certain tentative steps had already been taken in the scientific detection of crime during earlier centuries, the period from the last decade of Queen Victoria's reign to the present has seen a previously unimaginable escalation in the fight against serious crime – from the test to distinguish human from other animal blood discovered by the German biologist Paul Uhlenhuth in 1900, to the development by Professor Alec Jeffreys in England of digitalised DNA profiling in the early 1990s. New techniques of scientific analysis were enabling the law-enforcement agencies throughout the world to fully exploit a vital principle first propounded by Edmond Locard of the University of Lyon in 1910. The theory states simply that a criminal will always carry away with him some trace from the scene of his crime, and leave some trace of his presence behind. This has become the very foundation of forensic science. The practicalities of policing

were also being addressed – the bobby's bike was being supplemented by motor vehicles for fast response to crimes by detectives alerted via the newly invented wireless.

Society was changing rapidly as well, and attitudes towards sex, marriage and family were gradually throwing off the heavy cloak of a Victorian morality characterised by an appalling double standard which at one and the same time ostracised a woman for being divorced, but supported a huge trade in child prostitution. I often reflect on whether Crippen, if he had been able to take advantage of our enlightened view of relationships and accessible divorce laws, would ever have felt the need to poison poor Cora.

Another feature of homicide in the twentieth century has been the growing number of 'celebrity' murders. It is true, of course, that every age has had its famous cases – in 1551 Alice Arden with her crew of preposterous accomplices, Mosebie, Shagbag and Black Will, entered history with their bungling murder of Alice's husband Thomas Arden of Faversham. The murder of magistrate Sir Edmundberry Godfrey in 1678 was one bloody scene in the whole sordid drama of the so-called Popish Plot, and shook English politics as few crimes had done before or since. In 1725 a squalid vicious highwayman named Richard Turpin was hanged at York and entered the fabled world of the 'loveable rogue', sanitised for nursery fare and assured of immortality. The nineteenth century had more than its share of notable villains – Lizzie Borden, the parricide, and H. H. Holmes, the torture doctor, in the New World; Hélène Jegado, the mass poisoner, in France; and Gesina Gottfried, killer of at least thirty people, in Germany. And of our own, home-grown fiends, who but the enigmatic Jack the Ripper, most famous murderer in the world, could represent the darkest corners of British criminal history?

But for all that, the chronicler of the eighteenth, or even the nineteenth centuries would be hard put to find a truly notorious case for every decade, let alone every year. As for the twentieth century, the task of selection has at times been overwhelming, so great is the available material; and so the journey through the century's zoo of human monsters which lies ahead is an essentially subjective choice.

Frequently the relevance of cases will be that they do act as a mirror to the times, but the escalation of crime and its detection in the twentieth century has also been punctuated by what crime writers like to call 'classics' and criminologists refer to as 'landmarks'. Whichever title we choose to use, these are the cases that have endured not necessarily because they are of scientific, legal or social importance but because, often unaccountably, they have entered popular mythology – crimes such as those of Harry Thaw and Bonnie and Clyde, Dennis Nilsen, and mad Charlie Manson.

THE FIRST DECADE (1900–1910)

Although the end of Victoria's reign coincided conveniently with the turn of the nineteenth century (the Empress died in January 1901), the legacy of her reign persisted well into the first decade of the twentieth, and it is difficult not to associate the crime of, say, Dr Crippen with the earlier 'gaslight' period typified by those other poisonous medics Drs Palmer, Pritchard, Smethurst, Lamson and Neill Cream. I am often asked why members of the medical profession who turn to murder choose poison. The answer is simple. They, of all people, have a perfectly legitimate reason to keep cupboards full of toxic substances; and besides, they have the knowledge of how to use poisons and make the death appear to be from natural causes – heaven knows how many certificated deaths from 'gastro-enteritis' were in reality arsenic poisonings. Indeed, arsenic has become synonymous with the great poisoning cases of the gaslight age – in Britain Herbert Rowse Armstrong, Frederick Seddon and Madeleine Smith; Amy Archer-Gilligan and Johann Hoch in America; Daisy de Melker in South Africa and Hélène Jegado in France – plus the thousand and one less celebrated assassins. The fact is, it was difficult to *avoid* buying arsenic – it was an active ingredient in a vast range of products from cosmetics to sheep-dip, including the number of medicines! It is therefore no great surprise to find arsenic poisoning remaining a popular means of disposal throughout Victor-

ia's reign and beyond into the 1920s and 1930s – a steady flow of shadowy figures emerging from the dark annals of murder, the rat-poison, weed-killer and fly-papers in their hands.

But if the killers were up to their old tricks during this decade, the police were learning new ones. In two important cases – Albert T. Patrick in the USA and Samuel Herbert Dougal in England – analysis of forged documents led to the arrest and conviction of two vicious and greedy murderers. England saw the setting-up of Scotland Yard's Fingerprint Branch in 1901, and by 1904 its head, Detective Inspector Stockly Collins, announced that its records already exceeded 70,000 sets. Shortly afterwards a British court accepted fingerprint evidence for the first time in a murder case. However, as if to caution against too great a display of complacency, the High Court of Justiciary in Edinburgh wrongly imprisoned Oscar Slater for eighteen years for a murder he did not commit.

If the domestic killers were out in their customary strength, then the political assassins were hyperactive; indeed, it could almost have been called the 'Decade of the Assassin'. On 4 April 1900, the Prince of Wales escaped uninjured when a teenage anarchist shot at him as he sat in a railway carriage at Brussels station; the murder attempt was a protest at the war in South Africa. Less than four months later, the much-loved king of Italy, Umberto I, was shot dead by Angelo Bresci; he died instantly as three bullets pierced his heart. On 6 November 1900 Republican William McKinley was re-elected President of the United States amid national jubilation; on 14 September the following year, less than twelve months into his new term of office, McKinley was felled by an assassin's bullet. His last words, 'Nearer my God to thee', marked the death by assassination of the third, but not the last President of the United States. By 1903 it seemed the whole world had gone assassination mad. In the early hours of 11 June King Alexander and Queen Draga of Serbia were sleeping in the Royal Palace at Belgrade when a band of disaffected army officers forced their way in, first shooting down the King's bodyguards, and then murdering the royal couple in their bed. Grand

Duke Sergei, an uncle of Tsar Nicholas II, was sitting in his carriage as it passed through the gates of the Kremlin on 17 February 1905 when a bomb packed with nails was thrown on to his lap; the explosion was so powerful that it tore the Duke's body into unrecognisable tatters of flesh and pulverised bone. The murder was clearly connected with the dreadful events of Bloody Sunday, three weeks earlier, when the Tsar's troops opened fire on strikers in St Petersburg, massacring more than five hundred. Less successful was the would-be bomber who threw a bouquet of flowers into the carriage of the newly married King Alfonso of Spain and his bride Queen Victoria. The bomb went off under the horses killing eighteen people; the king was miraculously saved when his chestful of medals deflected a piece of shrapnel. To close the decade, on 26 October 1909, Japan lost its senior statesman to an assassin's gun. Sixty-eight-year-old Prince Ho was shot in a revenge attack by a Korean nationalist in retaliation for Japan's repression of the Korean insurgents. Soon this international political unrest would find its outlet in one of the bloodiest and most futile conflicts the world had ever witnessed.

INTO THE GREAT WAR (1911–1920)

The years leading up to the First World War saw Britain's troops being given unexpected target practice talking pot shots at civilians. The first occasion was at the notorious Siege of Sidney Street in 1911. The battle began around 4 p.m. when gun-toting policemen arrived at a house in Sidney Street, just off the Mile End Road in London's East End, searching for a group of anarchists who had already been involved in an armed fracas with the police during which three officers had been killed. Here, outside No. 100, detectives came under such heavy fire that troops were called in as reinforcements, bringing with them a Maxim gun and two thirteen pounders – all under the watchful eye of Mr Winston Churchill, then Home Secretary. The siege raged throughout the morning claiming several minor casualities among the soldiers and constabulary, and among the huge crowds which had gathered

from miles around, treating the whole incident as a sort or side-show. Suddenly, just before 1 p.m., smoke was seen billowing from the chimney of 100 Sidney Street. Although the fire brigade stood in readiness, Churchill refused to allow the blaze to be brought under control, and within the hour the building was gutted. When the house was cool enough to enter, police officers found the charred bodies of two men; however, despite the heavy gunfire, at least one of the anarchists, 'Peter the Painter', managed to escape.

Troops of the Worcester Regiment got their chance during rioting that accompanied the rail-strike at Llanelli, South Wales. On the night of 20 July 1911, they confronted a stone-throwing mob who were attempting to sieze a locomotive. As soldiers advanced with fixed bayonets, the rioters began burning and looting shops. Troops opened fire and killed three men, seriously wounding a fourth. By August the strike was nationwide, bringing much of the country to a standstill, forcing the government, through Winston Churchill, to augment the already stretched resources of the police forces with 50,000 troops.

On 28 June 1914, Europe witnessed another political assassination, one that would have deadly repercussions throughout the world. As Archduke Franz Ferdinand, heir to the Austro-Hungarian throne, drove in his open-top car through the Bosnian capital of Sarajevo, a nineteen-year-old student leapt out from the crowd lining the road and shot dead the Archduke and his wife. The incident provoked such feelings of outrage in Austria that anti-Serbian demonstrations erupted spontaneously, and the Austrian government broke off diplomatic relations with Serbia. In a move that would soon embroil the whole of the continent of Europe in a pointless and unjust war, Austria declared war on the Serbs on 28 July 1914. Between then and the Allied defeat of Germany in November 1918, more than ten million people would die.

But while the war was having its effect on a global scale, it was also influencing domestic crime – for a start, thousands of guns had gone into circulation, many of which were never handed back when hostilities were over. But it was in Germany where, in the wake of defeat, famine was stalking the nation, that the crooks swept in like vultures to put the already dispossessed into the grip of the 'black market'. At least two ruthless killers, Georg Grosz and Fritz Haarmann, the 'Butcher of Hanover', murdered scores of hapless victims in order to supply the black market with fresh meat.

THE JAZZ AGE (1920–1938)

The end of the bleak period of the 'War to End Wars' brought with it a new spirit of optimism – though to be truthful this was most apparent in the United States which had suffered few of the ravages of the recent conflict. But still, somehow, there was feeling of vitality. The 1920s heralded the rise of Hollywood and the cult of the movie star. Women fainted at Rudolph Valentino's *Sheikh*, they laughed and cried at Chaplin's first full-length feature *The Kid*, and they booed the once-adored 'Fatty' Archbuckle after a doubtful accusation of manslaughter. Jazz swept across the nation, exciting the young, infuriating the old, and forcing American church leaders to condemn the music as 'a return to the jungle'. In 1925 Britain imported the Charleston – 'the dance mothers detest' – as the jazz age spread to Europe. Radio was entering the home as a form of popular entertainment on both sides of the Atlantic, and in 1926 John Logie Baird proved the possibility of television. Affordable family motor cars were pouring off the production lines, and air travel, formerly reserved for those waging war, was being put to civilian use for both business and pleasure. The world was becoming smaller.

But if the land of the free had jazz and the movies, it also had Prohibition, and as a result would soon have Al Capone and a thousand and one other greedy hoodlums muscling in on the illegal booze market, laying the foundation stones of an empire of organised crime that has not been defeated to this day.

Not that Britain was enjoying an entirely trouble-free peace. It seemed that no sooner had the European conflict ended than problems in Ireland connected with partition necessitated the dispatch of nearly a thousand special constables – the notorious 'Black and Tans', so-called because of their uniforms – to help put down the disturbances. These officers were followed by troops when rioting erupted in Londonderry, and Ireland has not known peace and political stability since. At home, 1926 witnessed the first general strike in British history.

On the law-and-order front, however, new technology was being pressed into use in the fight against crime. Criminals had already taken advantage of the motor car to effect quick getaways and to operate further from home. In 1920 the Metropolitan Police also went mobile with the purchase of two vans; from these humble beginnings the celebrated Flying Squad would develop. In 1922 radio was fitted into the growing fleet of cars, and telephones were in increasing use for the transfer of information. In 1925 American ballistics experts Philip Gravelle and Charles White developed the single most important piece of apparatus in analytical ballistics, the comparison microscope, which made it possible to view two objects simultaneously. This facilitated the comparison not only of bullets and cartridges, but of any forensic traces such as hairs, fibres, glass and paint fragments, and revolutionised the forensic laboratory. Four years later, fellow expert Calvin Goddard was able to identify the guns used in the St Valentine's Day Massacre by this means.

The next decade would see further advances in the areas of police use of the public radio waves, and in 1933 Stanley Eric Hobday became the first killer to be apprehended as the result of a radio 'wanted' announcement. Hobday had fled the scene of a brutal killing committed during the course of a burglary in West Bromwich; he was identified when fingerprints left at the scene matched those on his criminal record, and a description was broadcast over the BBC radio network. Watty Bowman, a cowherd and the proud owner of a wireless set, recognised the description of the fugitive Hobday as a man he passed in a country lane and alerted the police.

The 1930s also witnessed the worst economic depression the industrialised world had known. In Britain the unemployed mobilised themselves into hunger marches, frequently clashing with the police in bloody battles which left casualities on both sides. Despite the best efforts of President Roosevelt to provide aid for the growing numbers of American poor and unemployed, the United States, too, slipped into depression. Even the lifting of Prohibition at the end of 1933 failed to raise the nation's spirits more than momentarily – and it certainly did nothing to suppress the gangsters who had risen to power on bootleg liquor, and now turned instead to drugs, prostitition and illegal gambling. In 1934 bank robber and murderer John Dillinger was elected Public Enemy Number One by the FBI, and in May of the same year the careers of Bonnie Parker and Clyde Barrow ended in a hail of Texas Rangers' bullets. On 22 July Dillinger as also shot down where he stood, outside a Chicago cinema.

THE WAR YEARS (1939–1950)

By 1935 the storm that was about to break over Europe for the second time in a quarter-century was gathering over Germany. Adolf Hitler had taken over as Chancellor of the German Reich in January 1933. Two months later Josef Goebbels, as Minister of Public Enlightenment, was denouncing the 'Jewish vampires', and in May the Nazis began their programme of publicly burning books considered to be anti-German. Now Jews were forbidden to marry Germans and were barred from public office. In 1937 Hitler was joined by the Italian fascist leader Benito Mussolini in a show of strength at a massive floodlit rally in Berlin, and having worked their way through the world's literature, the Nazis next began to destroy 'un-German' art – the 'decadent by-product of Bolshevik Jewish corruption'. Soon they would be destroying non-German people too. The German Army marched into Czechoslovakia in October 1938; three months later the British Home Office began to deliver air-raid shelters to private homes throughout London. Following France and Britain's official declaration of war on 3 September 1939, the Nazis invaded Poland. Once more the world was in the grip of a destructive war from which no winners would emerge – only greater or lesser losers.

The Second World War can be blamed for many things, but it cannot be said that it created any great escalation in civilian violence.

In fact the reverse was generally true – the old principle of comradeship in adversity counteracting the frustrations of wartime privation. For those impressed by statistics the British murder rates for the period were: 1939, 135; 1940, 115; 1941, 135; 1942, 159; 1943, 120; 1944, 95; 1945, 141. In fact with few exceptions, the same old murders were being committed for the same old motives – the only difference being that some of the killers wore uniform.

Of course the war did help in some ways – Harry Dobkin, for example, when he decided to dispose of his wife in 1946, hid her body in the bombed-out crypt of a London church, hoping that her remains, if discovered, would be taken for just another victim of the Luftwaffe. In fact bomb-damaged buildings became the last resting places of several wartime murder victims. The darkness imposed by the blackout may have been used to advantage by a number of murderers; it certainly made crime easy for Gordon Cummins, 'The Wartime Jack the Ripper'.

The war also brought the people of Britain into contact with the visiting US forces. Some of them, like the Walter Mitty GI Karl Hulten, did little for international relations. Hulten, with English-born Betty Jones, acted out their own Bonnie and Clyde fantasy on the streets of London. In France the war helped Dr Marcel Petiot to explain away the pile of dismembered corpses in his basement – Nazi collaborators, he told the men from the Sureté, assassinated by the Resistance fighters and entrusted to Petiot to dispose of. However preposterous the story sounds, at the time the good doctor escaped with a pat on the back!

By August 1945 the war was over; once again humankind was the only loser. But this time a horror more wicked even than the 55 million slain in the theatres of war; a new and terrible weapon, capable of unimaginable destruction, had been loosed on the world. We had just entered the age of the atom bomb.

THE ROCK 'N' ROLL YEARS (1951–1960)

Despite the Shadow of the Bomb, and the continuation of post-war rationing, the world was beginning to look forward to the future with optimism; after all, perhaps *this* had been the War to End Wars!

Technology developed as part of the struggle for military supremacy began to make itself useful in the civilian field. And nowhere was this more instantly apparent than in the manufacture of passenger aircraft. In July 1949, almost before the last echo of the last gun had died away, the De Havilland company flew their new Comet, the world's first jet airliner. Inside months, the largest passenger plane ever built took to the skies – the Bristol Brabazon weighed in at 130 tons, and could carry 100 passengers. 1949 was also the year Albert Guay planned to commit the perfect murder by planting a bomb on the Quebec Airways DC-3 on which his wife was travelling.

England was following the United States in the growing demand for consumer goods, and television was creeping into more and more of the nation's living-rooms. The police were not slow to exploit the immediacy of the medium in seeking assistance with tracking down suspects.

The first attempt was made during the search for William Pettit after his murder of Mrs Rene Brown at Chislehurst in Kent in October 1953; however, the estimated eight million viewers could offer the police no clues, and Pettit's decomposed body was subsequently discovered in a blitzed London building.

But above all the 1950s would be remembered as the Rock 'n' Roll Years – the age of the Juvenile Delinquent, the Teddy Boy; the decade teenagers were invented. In America a generation was being fed rebellion from a succession of films such as *Blackboard Jungle* and *Rock Around the Clock*, and was aping the sullen aggression of James Dean's *Rebel Without a Cause* and the leather-clad Marlon Brando. In Britain the 'youth problem' became epitomised by the tragedy of two young thieves named Craig and Bentley who got caught up in murder in 1953 and fuelled the already controversial debate on capital punishment. Apart from other considerations, the case forced the then Home Secretary to strengthen the laws on ownership of firearms, and to attempt to retrieve the thousands of weapons kept as 'sou-

venirs' after the end of World War II.

Guns were also beginning to play a part in the activities of London's underworld. As if nothing had been learned from Chicago and the 1930s, this became the age of the gangster London-style, with an escalation of violent gangland activity surrounding the Kray twins in East London and the Richardsons south of the Thames. It was in this climate of increasing aggression that Ruth Ellis gunned down her faithless lover on a North London street. Although she would almost certainly have been able to plead diminished responsibility in today's courts, Ruth was convicted of murder and, on 13 July 1955, became the last woman to be hanged in Britain.

It was increasingly clear that a kind of lawlessness was here to stay as the 1950s made was for the 1960s and 70s.

THE AGE OF VIOLENCE (1961–1970)

As a decade, the 1960s was a period characterised by opposites. Youth had grown confident enough to recognise its own collective strength, and nowhere was this more apparent than in America. While half that nation's youth seemed content with the power of flowers, others were engaged in using power of a very different kind in Vietnam, producing a generation of young men returning from a pointless and seemingly endless conflict, already battle-weary 'veterans' at the age of 22. Ironically members of both these extremes fell prey to a drug culture that was to spread its evil and suffering over the following thirty years – the hippies to 'expand' their minds, the vets to deaden their minds to the horrors of war. In China the Red Guards engaged in a rampage of violent fundamentalism; in Paris students and workers engaged in bloody street clashes with security police; the British Army moved in to police Northern Ireland. And everywhere, it seemed there were race riots. 'Love and Peace' may have been the benign battle colours that welcomed the dawn of the Age of Aquarius, but it was rapidly developing into the Age of Violence. A new kind of madness seemed to strike: the assassination of another American President on the open street, and the assassination of his

13

assassin, followed shortly by the senseless murder of the black peacemaker Dr Martin Luther King and, unbelievably, just two months later, the gunning down of the late President's brother. In Britain at least, it seemed that sanity was prevailing when an Act of Parliament abolished capital punishment for murder. Less than nine months later the retentionist lobby's worst fears seemed to have been realised – three policemen were shot dead on the streets of London by a gang of petty crooks. The criminals were arming themselves for their own war; and they were prepared to kill. In the Age of Violence the gun became the equaliser for the forces of disorder.

EMERGENCE OF THE SERIAL KILLER (1970–1979)

It is quite obvious that what we call 'serial' murder was not 'invented' in the 1970s – indeed, the stereotype sado-sexual serial killer was Jack the Ripper whose reign of terror took place in the autumn of 1888. However, what did emerge in the United States in the 1970s was the *identification* of this new and increasingly prevalent *type* of murderer: one who kills randomly and without apparent motive. An awareness of the need to make some positive effort to analyse and combat this baffling phenomenon coincided with the establishment in the early 1970s of the FBI's National Academy at Quantico, where senior instructors founded what was called   the Behavioral Science Unit. In response to the virtual impossibility of applying the time-honoured techniques of homicide investigation to some of the cases before them, FBI agents began work on a system of 'psychological profiling' which would use the disciplines of the behavioural scientist, the psychologist, and the psychiatrist to help analyse evidence, both tangible and intuitive, collected by officers at the scene of the crime. The profile is built by the careful analysis of elements such as victim traits, witness reports and the method and location of the killings. The profile attempts to indicate physical and psychological characteristics resulting in a 'portrait' of the suspect and his

behaviour patterns. For obvious reasons a considerable element of intuitive guesswork is involved, and no law-enforcement officer would dismiss a suspect from his investigation simply because he did not fit the profile. However, profiling has proved increasingly accurate in narrowing the field of inquiry.

THE SLAUGHTER CONTINUES (1980–1992)

The violence did not go away; it never does. The predominance of multicide which had begun with such household names as 'Son of Sam', Ted Bundy and the 'Boston Strangler' during the last half of the 1970s, escalated to epidemic proportions in the following decade. One study published in 1991 listed upwards of 50 serial killers active during the 1980s in the United States alone. In 1990 an 'unofficial' estimate suggested that in America as many as 5,000 people a year could be the victims of serial killers. In Britain the pattern was being repeated. In 1980 Peter Sutcliffe was arrested after a reign of terror lasting five years during which, as the 'Yorkshire Ripper', he had murdered thirteen women. Three years later Dennis Nilsen confessed to killing 'fifteen or sixteen' young men in London. Michael Ryan went on a shooting spree in the small English town of Hungerford in 1987, leaving fourteen people dead before turning the gun on himself; and at the University of Montreal, Marc Lepine cut down fourteen women in a hail of gunfire because he 'hated feminists'.

But at least in the 1980s Britain was able to lead the world in a revolutionary new scientific technique that could make the positive identification of criminals accurate beyond dispute: DNA profiling. It was in 1986 that 'genetic fingerprinting' was successful for the first time in convicting a savage double killer.

As for the 1990s, it is too early to tell. Certainly the curse of the serial killer persists, with seemingly ever greater excesses – like the cannibalism of America's Jeffrey Dahmer and Russia's Andrei Chikatilo. Patterns of crime can only be assessed in retrospect. One thing is certain: homicide statistics always rise . . .

Herbert John Bennett

Murder on Yarmouth Sands. *A case which pivoted on the identification of a gold chain in a beach photographer's snapshot. Bennett was held in such contempt in Norwich that the rarely invoked Palmer Act was used to have the trial moved to the Old Bailey.*

Herbert John Bennett married Mary Jane Clark in the register office at West Ham, London, on 22 July 1897; at the time they met Bennett was seventeen and Mary twenty years of age. Mrs Bennett had been a music teacher; Mr Bennett earned his living as a petty thief and con-man. It was not long before Mary Bennett joined her husband in the twilight zone on the edges of the criminal world. For a while they combined her musical knowledge with his unscrupulous sales tactics and sold matchwood violins as genuine antiques. Mary learned the trade quickly and was soon making good sales of her own; her most enduring role was that of a young widow obliged by strained circumstances to part with her late husband's cherished instrument. Later, Mrs Bennett felt confident enough to set up some profitable scams of her own, including, it is thought, a touch of blackmail.

In 1900 things began to go to the bad for the Bennetts. Herbert John had bought a grocer's shop, insured it, then burned it down and moved the family to lodgings in Plumstead,

south London. Whether it was Bennett's ambition, Mary's criminal independence, both, or neither we cannot know, but a rift was widening between the couple that took on most sinister undertones. Their landlady at Plumstead, Mrs Elliston, later recalled for the benefit of an Old Bailey jury a particularly fierce row in which Mrs Bennett had warned her husband: 'Herbert, I will follow you for the sake of the baby, but if you are not careful I can get you fifteen years.' To which Herbert threatened: 'I wish you were dead; and if *you* are not careful you soon will be.' Things had clearly come to a pretty pass.

It was around this time that Herbert Bennett transferred his affections to a young parlour maid named Alice Meadows. Bennett forgot to tell Miss Meadows that he was already married, and that he had a child; it is also likely that he forgot to tell his new friend about his lowly paid job at the neighbouring Woolwich Arsenal – preferring to maintain the mystique of the street-wise man-about-town. It obviously worked, because on 28 August 1900 Bennett proposed marriage, was accepted, the wedding was set for the following June, and the couple took a week's holiday to celebrate. But what of Mary Bennett?

Mrs Bennett was at this time living apart from Herbert, with her child, at an address in Glencoe Villas, Bexleyheath, Kent. On 14 September Bennett paid a visit to his wife in order to make what he described as a peace offering – he would send her to the seaside on a short vacation, and if possible would follow on later himself. Mary accepted, and on the following day journeyed by train to Yarmouth where, for reasons best known to herself (though in retrospect probably at Bennett's insistence) she adopted a false name and identity. At around

Herbert John Bennett
Mrs Mary Bennett

9 p.m. on 15 September 'Mrs Hood' and baby 'Rose' took a room at Mrs Rudrum's guest house in The Rows – an address given to his wife by Bennett. 'Mrs Hood' explained that she was a widow based in York, and that she had been accompanied to Yarmouth by her brother-in-law. Never one to sell a story short, Mary added that the gentleman concerned was hopelessly in love with her and passionately jealous. This at least might explain away in advance why the merry widow was frequently out till all hours drinking with a man friend.

Meanwhile, back in London, Bennett was inventing relatives of his own: to be precise, a grandfather in Gravesend who was critically ill. At least that is what he told Alice Meadows when he excused himself for leaving her for a few days, and on the morning of 22 September left his digs at Woolwich and took a train. It was not the service to Gravesend.

Further north, on the South Beach at Yarmouth at eleven o'clock at night, a young courting couple, Alfred Mason and Blanche Smith, were snuggled into a hollow doing who knows what. Looking up briefly they saw the silhouettes of another couple against the sky, just some twenty yards from them. Alfred and Blanche thought no more of it until their own reveries were interrupted by a woman's cry – 'Mercy . . . mercy!' – followed by a deep groan, and then silence. Alfred Mason took Blanche's hand and together they wandered back across the lonely beach, making a deliberate detour to where they had seen the other couple; as they passed they could just see through the darkness the figure of a woman lying on the sand and a man crouched over her. It is not difficult to imagine what our young couple thought was going on, and they retreated in discreet silence.

While this apparently everyday activity was going on at Yarmouth beach, an equally prosaic event was taking place in town, at the Crown and Anchor Hotel. At 11.45 p.m. a man walked into the lobby and booked a room for the night – he had, so he said, just missed the last train to Gorleston. Early next morning the man left.

Shortly afterwards the body of a woman was found on the beach – she had been sexually assaulted and a bootlace tied so tightly round her throat that it had embedded itself in the flesh.

Then Mrs Rudrum at The Rows was disturbed by the crying of a baby – Mrs Hood's baby. What's more, Mrs Hood's bed had not been slept in. The landlady told the police, of course, but what good was a false name? So the corpse remained anonymous for the next six weeks, until the enquiry wound its inexorable way down to Kingdom's Laundry of Bexleyheath where, on 2 November, a small laundry mark – just '599', the only means of identification left on the body – was traced to Mary Jane Bennett of Glencoe Villas.

On the sound principle that in cases of murder, particularly of a woman, look first for the husband or lover, on 4 November the police took Herbert Bennett into custody and made a search of his lodgings. Here officers found two wigs – a man's and a woman's – a false moustache, and a gold chain. It was the chain which was, metaphorically, to hang Herbert Bennett.

The trial of Herbert John Bennett opened at the Old Bailey in London on 24 February 1901. It should not have done so of course: trials were customarily heard at the assize court which sat in the locality in which the crime was committed – in Bennett's case, the Norwich Assizes. However, there is a provision in law (called the Palmer Act, after another notorious murderer) where, if it is felt that local prejudice precludes an unbiased trial, proceedings can be transferred to the Central Criminal Court. Local feeling against Bennett could not have been much worse.

The judge was Lord Justice Alverstone, recently appointed Lord Chief Justice of England. But Bennett also could also take some comfort in that one of the greatest criminal advocates of the day was on his side – the almost legendary Edward Marshall Hall KC. But even he, contrary to popular belief of the time, could not work miracles.

It was the prosecution's evidence of the chain that Marshall Hall found it most difficult to find a way round. A number of witnesses had already given statements that the gold chain found in Bennett's possession had been the one worn by Mary when she was staying in Yar-

mouth; the defence could find no evidence to the contrary. While she was in Yarmouth Mrs Bennett had a seaside snap taken of herself and her baby sitting on the beach; it is just possible to spot a gold chain around Mary's neck. Although the tiny tintype proved interesting, it was not in practice much use at all. The question was whether the chain was the same as that offered in evidence, the one found in Herbert Bennett's portmanteau in Woolwich, a simple *link* chain.

No, said Mr Marshall Hall, the chain shown in the photograph was of a pattern called a *rope* chain – 'of the Prince of Wales pattern'. It was a good try: a gallant effort by a great defender. But it amounted to nothing. Photographic enlargements of this celebrated picture were so blurred that the design of the chain could have been either or neither. However, Marshall Hall did, as was his style, cause at least one sensation when, on the fifth day of the trial, he suddenly produced a surprise witness.

Mr Douglas Sholto Douglas was a fancy-goods manufacturer who, on the evening of 22 September (when Mrs Bennett was murdered), encountered a man at Lee Green in south London. He had not known the man, nor had he particularly wanted his company, but the fellow was persistent and they fell into conversation. As they walked along the high street, Douglas's companion suddenly pointed up at the sign above a barber's shop which read 'F. K. Bennett'. 'It would seem a namesake of mine lives here,' the man announced. Though a porter at Yarmouth's Crown and Anchor Hotel had already identified Bennett as the man who booked a room on the night of the murder, from the witness stand Mr Douglas Douglas

The enigmatic Mr Douglas Sholto Douglas

17

unhesitatingly pointed his finger at Bennett and identified him as the man in Lee. All highly dramatic and calculated to bring total hush over the court.

There was just one drawback to all this: Herbert Bennett had not pleaded alibi as his defence. For the alibi to stand it would have required putting Bennett on to the witness stand to explain under cross-examination by Mr Charles Gill KC, leading for the Crown, exactly what he was up to in Lee on 22 September; and Marshall Hall knew that his client could not stand up to that. And so it was left.

From the Bench, Mr Justice Alverstone had clearly seen through Bennett, and although his Lordship was a model of impartiality in his final charge to the jury, some old hands at court-watching might have said that he summed up 'against' the prisoner. The jury required little longer than a half hour to convict Herbert Bennett. From beneath the black cap, Lord Alverstone read out the sentence with a quaver in his voice which betrayed this deeply humanitarian judge's evident distress at passing sentence of death on any man. As for Bennett, he did not seem too worried or, if he was, he certainly didn't show it. He displayed the same fortitude on the morning of 21 March 1901, when he was hanged from the scaffold at Norwich Gaol.

There is one curious postscript added here for the benefit of the superstitious. It was customary in former days to fly a black flag above the prison gate after an execution. As the flag was run up after Bennett was dispatched a strong gust of wind caused the flagpole to break and the flag to fall. Was it, as some have claimed, a divine sign that Bennett was innocent?

It seems unlikely.

The Love of Money . . .

One thing you can be sure of in life is that for every person who has a bit of money put by there are others trying to get their hands on it; and millionaire philanthropist William Rice – in honour of whose benefactions Rice University was so named – had plenty laid by. Albert T. Patrick, Rice's late wife's family lawyer, hatched a plan in which Charles Jones, the tycoon's valet, did the dirty work and Patrick collected. On 23 September 1900, Jones snuck into William Rice's bedroom under cover of night and chloroformed his master to death. The following day Patrick presented six cheques for various large sums of money bearing Rice's forged signature. The cheques were all payable to the lawyer, but one had been incorrectly made out to 'Abert T. Patrick'. The cashier asked Patrick to endorse the cheque, and he made the same spelling error. This was suspicious enough for the bank to check up and discover that William Rice was dead. Albert Patrick then produced a will, apparently signed by Rice, making Patrick a beneficiary of half his estate and executor of the rest. Examination by experts proved that the signatures at the foot of each of the four pages

Top, the authentic signature of William M. Rice; below, one of Patrick's forgeries

of the will were identical – an impossibility given Rice's advanced age. When a squared-up glass sheet was placed over the enlarged signatures, individual letters and parts of letters crossed at exactly the same points on the grid in each case; clearly Patrick had made tracings of a single signature. In a fine show of thieves falling out, Jones subsequently turned state's evidence, and Patrick was sentenced to death. This was later commuted to life imprisonment, and for some reason best known to himself, New York Governor John Dix pardoned Patrick just two years later.

1901

Harold Amos Apted

Terrible Tragedy at Tonbridge. *This particularly ugly child murder was notable for the painstaking way in which the prosecution case needed to be built in order to reinforce evidence of bloodstaining in the absence of reliable analysis at this date. The following account derives from contemporary newspaper reports, still written in the 'gaslight' era style.*

Nobody has ever seen a murderer – and everybody felt instinctively that he *was* a murderer – simulate innocence as well as the man in the dock. The man who had assented, in his quiet voice, that he was Harold Amos Apted. Neither in his clear voice, his boyish, open countenance, his placid and serious demeanour, nor his respectful behaviour towards the court was it possible to detect the slightest sign of guilt, the least lack of candour, the faintest indication of fear, the remotest approach to remorse . . . The evidence of your ears convinced you of his guilt; the testimony of your eyes made you doubt it.

The peculiar and sensational murder of Frances Eliza O'Rourke on the afternoon of 31 December 1901 created the greatest consternation and excitement throughout the districts of Tunbridge Wells, Southborough and Tonbridge. Imagination revolted at the idea of a young child, merely a well-developed baby, being induced to accompany the driver of a van, being outraged in the vehicle, being driven

– unconscious or possibly dead – towards a pond and being thrown therein, half stripped, and with the deadly weapon which had done the deed still caught in the child's hair. The place of the discovery was a lonely and secluded one near Vanshall Farm, about a mile from the outskirts of Tonbridge, Kent. A labourer passing that way early on the morning of New Year's Day observed, in a rank and shallow duck pond, separated from the road by a fence, the body of a female child. It was

Apted abducting young Frances Eliza O'Rourke

floating on the top, and was almost in a nude condition. The finder did not make any attempt to secure the corpse, but hurried to a public house at Pembury, known as the Vanshall Inn, and reported the discovery to the landlord, who immediately hurried to the spot. The poor little body was recovered and reverently carried to the parlour of the inn. The landlord, aware a horrid crime had been committed, lost no time in calling for a medical man, who stated that the child had been outraged and that her throat had then been cut, the left jugular vein being severed.

Entwined in the girl's hair was a blood-stained knife. Its larger blade was half open, and the hair had become twisted around the angles made by the steel and the bone handle. It seemed safe to conjecture that the most recent possessor of the knife was the murderer.

A complete search was made of the spot where the body was found and of its environs. No footprints were visible, but the police expressed their conviction that a cart or van had been driven close to the fence which divided the road from the pond, that the occupant had descended with the corpse in his arms, had scaled the hedge or the fence, and had thrown the body into the stagnant water. On the Wednesday night the remainder of the girl's clothing was found in a remote field about two miles from the pond in question. It had been strewn, rather than hidden, amid some brambles near a wood. Most of the garments, the underclothing in particular, were stained with blood.

A number of persons now came forward to declare that they had seen little Eliza O'Rourke sitting beside the driver of a van not far from the scene of the murder on the afternoon of 31 December. At least, they said, if it was not Eliza it was someone dressed similarly and about her age. It appeared that she was actually last seen about half-past four on the Tuesday afternoon in St John's Road, Tunbridge Wells, and that at that time she was sitting next to the driver in a dark-coloured van pulled by a brown horse. In consequence of this information, which was strongly corroborated, the police directed all their energies towards the discovery of this van and of its driver. Certain facts engendered a more or less general suspicion of one Harold Apted, who was known to drive a van for the local butcher, and had been seen therein by various people close to the scene of the crime on the afternoon in question. The police went to interview this youth, and his answers to certain questions, though given without any apparent hesitation, could not be accepted as altogether satisfactory. His own account of his movements on that day was vague and suspicious, and his statements were either uncorroborated or absolutely refuted when inquiry into them was made. The detectives began to entertain a strong suspicion of young Harold Apted; nevertheless his arrest was not considered advisable until 3 January, he being in the meanwhile strictly watched.

The theory of the police was – and everything points to it having been correct – that the murder was committed in the field or wood in which the bloodstained garments were found. There the poor mite, lured to the spot on some pretence, and trusting her devilish guide, was barbarously outraged. Her screams and cries probably alarmed her assailant, who cut her throat with relentless savagery, and the child died almost instantly. Then he placed the body again in his van, drove to the pond, and threw the corpse, mangled, bloody and half nude, into it.

On the Saturday after the discovery, at the Tonbridge police court [former name of the magistrates' court], Harold Apted, twenty years old and described as the son of a coal merchant, was put in the dock charged on suspicion with the murder of Frances Eliza O'Rourke. The building was beseiged by a curious crowd, who evinced the utmost animosity towards the accused man, of whose guilt most of the populace seemed already to have satisfied themselves.

Detective-Sergeant Fowle of the Kent Constabulary stated that at six o'clock on the Friday evening he arrested the prisoner at his residence, Woodside Road, Tonbridge. At the police station he told Apted he would charge him with suspicion of wilfully murdering Frances Eliza O'Rourke by stabbing her in the neck in Vanshall Lane, and he replied: 'I never came home that way. I know nothing about it.'

A Giant Step Forward for Serology

On 1 July 1901 two young boys failed to return home for supper to their father's house on the island of Rugen, in northern Germany. The following morning the mutilated bodies of eight-year-old Herman Stubbe and his brother Peter, aged six, were found in a wood. The children had been sexually assaulted, their limbs hacked off and their internal organs torn out and scattered around their tiny corpses. In the course of a subsequent police enquiry, a neighbour reported seeing the victims talking to an itinerant carpenter named Ludwig Tessnow. When he was picked up and routinely searched, Tessnow told police that the suspicious stains on his clothing were not blood, but the wood dyes used in his trade. It was learned that the car-penter had been similarly questioned over two other horrific child murders near Osnabruck in 1898 – and he had explained his soiled garments in the same way; and nobody could prove otherwise. What Tessnow did not know was that in three years the infant science of serology had made one giant stride forward – a German chemist named Paul Uhlenhuth had perfected a process for distinguishing between human blood and that of other animals. Tessnow's clothing was therefore sent to Professor Uhlenhuth's laboratory at the University of Griefswald, where some of the stains were proved to be human blood. Ludwig Tessnow was tried, convicted and, in 1904, executed.

Upon examining the clothes the accused wore on the night of the murder, Fowle found stains which appeared to be blood. He also examined the van which the accused was in charge of on the night in question, and found what appeared to be bloodstains on it. There were some stains on the body of the van and some on the straw lying within it. There were also marks of blood underneath the cart, where it had apparently been washed through. In further evidence the detective declared positively that the cart had been washed, and Apted said: 'I deny that. Do you say that the blood had soaked through the wood of the van?' DS Fowle said that he did.

After the other evidence had been given, the prisoner again said that he knew nothing at all about it, and he was remanded for trial, and sent to Maidstone Gaol.

The trial took place on Tuesday and Wednesday, 27 and 28 February 1902, at the Maidstone Assizes; Mr Justice Wright presided. The prisoner, who pleaded 'Not guilty' in a loud firm voice, was rather a good-looking young fellow of average height. He was slightly built, clean shaven and rather dark, with somewhat close-cropped hair. He was attired in a neat suit of blue serge and carried a bowler hat. He bowed politely to the court, and then took his seat in a chair provided for him, folding his arms and preparing himself to give full attention to the opening address by counsel for the Crown.

Dr Watts of Tonbridge was the medical gentleman who first examined the body. He stated that he found a deep wound in the left side of the neck, caused by a stab rather than a cut. The knife found in the child's hair almost certainly occasioned that wound. There was a bruise below the stab, and great violence had been used. Portions of the underclothing still adhered to the corpse, and these were much torn and bloodstained. The deceased had been outraged. She must have bled to death after the stab, which divided the carotid artery, in little more than a minute. Both the stab and the bruise had been administered by a person standing opposite her and using the right hand.

William Emery next gave evidence that he had assisted to load the van which Apted drove with calves on 31 December. A cord had required shortening, and the prisoner had produced a knife and cut it. The job of the accused was to take the calves to market. The witness denied there was any mess in the cart through a calf bleeding, though the prisoner had attempted to account for the blood in this way.

Thomas Hankins identified the knife found in the child's hair as his own property, lent to the prisoner three weeks before to kill rabbits. Apted had admitted that this witness had once lent him a knife, but declared that it was at least seven months before the murder, and that the one found with the deceased was not the same. Hankins, however, insisted that the knife was his and that Apted never returned it. He had, he pointed out, picked the knife out from ten others shown to him by the police.

Detective-Sergeant Fowle called on the prisoner at the house of his parents on the day after the crime. He asked Apted what had induced him to come home from Tunbridge Wells that way, and the prisoner had said: 'To call for a Christmas-box.' The detective had asked for and received the clothes worn by Apted on the previous day. There were distinct traces of blood on the shoulder of the coat, which the accused said 'came from the slaugh-ter-house'. He also remarked: 'I have never had a knife in my life. I did not come that way, and I know nothing about it.'

Dr Stevenson found mammalian blood on the floor of the van, but preferred not to state positively that it was human in origin. He had also found blood on the prisoner's clothing; it had soaked through the lining of his coat.

The jury retired to consider their verdict at about five o'clock, and shortly returned with a verdict of 'Guilty', recommending the prisoner to mercy on account of his youth. The judge expressed his concurrence in the verdict, but held out little hope of a reprieve.

Harold Apted remained in Maidstone Gaol and was there visited by his parents on two occasions. He had eaten very little since he heard that the Home Secretary had declined to interfere with the sentence of death, but, summoned to arise at six o'clock on the morning of 18 March, Apted made a fairly good breakfast, and at half-past seven he received the Holy Sacrament. He was pinioned by the brothers Billington, and the procession formed at three minutes to eight. The convict walked without any assistance and evinced the utmost fortitude on the gallows. Death was instantaneous.

Death of a President

The anarchist Leon Czolgosz visited the Pan-American exhibition at Buffalo, New York, and, on 14 September 1901 while apparently waiting in line to shake President William McKinley's hand, pulled a pistol from his pocket and shot the President in the stomach. Eight days later McKinley, 25th President of the United States (inaugurated 1896), died from his wounds, and on 29 October, Czolgosz was executed in the electric chair at Auburn Prison.

1902

Jane Toppan

Moved by a Dark Madness. *One of the earliest recorded female serial killers, and one of a long line of nurses who took advantage of their vulnerable patients. Jane herself, with a victim list of at least 100, claimed to be 'the champion female poisoner in American history'.*

Jane was born Nora Kelley in 1854 in Boston, Massachusetts. Her mother died when she was young, leaving Peter Kelley to look after Nora and her three sisters. Kelley, either through overwork or a weak constitution, was not entirely right in the head, a fact that was amply exhibited when one day he was found in his tailor's shop trying to sew his eyelids together. Kelley was sent to an insane asylum, and his daughters were cared for by their grandmother; when this good lady found things to much for her, the girls were committed to an orphanage, from where Mr and Mrs Abner Toppan of Lowell, Massachusetts, adopted five-year-old Nora in 1859.

The Toppans changed the girl's name to Jane, and encouraged her to attend church. She did well at school, and grew into a popular young lady. After an unfortunate engagement which ended when Jane's fiancé married another girl, she withdrew into herself, becoming a virtual hermit. During this time Jane became convinced that she could see into the future, and so bleak were her visions that she twice tried to end her own life.

Suddenly, at the age of 26, Jane informed her adoptive parents that she intended to take up nursing, and immediately enrolled as a student in a Cambridge, Massachusetts, hospital, where she was apparently an eager and well-liked trainee. If her fellow nurses had been asked to name any fault in Jane, they might have been tempted to refer to her unhealthy, almost morbid fascination with the activities of the post-mortem room.

One day a patient who had been in Jane's care, a man previously recovering well, unexpectedly died. Then another one, and Jane was called into the chief surgeon's office to answer a few questions. No official accusations were ever made against Nurse Toppan, but it did not go unnoticed that she was discharged from her post without a certificate of proficiency. Unbowed, Jane assured her parents: 'I will go to the old and the sick, to comfort them in their neediest hour.' In order to do so she forged her own qualifications.

Between 1880 and 1901, Jane Toppan served as a private nurse in many New England homes – and what did it matter if a large number of her patients died? At the turn of the century illnesses were frequently fatal.

On the warm early summer day of 7 July 1901, Jane was among a group of mourners in the small cemetery in Cataumet. When the service was over, she participated in the age-old custom of scattering a handful of soil on to the coffin as it rested in the grave. Inside was the late Mrs Mattie Davis, one of Jane's patients and a close personal friend; it was touching, everybody thought, how the nurse was so loyally devoted even to the last. So loyally devoted, in fact, that the unfortunate woman's family begged Jane to stay on and look after the rest of them who had also unaccountably fallen sick. Indeed Mrs Annie Goodman, the deceased's married daughter, was so sick that on 29 July 1901 it was necessary to summon a doctor. Then, as her patient appeared restless, Jane obligingly gave her an injection. When the doctor arrived a few hours later, Jane told him: 'I think she is sinking.' Dr Walters took the frail woman's wrist seeking a pulse, then gave his diagnosis: 'This girl is already dead.'

After the funeral Nurse Toppan again thought she ought to leave the house; after all, she was becoming something of a jinx on the health of its occupants. But the family would not hear of it. Next to suffer was Alden Davis; the regular funerals were proving depressing, and it was with gratitude that he accepted Jane's soothing nightcap. Next morning, Captain Davis was found dead in his bed. 'A stroke,' Jane explained to the sole surviving daughter, Mary Gibbs. However, Mrs Gibbs had been unsettled by so many tragic deaths in her family, not least because her husband was far away on a sea voyage. Eventually, she asked a cousin, Beulah Jacobs, to come and stay with her. Despite the presence of Beulah's watchful eye, Mary Gibbs succumbed to the ministrations of her nurse within days. The whole of the Davis family had been wiped out in just six weeks. Jane Toppan simply packed her bags and went back to her childhood town of Lowell.

When Captain Gibbs returned from sea he found his wife dead, and a distraught cousin Beulah who informed him that Nurse Toppan had refused to allow an autopsy because, 'such practices were against the religious beliefs of the family'. Gibbs lost no time in sharing his suspicions with Detective John H. Whitney, the result of which was that Mary Gibbs' body was exhumed, autopsied by a Harvard professor of toxicology, and found to contain an overdose of morphine.

By the time the police, in the person of Detective Whitney, caught up with her, Jane Toppan had murdered her foster sister, Mrs Edna Bannister, at Lowell, and moved on to nurse the Nichols family in Amherst, New Hampshire. On the night of 29 October 1901, Detective Whitney stood at the door in the rain and asked: 'Jane Toppan, the nurse?' 'Yes.' 'You are wanted in Massachusetts for questioning in connection with the deaths of Mrs Henry Gordon and Mrs Irving Gibbs.'

Jane went voluntarily back to Massachusetts, apparently amused by the thought that anybody should think her capable of murder: 'I have a clear conscience. I wouldn't kill a chicken, and if there is any justice in Massachusetts they will let me go.'

Police throughout New England began to disinter dozens of bodies – former patients of Nurse Toppan. Autopsies proved that all had died of morphine and atropine poisoning. Then Benjamin Waters was found, who remembered Jane making purchases at his Wareham pharmacy; a check of his poisons register confirmed frequent large prescriptions for morphine in Jane Toppan's name, all of which were forged. Meanwhile, from the Barnstaple County jail, Jane was beginning a triumphant confession: 'Yes, I killed all of them. I might have killed George Nichols and his sister that night if the detective hadn't taken me away. I fooled them all – I fooled the stupid doctors and the ignorant relatives; I have been fooling them for years and years . . .' Jane then rounded on the prosecutor who was there to witness her statement: 'I read your statements about me poisoning people with arsenic. Ridiculous! If I had used arsenic my patients would have died hard deaths. I could not bear to see them suffer. When I kill anyone they go to sleep and never wake up. I use morphia and atropia, the latter to hide the effects of the former.' After administering the injection of morphine Jane would sit back and watch her victim fade: 'I would have to watch and watch and watch as the pupils of the eye contracted and then at just the right moment inject the atropine and watch and watch until the pupils were again wide and vacant. This was hard, precise work, all of it. I had to dose the patients slowly, a little at a time. It took days sometimes to kill them.' 'I want,' she later claimed, 'to be known as the greatest criminal that ever lived. That is my ambition.'

Jane then began an inventory of her victims, but by the time she reached 31 she became a trifle confused; it was so annoying not being able to remember, she observed, because there were at least seventy deaths altogether, not counting the hospital deaths at the beginning, as they were only 'practice murders'.

On 25 June 1902, Jane Toppan was put on trial. Dr Stedman, the psychiatrist, gave evidence that 'Jane Toppan is suffering from a form of insanity that can never be cured.' At which Jane indignantly shouted: 'The alienist lies. I am not crazy, and all of you know it. I know that I have done wrong. I understand right from wrong – that proves I am sane.'

Even so, Jane Toppan was confined to the Taunton State Asylum for the Criminally Insane. Her behaviour alternated between the docile, almost morose, and raging fits of paranoia, during which she would, ironically, accuse the nurses of trying to poison her. 'After all,' she would say, 'I should know!' Jane lived a long and healthy life until, on 17 August 1938, she died at the age of 84.

1903

UNITED KINGDOM

Samuel Herbert Dougal

The Moat Farm Murder. *Tried and convicted of the murder of Miss Camille Holland, Dougal was sentenced to death. Questions were subsequently asked in Parliament about the conduct of the chaplain who was badgering Dougal to confess as he stood on the gallows. Dougal did confess, not to the chaplain, but to the* Star *newspaper for a lot of money!*

Samuel Herbert Dougal was a man both greatly attracted to and greatly attractive to women of all kinds. As an unashamed womaniser Dougal collected a string of broken hearts and illegitimate children dotted around the world like markers charting his career with the Royal Engineers. Although Dougal enlisted more in order to escape the pack of hungry creditors

baying at his modest East Ham door than out of any loyalty to King and Country, he nevertheless made the best of necessity and was, by the account of his senior officers, 'of very good character and conduct' – indeed, on his discharge from the force in 1887 Dougal was awarded a medal for long service and good conduct, given excellent testimonials and a satisfactory pension. He had married three times during his service, the first time in 1869 to a Miss Griffiths who had borne him four children. Despite the inevitable infidelities the marriage lasted until June 1885, when Mrs Dougal suddenly became ill with severe vomiting, and died in Halifax, Nova Scotia, where her husband was stationed. At that time there was no requirement for a death occurring on military property to be reported to the civil authorities, and Dougal was allowed positively to *rush* his late wife's remains into their early grave.

Dougal immediately applied for home leave and in September he returned to base with a new Mrs Dougal, whom he had married the previous month, and who was dead by the following month, October, after a sudden illness

Samuel Herbert Dougal with Miss Georgina Cranwell

and in the end he was obliged to set fire to the public house in the hope of raising some money on the insurance. As it turned out, the insurers, far from solving Dougal's liquidity problem, insisted that he be arrested forthwith on a charge of arson. Then Dougal's house (insured with a different company) also caught fire, and once again he suffered the indignity of being charged with arson. The case came up at the St Albans Assizes on 5 December 1889, but was dismissed through lack of evidence.

If he realised that he had enjoyed a lucky escape, Dougal certainly did not take it as a warning to change his ways. He did, however, move to Ireland where his military record went a long way to securing him a position at Dublin Castle, and his natural charms went a long way to securing him a wife. The luckless woman in this instance was Miss Sarah Henrietta White, and they married on 7 August 1892.

In 1894 Dougal was back in London and up to his old tricks. He met and quickly cultivated an intimate friendship with a woman named Emily Booty. It was Miss Booty's money which took out a three-year lease – in Dougal's name of course – on a grand house in Wattlington. If she ever noticed that her bank balance was being milked by Dougal, poor Emily never complained. And so it might have continued had Dougal not been so unwise as to bring his wife and children over from Dublin to live with them. When Miss Booty complained, Dougal used threats of violence to get her out of her own house. Clearly this was the final straw, and Emily Booty went straightaway to the police and had Dougal arrested. On 9 April 1895 he appeared at the Oxford Quarter Sessions charged with the theft of Miss Booty's possessions. Miraculously, Dougal was once again acquitted.

The year 1895 found Dougal in trouble yet again. He and his family were back in Ireland where he was working at the Royal Hospital – or at least he was until he began forging cheques stolen from the assistant military secretary, Colonel Childers. In October 1895 Dougal was arrested on a charge of forgery and uttering, and shipped back to London where he stood his trial at the Old Bailey. By now Samuel Dougal's luck had run out, and he was

characterised by severe vomiting. Her body, too, was interred with unseemly haste. Although they never married, Dougal next took up with a local Halifax girl of twenty, and on his discharge brought her back to England as his 'wife'. However, the violent assault and threats on her life, and that of their child, eventually drove the unhappy girl back to the safety of her family.

Although Dougal made several half-hearted gestures towards employment, it was not long before he had found a woman of some means with whom he took over the tenancy of a public house at Ware in Hertfordshire. They also took a small house a little way down the road from the inn. Apparently his new provider took against Dougal's continual financial demands sentenced to twelve months' hard labour; even so, he managed to feign insanity so successfully that he spent the whole year in the comparative comfort of the London County Lunatic Asylum at Cane Hill. Discharged as 'cured' at the end of his sentence, Dougal found himself without his army pension, which had been withdrawn as a result of his conviction. For a while he acted as caretaker for some properties owned by his brother Henry, moving his wife and children in with him. But such stifling domesticity soon took its toll, and it was not long before Mrs Dougal and her child were on their way back to Dublin, unable to stand any more of her husband's persistent violence and womanising. Shortly afterwards Dougal's appalling behaviour even antagonised brother Henry, and once again he found himself unattached and unemployed.

Miss Camille Cecile Holland was a cultured, single lady living in a small boarding house in London's Elgin Crescent. She was later described by her landlady as 'a rather pretty, faded, delicate-looking woman, who took to preserve her youthful appearance by means that were rare in those days. She powdered her face, dyed her hair a reddish-gold, and was careful over the details of her toilet. Although she looked sixty in bed, when she was finally "got-up" for the day she seemed ten or fifteen years younger'. In fact Miss Holland was, in 1898, the year she met Samuel Dougal, about 56 years of age. In particular she was, thanks to family legacies, a woman of rather more than comfortable means; in short, she was the perfect prey for a scoundrel like Dougal – or, as Miss Holland knew him, 'Captain' Dougal.

In her excellent introduction to *The Trial of Samuel Herbert Dougal** Miss Tennyson Jesse observed: 'There are men, criminals such as Dougal, George Joseph Smith and Landru, who recognise emotionally-starved women, who scent them from afar off, and who know exactly what they are about when they enter into a relationship with them. It is when meetings such as that of Dougal and Camille Holland take place that criminal history is made. The

Notable British Trials; published by Wm. Hodge, London, 1928.

Miss Camille Cecile Holland

potential murderer has met the born murderee.'

As a matter of fact we are not at all certain how the couple did first meet. One story is that they encountered each other at the Earl's Court Exhibition; other accounts suggest that they became acquainted via a matrimonial agency. Although Miss Holland was well educated, accomplished in fine art and music, and of a deeply religious inclination, she tended toward unworldliness, and this must explain her quite uncharacteristic passion for a man of Dougal's type. But win her heart he did, and was soon intent on winning her money and possessions. In 1899 Dougal persuaded Miss Holland to purchase a remote property near Saffron Walden, Essex, called Coldhams Farm, a name which Dougal later changed to Moat Farm. However, despite her continuing infatuation, Camille Holland still retained the good sense to have the contract name her as sole owner. While awaiting completion of the legal details and the arrival of Miss Holland's furniture from storage, the couple stayed as paying guests of Mrs Henrietta Wisken at Market Row, Saffron Walden. This arrangement lasted for some two months, during which time they maintained the appearance of loving devotion, though Miss Holland (or 'Mrs Dougal' as Henrietta Wisken knew her) was rather peeved at Dougal's overnight trips to London 'on business'.

On 27 April 1899 Henry Pilgrim, Moat Farm's general factotum, arrived in a trap to take Dougal and Miss Holland to their new home. They had been in residence less than a fortnight when, on 6 May, a nineteen-year-old servant named Florence Havies complained to her mistress that Dougal had put his arms round her waist and kissed her. Not surprisingly Camille Holland was furious and subsequently gave Dougal a taste of her sharp tongue. Not that it made any difference; the night of 16 May found Dougal tapping at Florence's locked bedroom door, which resulted in the terrified girl yelling at the top of her voice for her mistress. Miss Holland was just in time to catch Dougal trying to break the door down. Over the following couple of days tempers subsided, and on Friday the 19th Dougal drove Miss Holland in the trap on a 'shopping spree'. It was the last time Camille Holland was seen alive, for only Dougal returned that night. On the following morning, with her mistress still not returned and after a watchful night spent near an open window ready to jump if Dougal approached, poor Florrie Havies made off at first light for the safety of her mother's home at Newport.

Dougal next wrote to his wife in Ireland and invited her to join him at Moat Farm, introducing her to any who cared to inquire as his widowed daughter. To those who inquired after Miss Holland, Dougal said that she had gone on holiday. Thenceforth Mr and Mrs Dougal settled into a life of comfort and ease underwritten by Camille Holland's bank balance. Dougal did take the trouble, though, to get Henry Pilgrim and some local workmen to fill

in the moat surrounding the farmhouse. He frequently abused his long-suffering wife; so frequently, in fact, that she again left him and went to live in Tenby in Wales. This at least gave Dougal more time for his twin pursuits of drinking and bedding local women, to some of whom he gave children and some of whom, in return, served Dougal with paternity suits. In brief, things were once more becoming rather hot for Samuel Dougal.

Four years on, and with Dougal's increasingly high profile, people began to wonder what had become of Miss Holland after all this time. Indeed, rumours became so widespread that the chief constable instructed district superintendent Charles Pryke to make local inquiries. At last the game was up, and even Samuel Dougal must have sensed the hand of Nemesis feeling his collar. On 5 March 1902, the day following a visit from Superintendent Pryke, Dougal drew out his bank balance of £605 from two accounts and left Moat Farm for London. On the 12th, he returned and collected such valuables as he could transport and proceeded on to Bournemouth via London in company with a servant girl. Dougal must have known that the net would be closing, but he could not realise how quickly. When he returned to London from this brief holiday, and tried to change some £10 notes at the Bank of England (money he had withdrawn in Bishop's Stortford) they already had a bank stop order on them and Dougal was taken into custody.

An extensive search of Moat Farm had, nevertheless, revealed nothing directly incriminating, and Dougal was detained on a holding charge of forging Miss Holland's cheques. Meanwhile, the painstaking task of digging over the garden continued. Numerous eccentrics – spirit mediums, clairvoyants, dowsers and the like – offered their services but in the end it was the police searchers who found what they were looking for, what they feared to find. On 27 April 1902 – four years to the day since Camille Holland crossed the threshold of Moat Farm – her body was dug out of a drainage ditch. Identified by her clothing and by a pair of distinctive hand-made shoes, the sad remains of Miss Holland were passed on to Dr Augustus Pepper, a noted surgeon and the

Miss Holland's body as it was recovered from the ditch

Examiner in Forensic Medicine at the University of London, to establish cause of death. Once the mud and slime had been removed from the skull it became clear that Miss Holland had been shot through the head.

On 30 April 1903, Samuel Herbert Dougal was charged with the murder of Camille Holland; his trial opened before Mr Justice Wright at the Shire Hall in Chelmsford on Monday, 22 June 1903. Mr (later Sir) Charles Gill acted for the Crown (as he had in the Bennett case, see 1900), and Mr George Elliott led for the defence. The charge was all but unanswerable; as one spectator at the trial observed: '[Mr Gill] had built a prison wall round Dougal from which the latter was unable to dislodge a single stone.' The trial lasted just two days, and at 4 p.m. on 23 June the jury went into retirement; when they returned one hour later it was with a unanimous verdict of guilty. Under sentence of death, Dougal made a number of preposterous 'confessions', among which was one that may have been close to the truth – characteristically, it was made to a newspaper for money.

On the morning of 8 July 1903 Samuel Dougal was hanged at Chelmsford Gaol by executioner Billington.

As for Miss Holland, her remains were laid to rest in the cemetery at Saffron Walden beneath the inscription: 'In sympathetic memory of Camille Cecile Holland of Maida Vale, London, who died at Clavering under distressing circumstances on 19 May 1899, aged fifty-six years. *Nunc demum requiescat in pace.*'

1904

The Nan Patterson Case

Third Time Lucky. *Showgirl Nan Patterson was accused of shooting dead her lover in a New York hansom cab. At her first trial the judge declared a mistrial when one of the jurors died, at her second trial the jury failed to agree, and at a third trial the jury was again deadlocked. Such was the strength of public sympathy that Nan Patterson was released from custody.*

His name wasn't really Caesar, but for a flash gambler and prince of the race-tracks, 'Caesar' Young certainly had the edge on Francis Thomas Young; and Caesar liked to have the edge. It showed in the snappy way he dressed; it showed in his expensive taste in entertainments; and it showed in his choice of female company. Of course Young was married, but that was before he reinvented himself as Caesar – he had left Mrs Young at the starting post long ago, as Caesar's racing cronies might have put it. No, the big love of Caesar Young's life was a 22-year-old showgirl hand-picked off the chorus line of the ever-popular musical *Floradora*. (Students of coincidence might care to recall that Evelyn Nesbit, catalyst in the notorious Thaw/White killing of 1906 had also been one of the *Floradora* chorus girls.) Nan Randolph Patterson was also married, and it was quite consistent with her romantic nature and Young's love of the dramatic gesture that they tried to elope, an escapade foiled by Mrs Young

and Mr Patterson. Mrs Young had clearly not finished with her husband yet even if he had tired of her, and by one means or another she managed to effect an uneasy reconciliation. At any rate, she persuaded Caesar to take her on a vacation to England, and before he had a chance to say no, booked their passage for 4 June 1904. Nan, meanwhile, had announced that she was pregnant, and Caesar had responded equally dramatically by asking her to flee to Europe with him; wisely or not, Nan refused. They were still squabbling about it on 3 June, the night before Mr and Mrs Young embarked on what Mrs Young clearly saw as the opportunity for a second honeymoon. In fact Caesar drank just a little bit too much that night and became a little bit too quarrelsome, leaving Nan in quite a state – such a state that Caesar felt obliged to meet her the following morning, before his ship sailed, to make some sort of apology. They chose to say their fond *au revoirs* in the comfort of a horse-drawn cab, and it was as Nan and Caesar were being transported at a leisurely pace down New York's Broadway that a shot rang out from the inside of the hansom. By the time the driver had got to the Hudson Street Hospital, Caesar Young was dead, a bullet through his chest. Not surprisingly a distraught Nan Patterson was detained and eventually charged with his murder.

By the time the case got to trial it had already become a sensation – crimes of passion have that effect on people. It was going to get even more sensational. The first hearing was opened in New York in November, but jerked to a halt when one of the jurors died; the judge declared a mistrial, and Nan had to wait until the following month to make her side of the story public. In this second trial, Nan Patterson gave evi-

30

Arsenic: Poison for Cats

In 1904 Florence Maybrick was released from her fifteen-year ordeal in prison. There can be few who have not heard or read of the crime of Mrs Maybrick; it was she who, in 1889, is supposed to have murdered her husband James by spiking his meat extract with arsenic. Prejudice ran high against Florence on account of her infidelity to James – considered in the morality of the day, adultery was not much further down the criminal scale than murder itself – compounded by an irrational xenophobia (Florence was a citizen of the United States) and the fact that her mother was already on her *third* husband. The case is of great social interest, illuminating as it does the repressive Victorian atmosphere by which Florence was surrounded, and the stifling middle-class climate in which she spent the whole of her married life. At her trial the evidence against Mrs Maybrick appeared strong, though there is still considerable doubt as to her guilt, and the judge (who was subsequently certified insane) summed up heavily against her. Florence Maybrick's death sentence was commuted to life imprisonment, of which she served fifteen years. On her release Florence returned to the United States where she died in 1941.

While this manuscript was being prepared, the Maybrick case again made the headlines. This time it was not Florence but James who was in the news. According to a London publisher, James Maybrick's diary – hidden for more than a century in the family home of Battlecrease House, Liverpool – revealed that he was none other than Jack the Ripper! Red herring or not, the thought of discovering the identity of their *bete noire* has thrown Ripperologists the world over into quite a tizzy, and crime historians wait with baited breath . . .

Contemporary 'highlights' from the Maybrick case

dence from the witness box, protesting, as one might have guessed, that the late Caesar Young had pulled the trigger on himself. Nan's attorney had found an eye-witness who would testify on oath that he heard the shot come from the cab, followed by a woman's voice lamenting: 'Look at me Frank, [Frank?]. Why did you do it?' He must have had very acute hearing, you might think, to have picked up the words so clearly coming from the inside of a cab; or perhaps the windows were open. At any rate, the jury could make neither head nor tail of it and Nan Patterson's second trial was abandoned when they could not agree on a verdict.

It was not until April of the following year that the state made a further attempt to secure a conviction against Nan Patterson. By now the unhappy woman's plight had gone to the heart of the nation, and to that of many individuals as well, if the proposals of marriage she received were anything to go by.

Nan's third trial was a repeat of the second, and the jury, probably swayed as much now by emotion as by hard evidence, once again failed to agree. Even so, it was almost a further fortnight before the District Attorney, through the trial judge, announced that the trial would be dismissed and the defendant discharged. There could have been no more welcome sight to Nan Patterson's eyes as she stepped free from the New York court house than the thousands of cheering supporters who surrounded her. And in playgrounds across the city, children immortalised her in rhyme:

> Nan is free, Nan is free,
> She escaped the electric chair,
> Now she's out in the open air.

GERMANY

Another Forensic First for Germany

Confirming Germany's pre-eminence in the science of serology (see also 1901), the case of Theodore Berger gave the world its first murder solved by *matching* bloodstains. Berger acted as pimp to a prostitute named Johanna Liebstruth, who worked from a flat in the centre of the city of Berlin. In June 1904 nine-year-old Lucie Berlin went missing from another apartment in the same block, and on the 11th of the month her limbless, headless torso was dragged from the River Spree, followed by a suitcase containing the other pieces of her body. A horrified Fraulein Liebstruth now confided to the police that on the day she disappeared, Berger had invited the child into her flat; bloodstains found on the floor of the apartment were proved to match the group of Lucie Berlin. In custody Berger confessed how he had lusted after the girl and, when she resisted his sexual advances, strangled her and dismembered the body for disposal. Berger was executed in the same year.

1905

Alfred and Albert Stratton

Hanged by a Fingerprint. *The first occasion on which fingerprints were accepted as evidence of identity in a British murder trial.*

The early morning of Monday, 27 March 1905 was characteristic of that season's generally inclement weather. To one young man named William Jones, already soaked through by the penetrating rain, the oil and colour shop where he worked offered the welcome opportunity at least of warmth and shelter. There was nothing at all impressive about 34 Deptford High Street – indeed, there still isn't; it was a small rather run-down shop, with rooms above in which Thomas Farrow, manager of the business for 25 years, lived with his wife Ann. Farrow was nearing 70, Mrs Farrow just a little younger. It was before eight o'clock, but the boy was familiar with old Mr Farrow's obliging habit of opening up early to supply painters and decorators starting their day's work. So he was surprised and not a little irritated to find the shutters still up and the door locked. Even more unusually, Jones could not raise anybody by knocking, and so he set off for Greenwich where George Chapman, who owned the small chain of shops of which Farrow managed the Deptford branch, had his own business. Chapman sent one of his assistants back with Jones, and together they forced an entry at the back of the shop.

It was a badly shaken pair of lads who rushed back out the door just minutes later and sped through the rain to the nearby police station.

It was Mr Farrow that the police found first when they accompanied the shop-boys back to the High Street; he had been beaten to death in the shop's back parlour. In the bedroom they found his wife, still alive, but with such dreadful injuries that she died in the Seamen's Hospital at Greenwich three days later without once regaining consciousness.

It was clearly a case for Scotland Yard's Murder Squad, and Chief Inspector Frederick Fox took command of a group of experienced detectives in a thorough search of the scene of the crime. This exercise yielded two vital clues, one of which would change the whole course of the criminal identification procedure.

Near the doorway through which the murderers were presumed to have fled were found two crude home-made masks fashioned from the top of a lady's black silk stocking. To the experienced reasoning of Fox this indicated that almost certainly the criminals were local men, men whose faces were familiar enough to need hiding. This theory was given extra credence when it was learned that it was Mr Chapman's practice to collect the weekly takings on a Monday morning; it would have required local knowledge to be sure that was the best time for a robbery.

But it was the second clue that was to elevate this simple, sordid crime into national headlines and, more importantly, to introduce a completely new feature to future crime investigation. The police found a cash box close to the body of Thomas Farrow. The box had obviously been forced by the robber/killer and plundered of its contents, in the course of which, it was

33

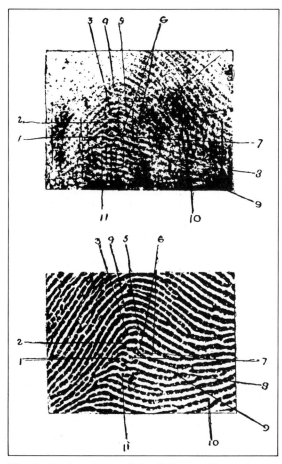

The fingerprints that made legal history. Above, the thumb-print left by Thomas Farrow's killer on the cash box he robbed; below, the thumb-print of Alfred Stratton showing a convincing eleven points of similarity

been difficult enough for the pioneers of the new system to convince *scientists* of the remarkably individual characteristics of fingerprints – what chance with a jury of twelve ordinary people?

With this doubt in mind, the enquiry continued to focus on finding Deptford-based criminals with no alibi for the night of 26–27 March. The first breakthrough came with Henry Jennings, a milkman, and his eleven-year-old assistant Edward Russell. They had been passing the oil and colour shop at about 7.15 a.m. on the day of the murder and had seen two men hurry out the door and down Deptford High Street. The taller of the two men, according to Jennings's recollection, was wearing a blue serge suit and a bowler hat; the second man had on a brown suit, brown shoes and a cap.

It was not long before the names of Alfred and Albert Stratton began to crop up with sinister regularity. The brothers, aged 22 and twenty respectively, were already known to the police as housebreakers, thieves with a vicious enough record to make them suitable candidates for the murders. Strong confirmation was subsequently provided by a boxer named Henry Littlefield. At the early hour of 2.30 a.m. on 27 March (before the murder took place) Littlefield had met the two men he knew as Alfred and Albert Stratton in the street. Alfred, he remembered, was wearing a brown suit, brown shoes and a cap; Albert was dressed in a blue serge suit and had on a bowler.

Under police questioning, Hannah Cromerty, with whom Alfred had shared a room at a lodging-house in Brookmill Road, Deptford, revealed that he and his brother Albert had not been home all night on the 26th, and that when he returned the next morning, Alfred destroyed the coat that he had been wearing. Hannah had also been puzzled as to why Alfred had put black boot polish on his brown shoes. Albert's partner, Mrs Kate Wade, with whom he lived in Knott Street, recalled that he had recently asked her if she had an old pair of stockings he could have.

On 3 April, the Sunday after the murder, Alfred Stratton was arrested in a public house in Deptford, and his brother was picked off the

discovered, the impression of a right thumb had been left on the metal tray. When comparisons had eliminated those persons known to have handled the cash box it became clear that the print belonged to the killer. It was a simple enough deduction, but this was 1905, and Scotland Yard's small Fingerprint Department had been founded only four years previously. Besides, there was no precedent for such evidence being acceptable in a capital case. It had street the following morning. Both men were taken to Greenwich police station where Detective Inspector Charles Stockley Collins of Scotland Yard's Fingerprint Department was waiting to take samples of both men's prints. It was established beyond doubt that the thumbprint on the cash-box tray belonged to Alfred Stratton.

At their committal proceedings at the Tower Bridge magistrates' court (then called 'police courts') on 18 April, both Alfred and Albert Stratton entered pleas of not guilty. However, I am indebted to Commander Gerald Lambourne, head of the Yard's Fingerprint Department until his retirement in 1980, for the following extraordinary conversation which took place between Albert Stratton and his gaoler, PC Giddens, during the lunch adjournment.* The two brothers were in separate cells and Albert asked the officer how he thought he would get on; Giddens replied that, quite frankly, he didn't know. Then Albert began to get very conspiratorial, and in a quiet voice asked the gaoler if his brother Alfred could overhear their conversation. Satisfied that Alfred was engrossed in a newspaper, Albert confided: 'I reckon he will get strung up, and I shall get about ten years. He let me into this. He is the cause of my living with that woman. Don't say anything to him. I shan't say anything until I can see he has got no chance, and then . . . I don't want to get strung up . . .'

When the case opened at the Old Bailey before Mr Justice Channell in May 1905 it was not only the brothers Stratton that were on trial but the credibility of the technique of fingerprint identification. For although the police knew with certainty that they had the culprits in custody, they still had to convince a court.

It was for this reason that the Crown led with one of the greatest counsels of his time, Mr (later Sir) Richard Muir. Less than three years previously, in September 1902, Richard Muir had prosecuted the very first case in which fingerprints had been used as evidence. Muir had been successful in convicting housebreaker Harry Jackson on the evidence of a fingerprint

*Recalled in *The Fingerprint Story*, Gerald Lambourne QPM. Harrap, London, 1984.

left at the scene of the crime. The present case was a different matter entirely; this time two men's lives were at stake. Muir, in partnership with Charles Collins in the witness box, patiently inducted the jury in the technicalities of fingerprinting. With the aid of giant enlargements, they were shown how comparisons were made, and in particular the conclusive eleven points of similarity between Alfred's thumbprint and the impression left at the scene of Thomas Farrow's murder. The jury, clearly impressed with their newly acquired information, had one of their own members fingerprinted in order to test the theory in comparison with the prisoner's prints.

For Stratton, Mr H. G. Rooth dismissed the whole principle of fingerprint evidence as 'savouring more of the French courts than of English justice' – whatever that may mean. He then called his own witness, in the person of Dr John Garson, to swear that the print on the cash box was not made by Alfred Stratton. When his turn came to cross-examine, Muir was able in a stroke to completely undermine the credibility of this 'expert' witness.

'Did you,' he demanded of the witness, 'when you read of this case in the press, write two letters offering your services as an expert? Did you, on the very same day, write one letter to the defence offering your services and another to the Treasury asking to be retained for the prosecution?'

'Yes,' barely audible.

'How, then, do you reconcile the writing of those two letters on the same day? One offering to swear to the infallibility of the system, and the other to its fallibility?'

'I am an independent witness.'

Mr Justice Channell: 'A very unreliable witness I should think, after writing two such letters.'

Even so, it could not be said that the judge himself was entirely convinced by this newfangled system, going only so far in his summing up as to acknowledge a strong resemblance between the two fingerprints under consideration. The jury, however, entertained no such doubts, and after a brief retirement announced a verdict of guilty against both prisoners. And so the end of Alfred and Albert

Stratton – hanged by a fingerprint – was the beginning of a new era in the fight against crime. They met their deaths on 23 May 1905; and ironically the killers Alfred and Albert Stratton were executed by the hangmen John and William Billington.

Henri Languille

The Head of Languille. *Did the severed head of the murderer Languille really wink twice at Dr Beaurieux as he lifted it from beneath the guillotine?*

On 25 June 1905, at Orléans, what began as the routine execution of a bandit convicted of murder turned into one of the most extraordinary episodes in the colourful history of France's guillotine. The following account of Henri Languille's death has been derived from contemporary newspaper reports:

EXECUTION

The day breaks with that pale light that makes figures look like ghosts. Now and again agitated shouts resound from behind the barriers to the left and the right of the Rue de Bel-Air; barriers which have several times almost been broken down despite the three ranks of soldiers holding back the crowd and the knots of gendarmes. Suddenly a movement is seen in the Rue Verte; it is the enclosed wagon, escorted by a detachment of gendarmes, which transports Languille from prison. It is half-past three.

The melancholy procession arrives at the end of Rue Verte and emerges on the Place, the wagon being reined in beside the guillotine. The prison chaplain, the Abbé Marcais, himself as pale as the prisoner, steps from the wagon first. Behind him comes Languille, his arms tied behind him, supported by the executioner's assistants.

The killer of Nibelle is white as a shroud, his half-bare shoulders shivering with the morning chill. Nevertheless he seems resolved, and to the end maintains his previous courage. Despite his apprehension Languille hurls an insult into the expectant crowd: 'Muck-heap of peasants!'

The assistant executioners now take hold of their prisoner and push him on to the *bascule*. It seems almost as if the condemned man's muscles conspire to throw him backwards, but he is swiftly laid on the plank. His neck is encircled with the *lunette*. A few seconds pass, then the young Deibler – quicker and more off-hand than his illustrious father who was always hesitant – steps up to the machine. 'Monsieur de Paris' puts the spring in motion, the glittering knife falls with a dry sound; a thin stream of blood spurts up into the air, and the head falls into the tray. The decapitated corpse is rolled to the right into the coffin-shaped basket of sawdust.

THE HEAD OF LANGUILLE

As soon as Languille's head had dropped into the tray, a Dr Beaurieux, with the permission of the Public Prosecutor, lifted it out in order to conduct a most bizarre experiment. The doctor held the severed head between his hands, and looking into the apparently dead face of the bandit, called: 'Languille! Languille!' Slowly but deliberately, the eyelids opened, revealing eyes still sparkling with life; they stared into the eyes of Beaurieux for a long moment, and then the lids fell again. 'Languille,' the doctor called for a second time. And again the eyelids were raised; again the eyes stared out from the disembodied head, before closing for the last time. When his name was called for the third time, Languille's eyes remained for ever more shut tight. Although the experiment lasted some thirty seconds according to the newspaper, other medical experts at the foot of the guillotine are said to have insisted that the spark of life lasted no longer than ten seconds after the execution. Which may be purely academic, because since that June day in 1905 sufficient scorn has been poured on the remarkable occurrence at Orléans to incline many to view the original newspaper report a hoax.

1906

Harry Thaw

You Can't Convict a Million Dollars. *One of the century's most celebrated cases, which sees 'Mad' Harry Thaw shoot dead America's most famous architect in a jealous rage over his former relationship with showgirl Evelyn Nesbit, now Harry's wife. A story of corruption, with the Thaw millions trying to buy Harry out of trouble, and when that fails, out of the asylum to which he is sent.*

On the evening of Monday, 25 June 1906, a fashionable audience was gathered for the opening of a much-publicised new musical comedy to be staged in the roof-top theatre of Madison Square Gardens, New York.

Among that audience were three members of the cast of what was to become one of the most controversial real-life dramas in the history of the American legal process.

Stanford White, a handsome 52, was arguably America's most distinguished architect. As well as being known as the creator of the Madison Square Gardens complex in which they were sitting, he also had a formidable reputation as a lecher and seducer.

Harry Kendall Thaw was the 34-year-old heir to a Pittsburgh railway fortune; celebrated in his own circle as a playboy, gambler and big-spender, whose more outrageous escapades had earned him the nickname 'Mad Harry'. Harry was a psychopath.

A character common to both these male leads was sitting with the Thaw party. Evelyn Nesbit, young, exquisitely beautiful, a top model and former chorus girl with the famous *Floradora* sextet. A former girlfriend of Stanford White, she was now Mrs Harry Thaw.

The auditorium was not a conventional one – it was open-air for one thing, and for another the spectators were seated around at tables. *Mam'zelle Champagne*, the new offering, was not proving to be the most riveting of entertainments, and people were walking about among the tables chatting to friends; some were already drifting towards the exits. So it was

Evelyn Nesbit

unremarkable when, in the middle of the second act, the Thaw party – Harry, Evelyn and two friends, Thruxton Beale and Thomas McCaleb – got up and prepared to leave. It was equally unremarked that Harry Thaw detached himself from the party and moved between the tables to where Stanford White sat alone sipping his drink and awaiting the company of one of the chorus girls from *Mam'zelle*'s cast.

What followed, however, was highly remarkable. Taking up a position behind White, Harry Thaw held a pistol to the architect's head and pulled the trigger three times. Then he walked slowly away, leaving Stanford White in a pool of blood and broken glass and with two bullets in his brain and one in his left shoulder. By this time, Evelyn had been attracted by the general air of panic and had rejoined her husband in time to see him apprehended. 'Good God, Harry,' she cried, 'what have you done?' 'I have probably saved your life,' he replied, and was rewarded with the touching rejoinder: 'I'll stick by you Harry, but my! you're in an awful mess.'

It was certainly no understatement.

By the following morning Harry Thaw was in a police cell refusing to say anything until his lawyer was present; and the front pages of the newspapers across the United States were dominated by the murder. At 9 a.m. the prisoner was photographed for the Rogue's Gallery at police headquarters, and taken to Jefferson Market Police Court for formal committal to New York's Tombs prison. It is just at this point that the delicate balance of Justice's scales began to be upset by the solid weight of the Thaw fortune. Harry's mother, Mrs William Thaw, received the news of her son's delinquency when her liner docked at Southampton, on a visit to England. 'My son is innocent,' she announced. 'If it takes the fortune of my entire family to clear him, every dollar we possess will be used to help Harry regain his freedom.' As District Attorney William Jerome, who was to lead the case for the prosecution, said afterwards: 'From the very hour when Stanford White lay dead on the roof-garden in the city of New York, it was clear that his life had been taken either by a murderer or a lunatic, and from that time to this it has been said that in the end the Thaw money would defeat the ends

of justice. But the State of New York will not permit justice to be defeated by the corrupt use of money if it can prevent it.'

By the time Harry came to trial seven months later the Thaws had not used the 'fortune of the entire family'; but they had certainly made a dent in it. All the stops were being pulled in a defence that had every appearance of an attack. One of the first steps was to engage a press agent, Ben Atwell, to stage-manage an extensive programme of slander and character assassination against the memory of Stanford White, while victims of Harry's own indiscretions were bought off – all part of the necessary prelude to the main nub of Harry K. Thaw's court defence.

It had been decided at first, on the advice of the powerful lawyer Judge William Olcott, that a plea of insanity would be appropriate. Dr Hamilton, one of the foremost mental experts of the day, had been persuaded to support this view, and there appeared to be no shortage of medical examples on both sides of the Thaw family to corroborate it. Harry, though, took this as a blatant attempt by Stanford White's supporters to have the good name of Thaw tainted with suggestions of congenital madness – a view wholly endorsed by Mrs Thaw senior, who promptly sacked Olcott for daring to suggest it.

This made the job of Messrs Hartridge and Peabody, the second firm of lawyers, no easier – to them remained the task of proving a defence of temporary insanity on the night of the killing, backed up by appeals to the spurious *dementia Americana* invented for the occasion by Thaw's leading counsel (engaged, unsurprisingly, at a record fee) and defined by him as 'That species of insanity which makes a man believe that the honour of his wife and daughter is sacred ... It is that species of insanity which makes him believe that whoever invades the sanctity of that home, whoever brings pollution upon that daughter, whoever stains the virtue of that wife, has forfeited the protection of human laws and must look to the eternal justice and mercy of God.'

So what was this 'unique' defence, this defence which was to shake the faith of a generation in its own system of justice?

Harry Thaw, it was deposed in court, proposed marriage to Evelyn Nesbit in June 1903. A recollection of the occasion was given by Evelyn in her own evidence: 'Mr Thaw was sitting opposite me and he suddenly said that he loved me and wanted to marry me. I stared at him for a moment and then he said "Don't you care for me?" I said "Yes", and he said "What is the matter?" I said "Nothing at all". He said, "Why won't you marry me?" And I said "Because." '

To cut a long story short, Evelyn's feeling of unworthiness was, so she claimed, occasioned by an incident in which Stanford White had lured her by deception into his studio and, following the administration of drugged champagne, had ravished her. Thaw's outrage at this, it was to be claimed at trial, was to become an obsession. It seemed irrelevant to Harry Thaw that the incident had occurred almost four years previously – before he had, so to speak, 'stolen' Evelyn from her secure position as White's mistress and made her his own. As the obsession with the supposed wrongs committed by his 'enemy' festered and grew to bursting point, he could no longer think of this 'foul perverted satyr' living. It was Harry Thaw's destiny to put on the mantle of avenging angel and saviour of maidenhood – or so it was claimed by his defence attorney.

Now it must be said at the outset that the relationship between Evelyn Nesbit and Stanford White was never, could never, be denied. Nor was it ever denied that White had very strong sexual inclinations in the direction of pretty young girls, inclinations attested to by more of that species than Evelyn alone. But it was only under determined cross-examination by District Attorney Jerome that the jury learned the real colour of the girl Harry Thaw had elected to champion. Having been introduced to White by a fellow chorus girl in the

A contemporary view of 'America's Most Sensational Murder Trial'

Floradora troupe Evelyn was, at the time of the alleged seduction, already receiving regular gifts of money from White. It was learned later that Evelyn had maintained extremely 'friendly' relations with her benefactor even after he is supposed to have drugged and assaulted her – the same kind of friendly relationship that had been enjoyed by quite a number of men, on two occasions resulting in Miss Nesbit being cited as a co-respondent in a divorce action. Finally, as if all this were not damaging enough to her masquerade as an ill-used innocent, Evelyn was obliged to confess that she had been a regular partner in Harry's bed long before they were married.

But nor was Harry Thaw quite the Sir Galahad that the defence were to pretend. While

The 'Tombs' prison, New York, where Thaw awaited trial

Evelyn Nesbit was in the clutches of the monster into which Stanford White had been distorted, the unhappy Ethel Thomas was having her own battle with another monster. In the law suit that Ethel brought against Thaw in 1902, she alleged: 'At first he lavished much affection on me. He took me on automobile rides to theatres and other places of amusement, and bought flowers and jewellery for me . . . One day, however, I met him by appointment, and while we were walking towards his apartment at the Bedford, 304 Fifth Avenue, he stopped at a store and bought a dog whip. I asked him what it was for and he replied, laughingly, "That's for you dear!" I thought he was joking, but no sooner were we in his apartment and the door was locked, than his entire demeanour changed. A wild expression came into his eyes, and he seized me and with his whip beat me until my clothes hung in tatters.' Even Evelyn was to swear a legal affidavit recording the sadistic brutality to which she had been subjected by Thaw on one of their trips abroad.

When all this information was assembled and finally taken to court on 23 January, 1907, the Thaws' injection of money into the legal system had reached farcical proportions. So many lawyers were retained that they were literally falling over each other at times – even the leading counsel who was to plead the case, Delphin M. Delmas, was initially misinformed as to the plea, and defence witnesses were arriving at the court to find that nobody knew why they had been called.

One sublime gesture had been the backing by Mrs Thaw senior of a play based crudely on the more lurid incidents in the case. The melodrama was enacted in Brooklyn's Amphion Theater, and had as its three main characters Harold Daw, Emeline Hudspeth Daw, and Stanford Black. After committing a series of unspeakable crimes – against humanity in general and against womankind in particular – the villainous Black is shot down by Daw at a roof-garden theatre. The avenger addresses his audience from a prison cell (in the Tombs): 'No jury on earth will send me to the chair, no matter what I have done or what I have been, for the killing of the man who defamed my wife. That is the unwritten law made by men themselves, and upon its virtue I will stake my life.'

As it turned out, the jury at the Criminal Branch of the Supreme Court of the State of New York didn't send Harry Thaw to the electric chair either. Despite all attempts by District Attorney William Travers Jerome, a tireless campaigner against corruption in the legal system, the Thaw fortune had managed to generate such confusion, such doubt, that *all* issues, let alone the main ones, had been tactically camouflaged; dollars had on the one hand bought a lot of silence, and on the other such extensive campaigns of vilification that even after 24 hours the jury was unable to agree on a verdict. Subsequently it was revealed that the division had been seven for first-degree murder and five for not guilty by reason of insanity.

A retrial opened nine months later on 6 January 1908. Leading the defence on this occasion was Martin W. Littlejohn. District Attorney Jerome once again led for the prosecution, and after a re-washing of the previous year's dirty laundry, Foreman Gremmels announced the result of another gruelling 24-hour jury retirement: 'We, the jury, find the defendant not guilty as charged in the indictment on the ground of the defendant's insanity.' It was not the conviction for first-degree murder that he would have liked, but there must have been a certain amount of satisfaction for William Jerome as he listened to Justice Dowling read out the sentence: '. . . the Court therefore orders that the defendant, being in custody and being a person dangerous to the public safety, the said Harry K. Thaw shall be kept in custody and shall be sent to the Asylum for the Criminally Insane at Matteawan forthwith. The Sheriff of New York County is charged with the duty of immediately executing this order.'

But the iniquities this brutal psychopath would not be contained behind the bolted doors of the Matteawan Asylum; the Thaw millions had by no means been exhausted. Within three months of committal, in May 1908, Mrs William Thaw employed a new team of legal talent to take out a writ of *habeas corpus*. This writ was dismissed. So was a second, in which Thaw's case was not helped by the evidence of Mrs Susie Merrill, described by one observer as 'fat, breathless, with nerves on edge [looking like] the pallid and bloated beast of dark caverns drawn out into strange sunlight, and squirming under it'. To Harry Thaw she must have looked like Nemesis as she stood in the box and recounted how Thaw regularly rented rooms at her bawdy-house for the purpose of submitting young girls to sadistic whippings – indiscretions which he had hoped to silence with a sum of $40,000 (his appetite can be judged by the fact that this was to be divided between 233 girls). It was also at this time that Evelyn Thaw decided that enough was enough and threw her lot in with the opposition.

A third writ in 1912 was again steered to defeat by Evelyn; this time accompanied in court by a baby son; the boy had been named Russell William Thaw, even though Harry had denied that it was his child. Evelyn also testified that Thaw had threatened her with extermination as soon as he was released – his exact words were: 'I suppose I'll have to kill you next.'

The following year the Thaws put hand in pocket for the purpose of bribing Matteawan Superintendent John W. Russell to certify Harry sane; the result was the forced resignation of Russell and the conviction of the lawyer John Anhut, who acted as go-between. However, money saved on this exploit was put to good use in hiring the New York Gopher Gang for $25,000. Their instructions were to spring Harry Thaw from the asylum and transport him to Canada, which, with considerable help from bribed warders at that establishment, was done on Sunday, 17 August 1913. It had taken seven years, but the Thaw fortune had at last secured the release of a miscreant son. With great good sense the Canadian Minister of Justice returned Mr Thaw to the United States, though it was not a popular move among the common people, for whom Harry had become something of a celebrity; he remained for another year at liberty while the lawyers wrangled.

Finally ordered to New York, Harry Thaw renewed his acquaintance with the Tombs, and with the courtroom in which he had starred twice before. By 16 July 1915, it was all over. With the judgement of the court at his third

Harry Thaw covers his face as he is taken from court to jail

trial declaring that he was not insane, Harry Thaw was acquitted of all charges and returned once more to the streets, on which he was feted like some conquering hero.

The final bill to the Thaw family was estimated to have been close to a million dollars. And as they say on Broadway, 'You can't convict a million dollars.'

It was left to the *New York Sun* to sum up for sanity. An editorial headed 'How To Be A Hero' concluded with the words: 'In all this nauseous business we don't know what makes the gorge rise more, the pervert buying his way out, or the perverted idiots who hail him with wild huzzas.'

This *could* have been the end of the Harry Thaw story; but eighteen months after his release Thaw was in trouble again, this time for the kidnapping of nineteen-year-old Frederick Gump Jr. Surviving an attempted suicide, Thaw was once again judged insane and committed to the mental ward of Pennsylvania State Hospital, leaving the family to settle the Gump lawsuit in the only way they knew how – it cost them an alleged $25,000.

At the beginning of 1924 a brief hearing found Harry Thaw sane again, despite evidence that one of his favourite pastimes in the

hospital had been hurling pet rabbits high in the air and, when they landed, torturing them. One tends to concur with Evelyn's view: 'I am not surprised at the verdict, there was dirty work at the crossroads that's all.'

This *should* have been the end of the Harry Thaw story. Beyond enjoying New York society life and penning a rambling autobiography of little literary merit, Harry's activities passed mostly without notice for several years. True, he was refused entry into England in 1928, but that was only because they held old-fashioned views on the correct place for murderers; and it is true he caused a violent scene in *Chez Evelyn*, a café run by his former wife. But Harry's real problem was that he couldn't resist beating people up. Of course he paid for the privilege, and the privilege of beating up nightclub hostess Marcia Estardus cost him $16,000 in 1931. Six years later Paul Jaeck was a couple of thousand dollars richer for a black eye which he earned in his capacity as wine waiter – he made the mistake of asking Harry Thaw to pay his champagne bill.

On 21 February 1947, Harry K. Thaw finally faced an adversary that he couldn't buy off. The Grim Reaper left 'Mad Harry' dead from a heart attack.

1907

Maria Vere Goold

The Body in the Trunk. *A classic case of the 'Trunk Murder' genre, where the body was cut up and boxed for shipping to London. The plot was betrayed when the putrefying remains came to the unwelcome attention of the left-luggage clerk.*

The two passengers arrived with their luggage at Marseilles off the Monte Carlo Express on the morning of 5 August 1907. Their first stop, having secured the services of a porter, was at the baggage office where they deposited their large trunk in the care of a clerk named Pons. It had been labelled for dispatch to London's Charing Cross station, and Pons was left to complete the paperwork while the trunk's owners took up their reservations at the Hotel du Louvre de Paix, carrying with them a heavy bag which had not left the woman's grasp since they disembarked from the train.

As young Monsieur Pons attended to his duties he became uncomfortably aware of a strange, not entirely pleasant odour circulating about the office, the origin of which turned out to be the London-bound cabin trunk. As he attempted to move it, the clerk's hand met a sticky patch of reddish-brown liquid which appeared to have seeped from the luggage. Perhaps he was just being efficient, or perhaps he was simply inquisitive, but the youth made straight for the Hotel du Louvre to confront his customers. 'It must be the poultry,' the woman

snorted, 'they might bleed a little.' If she were him, the lady went on, she would get the trunk off to London as quickly as possible.

Instead, Pons went to the railway police where an Inspector listened to his story and decided that on no account should the owners of the trunk leave Marseilles until it had been opened and checked. For some extraordinary reason known only to himself, the Inspector sent the youth Pons back to the hotel to persuade the mysterious couple to go back to the railway station, and the unlikely trio took a cab back to the baggage office. *En route* the woman tried to buy the clerk off with several thousand francs, but Pons was too deeply involved now, even if he felt tempted.

Before long the cause of the smell coming from the cabin trunk was explained; it arose from the dismembered human torso and arms which were putrefying inside it. As for the kitbag which had seemed so precious to its

Fanciful impression of the discovery of Madame Levin's dismembered body

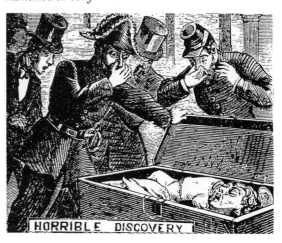

HORRIBLE DISCOVERY

43

owners, that contained the legs and head belonging to the same body. It was later identified as that of a lady named Emma Erika Levin.

More important, who exactly were the apparently aristocratic couple who were trying to send one half of a corpse across the Channel to England, and carried the other half around with them? The woman introduced herself to the police as Lady Vere Goold, and her companion as Sir Vere Goold – in reality neither of them had any right whatever to such titles. Maria Girodin had been born in Switzerland in 1877, and had already been widowed twice in suspicious circumstances when she met an Irishman named Vere Goold in London. For a year or so after their marriage the Goolds sponged off relatives, and when they had worn out their welcome, transferred their activities to Monte Carlo where they drank and gambled away such funds as remained. Things were beginning to look decidedly bleak on the financial front when 'Lady' Vere Goold cultivated the acquaintance of Madame Levin, a wealthy Swedish widow. How was Maria to know it would be so difficult to prise Madame's money from her? How was she to know that even when she did manage to scrounge £40 the wretched woman would want it back?

On 4 August 1907, a Sunday, Her Ladyship invited Emma Levin out to the Villa Menesimy where she and 'Sir' Vere Goold rented rooms. Lured on the pretext of having her loan repaid Madame Levin was attempting to engage in conversation with an, as usual, inebriated host, when her hostess snuck up behind and stunned the poor woman with a blow from a fire-poker and finished the bloody deed with a knife. After helping themselves to Madame's jewellery, the couple dismembered her body in the bath, packed the parts into the trunk and the hold-all, and fled to Marseilles ... which is where they had the misfortune to encounter baggage clerk Pons.

'Sir' and 'Lady' Vere Goold were put on trial in Marseilles, and after scenes of histrionics that earned her the popular soubriquet *La Grande Comédienne*, Maria was sentenced to death for being the dominant force in the killing. The sentence was later commuted, and both she and her husband were condemned to life

imprisonment on the French penal colony of Cayenne in French Guiana. In July 1908 Maria contracted typhoid fever and died; Goold committed suicide the following year.

UNITED KINGDOM

Horace George Rayner

The Case of the Unwanted Son. *In which William Whiteley, the self-styled 'Universal Provider', was killed by his illegitimate son in a dispute over paternity. The subsequent trial was notable for exposing the sexual intrigues of the Whiteley family.*

January 24 1907 found 75-year-old William Whiteley striding with satisfaction around his famous Queensway emporium. He had some reason for complacency – the self-styled 'Universal Provider' had founded the first British department store in the 1880s, and was now indisputably the foremost shopkeeper in London. True, his rise to success had earned Whiteley some unpopularity and the jealousy of his business rivals but now, a quarter of a century later, on this busy January afternoon, the thin winter sun shone through the windows on a man at peace with the world, or at least with his part of it.

Suddenly the calm efficiency of Whiteley's was disturbed by a young man striding purposefully into the master's office and, after a brief but violent quarrel, drawing a revolver from his pocket and firing three shots in full view of witnesses.

Either of the first two bullets would have proved fatal to old Whiteley as he slumped to the carpet, but the third shot, from a gun now turned on himself, failed to despatch the assassin, entering his right eye-socket and exiting at the root of his nose.

As the man identified as Horace George Rayner was rushed to St Mary's Hospital for emergency surgery, a message was found in a notebook among his possessions, reading: 'To all whom it may concern: William Whiteley is my father.'

George Rayner – Horace's foster-father – once had a mistress named Emily Turner, who had a sister Louisa. It transpired that George and Emily, and Louisa and William Whiteley, made up a fairly frequent foursome – the result of which fun and games was the birth of two illegitimate children to Emily and one to Louisa.

The brief trial of Horace Rayner took place in March 1907, the first murder case to be heard in the newly rebuilt Old Bailey. Rayner pleaded not guilty by reason of temporary insanity, and the sordid story surrounding his disputed paternity went a long way to arousing sympathy which, while it did not excuse an act of cold-blooded murder, did ensure Horace's merciful reprieve from the statutory death sentence. Horace Rayner tried to commit suicide twice before being released from prison in 1919, having served twelve years of his life sentence.

Rayner strode into his father's office . . .

Contemporary scenes from the Rayner trial

HORACE GEORGE RAYNER IN THE WITNESS BOX

RAYNER IN THE DOCK

MR MUIR THE PROSECUTING COUNSEL FOR THE PROSECUTION

THE RAYNER TRIAL AT THE NEW OLD BAILEY

LOUISA TURNER

ALICE MAY RAYNER PRISONER'S WIFE

ANNIE KNOWLES

1908

Oscar Slater

Rough Justice. *Classic miscarriage of justice which resulted in Oscar Slater being imprisoned for eighteen years for a murder of which he was clearly innocent. His eventual release was due in great part to the efforts of Sir Arthur Conan Doyle, creator of Sherlock Holmes.*

There lived in Glasgow in 1908 a maiden lady of 81 named Marion Gilchrist. She had occupied her first-floor flat at 15 Queen's Terrace for the past 30 years. On the floor below lived the Adams family, and the flat above was, at the

Miss Marion Gilchrist

time of which we speak, untenanted. Miss Gilchrist had one servant, Helen Lambie, a girl of 21 who had been with her for three years. The old lady was comfortably off, and throughout her life had taken great pleasure from acquiring a collection of jewellery, the value of which had caused her several times to voice the fear that she may one day be robbed. As a consequence of this apprehension, she had two strong locks attached to her outer door, and, further, arranged with Mr Adams below a system of knocks on the floor that would signal distress.

It was customary for the maid to go out at about seven o'clock each evening to buy an evening newspaper, after which the girl would go out again to do any necessary shopping. On the night of 21 December, Lambie left her mistress reading by the dining-room fire and took the keys with her, locking the doors on her way out.

Helen Lambie's recollection of her movements that evening were related at the trial:

I went out for a newspaper that night, and I had some other messages to do after that. Miss Gilchrist gave me a penny for the newspaper, and ten shillings for the other messages. I looked at the kitchen clock just before I went out and saw it was just seven o'clock. I intended to go for the newspaper first and come back to the house, and then go out again for my other messages; I had done that before . . . I had to go to St George's Road for the newspaper; it would take me about three minutes to walk from the house to the newspaper shop; I would be away from the house about ten minutes altogether. When I got back to the house I noticed that the door was open, and was not as I had left it. I went upstairs. I did not have to use my key to open the hall door. I saw a wet footmark on two of the steps when I got inside the door. When I got up to the landing I found Mr Adams there, a neighbour who lived below. He

46

was never a visitor at the flat, and I was astonished to find him there. He said to me that there was a noise in our flat, and that the ceiling was like to crack. The flat door was locked. When I unlocked the door I saw a man coming, and I stepped back. The man was coming from the direction of the spare bedroom. He came through the hall and passed me, and went downstairs. I then went into the kitchen and saw that everything was all right there; I went into the bedroom, it was all right there. Then I went into the dining-room and saw Miss Gilchrist lying on the rug in front of the fire. The rug was over her head; I did not see her face. I went out and told Mr Adams that something was wrong, that the man had done something to Miss Gilchrist. The man, when he passed me, was very close. I noticed that he held his head down. When he passed I turned round and got a good look at him. I heard him going down the stairs, not rapidly, but deliberately. When I first saw him coming from the bedroom he had nothing in his hand. He was wearing a dark cap, a fawn overcoat, and dark trousers. I did not notice what else he was wearing. His coat was open. He was about five feet seven or five feet eight high. He did not say anything as he passed. I noticed his walk; he was forward a little; it was a bit shaky. When I saw my mistress lying on the floor with the rug over her, I ran downstairs . . . Mr Adams also ran downstairs, and then he went in the direction of Queen's Crescent. When I returned to the house I saw Constable Neil there. Dr Adams [no relation to Mr Adams] was summoned. I did not find anything out of place in the dining-room, but in the spare bedroom I saw the box there with the papers taken out and scattered about on the floor. I never saw anybody visiting the house the least like the man who came out of the bedroom when I opened the door that night. That same night I missed a brooch belonging to Miss Gilchrist; it was usually kept in a small open dish on a dressing-table in the bedroom. It was a diamond crescent brooch, about the size of a half-crown. I saw it in the dish on the day before the murder. I saw beside it a gold and diamond ring which was left, while the brooch was taken.

The subsequent testimony of Mr Adams, the neighbour, agrees in all major respects with that of Helen Lambie. He had been in his flat with his sisters, Laura and Rowena, when he heard 'a sound like a thud, and three distinct knocks, as if wanting assistance'. Laura Adams immediately sent her brother up to investigate. He had returned to his own flat, and been sent back again to Miss Gilchrist's by his sisters at the time the servant, Lambie, came in from her errands, and he was standing outside the front door when she opened it and went inside. Adams clearly recalled the mysterious stranger, who immediately left Miss Gilchrist's flat:

I stood on the threshold, half in and half out, and just when the girl had got to the kitchen a well-dressed man appeared. I did not suspect him, and she said nothing, and he came up to me quite pleasantly; I did not suspect anything wrong for a minute. I thought the man was going to speak to me, till he got past; then I suspected something wrong, and by that time the girl ran into the kitchen and put the gas up . . . I said 'Where is your mistress?' and she went into the dining-room. She said: 'Oh, come here'; I just went in and saw the horrible spectacle, and I said: 'Go to the house door and stand there till I come back.' I went down to St George's Road, and I could see nobody there, but I could see up to Park Road, and could see people in the distance, and I made after them as fast as I could go, but it was no use.

I had seen the man go downstairs. I saw him walk quite coolly till he got up to me, and then he went down quickly, like greased lightning, and that aroused my suspicions. He was a man a little taller than me, a little broader in the shoulders; not a well-built man, but well-featured and clean-shaven, and I cannot exactly swear to his moustache, but if he had any it was very little. He was rather a commercial traveller type, or perhaps a clerk, and I did not

Miss Helen Lambie

know but what he might be one of Miss Gilchrist's friends. He had on dark trousers and a light overcoat; whether it was fawn or grey I could not really say. I do not recollect what sort of hat he had; I am not sure on that point. He seemed gentlemanly and well dressed. He had nothing in his hand as far as I could tell. I did not notice anything about his way of walking at all. When I failed to get on his track I came back to the house. I then found the servant and a constable there. The constable and I entered the dining-room together. We uncovered the body and found she had been battered to death, but she was breathing – just breathing. I went for Dr Adams as hard as I could go. I brought another constable, and I phoned to the police office. I myself waited in the house for the police. I had not my spectacles on at the time.

The relevant testimony of Dr Arthur Adams and Police Constable Neil was as follows.

The dining-room was a fairly large apartment. Its windows (two in number) look into West Princes Street. Along the east wall of the room is the fire-place. On a carpet rug in front of this fire-place the body was lying. The head was pointing diagonally to the fire-place, and the feet towards the dining-room door. The right arm was extended at right angles from the body, and the left arm was lying alongside of, and parallel to, the body. The left leg was crossed over the right below the knees.

Without disturbing the body, it was observed that the head and face had been very much smashed.

Inside Miss Gilchrist's dining-room; her body was found just in front of the fireplace

There were wounds on the right cheek extending from the mouth, wounds of the right forehead, and of the right side of the head. There was a deep hole on the left side of the face between the eye-socket and the left ear.

The left eyeball was entirely missing, having either been driven into the cavity of the brain or having been gouged out. The right eye was partially torn out of its socket by the deep fracture of the right side of the brow. There was much blood on and among the hair of the head. On the carpet rug beneath the head on both sides was a considerable amount of clotted blood, and fluid blood had soaked into the substance of the rug. Between the head and the fender of the fire-place a piece of brain tissue weighing about three-quarters of an ounce, as well as smaller pieces, and several pieces of bone covered with blood were found. Two of these pieces were retained.

The fire-irons were in their places. They were bespattered with blood, as were also the grate and the fire-bars. The legs of some of the chairs in the neighbourhood and the coal-scuttle were also bespattered with blood. All these signs indicated that the injuries had been inflicted in the neighbourhood of where the body was found lying, and that the injuries had been produced by very forcible application of some instrument.

There was also found between the head and the fender a complete plate (gold) of artificial upper teeth.

Both hands were remarkably pallid. There was no blood on the right hand or fingers, but there was dried blood between the fingers of the left hand. The skin rug already referred to was found when the body was first discovered to be more or less covering the body. On examination of it blood was found among the hair about the middle of the rug.

The spectacles of the deceased were found on the table in front of an open magazine. The chair, referred to as having been removed, originally stood, when the body was found, in front of the magazine, standing on its four legs.

On 22 December, the morning after the murder, the Glasgow police circulated a description of the man they suspected of being Marion Gilchrist's killer, a description based on the observations of Adams and Lambie:

Male; between the ages of twenty-five and thirty years, five foot eight or nine inches in height, slim build, dark hair, clean-shaven, dressed in light grey overcoat and dark cloth cap.

Four days later – Christmas Day – they were able to publish a more detailed description:

The man wanted is about twenty-eight or thirty years of age, tall and thin, with his face shaved clean of all hair, while a distinctive feature is that his nose is slightly turned to one side. The witness thinks the twist is to the right side. He wore one of the popular tweed hats known as Donegal hats, and has a fawn-coloured overcoat which might have been a waterproof, also dark trousers and brown boots.

These additional points came from the statement of a further eye-witness to the mysterious man who left 15 Queen's Terrace, a young girl named Mary Barrowman:

I am now fifteen years of age. I am employed with Mr Malcolm M'Callum, bootmaker, Great Western Road, Glasgow, and I live at No. 9 Seamore Street. I remember that on the night of the 21st December last I left my employer's shop in the Great Western Road at about seven o'clock with a parcel to be delivered at Cleveland Street, off Vincent Street . . . I walked along West Princes Street in the direction of St George's Road. When I came opposite the house a man came running out of it and knocked up against me. He wore a fawn overcoat, a dark suit of clothes, and a Donegal hat; he had dark brown boots. He ran towards West Cumberland Street, and I could see he turned down there. I was just at the lamp-post near the house when this happened. I got a good look at him, both when he was coming up to me and when he knocked against me. He was tall and broad-shouldered, and he had a slight twist in his nose. He was clean shaved and had dark hair. He had a Donegal hat on, and was wearing it down over his face. I got a look at his face, and I would know him again if I saw him.

It was on the evening of Christmas Day that the police came at last upon a definite clue. It was brought to their notice that a German Jew of the assumed name of Oscar Slater had been endeavouring to dispose of the pawn ticket of a crescent diamond brooch of about the same value as the missing one; also that, in a general way, he bore a resemblance to the published description. Still more hopeful did this clue appear when, upon raiding the lodgings in which this man and his mistress lived, it was found that they had left Glasgow that very night by the nine o'clock train with tickets (over this point there was some clash of evidence) either for Liverpool or London. Three days later

the Glasgow police learned that the couple had sailed on 26 December on the *Lusitania* for New York under the names Mr and Mrs Otto Sando.

Oscar Slater was at once arrested upon arriving at New York, and his seven trunks of baggage were impounded and sealed. On the face of it there was a good case against him, for he had undoubtedly pawned a diamond brooch, and he had subsequently fled under a false name for America. The Glasgow police had reason to think they had got their man. Two officers, accompanied by the witnesses to identity – Adams, Lambie and Barrowman – set off at once to carry through the extradition proceedings and bring the suspect back to trial. In the New York court they first set eyes upon the prisoner, and each of them expressed the opinion that he was at any rate exceedingly like the person they had seen in Glasgow. Their actual identification of him was vitiated by the fact that Adams and Barrowman had been shown his photographs before attending the court, and also that he was led past them, an obvious prisoner, while they were waiting in the corridor. Still, however much one may discount the actual identification, it cannot be denied that each witness saw a close resemblance between the man before them and the man whom they had seen in Glasgow.

On 21 February Oscar Slater was back in Glasgow, having voluntarily consented to return. On 3 May his trial took place at the High Court in Edinburgh.

But already the bottom of the case had dropped out. The starting link of what had seemed an imposing chain of incriminating evidence had suddenly broken. It will be remembered that the original suspicion of Slater was founded on the fact that he had pawned a crescent diamond brooch. The ticket was found in his possession, and the brooch recovered. It was not the one which was missing from the victim's room; in fact it had belonged to Oscar Slater for many years, and he had pawned it frequently before.

Apart from this fact, several of the other points of the prosecution case had shown themselves to be unreliable. It had seemed at first that Slater's departure had been sudden and unpremeditated – in short, the flight of a guilty

Oscar Slater

man. It was quickly proved that this was not the case, and documents were produced to show that the arrangements for his emigration had been made long before the tragic death of Miss Gilchrist.

Further details came out at the trial: first, as to Slater's movements on the day of the crime. He began the day, according to his own account and that of his mistress and their maid, by receiving two letters which had the effect of hastening his journey to the New World. Indeed, the whole day seems then to have been spent in preparations for their departure. He gave notice to his servant Schmalz as from the following Saturday, and shortly before five in the evening Slater wrote a letter to a London post office where he had deposited a small amount of money. At 6.12 p.m. a telegram was sent in his name – and presumably by him – from the Central Station to Dent's in London for the return of his watch which had been under repair. According to two witnesses Oscar Slater was seen at 6.20 p.m. in a billiard hall. The murder, the court was reminded, was committed at seven o'clock.

Slater was observed to spend about ten minutes in the billiard hall, and left some time between 6.30 and 6.40 p.m. One of the witnesses, a man named Rathman, testified that at the time Slater was wearing a moustache about a quarter of an inch long – so noticeable that he could not possibly be mistaken for a clean-shaven man. Antoine, Slater's mistress, and Schmalz, the servant, deposed that Slater dined

at home that evening at seven o'clock, and at 9.45 p.m. he was to be found 'trying to raise the wind' at a favourite gambling club.

The evidence for the prosecution rested in essence upon two sets of identity witnesses. The first were those who had actually seen the murderer, including Adams, Helen Lambie and the Barrowman girl. The second set consisted of twelve people who had, at various dates, seen a man loitering suspiciously in the street in which Miss Gilchrist lived. All of these witnesses – some with confidence, most with some reserve – were prepared to identify the man as Oscar Slater.

Apart from this evidence, the only thing which might connect Slater with the crime was a hammer found by the police among his baggage; the prosecution undertook to prove that this was the weapon with which he had committed the murder. On this point there was a sharp divergence of opinion among the medical experts. Professor Glaister for the prosecution stated:

I did not find in the dining-room any implement which looked as if it had been used for the purpose of murdering Miss Gilchrist. The fire-irons were undisturbed in their places, and all the ornaments were undisturbed. The fire-irons, the tongs, the poker, the fender and the fire-bars and the sides of the grate all bore bloodstains as did other objects and pieces of furniture in the room ... It was clear that the injuries had been produced practically at the point where the body was found. I inferred that from the spattering of the blood in the neighbourhood, and also from the fact that round the head there was a considerable quantity of blood. From my experience my view is that the assailant knelt on the woman's chest and struck violently at the head with the implement that he held. The weight of his body plus the force exercised in violently attacking the head, accounted for the rib fractures and other fractures of the chest bone. The bones in a person over eighty years of age are much more brittle than in a younger person. I formed an opinion as to the character of the weapon with which the injuries to the face and head had been inflicted. From the nature of the wounds I arrived at the conclusion that the weapon was not uniformly the same at the striking part, for this reason: we found several wounds of different sizes and of different shapes. Also we found the left eyeball, in a burst condition, driven into the brain. That indicated the weapon must have been of a pointed character to have enabled the eyeball to have been driven into the brain because a large weapon that would have been likely to have caused the larger wounds could not have entered the orbit, because the orbit is bounded by bone.

The spindle-shaped wounds were either produced by a relatively sharp surface of a blunt instrument, such as the head of a hammer or any such implement. I have examined this hammer before for another purpose, and in my opinion it could, in the hands of a strong man and forcibly wielded, have produced the injuries found on the body. I carefully examined the claws of the hammer and made measurements. I can only say that this instrument accounts most easily for the different classes of wounds, and particularly the eye mischief. I cannot see any other instrument that could do it unless it was of the same type – the head of a crowbar of varying sizes, for example.

The hammer had the appearance of having been scrubbed, and between the danges by which the head is joined to the wooden shaft, and particularly at the sides and half-way down, the shaft looks as if it has been washed, scrubbed or sand-papered. The iron has the same appearance, though that effect I have seen on a comparatively cheap hammer where the polishing has not been very carefully done.

This evidence was supported by Dr Hugh Galt.

For the defence, Dr Robertson deposed:

I consider this small hammer a very unlikely weapon. I examined it for bloodstains, but there are no bloodstains on it; it has no appearance whatever of having been washed or scraped. It has absolutely no signs of blood about it. I do not think it is the instrument. I should expect to find one of heavier weight than this – a heavy poker, it may be – a crowbar. I do not see how these spindle-shaped wounds could ever have been inflicted by this hammer.

With all the problems of this conflicting evidence before them, the jury, on the fourth day of the trial, retired to consider their verdict. They were out for one hour and twenty minutes, before returning to announce the verdict that few in the court expected: 'guilty' by a majority. Lord Guthrie now had no alternative but to pronounce sentence of death, condemning the prisoner to be hanged at Glasgow on 27 May.

Two days before the sentence was due to be carried out, Oscar Slater's sentence was commuted to penal servitude for life.

It was apparent to a great many people that if ever there was a reasonable doubt in a case, then it was the case of Oscar Slater. Immediately the trial was over, a vigorous campaign was launched for an inquiry into the possibility of a miscarriage of justice.

One of the influential men of the time enthusiastically to espouse Slater's cause was Sir Arthur Conan Doyle, who, over the succeeding years, penned thousands of published words in an attempt to secure Slater's release. Doyle's initial response to the verdict and sentence was the following:

Having just got clear of the Edalji case*, I became entangled in that of Oscar Slater. The one was in a way the cause of the other, for since I was generally given credit for having got Edalji out of prison, it was hoped by those who believed that Slater's condemnation was a miscarriage of justice, that I might be able to do the same for him. I went into the matter most reluctantly, but when I examined the facts I saw that it was an even worse case than the Edalji one and that this unhappy man had, in all human probability, no more to do with the murder for which he had been condemned than I had. I am convinced that when on being convicted he cried out to the judge that he never knew that such a woman as the deceased existed, he was speaking the literal truth...

Conan Doyle then proceeded to analyse the evidence against Slater: the supposedly stolen diamond brooch, which proved to have been Slater's all along, and quite unconnected with the Gilchrist murder; the fact that his 'hurried flight' had been planned for some length of time, and that the flimsy hammer, part of a set of cheap tools that came on a card, could by no stretch of the imagination have caused the savage wounds suffered by the unfortunate Miss Gilchrist. More alarming still were the appalling circumstances under which the witnesses to Slater's identity were coerced,

*In 1903 young George Edalji, a solicitor and the son of the vicar of Great Wyrley, Staffordshire, was accused in a series of ugly poison-pen letters of being responsible for a local outbreak of cattle mutilating. Edalji, though clearly innocent, was sentenced to seven years' imprisonment, and only the most intense campaign by Conan Doyle and others secured his release after three.

wittingly or not, into pointing their finger at the wrong man: how this sallow-complexioned, dark-haired Jew had been paraded among a group of fair Scots; how the girl Barrowman had been shown photographs of Slater before being asked to identify him. And when it came to identifying the mysterious man said to have been loitering around Marion Gilchrist's home, most of the witnesses described a man either unlike or totally the opposite of Oscar Slater. On the matter of Slater's alibi – that he was taking his supper at home at the time of the murder – neither his mistress nor the servant were allowed to give evidence in court.

Finally, Conan Doyle emphasised that the crown secured their conviction by only nine jury votes to six (five were 'Not Proven', one 'Not Guilty'):

The scaffold was actually erected and it was only two mornings before his execution when the order came which prevented a judicial murder. As it was, the man became a convict – and is one still.

It is a painful story, and as I read it and realised the futility of it all I was moved to do everything I could for the man. I was abided by the opinion of Sir Herbert Stephen, who read the evidence and declared that there was not even a *prima facie* case against the man. I, therefore, started a newspaper agitation and wrote a small book with an account of the whole matter.

For example, at the trial it had been stated that Slater on reaching Liverpool from Glasgow had gone to a Liverpool hotel under a false name as if he were trying to throw the police off his track. It was shown that this was not true, and that he had signed the register with his own Glasgow name. I say his Glasgow name, because he has had several pseudonyms in the course of his not-too-reputable career, and, as a fact, he took his actual passage under a false name, showing that he intended to make a clear start in America . . .

On the whole, if I had to reconstruct the crime, I should judge that the jewellery had nothing to do with the matter, since other articles of value which were exposed were untouched. On the other hand a box was opened, and if it were violently opened it would account for that sound of 'breaking sticks' heard by Adams. There were papers in this box and their nature has, so far as I know, not been disclosed in the trial. They may have been securities of value, or the murderer may have thought that such deeds were to be found there. It is along this line of investigation, as it seems to me, that the inquiry should have moved, and I do not see how it could have led to a Bohemian foreigner who never had any connection with the household, nor any knowledge which would have led him in so short a time to the very room and the very box in which the old lady's papers had actually been stored. Some day, doubtless, the truth will out, but meanwhile the unfortunate Slater grows old in his prison cell.

In fact the truth never did out, though happily for Oscar Slater the immense effort applied to his case by such tireless supporters of justice as Sir Arthur and the celebrated criminologist William Roughead ended in his release from Peterhead jail after eighteen years' incarceration. For this injustice Slater was awarded compensation of £6,000; he died in 1948.

UNITED STATES

A female Bluebeard

Belle Gunness had already disposed of two husbands and committed a couple of insurance frauds before settling on the career of a female Bluebeard. Establishing herself on a remote farm at La Porte, Indiana, Belle attracted 'suitors' via the newspaper matrimonial advertisements: 'Rich, good-looking woman, owner of a big farm, desires to correspond with a gentleman of wealth and refinement, object matrimony.' Belle Gunness slaughtered fourteen prospective partners, banked the large sum of money they had been persuaded to bring with them as an investment in the future, and buried their bodies on the estate. In April 1908 a fire at the farm led to the discovery not only of Belle's victims, but of Belle herself and her three children. Ray Lamphere, a local handyman and Belle's lover, was acquitted of her murder, but sentenced to a term in prison for arson.

1909

The Gorse Hall Murder

One of the most celebrated and enduring mysteries of crime took place in the quiet borough of Dukin-field in Cheshire, a most unlikely stage on which to focus the national spotlight.

Gorse Hall – a name fated to be on the lips of a nation – was a large private residence in its own extensive grounds; in 1909 it was occupied by Mr George Henry Storrs, a building contrac-tor with interests in a number of textile mills. Storrs was a wealthy man, and held in high respect locally. On the evening of 1 November he was at home with his family and the regular household staff. He, his wife and his adopted daughter Miss Marion Middleton Lindley were in the dining-room taking supper; Ellen Cooper the housemaid and Mary Evans the cook were in the kitchen; and the coachman and his family were in their quarters over the stables.

At about 9.20 p.m. Mary Evans went down to the cellars, and as she returned was sur-prised by a man pointing a revolver at her; with commendable pluck Mary turned on her heel, fled upstairs and raised the alarm. George Storrs rushed out of the dining-room and closed with the gun-toting intruder, much to the disadvantage of the latter. Storrs was a powerfully built six-footer, still in his prime at 49 and more than a match for the intruder, who also had Mrs Storrs to contend with. Clearly infuriated by having her repast interrupted by

this murderous attack on her husband, she flew at the man, brandishing a stick, and disarmed him. She then ran upstairs and sounded the alarm bell. During this brief respite in what was turning into a decidedly uneven fight, the intruder decided to shorten the odds by bring-ing out a knife and stabbing George Storrs several times in the back. Still Storrs fought back, even managing to haul his assassin down to the scullery and locking him in before col-lapsing on to the floor mortally wounded. In the confusion which followed, however, the mystery attacker broke out through the scullery window and fled. The gallant George Storrs lived for only another twenty minutes.

Police from Stalybridge, led by their Chief Constable Captain John Bates, and from Dukin-field, under Superintendent Croghan, joined in the inquiry and the search of the grounds; bloodhounds were brought in, but at the end of the day all the police had was a vague

X marks the spot in the kitchen at Gorse Hall where Storrs was found

53

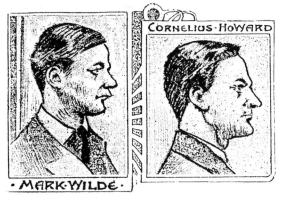

CORNELIUS·HOWARD

·MARK·WILDE·

Portrait drawings of Mark Wilde and Cornelius Howard

description of the attacker, so general as to fit half the population of the North-West. It certainly fitted 31-year-old Cornelius Howard, former butcher, Army reservist and petty criminal. It so happened that Howard was also a first cousin of the murdered man.

The case against Howard had been shaky from the start, despite his possession of a knife and the discovery of bloodspots on his clothing. The female servants of the house could make no positive identification, and Mrs Storrs could make no decision at all at the identity parade because 'they all look so untidy'; Marion Lindley was alone in feeling 'positive' that Howard was the intruder. There was no connection established between the accused and the gun, and his corroborated alibi was that he was playing dominoes at the Ring O'Bells in Huddersfield on the night of the murder. However, the coroner's jury returned a verdict of wilful murder against Howard and he was remanded to Assizes.

The case was heard at Chester before Mr Justice Pickford (later Lord Sterndale) on 3 March 1910; Howard was defended by Mr Austin Jones (later Mr Justice Jones). His alibi was unshakeable and the prosecution case amounted to nothing: Mr R. W. James in his short history of the Cheshire Constabulary* says: 'What is amazing about the proceedings is that they ever began on nothing more than

*To the Best of Our Skill and Knowledge, R. W. James. Published by Chief Constable of Cheshire, Chester, 1957.

mere suspicion and that the Director of Public Prosecutions could have been induced to take charge of the prosecution.'

And so the case was relegated to the 'Unsolved' file, where it would perhaps have been better to leave it. But the police seemed determined to compound the errors of the Howard case. In July 1910 they arrested Mark Wilde, a native of Stalybridge, on a charge of wounding a young man with a knife. While serving his sentence for this crime Wilde was put into an identity parade, where the Storrs servants owned that he looked to them 'even more like the murderer than Howard'. A former Army colleague (who later became a constable in the Liverpool City Police) was found who claimed that the service revolver used in the attack belonged to Wilde, and further identified it by its mechanical faults. Mark Wilde was put up before Mr Justice Horridge at the Chester Assizes.

The trial, which opened on 24 October 1910, lasted five days. Mrs Storrs was forced to relive the tragedy that she had been trying to forget for six months, and collapsed in the witness box; Cornelius Howard was put into the dock alongside Wilde in order that the jury might compare their features. Home Office senior analyst Dr Herbert Willcox testified that blood found on Wilde's clothing was human (at the time a great achievement for forensic serology), though the prisoner's contention that he had become bloodied in a fight in a pub was as good an explanation as any in those days before accurate blood grouping. Indeed, the jury must have felt that this was the best explanation, for they acquitted Wilde as their predecessors had acquitted Howard.

The police did not try for the proverbially lucky third time, and the Gorse Hall Murder became the Gorse Hall Mystery. The culprit was never caught, and it would probably be unwise to attach any importance to the fact that Storrs' coachman committed suicide shortly after Howard's arrest.

R. W. James sums up: 'The case of the Gorse Hall murder was not a good example of police work. No motive for the murder could be found except in the imagination of the press, and public.'

1910

Dr Bennett Clarke Hyde

Doctor Death. *The case of a physician who turned to murder, using – as so many healers-turned-killers do – poison to dispose of his victims. In this case, Dr Hyde killed more than once, setting his sights on an entire family.*

A thoroughly unscrupulous opportunist, Dr Bennett Clarke Hyde, a 40-year-old physician, married Miss Frances Swope, the niece of octogenarian Kansas millionaire Thomas Swope, in 1909. After the wedding Hyde not unnaturally became old Mr Swope's medical adviser and moved into the Swope mansion in order to be that much closer to the family fortune. Thomas Swope was not, at the age of 82, the strongest of men, and his health was deteriorating to the extent that he felt it was prudent to appoint an executor to handle the administration of his estate. To Hyde's evident disappointment Swope entrusted this responsibility to an old family friend, James Hunton. It was well known that under the terms of his will, all Swope's estate was to be divided equally between the nieces and nephews; if any died, their share would be divided among the survivors.

In September 1909 James Hunton fell ill and was attended by Dr Hyde. He did not long survive these ministrations, and his death – at least according to the certificate written by Hyde – was due to apoplexy.

Shortly afterwards Thomas Swope took to his sickbed, treated by Hyde and looked after by the trusted family nurse. As Swope became weaker so the sense of urgency grew within his physician, to the degree that Hyde was obliged to ask the nurse to intercede on his behalf and advise Mr Swope to make him, Hyde, the new executor of his will. The nurse said she would do no such thing, and the next she knew Hyde was shovelling pills down his patient's throat. Whatever they were, they did the old man no

Dr Bennett Clarke Hyde

good at all – in fact, within the quarter-hour he died. Hyde announced to the nurse: 'He's passed on, poor soul.' So soon? the nurse asked; oh yes, Hyde replied, at that age they can succumb very quickly to apoplexy.

Having failed to get control of the administration of the Swope estate, Bennett Hyde had to console himself with administering his wife's share – $250,000. Within weeks no fewer than five of the other beneficiaries were mysteriously stricken with typhoid; one of them, Christian, died in November 1909. Then Dr Hyde, who had been treating them, was called away on business, and the others recovered under treatment by another doctor brought in by the family nurse.

Now that Dr Hyde was officially under suspicion by the Swopes, the bodies of old Thomas and James Hunton were exhumed and subjected to post-mortem examination. Both corpses showed traces of strychnine *and* cyanide. On 9 February 1910 Dr Bennett Clarke Hyde was charged with the double murder of Swope and Hunton.

At a sensational trial, a horrified nation learned how Hyde had planned to dispose of the entire Swope family in order that he, through his wife, would inherit all the portions of Thomas's estate. A pharmacist was called to testify that Dr Hyde had made purchases of cyanide and strychnine on the pretence of killing vermin. A bacteriologist, Dr Stewart, told the court that Hyde had invented some cock and bull story about taking up bacteriology as a sort of hobby, and Stewart had reluctantly provided him with some typhoid cultures. Indeed, Stewart had been so apprehensive that he had later visited Hyde in order to ask for the samples back. Hyde claimed that he had got rid of them – which he had, of course; Christian Swope had died the following day to prove it.

UNITED KINGDOM

The Infamous Dr Crippen

Meanwhile, on the other side of the Atlantic, another American medic was committing the most famous of the 'Classic' English murders; even today, more than 80 years later, Dr Hawley Harvey Crippen is still a household name, epitomising the theatricality of murder: he murders a spiteful, domineering wife in favour of a young mistress, Ethel Le Neve, with whom he is desperately in love, cuts up the body and disposes of it heaven knows where – most of it was never found. He and Ethel then put on disguises (Ethel dressed as a young boy) and take a steamship to America, to the New World. Unfortunately the captain is something of an amateur detective, and via the newly invented wireless telegraph system alerts Scotland Yard to his suspicions about two of his passengers. Meanwhile the police have found a few fragments of Mrs Crippen buried in the cellar. There is a subsequent chase across the Atlantic by Chief Inspector Walter Dew (also in disguise) who overtakes and arrests the fugitives aboard ship. Then follows the ritual of the trial at the Old Bailey – the most famous criminal court in the world – where Crippen is literally fighting for his life in the shadow of the gallows. He loses the battle. Crippen is hanged, and according to his last wishes is buried holding a photograph of his beloved Ethel and surrounded by her love letters. Ethel herself is acquitted and builds a new life for herself.

Popular illustrations of the arrest of Crippen and Ethel Le Neve

Dr Hawley Harvey Crippen

At the end of the four-week trial there was little doubt remaining in anybody's mind that Hyde was an avaricious, murdering scoundrel who well deserved the sentence of life imprisonment that was imposed on him. Only one person remained convinced of his innocence: Mrs Frances Hyde, which was lucky for her husband, because she spent a large part of the family wealth on slick lawyers and cute publicists in a battle for Bennett Hyde's release. The lawyers found some minor irregularities in the conduct of the original trial, and the publicists made enough fuss about them for the Kansas Supreme Court to order a retrial.

There followed a sequence of legal oddities which almost challenged the Harry Thaw case of 1906 for the stench of corruption. At the first retrial in 1911 a juror fell sick and a mistrial was announced; it was later rumoured that this juryman's 'illness' had been bought with Swope money. At a third trial the jury was unable to agree on a verdict, and once again more cynical observers thought they smelled the whiff of largesse from the Swope's seemingly bottomless purse. By this time the District Attorney's office must have lost count of the number of trials, retrials and mistrials, because the state announced that Dr Bennett Hyde would stand trial for an incredible fourth time. And this was just what Hyde's lawyers were hoping for; at last they had an honest legal leg to stand on. According to the statute, they crowed, no man could be tried more than three times for the same crime. And so, on a technicality. Hyde was released from custody.

There is a postscript. After his release, Hyde returned to live with his ever-faithful wife Frances; but almost ten years later, she left their home and filed for divorce – it seems she had started suffering some sudden and rather worrying stomach pains . . .

THE PRISONERS' LANDING AT QUEBEC.

MISS LE NEVE RESUMES HER PROPER CLOTHES

MME GINNETT DENOUNCES CRIPPEN IN COURT.

1911

George Baron Pateman

Betrayed by Blood. *In the first decade of the 1900s forensic science as it is understood today – the application of medicine, physics, chemistry, and all the battery of new technological developments to the specific purpose of legal investigation – was in its infancy. The case that follows was a milestone in one branch of that blossoming science, the analysis of blood samples.*

Alice Isabel Linfold was a 22-year-old chamber maid in the employ of a large household in North Finchley. On her regular day off, it was Alice's custom and pleasure to visit her parents. The senior Linfolds had for some years taken in lodgers, the better to stretch family finances, and it was during one of Alice's visits that she was introduced to the son of Mr Pateman, the latest in a sequence of paying guests. In no time the young couple, seemed for all the world to have fallen victim to fancy; romance bloomed, and despite an eleven-year difference in their ages (George was 33) they became engaged to be married.

It will probably never be ascertained exactly what went wrong. It may have been, as some of their sharp-tongued critics claimed, that the age difference really *did* make a difference. Perhaps, like many other couples they simply became disenchanted with each other and the prospect of being manacled together in wedlock 'till death you do part'. And like so many

other couples, they found this split difficult; especially George, who made his exit during a turbulent farewell scene accompanied by threats of his imminent suicide.

The following Thursday, 27 April 1911, found Alice back in her accustomed place on her parents' sofa, Mr Pateman senior making up the four; all engaged in earnest discussion of broken hearts and severed ties. It was a dark night, and they talked deep into it, prompting Pateman to do the chivalrous thing and escort Miss Linfold back to the safety of her employers' home at Ryhope House. As he turned to leave the girl at the front gate, Mr Pateman saw a shadowy figure approach and greet Alice as she made her way to the door; though he could not identify the person, it was clearly somebody known to the girl, and he gave it no more thought. Which was a great pity for Alice. Within minutes the household was awakened by the unfortunate girl staggering and stumbling about in the kitchen, blood pouring from a savage gash across her throat. Unable to utter a single last word, she fell and died.

Early the next morning, the excitable George was brought in for questioning, and subsequently arrested for the murder of his ex-fiancée. On examination his clothing exhibited what appeared suspiciously to be bloodstains, presenting police experts with the opportunity to test a method of biological analysis that had only recently been developed. Compared with modern techniques, the result may seem crude; but for the time it was startling – and gave prosecuting counsel the evidence needed to secure a conviction. It was, incidentally, Dr (later Sir) Bernard Spilsbury's first appearance as pathologist for the Crown. As a medical witness at the Old Bailey trial, he summed up:

'The science of evidence with regard to bloodstains has taken a step further in this case than any other in my experience. It appears that this was an anaemic girl, and the skilled analyst is able by modern methods to say that the stains on this man's clothes are of human blood. Further, they are of anaemic blood, as were also the stains on the girl's clothes.'

A small step forward for forensic science led to a long drop downwards for George Pateman.

1912

The Death of Jean Milne

The Broughty Ferry Mystery. *Few people have been judicially executed in error (though enough to make capital punishment a questionable tool of justice), but there are an uncomfortable number of cases in which, but for the intervention of luck, an innocent party could have lost their liberty . . . or worse. This is the story of one such man, and his unwitting involvement in a crime which remains an unsolved mystery to this day.*

On Sunday, 3 November 1912 the battered body of Jean Milne was discovered in the hallway of her fourteen-roomed mansion at Broughty Ferry, close to Dundee. Miss Milne was 65 years old, wealthy and considered rather eccentric in her habits, though much of this local 'reputation' rested on the fact that she chose to live alone and enjoyed wearing flamboyant clothes. It was estimated from the state of decomposition of the body that Miss Milne had been killed – with the poker which lay beside her – on the 15th–16th of the previous month. Her ankles had been tied together with curtain cord and, a bizarre feature never explained, she appeared to have been pricked on the body with some kind of two-pronged fork. Robbery was immediately ruled out as a motive, as Miss Milne's diamond rings were still on her fingers, and her purse, containing £17 in gold, was untouched. Furthermore, it was apparent that whoever put such a cruel end to her life had been known to the victim – there were no signs of forcible entry, and the dining-room table was laid for tea for two. It did not take detectives long to collect together a body of useful information from the local residents; after all, Miss Milne being something of a village curiosity, her movements tended to be monitored by her gossip-hungry neighbours. Margaret Campbell, a servant employed in the house next door, recalled seeing a tall, handsome stranger walking in the grounds of Elmsgrove House around the date on which its occupant was killed. This seemed to confirm the local belief that, despite her advancing years, Jean Milne had far from forsaken the romantic idealism that was the stuff of the magazines in which she took such delight. Indeed, the lady herself had done nothing but encourage such speculation. After one of her lengthy sojourns in London in the spring of that same year, she had confided to a friend that she had met a 'gentleman' at her hotel (the Strand Palace), who had 'taken her

59

about' and paid her much attention; Miss Milne had even gone so far as to suggest that this might prove to be the beginning of a partnership for life.

There was a further sighting of the mysterious stranger in the early hours of the morning of 16 October. James Don, a scavenger about his cleaning duties, had seen a man in a bowler hat and dark overcoat walk out of the gate to Elmsgrove House and turn down the lane. Then John Wood, a gardener employed by Miss Milne on a casual basis, remembered a gentleman calling at the house while he was there in the previous September. His recollection was that Miss Milne 'skipped along the passage just like a lassie' to greet her visitor.

On the basis of these observations, Detective-Lieutenant Trench, who was leading the investigation, issued a description of a man they wished to interview in connection with Miss Milne's murder. Among the recipients of this document were the prison authorities at Maidstone Gaol, Kent, who connected it with one of their guests, a Canadian by the name of Charles Warner. Warner had been convicted of defrauding an innkeeper in Tonbridge, and was currently serving his sentence. Consequently, a party of witnesses was transported from Broughty Ferry to inspect the hapless Canadian in his cell.

James Don identified Warner immediately as the man he had seen leaving Elmsgrove House; James Wood, the gardener, was convinced that he was Miss Milne's welcome guest, and two sisters named M'Intosh swore that Charles Warner was the man they saw leaving the mansion on 9 October. Margaret Campbell was less certain until she saw Warner's eyes – 'I cannot forget his eyes'.

All this clearly came as a great surprise to Charles Warner, not least because, he said, he had never even been to Scotland. In fact at the time of Miss Milne's murder he had been in Antwerp, whence he had arrived via Paris, London, Liverpool and Amsterdam – which would have been a perfect alibi had Warner been able to prove it. What hotel was he staying at? None; he had been so completely out of funds that he had slept rough in the park. Was there anybody who could vouch for his being

in the city? None; he had wandered friendless, penniless, and anonymous. If his recent past had been bleak, Charles Warner's future looked even bleaker. With no supportable alibi, and five witnesses who placed him at the scene of a murder, he now stood a chance of losing a great deal more than his freedom.

It was luck that literally saved Charles Warner's neck. He suddenly remembered that on the very day of the incident at Broughty Ferry he had been constrained by circumstances to exchange his overcoat for a few guilders in an Antwerp pawnshop. And this time he could prove it.

When Detective-Lieutenant Trench arrived in Belgium, he had with him a pawn-ticket; a crumpled scrap of paper that for no good reason had remained in a corner of Warner's jacket pocket. It was the scrap of paper that drew Charles Warner out from the shadow of the gallows. More important, and more disturbing, it prevented a gross and irreversible miscarriage of justice.

Lieutenant Charles Becker

'The Crookedest Cop Who Ever Stood behind a Shield.' *The story of a twilit world of gangsters, gambling and bent cops.*

'The crookedest cop who ever stood behind a shield', that's what they called Lieutenant Charles Becker; and nobody was going to take that title away from him. For a start, he was using his own force to operate a city-wide protection racket covering most of New York's underworld; Becker's cut was 25 per cent of whatever crooked deal was going down – gambling, drugs, prostitution, robbery . . . Becker's

Charlie Becker, the crooked cop

particular pal in that twilit gangster world was Herman 'Beansie' Rosenthal, and they each owned a half share in a gambling club called the Hesper – but Becker wanted the biggest half. So he just got a couple of bent cops to close the club down for a while, throw 'Beansie' out, and make his life generally uncomfortable by having officers stationed outside his apartment when he was at home and officers following him down the street when he was out. Now clearly 'Beansie' was smarter than the average hood, because instead of ordering his partner's execution, he went to New York's tough reformist District Attorney, gave him a detailed account of Lieutenant Becker's extracurricular activities, and let the state sort him out. But it was equally clear that Charlie was not as smart as 'Beansie', because on 16 July 1912, Charlie had 'Beansie' shot dead on the sidewalk where he stood. Before long the assassins were behind bars, and when they realised Becker wasn't going to lift a hand to save them they began to sing, as they used to say in New York gangster circles; in short, they turned state's evidence, leaving Charlie to face the murder charge on his own. In October 1912 he was put on trial for the first time, and after a session of protracted hearings lasting almost three years he was sentenced to death and put into the execution chamber to be electrocuted on 7 July 1915.

1913

Jeannie Baxter

A Tragic Accident. *That pre-eminent defender Mr Edward Marshall Hall, never at a loss for an elegant turn of phrase, introduced the Jeannie Baxter case as one which would require 'the pen of a Zola and the brush of a Hogarth' to do full justice to it. A lot to live up to, perhaps, but in retrospect one can certainly see his point.*

In her early twenties, Jeannie Baxter was being comfortably 'looked after' by a wealthy middle-aged northerner, and would no doubt have continued to enjoy this mutually convenient relationship but for the intrusion into her life of Mr Julian Bernard Hall. A younger, wholly more glamorous man than Jeannie was accustomed to, Hall was not only rich but adventurous, being a pioneer of the aircraft and a patron of the art of boxing; less attractive was his serious drink problem. Nevertheless, Jeannie consented to be his mistress, and while Hall lived in luxury in a flat just behind London's Piccadilly, he installed Jeannie in a comfortable apartment just across town at Carlton Mansions, Maida Vale.

There was just one obstacle – Jeannie's former lover whom we will call, to preserve his blameless name, 'Jennings'. Now, while Mr Jennings was conveniently far away at the other end of England, he was, nevertheless, making increasingly persistent demands for Jeannie to return to him and the country cottage which he had provided for her use. In December 1912 Mr Jennings journeyed to

London in order to visit Jeannie at Carlton Mansions. Unhappily for all concerned, Julian Hall had arrived ahead of him. Hall had opened the proceedings by swigging down a magnum of champagne and loosing off a few random shots around the room from a revolver he was wielding. By the time a now very apprehensive Jeannie opened the front door to her former lover, Hall was best part down a second bottle of bubbly, and in pugilistic mood. Jennings, sober as always, found himself confronted by the gun-toting Hall who challenged him to a duel. Hall produced another revolver from his pocket and proposed that he and Jennings should each light a cigarette, Jeannie would turn the light out, and they would shoot at each other using only the glowing tips of the cigarettes for guidance. Wisely, Jennings declined to participate and Hall, lurching around and muttering oaths, shot at a framed photograph of Jennings instead. 'Are you in love with this girl?' slurred Hall, gesturing menacingly at Jeannie. 'I am,' replied the older man, with more courage than sense. Hall grunted again, turned the lights out anyway, and shot a few more wild slugs into the sitting room walls; this time, quite by chance, he hit a photograph of Jeannie. As a parting gesture of defiance, Julian Hall swore that if Jeannie would ditch her former lover, then they could be married. He then stumbled out of the door, firing a parting shot over his shoulder.

One might have thought that this display would have given Jeannie Baxter pause to think of the wisdom of any permanent relationship with the crazy drunk who had just shot up her flat; but this sort of behaviour clearly appealed to the girl, for she promptly dismissed the nice Mr Jennings and announced to Hall that she wished to get married the following spring, on

15 April. She left it up to Hall to make the arrangements.

On 14 April, the day before the wedding, Jeannie, who had hardly been able to think about anything else for days, arrived at Hall's Denman Street apartment to go over the final arrangements. She was irritated, though by no means surprised, to find her fiancé propped up in bed guzzling brandy. The irritation turned to fury when Jeannie learned that no arrangements had been made for the wedding at all – just this gibbering alcoholic moaning, 'The drink is killing me.' How prophetic those words proved to be.

Minutes later a friend of Hall's who had been staying at the flat heard the loud report of shots coming from behind the bedroom door, followed by a woman's voice pleading: 'Come here; come and look. I have shot Jack.' And when the bewildered guest leaped up and into the bedroom, sure enough there lay Julian Hall, bullet wounds in his arm and chest. 'Oh Jack,' Jeannie was crying, then: 'He made me do it!'

By the time her trial for murder came up at the Old Bailey in June of the same year, Jeannie Baxter had expanded her story into the defence which her learned counsel, Edward Marshall Hall, was to present to the jury. Jeannie, he explained, had arrived at the flat late in the morning and found 'Jack' drinking; she also found that he had done nothing about organising the impending wedding. Angry and frustrated, she had yelled: 'Jack, I think you are a coward to treat me like this!' He seems to have taken exception to the tone of Jeannie's voice and punched her in the face; then he pulled a revolver out of the bedside cupboard and laid it on the bed. After pouring himself another tumbler of brandy Hall shouted: 'You and I will never be married, I cannot keep my promise; it is better to finish it.' He then picked up the gun and began to wave it in the air. Jeannie, fearing for her safety, told him to put it down. 'Do you think you could take it from me?' Hall sneered, and turned the gun to point at his own chest, asking Jeannie to pull the trigger. By now Jeannie clearly felt that enough was enough and tried to take the weapon away before Hall got any drunker and any more dangerous. According to her story, that was when the gun went off. A tragic accident, Marshall Hall told a spellbound court – a tragic accident.

Well, the jury didn't go all the way with him on that. They may have wondered why, if the fatal shot had been accidental, Jack Hall also came to be shot in the arm; they may also have been puzzled as to why, on her own admission, Jeannie Baxter had picked up the gun and fired a couple of shots into the bedroom ceiling. However, they did meet Marshall Hall halfway; they convicted Jeannie on the lesser charge of manslaughter. She was sentenced to three years' imprisonment.

UNITED STATES

The Murder of Mary Phagan

One of the most shameful incidents in America's legal history; Leo Frank, a Jew, was sentenced to death on corrupt evidence for the murder of fourteen-year-old Mary Phagan. On hearing that his sentence had been commuted to life imprisonment an anti-Semitic mob abducted Frank and lynched him.

On 27 April 1913 Mary Phagan's body was found in the basement of the National Pencil Company factory at Atlanta, Georgia. Newt Lee, the black watchman, had been making his regular tour of inspection when he found the girl's corpse, and immediately raised the alarm; for this he found himself under arrest and charged with murder.

Mary, a fourteen-year-old white girl employed by National Pencil, had been battered over the head, raped and strangled; the scribbled illiterate notes found beside her body did at first glance seem to point a hesitant finger at the nightwatchman: 'Mam, that negro hire down here did this i went to make water and he push me down that hole a long tall negro black that ho it was long sleam tall negro i write while play with me.'

Although Newt Lee had been taken into custody, the police routinely questioned other employees of the company, among them Leo Frank, a 29-year-old American-born Jew who served as superintendent at the pencil factory. On the day of the murder in the absence of the regular paymaster, he had been handing out the weekly wages to staff, including Mary Phagan. For good measure, Frank's clothing was examined for bloodstains, but none were found.

At the formal inquest into Mary's death, another of the company's black workers, James Conley, made a startling accusation against Leo Frank that was to result in his arrest and, ultimately, his death. According to Conley's evidence, Frank had asked him to write the notes found next to the victim's body, and later to help him move the body. And so Leo Frank replaced Newt Lee in the jailhouse, and on 28 July 1913 was put on trial at Fulton County Superior Court.

Once again James Conley appeared as the star witness and repeated the evidence which he had given to the coroner; and just for good measure he added that he had sometimes seen Leo Frank engaging in acts of 'sexual perversion' with the factory girls. Although under Georgia law an accused was not allowed to give evidence in his own defence, Leo Frank submitted a written denial to the court accusing Conley of lying and insisting that he, Frank, had no part in the killing of Mary Phagan. And there it was; the prosecution offered no tangible evidence save Conley's testimony, and as no white man had ever been convicted on the testimony of a black, the defence camp was confident of an acquittal.

But this was to ignore blind prejudice. Sure, nobody put much store by what blacks had to say – but folks weren't too keen on Jews either.

Leo Frank was found guilty of first-degree murder and Judge Roan sentenced him to death – a popular verdict. Applications were made for a retrial through State and Federal courts, right up to and including the United States Supreme Court, but all were rejected. A plea of deprivation of liberty resulting from the conduct of the trial, in violation of the Fourteenth Amendment of the Constitution, was refused, as was an appeal to the State Prison Commission. However, despite threats to his own life, State Governor John M. Slaton commuted Leo Frank's death sentence to one of life imprisonment. It was not a popular decision, and, whipped into a frenzy by press and public opinion, a ragbag armed mob calling themselves the 'Knights of Mary Phagan' broke Leo Frank out of jail on 16 August 1915 and drove him 175 miles to the town of Marietta, where Mary had been born and where she was now buried. Here, close to the cemetery, Leo Frank was lynched from a tree, to the evident delight of the gathered crowd. When the body had been hanging long enough to ensure death, the souvenir hunters moved in to tear bits off Frank's clothing and be photographed next to his swinging corpse; photographs of the lynching were displayed in the windows of shops statewide, and one of the mob's ringleaders claimed the killing had been 'a duty'.

This sordid episode in the development of America's Southern states might yet have been forgotten, for despite the periodic efforts of Jewish organisations to have the case reopened, the Georgia Board of Pardons has consistently refused a retrial. However, in 1982 the *Tennessean* newspaper carried an article headed 'Leo Frank Did Not Kill Mary Phagan'. In the report a former employee of the National Pencil Company swore that he had seen James Conley holding the body of Mary Phagan, and had been threatened with his own life if he breathed a word. Information which came, alas, too late to save poor Leo Frank.

George Joseph Smith

The Brides in the Bath. *At trial, against all customary practice, evidence was allowed to be presented to the jury of more deaths than that on the charge sheet. This is permissible only in cases where there is a defence of accidental death, and a prosecutor is permitted to introduce what is called 'evidence of system'.*

Smith's story began in London's Bethnal Green; born on 11 January 1872, the son of an insurance company agent. Always a troublesome child, at nine years old he was sent to one of the harsh and brutalising reformatories that characterised the era; at eighteen he was serving six months for stealing, and in 1896, after two years' service with the Northamptonshire Regiment, he was sentenced, in the name of George Baker, to twelve months' hard labour for larceny, followed in 1901 by another two years. By this time Smith, under the alias Oliver Love, was already married to his first wife, Caroline Beatrice Thornhill, a domestic servant. 'Love' shortly persuaded her to act as his accomplice in a series of break-ins in London and along the prosperous south coast, though it is unlikely that she needed much persuading; at any rate, Caroline was caught in 1899 and sentenced to three months' gaol; he managed to escape. On her release Mrs Love evidently decided that she had had enough not only of the life of crime into which she had been introduced, but of Oliver Love as well, and made a strategic escape to Canada.

Smith flirted with several occupations before finding his true vocation in theft and murder – he was a baker and a gym instructor among other things, and in his spare time was an enthusiastic writer of letters on such subjects as Manners, Objectionable Literature, and other social dilemmas, a number of which were published in the *Bath and Wilts Chronicle*.

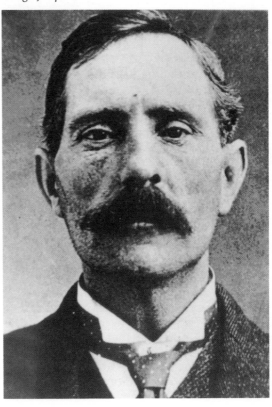

George Joseph Smith

Bessie Mundy   *Alice Burnham*   *Margaret Lofty*

In July 1908, despite his previous marriage, Smith 'married' Edith Pegler in Bristol under his own name; of all his subsequent marriages and affairs, Edith seems to have been the only woman for whom he had any real or lasting affection. Time after crime he would return to her welcoming arms, and it was to her that he sent his last farewell from the condemned cell.

Smith found work of the sort for which he was qualified uncongenial, and hungered for more lavish rewards. He could not help but be aware that women of nearly all stations and ages found him inexplicably attractive, and so, with what were to be horrendous consequences, George Joseph Smith set about perfecting the art of living off his charms . . .

In 1909, as George Rose, he married a Miss Faulkner at Southampton, and on her he developed a technique that was to become something of a trademark. He persuaded the poor woman to make over to him any money that she had, and then one day, during a pleasant walk in the park or, in Mrs Rose's

case, a visit to the National Gallery, he excused himself on some pretext and while the unfortunate woman was waiting, hastened to her home, stole everything of value – in one case going so far as to take the furniture and a piano – and disappeared for ever, leaving the lady without even a change of clothing to her name.

However, horrible as the crime against Mrs Rose had been, the fate of Smith's *next* wife was incalculably worse – for she was to be robbed of her very life. Bessie Mundy married 'Henry Williams' in Weymouth in August 1910, and although he robbed and deserted her soon after the ceremony, they ran into each other again in 1912, and Bessie, silly girl, forgave him. They set up home once again, this time at 80 High Street, Herne Bay. Smith accorded her the distinction of becoming the first of the 'Brides in the Bath', and the one on whom he perfected his silent and ingenious slaying technique. The format never varied – from the preliminary visit to the doctor (in Bessie's case for an 'epileptic fit') through to his appearance at the street door with 'something for my wife's supper' after he had committed his victim to a watery grave.

After his success with Miss Mundy, Smith was ready to murder again. He met Alice Burnham at a Congregational Chapel and, greatly against her father's wishes, married her – as George J. Smith – in Portsmouth on 4 November 1913. A month and a half later, in Blackpool, he was collecting £500 life assurance on her, after a verdict of 'accidental drowning' had been pronounced by the Coroner's inquest.

Then came Alice Reavil, who became Mrs 'Oliver James' in Woolwich in September 1914. She escaped with her life, but not much else; using the classic desertion technique – this time in southeast London's Brockwell Park – Smith got away with what was left after he had already relieved Alice of her life's savings.

In between the 'marriages', George Smith was also finding the time to practise his love-'em-and-leave-'em-penniless tricks on several other ladies to whom he clearly felt no constraint to offer his hand in marriage; and he was also returning each time to the unsuspecting Edith Pegler, explaining his extended absences as 'business trips', an excuse made thinly credible by their ownership of an antique shop in Bristol.

The beginning of the end came for the vile Smith when Charles Burnham – father of wife number five, Alice – saw an account of the inquest on Margaret Lloyd, whom Smith had married in Bath (!) on 17 December 1914 and drowned the following day, in the *News of the World*. The circumstances of the death were identical to those in which his own daughter had so tragically and unexpectedly lost her life, and Burnham's deep dislike and mistrust of his daughter's husband immediately galvanised him into action. He was convinced that this John Lloyd was one and the same person as the George Smith who had coolly collected life assurance on the late Alice. He instructed his solicitor to contact Scotland Yard, and a long and painstaking investigation was launched into the activities of George Joseph Smith. Chapter by chapter, the story was fitted together; the first link was an examination of the circumstances in which Mrs Williams (poor Bessie Mundy) had also died in her bath at Herne Bay in 1912. It was then that police realised that Lloyd, Smith, and Williams were the same gruesome killer. And so the manhunt for Smith began, and just as police were beginning to think that their quarry might have escaped abroad he was run to ground and arrested in a solicitor's office in Shepherd's Bush. As a holding measure, Smith was initially charged with the bigamy at Bath (Edith Pegler). The next step was to exhume, one by one, the bodies of the three dead 'brides'; and this time the medical experts were of the unanimous opinion that accidental death in baths of the size of the three murder tubs was virtually impossible. With no reason to suppose that all three women suffered from suicidal tendencies, they concluded that the deaths were therefore homicidal. Forensic experts later unravelled the silent murder technique used by the ingenious Smith, and demonstrated it in court.

At an identity parade, a large number of witnesses successfully picked out Smith as the man they knew under one or another of his soubriquets. Among them, triumphant in avenging his daughter, was Charles Burnham.

Smith's hearing at Bow Street Magistrate's Court, where he was charged with the murder of his three 'wives', took six weeks and, six weeks after that, on 22 June 1915, he came to trial at the Old Bailey charged with the murder of Mrs Williams (*née* Mundy) at Herne Bay. As 112 witnesses filed before the court during the eight-day trial, the proceedings were nearly brought to a nasty, if wryly appropriate, close when an over-zealous young detective nearly drowned a swim-suited nurse who had volunteered to help in the reconstruction of the murder method; it proved necessary to give her artificial respiration on the courtroom floor.

The story broke in the middle of the Dardanelles campaign of the Great War, and the grey pages of the national Press, devoted almost entirely to military news, gratefully accepted the spicing of the terrible tale of 'The Brides in the Bath'. Smith became the monster antihero almost overnight, and women fought for places in the public gallery to catch a shuddering glimpse of the creature whose reputed magnetism had lured so many susceptible members of their own sex to ruin and violent death.

On 1 July, after retiring for only 22 minutes, the jury brought in their verdict, and Mr Justice Scrutton passed sentence in accordance with that verdict. Friday, August 13th, was an unlucky day for George Joseph Smith; they hanged him at Maidstone Prison.

UNITED STATES

Frederick Mors

Call me 'Herr Doktor'. *The story of an unbalanced émigré male nurse who became one of America's earliest serial killers.*

Mors arrived in New York from Vienna on 26 June 1914, every inch the picture of a well-heeled European gentleman. But within a week of disembarking Mors seemed inexplicably to have lost whatever fortune he might have had, and exchanged his luxury hotel accommodation for a room in a cheap boarding house. In due course his native tongue enabled Mors to obtain modest employment as a porter at the German Odd Fellows Home in the Bronx; his wage was just $18 a week. Shortly after starting work there, Mors began to exhibit signs of megalomania which manifested itself in his dressing up in white uniforms with a stethoscope round his neck, adopting an arrogant air and ordering the elderly patients to address him as 'Herr Doktor'. His manner instilled no little fear into the old, though for less explicable reasons he seemed to be liked by the orphaned child residents. Mors took his masquerade a step further when he began purchasing items of pharmacy, including chloroform, from Oxmann's, a local druggist. During the four months from September 1914 to January 1915, the death rate in the Home escalated alarmingly, and in all seventeen passed away. Fearing foul play, the administration called in the police who, hearing of the elderly patients' terror of Mors, decided to elevate him to the top of their

suspect list. Mors could not have been more obliging if he had tried. Detective Cornelius W. Willemse interviewed him, and in his own account recalled that his prisoner behaved 'just like a man who has popped in for a pleasant chat with friends'. Willemse opened the interrogation by asking Mors his name:

'Frederick Mors.'

'What is your real name?'

'I do not care to give it.'

'How did you come to be a nurse; I mean what qualifications have you?'

'I studied medicine in Europe, and worked for some time in a hospital.'

'Which university?'

'I do not care to tell you.'

'How about all those deaths up there?'

'Oh, I killed them.'

'How many?'

'Eight.'

Mors went on to name his victims, and to explain: 'I killed these people and I believe I did the right thing. All of them were suffering and all of them were great nuisances. So I got rid of them. First I would pour a drop or two of chloroform on a piece of absorbent cotton and hold it to the nostrils of the old person. Soon my man would swoon. Then I would close the orifices of the body with cotton, stuffing it in the ears, nostrils, and so on. Next I would pour a little chloroform down the throat and prevent the fumes escaping in the same way.' He had perfected this method, apparently, after encountering problems with the arsenic poisoning of his first victim. 'The only difficulty was in devising a way to prevent the fumes of the chloroform escaping into the air of the room and becoming noticeable to anyone who entered.' Not surprisingly, Frederick Mors was speedily transferred to Bellevue mental hospital, where he offered to solve the institution's overcrowding problem! He was certified a criminal lunatic and committed to the Matteawan Institution for the insane, which at the time was home to 'Mad' Harry Thaw, who had shot dead America's most famous architect, Stanford White, in a fit of jealousy (*see 1906*). Mors escaped from the institution some time in the late 1920s and was never heard of again.

1915

William Burkitt

The Man Whose Luck Ran Out. *Tried for murder an extraordinary three times; each time a verdict of manslaughter was returned by a jury who had been prevented from hearing details of his previous record. (Compare with George Joseph Smith, 1914.)*

Burkitt was a fisherman out of Hull, and it was not until 1915 that he achieved any notoriety. That was the year in which he appeared before the York Assizes charged with murdering his mistress, a Mrs Tyler. Burkitt had stabbed the unfortunate woman several times in the throat, and was now on trial for his life. As it turned out, Burkitt was as lucky as his victim was not, and a sympathetic jury reduced the conviction to twelve years' worth of manslaughter.

With a few years' remission, Burkitt was back on the streets by 1924. He was now living with Mrs Ellen Spencer, who had left Mr Spencer for Burkitt, presumably to effect some kind of change in her fortunes. Although she didn't know it, her luck was running out fast; within the year Mrs Spencer had joined Mrs Tyler, and William Burkitt was back in the dock at York.

Helped by the unfailing fairness of the British legal system, which does not allow a prisoner's previous record to be made known to the jury, Burkitt once again had his murder charge reduced to manslaughter, and the hangman's noose exchanged for ten years inside. He was released in August 1935, and for the next few years enjoyed the home comforts of Mrs Emma Brookes.

In the early hours of 1 March 1939, William Burkitt succeeded in frightening the wits out of his sister by arriving at her door, foaming at the mouth and claiming to have swallowed 600 aspirins. Either he had miscounted, or his guardian angel was working overtime, because Burkitt was still active enough by the afternoon

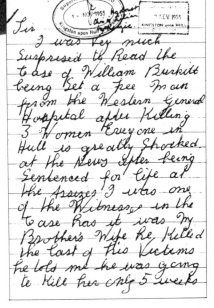

Police photograph of William Burkitt, with one of the many letters received by the police from frightened women in Hull

69

to hurl himself suicidally into the cold waters of the Humber. Such behaviour cannot long go unnoticed, and by the time Burkitt had been tucked into a hospital bed, police officers had broken into his home and discovered the bloody corpse of Mrs Brookes.

In May 1939, William Burkitt stood before the bench at Leeds Assizes facing his third trial for murder. Unbelievably, the jury reduced the charge to manslaughter.

It was quite apparent that the judge knew a rogue when he saw one, and was not prepared to exercise such clemency. He was, of course, privy to the information from which the jury had been so carefully shielded, and in passing sentence on Burkitt, Mr Justice Cassels gave muted voice to his misgivings when he told the prisoner: 'They did not know what you know and what I knew, and what they were not allowed to know – that this was the third time you have stood in the dock on a charge of murder. Each time it has been the murder of a woman with whom you had been living. Each time the jury have taken a merciful view . . . I can see in your case not one redeeming feature. You will be kept in penal servitude for the rest of your natural life.' Fate had clearly decided that William Burkitt had already enjoyed more than his share of good luck.

1916

RUSSIA

The Assassination of Rasputin

If at first you don't succeed . . . *Despite being fed enough cyanide to kill a score of men, Rasputin refused to die. He was then stabbed, shot, and thrown through a hole in the frozen River Neva after being kicked and bludgeoned to the head. If he could have broken free from the ice, Rasputin would have survived; instead he drowned.*

It was the supreme irony that the man credited first with almost total influence over the course of Russian affairs and then with the fall of the Romanov dynasty should be not a powerful prince or politician, but an ungainly Siberian peasant known as an habitual drunk and a lecher. By the time he had reached the Tsarist capital of St Petersburg in 1903, Gregory Rasputin had already become celebrated as a wandering holy man, a healer and prophet. Through one of his supporters, Anna Vrubova, one of the Tsarina's maids of honour, Rasputin was introduced to the imperial family.

It happened that Nicholas and Alexandra's son, the Tsarevich Alexis, had been born with haemophilia. When he was just three years old Alexis had a bad fall in the garden and suffered considerable pain from the bleeding in his joints. As a 'Man of God' Rasputin was summoned by the Tsarina Alexandra and set to pray by the boy's bedside; come the following morning, it was clear that little Alexis was going to make a full and fast recovery. And so Gregory Rasputin began his inexorable rise to the top.

In 1912 the Tsarevich was on holiday in Poland when he injured himself again, triggering severe internal bleeding which no amount of medical attention could stem. This time Rasputin sent a telegram assuring the Tsarina that her son would not die; the bleeding stopped immediately. Unsurprisingly the royal couple now viewed Rasputin as some few degrees above a saint.

Fortunately for the future of Russia, perhaps, not everybody was so impressed by the Holy Man; news of his debauchery was spreading like wildfire, and the Duma – the Russian parliament – was becoming openly critical of his interference in the country's politics. In June 1914, on a visit to his native Siberia, Rasputin was attacked and stabbed by a peasant woman who yelled 'I've killed the Antichrist'.

Soon events in Europe were to embroil the world in bloody conflict, signalling the collapse of Rasputin's personal world. He had already begun to attract some very powerful enemies, and as the result of a suspicion that Rasputin was engaged in a pro-German conspiracy, a wealthy young noble, the 29-year-old Prince Felix Yusupov, plotted with close friends to bring about his death. Yusupov was married to one of the Tsar's neices, and it was on the pretext that the Princess was sick and wanted his blessing that on the night of 29 December 1916* Rasputin was lured to the palace. When he arrived, the man of God was escorted to a lavishly appointed basement room where he was entertained with madeira wine and cake – both heavily laced with cyanide. But far from dropping to the floor dead, Rasputin seemed to cheer up with the wine, and even asked Yusupov to play to him on the guitar to while away the time till the Princess was ready to receive him. Thoroughly unnerved, Prince Felix fled upstairs to warn his fellow conspirators that the 'Mad Monk' was still alive, and to borrow a gun to shoot him. On his return to the basement Yusupov was startled by Rasputin's request for more wine! But distracting his attention, the assassin raised his revolver and fired one shot at close range. Rasputin slumped to the ground with an angry roar. At this signal

*16 December on the old Gregorian calendar.

Gregory Rasputin (Popperfoto)

the conspirators rushed to the basement where one of their number, a physician named Lazovert, pronounced Rasputin dead, and they all went off to celebrate.

It was about an hour later that Prince Felix returned to the scene of the murder to check arrangements for disposing of the body. As he approached his victim, one eye flicked open, fixing Yusupov with a glare of sheer hatred, and the next moment the huge form of Rasputin leapt up and lunged at his attacker, pursuing the terrified Prince up and out of the palace where his yells attracted the other conspirators. Vladimir Purishkevich chased after the fleeing Rasputin and fired two shots, bringing the holy man to the ground where he was kicked and cudgelled as he lay. Convinced that the Mad Monk was finally dead, Yusupov ordered Rasputin's corpse to be roped up in a heavy curtain and pushed beneath the frozen-over River Neva.

Most remarkable of all was that when the body was recovered from the water two days later and autopsied, it was revealed that Gregory Rasputin had died not of poisoning, not from gunshot wounds, not from bludgeoning, but from drowning – the 'holy devil' had still been alive when he was pushed into the icy waters of the Neva.

In many ways the death of Rasputin led directly to the collapse of the Romanov dynasty and ultimately to the Russian Revolution, because although it proved a simple matter to detain the conspirators, the murder was so widely approved by all levels of society that Tsar Nicholas was powerless adequately to punish the assassins. By the same token, to allow a royal favourite to be slaughtered without raising a hand against his butchers proved Nicholas to be in a position of weakness. On 15 March 1917 the Tsar was forced to abdicate, and in July of the following year many of the Romanov family were massacred by the Bolsheviks at Ekaterinburg. During the early months of the Revolution, Rasputin's remains were dug up and publicly burned.

UNITED STATES

The Birdman of Alcatraz

Robert Franklin Stroud first got into the US prison system in 1905, when he became involved in a bar-room brawl over a woman and killed the bartender. This earned him twelve years on a manslaughter conviction, much of which he served at Leavenworth Prison, Texas. On 26 March 1916 Stroud attacked and killed a prison officer with a knife in an apparently unprovoked, motiveless crime carried out in full view of prisoners and staff with no possibility of a denial. More extraordinary still, Stroud had been within a whisker of being released at the time. Although he eventually offered a cynical defence that the guard had died of a heart attack (Stroud had stabbed him in the heart!) he was convicted of murder and sentenced to death. As a result of the intercession of Stroud's mother with President Woodrow Wilson's wife, Stroud was given a commutation of sentence to life in solitary confinement in Leavenworth. One concession was that Robert Stroud was allowed to continue the ornithological studies which he had begun during his earlier sentence, and which was gradually earning him wide acknowledgement as the country's leading authority on diseases of the canary. Stroud was later transferred to Alcatraz, where he was given a specially enlarged cell to contain his scientific apparatus and caged birds, and where he established his unique reputation as the 'Birdman of Alcatraz', publishing *The Digest of Bird Diseases* in 1943. Stroud was later moved to Springfield Jail, Missouri, where in 1963, aged 76, he died of natural causes.

Robert Stroud, the 'Birdman of Alcatraz'

1917

Louis Voisin

The Butcher of Charlotte Street. *Murdered and dismembered his mistress leaving the scribbled message 'Blodie Belgium' with her remains. When asked by DI Frederick Porter Wensley to write this message, Voisin made the same error – sealing his guilt. It was a tactic heavily criticised by defence counsel at trial.*

The Voisin case opened, as do most murder inquiries, with the discovery of a body in suspicious circumstances; and there can have been few circumstances more suspicious than those which revealed themselves in Bloomsbury on 2 November 1917. On that morning a road-sweeper about his job in Regent Square, in London's Bloomsbury, found a large sacking-covered parcel in the central garden of the square. When the package was opened it was found to contain the bloody trunk of a woman, dressed incongruously in delicate lace underwear; around the remains was another partial paper wrapper on which the misspelt message 'Blodie Belgium' had been scribbled.

Medical examination put the time of death within the previous two days; more important, the dismemberment indicated some understanding of anatomy. A bloodstained sheet wrapped around the torso provided the most important clue – in one corner a laundry mark, 'II H', had been embroidered; it was at least possible that the sheet had belonged to the victim. And so it proved. A trawl of laundry

shops led to 50 Munster Square, a rundown district of Regent's Park, where it was learned that Emilienne Gerard, a 32-year-old French-woman, had been missing from her rooms since 31 October. A search of Mme Gerard's apartment produced a written IOU for the sum of £50, signed by a Louis Voisin, and a framed portrait of the same man, later identified as her lover.

Voisin was traced to a tenement at 101 Charlotte Street, Fitzroy Square, where he lived with Berthe Roche. Voisin's trade was that of a butcher.

Though there was no more connection than *l'amour* provable between the butcher and Mme Gerard (if indeed hers was the body in the parcel), Chief Inspector Frederick Porter Wensley, in charge of the case, thought it wise to have Voisin and Roche along to Bow Street for questioning. Wensley remembered Voisin as 'a short, thick-set man, heavy-jawed and exceedingly powerful of frame'. The man's story was that he had known the missing Emilienne Gerard for about eighteen months, during which time an intimacy had developed between them. On 31 October they had met to say *au revoir* on the eve of her departure for France where she was to visit her husband, a cook with the French army. She had taken this opportunity to ask Voisin to pop in and feed her cat while she was away, and this he had dutifully done on two occasions.

After a night in detention, Voisin again faced Frederick Wensley 'with a sort of aggressive determination'; on this occasion the detective asked him, through an interpreter, if he had any objection to writing out the words 'Bloody Belgium' for him. Voisin had no objection, and with the painstakingly slow hand of the border-

Detective Chief Inspector Frederick Porter Wensley of Scotland Yard

line illiterate, inscribed 'Blodie Belgium' – five times. Wensley recalled, 'The final copy bore a very close resemblance in every particular to that of the original. I knew then that it was only a question of time before the other points of the case would be cleared up.'

And cleared up they very speedily were. A return visit to Charlotte Street resulted in the first positive link between the dismembered trunk, Emilienne Gerard and Louis Voisin – in the cellar beneath Number 101 Madame's head and hands were found in a barrel of sawdust. Furthermore, Voisin's kitchen was seen to be heavily stained with human blood. When he was charged with murder the Charlotte Street butcher simply shrugged his shoulders and muttered, in broken English, 'It is unfortunate.'

The forensic brilliance of Bernard Spilsbury, combined with the experience and imagination of Frederick Porter Wensley, was not long in piecing together a coherent reconstruction of the last hours of the unlucky Emilienne Gerard.

The night of 31 October had been marked by one of the worst Zeppelin raids yet suffered by the capital, and at around 11 p.m., in response to the sirens, Emilienne Gerard fled first to the safety of the Underground, and from there to her lover's basement in Charlotte Street. The confrontation between the excitable Berthe and her rival – of whom she was until then unaware – must have been terrible to behold. Both women, their nerves already strained by the air raid outside, began a mutual tirade of accusations, recriminations and threats; the volatile Berthe pounced on the defenceless Madame Gerard, knife in hand, stabbing and slashing. This is the theory that supported Spilsbury's observation that a large number of the wounds suffered by the victim were by a far weaker hand than the powerful Voisin. It was at this point that Voisin – probably awakened by the fierce struggle – joined

UNITED STATES

Kidnap

On 30 May, fourteen-month-old Lloyd Keet was kidnapped from his home in Springfield, Missouri. Later, the boy's father, a wealthy banker, received a $6,000 ransom demand, and made the drop as instructed at an isolated spot in the Ozark foothills. A few days later the child's body was found battered to death at the bottom of a well at a disused farm not far from the Keet residence. Five men and a woman were eventually apprehended, and transported to Jefferson County prison; however, a lynch mob overtook the police vehicles and hauled out the ringleader, a man named Piersol, and strung him up from a tree. Only the pleading of the sheriff saved the skins of Piersol and his unlovely gang, and they were eventually put on trial. Piersol was convicted of kidnapping little Lloyd Keet, and sentenced to 35 years; he was never charged with the child's murder.

The popular conception of the Voisin case

the fray to strike out the remaining life in the body of his hapless paramour. He then put in a little overtime with meat cleaver and saw.

Confronted with the findings at Charlotte Street and Munster Square (where closer examination had rewarded detectives with further bloodstains), Voisin decided to modify his statement accordingly:

I went to Madame Gerard's place last Thursday at 11 a.m., and when I arrived the door was closed but not locked. The floor and carpet were soaked with blood. The head and hands were wrapped up in a flannel coat that is at my place now. They were on the kitchen table. The rest of the body was not there. I was so shocked by such a sight I did not know what to do . . . I remained there five minutes stupefied. I did not know what to do. I thought someone had laid a trap for me. I started to clean up the blood and my clothes became stained . . . Then I went back to my place and had lunch, and later returned to Madame Gerard's flat and took the packet [the head and hands] back home. I had no intention to harm Madame Gerard. Why should I kill her?

At the end of an unremarkable trial, Mr Justice Darling passed sentence of death – in French – on Louis Voisin. At his direction Berthe Roche was acquitted of murder, but charged as an accessory in a separate trial, before Mr Justice Avory, on 1 March. The jury found her guilty, and two years into a seven-year prison sentence Berthe Roche went mad and died in an institution at Holloway.

Voisin was executed on 2 March 1918; his 'Blodie Belgium' message, devised to mystify the police and send them tracking a false scent, had ended up hanging him.

1918

David Greenwood

The Button and Badge Murder. *The murder of sixteen-year-old Nellie Trew by ex-soldier Greenwood was solved when the button and regimental badge torn from his greatcoat during the struggle were identified.*

It is only when it is all over, and any survey of it is tinged with hindsight, that we have the opportunity to 'read' the background and consequences of a recent murder case. For the most part the narrative unfolds piecemeal, some of the aspects remaining isolated until perhaps the very end, when they can be fitted like pieces into a puzzle. This is particularly true of multiple, or 'serial', killings, where a small reported paragraph – perhaps covering the discovery of a body in suspicious circumstances, may require weeks, or months, sometimes years, of patient investigation before the next paragraph can be written, and longer before all the pieces can be assembled for the trial; post-mortem, inquest, magistrate's hearing. After the trial, the appeal. After the appeal, the punishment.

The case of David Greenwood and his senseless killing of young Nellie Trew is not a complicated one, but in the course of researching it, the writer became aware of this gradual unfolding of the narrative through the columns of the local newspapers, which reflected the fact that, though not of global importance, every death in such circumstances is a notable local tragedy.

It might also serve as a tribute to the contribution made by newspapers to police inquiries; it was, after all, the nationwide co-operation of the Press in publishing illustrations of the 'button and badge' that led to the identification of David Greenwood as the killer.

SHOCKING DISCOVERY ON ELTHAM COMMON
Young Girl Ill-Treated and Murdered

Seldom has the Woolwich district been so deeply stirred as on Sunday morning, when the news spread that a young girl had been found dead on Eltham Common in circumstances which pointed to outrage and murder. The victim proved to be Nellie Grace Trew, aged 16, who had been living with her parents at 5 Juno Terrace, on the new Government estate at Well Hall, and had been employed as a clerk in the Central Office, Woolwich Arsenal. The girl left home on Saturday evening to change a book at Plumstead Library, and as she did not return home her father communicated with the police at Shooters Hill Station. En route, oblivious to the terrible tragedy which had taken place, he passed and repassed the spot where his daughter lay dead.

The scene of the crime is remarkable for the fact that it is a small and lonely area lying between two comparatively busy centres. At the spot where Shooters Hill Road crosses the main thoroughfare, which on the Woolwich side is known as Academy Road, and on the Eltham side becomes Well Hall Road, stands Shooters Hill Police Station, faced on one side by officers' quarters and on the other by wings and outbuildings of the Royal Herbert Hospital. A few hundred yards down Well Hall Road is that huge Government estate of houses and many hundreds of hutments. On the left-hand side, proceeding Elthamwards, lies a waste of land covered with trees known as Eltham Common, fronted by ample pavement, and as well lighted as the times permit, whilst along the road runs a tramway to Eltham. It was on this waste land that the body was noticed by a tramway worker on Sunday morning, and he at once gave information to the neighbouring police station.

The murdered girl was found on the grass about 40 yards from the roadway, and she had evidently been carried there after succumbing to attack at a different point. A few yards from the pavement, and about 200 yards from Shooters Hill Police Station, there were signs of a severe struggle, and indistinct footprints in the mud leading to the place at which the body was discovered. The condition of the girl's face showed she had received a severe blow in the mouth, which had probably stunned her, and marks on the neck indicated that she had been strangled, whilst other appearances suggested maltreatment in other directions. It was apparent that as a result of her injuries the girl had lost a considerable amount of blood, which it is hoped will afford one clue to the discovery of the culprit or culprits. The case was at once taken in hand by Divisional Detective Inspector Brown, of Blackheath, who initiated the most vigorous and vigilant enquiries . . .

The victim of the murder was a quiet dark-haired girl . . . She had been employed since July last year in the card index department of the Wages Branch of the Central Office of the Arsenal, where she enjoyed the greatest popularity amongst her colleagues and had won the approval of her superiors by her good

behaviour and attention to her duties. A feature of her character which is of interest, as it somewhat deepens the mystery of her death, was her indifference to the society of men; all her acquaintances remark upon the fact that she never associated with men and had not the least suggestion of 'flightiness' in her disposition, she was, on the contrary, a quiet, industrious and home-loving girl, and was in the habit of hurrying home from work to assist her mother whose health is not good.

The prolonged and close search that was instituted by the police for clues that would assist in establishing the identity of the assailant or assailants has not so far been very successful. Two articles were found near the spot at which the initial struggle had occurred, and they may have some association with the tragedy. One was a large overcoat button which had been attached to the garment by wire, and had evidently been torn off as the wire still remained twisted. The other was [a] military badge. The badge is of white metal, fastened with a shank of copper wire, and is believed to be the full dress collar badge of the Gordon Highlanders* – not worn at the present time . . .

The police are anxious to know if any member of the public can recognise the badge or button as having been worn by any person known to them. It is possible that persons who let lodgings may have seen a lodger wearing such articles.

Any information to CID, New Scotland Yard, or any police station, will be welcomed.

(*Kentish Mercury*, Friday, 15 February 1918)

At once police made close enquiries regarding

*In fact it was the Lancashire Regiment.

The button and badge found at the scene of the murder

FRONT VIEW OF BADGE. BACK VIEW OF BADGE. BACK VIEW OF BUTTON

1918

leave in all the barracks and billets in the immediate neighbourhood but without tangible result. The murderer, or murderers, for it is believed that the outrage was done by two men, must, it is thought, have blood stains on their clothing, as Miss Trew's injuries were terrible.

(*Lewisham Borough News*, Wednesday, 13 February 1918)

MURDER OF A GIRL AT ELTHAM
Ex-Soldier Arrested and Charged

The police very rapidly carried out their plans for the elucidation of the mystery surrounding the death of Nellie Grace Trew, who, in circumstances related last week, was found strangled on Eltham Common on February 10th. The result was that on the 14th inst., David Greenwood, 21, a turner and discharged soldier, of Jupiter Street, Well Hall, was detained on Friday and was brought up at Woolwich Police Court on Saturday afternoon, to answer the charge of murder...

(*Kentish Mercury*, Friday, 22 February 1918)

[It appears that his workmates in the City, after seeing in the newspapers the photographs of the badge and overcoat button found near the body, noticed that he was no longer wearing a similar badge which he had worn for some time. In reply to their questions he appears to have made a statement to the effect that he had sold the badge to a man on a tramcar for two shillings on Saturday afternoon at Well Hall. His workmates advised him to give the information to the police, which he did, but they were not satisfied and detained him until he could be seen by Chief Inspector Carlin and Divisional Detective Inspector Brown, as a result of whose subsequent enquiries he was arrested and brought to Woolwich.]

(*West Kent Argus*, Friday, 22 February 1918)

... The prisoner, who stepped briskly into the dock when the charge was called, is a tall, thin young fellow, with a face that is rather intellectual than otherwise, and he followed the proceedings with a keen interest.

The only witness called was Chief Inspector Carlin of New Scotland Yard, who deposed to the finding of the body of the girl, and proceeded to say that on Thursday morning the prisoner was brought to Scotland Yard by Divisional Detective Inspector Brown, who said in his presence, 'This is the man who called at Tottenham Court Road police station this morning about the badge.' Greenwood said, 'I sold it to a man on a tramcar for two shillings.' Witness noticed that the buttons of his overcoat were missing, and pieces of thread were sticking out as though the buttons had been recently pulled off. Accused was very agitated whilst witness was making this examination. Witness said, 'I would like you to wait in the waiting-room while Inspector Brown and I make some enquiries', and he was left in the charge of Detective Sergeant Crawley. Later that day witness again saw the prisoner in company with Inspector Brown, and said to him: 'It is open to you to give an account of your movements on Saturday; you can do so if you like, but you must thoroughly understand that what you do say will be taken down in writing by Inspector Brown and may be used in evidence against you.' Accused said, 'I should like it taken down,' and witness replied, 'Very well, you can say what you like, and Mr Brown will write it down.' He made the statement and Inspector Brown took it down. It was afterwards read to him, and the accused signed the bottom, 'I made this statement myself, I made it of my own free will.' Witness had the statement there but would rather not read it out at that stage. After making the statement he picked up the button produced, which was lying on witness's desk beside the badge, and said, 'If I say that is my button, what will it mean?' Witness said, 'I cannot tell you.' He said, 'Well, I won't say anything then.' Witness told him he should detain him pending enquiries, and he made no reply. He was detained at Cannon Row police station. About 3.30 p.m. on Friday he saw him there, and said, 'I shall charge you with the wilful murder of Nellie Grace Trew, on February 9th, at Eltham Common.' He said, 'Yes.' He then brought him to Woolwich police station. He was charged and made no reply.

Prisoner replied 'No, sir', when asked if he had any questions to ask, and was remanded for one week.

FUNERAL

The murdered girl was buried on Saturday at Plumstead cemetery, and a huge concourse of people lined the streets along which the cortège passed. There were many wreaths, including a number sent by employees of Woolwich Arsenal, in which the deceased's father is employed.

(*Kentish Mercury*, Friday, 22 February 1918)

. . . Dr Spilsbury, who had made a post-mortem examination, said the girl was apparently healthy and strong. There were marks on the throat as of fingers and finger-nails, and the cause of death was asphyxia from strangulation, presumably by throttling. Considerable violence must have been used, and the girl had offered resistance. Mr Hay Hackett committed the prisoner for trial at the Central Criminal Court.

(*West Kent Argus*, Friday, 22 March 1918)

At the Central Criminal Court on Wednesday, David Greenwood pleaded not guilty to an indictment charging him with the murder of Nellie Trew.

Mr Travers Humphreys detailed the circumstances, which have been reported.

Dr Spilsbury asked whether a man who had been discharged from the army suffering from disordered action of the heart and subsequent fainting fits would be likely to have caused such injuries as were found upon the girl, replied that he could not say that such a man would be unable to do so.

The trial was adjourned.

(*West Kent Argus*, Friday, 26 April 1918)

THE ELTHAM COMMON MURDER
Discharged Soldier Found Guilty

The trial of David Greenwood, the young discharged soldier, on a charge of the murder of Nellie Trew, was concluded at the Central Criminal Court on Friday.

Mr Travers Humphreys for the prosecution, pointed out that his [Greenwood's] evidence was entirely different from that given by him at the inquest on March 6th. Prisoner replied that he remembered the circumstances better now than he did then.

Mr Slesser, for the defence, said that the prosecution had failed to connect the prisoner with the murder. He was a young man of excellent character, and he had never shown any tendency likely to cause him to commit so terrible a crime.

The jury, after an absence of two hours and forty minutes, found Greenwood guilty, but recommended him to mercy on account of his services to his country and of his youth.

Asked if he had anything to say, he replied, 'I am not guilty of this crime. I know nothing about it. I have never spoken to Nellie Trew in my life. I hope your Lordship will not take any notice of the recommendation of the jury, as it would always be a disgrace for me, and I would rather face the full penalty.'

Mr Justice Atkins (addressing the prisoner) said: 'You have been found guilty of a most heinous crime. You have taken your unfortunate victim's life, and for that crime there is only one penalty. At the same time I shall forward the recommendation of the jury to the proper authorities where, I have no doubt, it will receive every consideration. It is not right, however, that you should anticipate that the course of the law will necessarily be interfered with on account of that recommendation.'

Sentence of death having been passed, prisoner walked out of the dock. His mother, who was in court, collapsed and was removed weeping.

Greenwood has, we understand, made an application for leave to appeal against his sentence.

(*Kentish Mercury*, Friday, 3 May 1918)

GREENWOOD APPEAL

The Court of Criminal Appeal has dismissed the appeal made by Frederick [*sic*] Greenwood against the sentence of death for the murder of Nellie Trew at Eltham Common. Mr Justice Darling, in delivering judgement, said there was evidence on which the jury could come to the conclusion at which they had arrived, provided they were properly directed by the learned Judge. The summing-up took a considerable time of a case which had lasted three days, and the Court held that there was no justification for saying that the learned Judge had misdirected the jury. Although the evidence was circumstantial, it was sufficient to justify the verdict.

The execution of Greenwood has been fixed to take place at Wandsworth Gaol on the 31st.

(*West Kent Argus*, Friday, 24 May 1918)

THE ELTHAM MURDER
Petition for Greenwood's Reprieve

The Rev Frank M. Smith, of Catford Central Hall Mission, 39, Culverley Road, Catford, writes: 'Knowing your love of fair play and your sense of justice, I am writing to ask you to insert this letter in your widely-circulated and influential newspaper. I know there are very many of your readers who are convinced that the evidence at the trial of the young ex-soldier David Greenwood – who was discharged from the Army on account of shell-shock – wholly circumstantial, and, as they think, very unsubstantial – is sufficient to warrant the death sentence, and that the strong recommendation to mercy on the grounds of his youth, his blameless character, and his services to his country should have great weight in this momentous decision. I understand that the date of the execution is fixed for the 31st inst., and if this extreme measure be allowed to take effect there will be a large number of the public in the South-East of London, who will feel that justice has been outraged. Petitions to the Home Secretary for the reprieve of David Greenwood are being signed by thousands all over the district. I shall be glad to hear from any who are in sympathy with the case.'

(*Kentish Mercury*, Friday, 24 May 1918)

A REPRIEVE

It was announced yesterday that David Greenwood, the ex-soldier and munition worker, who was convicted for the murder of Nellie Grace Trew on Eltham Common and sentenced to be hanged, has been reprieved. The execution was fixed for today.

(*Kentish Mercury*, Friday, 31 May 1918)

UNITED STATES

The Rose Man of Sing Sing

Although Charles Chapin was assured of a good salary in his position as editor of the New York *Evening World*, his extravagant millionaire lifestyle was financed by well-placed investments in speculative stocks. Despite an ugly incident when he narrowly escaped prison trying to recover his fortunes after a disastrous collapse in the sugar markets, Charles Chapin continued to risk every cent he made on the stock market. In 1914 he lost $100,000 in a single day when Germany declared war, and spent the next four years fighting off bankruptcy with increasing desperation. By September 1918 Chapin could see no alternative to the spectre of imminent poverty for himself and his wife, so he bought a gun. On 16 September Chapin shot his wife and planned to kill himself; however, Mrs Chapin took so long to die that he had time to think better of suicide. Although 60-year-old Chapin refused to offer any defence of himself at the subsequent trial, a charity lawyer succeeded in getting the charge reduced from first- to second-degree murder, and Chapin's sentence reduced from death to twenty years. During his time in jail, Charles Chapin made use of his former publishing talent in editing the prison magazine. Later, Governor Lewis Lawes encouraged Chapin to lay down a garden in the prison compound, which was so successful that its creator was given the nickname 'The Rose Man of Sing Sing'. Charles Chapin died in prison in December 1930; he was 72 years old.

1919

William Nelson Adams

The Tax-Man Cometh. *According to William Adams, his victim had been 'worried out of his mind' by an impending tax demand. It was a unique, though unsuccessful, defence of 'murder by request'.*

When seventeen-year-old Adams, homeless, penniless and hungry, met George Jones on a bench by the Thames Embankment he would never have believed the price he was going to be asked to pay for Jones's friendship. At least that is what he told the jury at Guildford Assizes in July 1919.

Adams's story was that after taking him back to his modest room for a meal, the ageing ex-con began to regale his guest with desperate tales of huge income-tax demands that were 'worrying him out of his life'; Jones ended his pathetic story: 'I've done you a good turn, now you do me one. Will you kill me?'

One week later, on 10 June 1919, Adams and a man named Charlie Smith travelled by tram to meet George Jones at a pub in Tooting. After a few drinks, the odd trio set out on foot for Jones's home at Sutton. *En route* Jones, perhaps the worse for drink, cried out: 'God help me; will you kill me?' Adams reluctantly indicated

that he would 'try', and they turned into a field behind Ridgeway Road. According to Adams, Jones pressed a shoemaker's awl into his hand and renewed his plea to be put out of his misery: 'The best way is to stab me on the left side of the neck.' Despite his best efforts – a generous three blows with the awl to the neck and three in the stomach – William Adams failed to despatch his victim beyond the reach of the Inland Revenue. He then tried, but failed, to drag Jones to a nearby pond to drown him. In the end both he and the no doubt thoroughly bewildered Charlie Smith fled in panic, having first helped themselves to the few shillings Jones had in his pocket. As for Smith, he simply vanished, and despite a police hunt was never heard from again. Jones was found where he had fallen, but in an odd state of undress. He was wearing just trousers and a string vest, and somebody – either Adams or, perhaps, Jones himself – had tied his shirt around his stomach in an attempt to staunch the blood from his wounds. Jones was rushed to hospital where he lingered for three days on the boundary of life and death. During this time of grace he expressed considerable puzzlement at his predicament, wondering the while why Adams should have wanted to attack him: 'I had done nothing to him!' This was exactly what the jury wondered as well, before they rejected William Adams's preposterous story and convicted him of murder. Adams was not, however, asked to pay the ultimate penalty for his crime. The then Home Secretary, Mr Edward Shortt, commuted his death sentence to one of life imprisonment.

The Butcher of Hanover

Between the years 1919 and 1924 the monster known as the 'Butcher of Hanover' was responsible for the deaths of at least 27 and possibly as many as 50 young men and boys. Fritz Haarmann was born in 1879, and was already an accomplished petty criminal and child molester before he started killing. At the end of the First World War, Germany, in common with many other European countries, was ravaged by four years of senseless fighting, and home to countless homeless refugees who were flocking to the cities, congregating like lost sheep around the main railway stations. It was from among this riff-raff of orphans and drifters that Fritz Haarmann chose his victims – the friendless and the rootless who would be missed by nobody. Haarmann found it expedient to pose as a policeman and 'arrest' a vagrant boy, then feign sympathy and take the wretched youth back to his squalid apartment on the Kellerstrasse where he would be sexually abused before Haarmann bit through his throat until he was dead. Their clothing he sold, the flesh from their bodies he sold as meat for human consumption on the black market, and the bones and skulls he threw into the River Leine. In September 1919 Haarmann teamed up with another degenerate homosexual named Hans Grans, and with Grans selecting the victims (usually because he wanted their clothes) and Haarmann doing the killing, they became the perfect killer couple. It was only in 1924, when the skulls started to be dragged from the Leine, that a full enquiry began, and when Haarmann was pulled into the net after trying to molest a young boy in the street, he made a full confession implicating Grans. After a two-week trial at the Hanover Assizes, Haarmann was sentenced to death and beheaded; Hans Grans received a more lenient twelve years' imprisonment.

Fritz Haarmann returned to prison after sentencing

1920

The Green Bicycle Mystery*

One of the most celebrated murder cases of the decade and one of the most controversial. Although the weight of the ballistics evidence was in favour of Light's defence, and despite the fact that a jury acquitted him, there were few who considered him innocent.

On the evening of Saturday, 5 July 1919, a 21-year-old girl left her home at Stoughton (where her father was a farm worker) and cycled to Evington to get a stamp at the post office and to post a letter. She then returned, and proceeded on the road to Gaulby to visit her uncle, a Mr Measures.

At about the same time a man of 34, who lived in Highfield Street, Leicester, went out for a cycle ride and arranged to be back for supper at around 8 p.m. He turned left into London Road and proceeded through Stoneygate and Oadby to Great Glen. He then turned left and proceeded to the left turn into Gartree Road. This would have taken him back to Leicester, but he looked at his watch just before he reached Great Stretton and realised that he would be home too soon; so he decided to

*This text has been based on the researches of Mr A. W. R. Mackintosh into the murder of Bella Wright. With his colleague, Mr W. Richardson, Mackintosh has for many years pursued the minutiae of the Green Bicycle Mystery, and has opened many new avenues for investigation. By no means the least of their achievements has been to identify the spot where Bella was buried.

return through Houghton-on-the-Hill. He therefore turned right, and when he came to the cross-roads where the Gaulby Lane crossed the Houghton Lane he saw a girl bending over a bicycle. She raised her head as he approached and asked him if he had a spanner. He replied that he hadn't, but asked what the trouble was. She said that her back wheel was loose and as he did what he could to put it right he asked where she was going. When she said Gaulby, he thought he might as well go

Ronald Light with (inset) Bella Wright

Joseph Cowell finds Bella's body on the Gartree Road

with her as he could easily get to Houghton from there. When the couple arrived at Gaulby she said that she would only be about ten minutes and as that appeared an invitation to wait, he went with her to her uncle's house and waited outside. Mr Measures's daughter and her husband, a Mr Evans, happened also to be on a visit, and they asked about the man who was waiting outside. When she told them of the circumstances they advised her not to go back with him as he looked 'too old' for her. So she prolonged her visit until the man eventually tired of waiting and set off for home. His route took him uphill to Gaulby church, and when he arrived there he found he had a puncture. It took nearly an hour to mend it, and as the girl hadn't passed him during that time he went back to the house and got there just as she was coming out. They then cycled back together the way they had come. When they got to the road junction beyond King's Norton the girl said she would have to bid goodbye to

her companion as her route was to the left. He then, according to his subsequent evidence, proceeded directly back to Leicester via Stoughton and Evington.

At about 9.20 p.m. Mr Cowell, a farmer, was going along the Gartree Road when he found a girl lying on the road alongside a bicycle; when he examined her he found she was dead. Returning to his farm at nearby Little Stretton, Cowell harnessed his pony and trap, and after arranging for someone to guard the body, proceeded to Great Glen to report the matter to Constable Hall, the local policeman. From there he phoned Dr Williams at Billesdon, and then returned to Little Stretton. It was dark by the time Dr Williams arrived so he gave instructions that the girl's body be removed to an unoccupied house at Little Stretton. At this point it was assumed that she had died in a cycling accident.

The next day, Sunday 6 July, PC Hall returned to the scene and after a careful search found a bullet on the road. He then went to the house where the body had been deposited, and after washing the congealed blood from the face discovered a bullet wound. Dr Williams was immediately informed and he and another doctor carried out a full post-mortem.

It was subsequently established that the girl's name was Bella Wright and that she lived in Stoughton. When her relatives at Gaulby got to hear of her death the hue and cry went out for the 'Man on the Green Bicycle', as everyone jumped to the conclusion that he must have been the killer.

Although the identity of the 'man on the green bicycle' was not to be known for many months, his name was Ronald Light, and at the time of Bella Wright's death he was living in Highfield Street, Leicester. Light was born in October 1885 and the first family home had been in Granville Road, Leicester. It is understood that his father had been the manager of Ellistown Colliery, near Coalville. After graduating as a civil engineer at Birmingham University, Ronald Light was employed as an engineer and draughtsman at the Midland Railway Works at Derby, but he usually returned to Leicester at weekends.

In May 1910 he purchased a green BSA bicycle from a firm named Orton & Co. of Derby. At about that time he also became a member of the Fortress Company, Royal Engineers, whose headquarters were at Buxton. From time to time, Light used to hire a motorcycle from Orton's to enable him to get into Buxton.

The Great War broke out in August 1914 and in February 1915, after undergoing training at Chatham, Newark and Ripon, Ronald Light was granted a commission as a Second Lieutenant in the Royal Engineers. He was later posted abroad on active service, though for some reason he left the Royal Engineers in August 1916, and in September rejoined in the Honourable Artillery Company as a private. After undergoing further training Light was sent overseas again. He eventually suffered badly from shell-shock, and was invalided to a

number of hospitals in England before his demobilisation in January 1919.

Sometime in 1916 or 1917 Ronald's father died accidentally at Granville Road, and in May 1917 the family home was moved to Highfield Street where Ronald lived with his mother and a maid-servant.

It was not until the Tuesday evening (8 July) following his encounter with the girl cycling to Gaulby that Ronald Light read of the tragedy in the *Leicester Mercury*, and learned that the dead girl's name was Bella Wright. By this time the public and the press had decided that it was the man on the green bicycle who had been responsible for her death. According to his later evidence, Light was now in a serious dilemma. He worried over the matter for some

UNITED STATES

The Anarchists

The robbery and murder took place on 15 April 1920; but that was the simple part of the story. Just another payroll heist – two men shot dead, their killers richer by $16,000. The consequences of this crime, however, were set to reverberate around the world, and even now, 70 years and more after that fatal shooting in Massachusetts, the names of two men live on as enduring reminders that mistakes can be and are made by courts of law; that justice is as fallible as the mortals who are its guardians. Nicola Sacco, shoemaker, aged 29, and Bartolomeo Vanzetti, fish-seller, aged 32, both Italian immigrants, were picked up by the police as the result of descriptions given by witnesses to the robbery. Sacco and Vanzetti were both armed with pistols, but worse by far, they were known political activists – anarchists! The trial opened in Dedham, Massachusetts, on 31 May 1921, and made news nationwide. Despite a complex and convincing defence, Sacco and Vanzetti were convicted of first-degree murder and sentenced to death. The trial judge, who had little time for 'these anarchist bastards', was constantly criticised for his undisguised bias. Over

the next seven years no fewer than seven motions for retrial were dismissed, and Sacco and Vanzetti exchanged their cell on Death Row for the execution cell.

In 1977 the then Governor of Massachusetts, Michael S. Dukakis, issued a special proclamation clearing their names.

Nicolo Sacco (left) and Bartolomeo Vanzetti

Telephone 357 and 862.

LEICESTERSHIRE CONSTABULARY.

£5 REWARD.

At 9-20 p.m., 5th instant, the body of a woman, since identified as that of ANNIE BELLA WRIGHT, was found lying on the Burton Overy Road, Stretton Parva, with a bullet wound through the head, and her bicycle lying close by.

Shortly before the finding of the body the deceased left an adjacent village in company of a man of the following description :—

Age 35 to 40 years, height 5 ft. 7 in. to 5 ft. 9 in.; apparently usually clean shaven, but had not shaved for a few days, hair turning grey, broad full face, broad build, said to have squeaking voice and to speak in a low tone.

Dressed in light Rainproof Coat with green plaid lining, grey mixture jacket suit, grey cap, collar and tie, black boots, and wearing cycle clips.

Had bicycle of following description, *viz.* :—Gent's B.S.A., green enamelled frame, black mudguards, usual plated parts, up-turned handle bar, 3-speed gear, control lever on right of handle bar, lever front brake, back-pedalling brake worked from crank and of unusual pattern, open centre gear case, *Brooke's* saddle with spiral springs of wire cable. The 3-speed control had recently been repaired with length of new cable.

Thorough enquiries are earnestly requested at all places where bicycles are repaired.

If met with the man should be detained, and any information either of the man or the bicycle wired or telephoned to E. HOLMES, ESQ., CHIEF CONSTABLE OF COUNTY, LEICESTER, or to SUPT L BOWLEY, COUNTY POLICE STATION, LEICESTER.

County Constabulary Office,
Leicester, 7th July, 1919.

T H JEAYS & SONS, PRINTERS 7 ST. MARTINS, LEICESTER.

Reward notice issued by the Leicester police
The bicycle as it was recovered from the canal

time before eventually deciding to do nothing except remove the bike from where he usually kept it to the attic.

In October 1919, Ronald Light decided to get rid of his bicycle. He filed off the number at the top of the saddle column and took it down to the canal to a point near the Gas Works, and after detaching the back wheel (because it had a distinctive back-pedalling brake) he threw the parts separately into the canal.

As an officer in the Army Light had had a .45 revolver; when he reverted to being a private and was posted overseas, he took the revolver with him but not the holster. According to his evidence, when he became a casualty, all his belongings, including the revolver, were left behind in France. But he still had the holster and some rounds of ammunition at home which he also threw into the canal. And so things rested until January 1920, when Ronald Light took up an appointment as a mathematics master at a school in Cheltenham.

On 23 February a horse-drawn barge was going along the canal when suddenly its tow-rope tightened and up came a green bicycle. The manager of a cycle shop in Leicester, who examined the bicycle, found a number on the inside front fork, the duplicate of one usually stamped at the top of the saddle column. In no time ownership of the bike was traced to Ronald Light.

After the preliminary police-court proceedings, Light's trial was fixed for 20 June 1920, at Leicester Castle. He was defended by the celebrated advocate Sir Edward Marshall Hall, and to everyone's surprise, he was found not guilty.

If you ask any of the older generation today, you will almost invariably be told that 'he done it', and it was only through the brilliance of Marshall Hall that he got off. What they don't tell you is that at the inquest proceedings Mr Robert Churchill, the ballistics expert, revealed that a carrion crow which was found dead nearby had also been shot. So it is almost certain that whoever shot the crow also shot Bella Wright. As this evidence was not given at the trial, it would appear that the police were very remiss in not properly following through with this line of investigation.

Madame Bessarabo's Luggage

Born in Lyon in 1868, Hera Myrtel was of a somewhat esoteric disposition, much given to writing mystical verse and assembling around her an enthusiastic entourage of young sycophants. Hera had already narrowly escaped the full penalty of the law when her first husband had been mysteriously shot dead in Mexico; the police seemed to fall for Madame's story about four hooded bandits, but local speculation made things uncomfortable enough for Hera to seek the security of Mexico City with her young daughter Paule. There, she met and charmed into marriage a wealthy Romanian wood merchant named Bessarabo, and in 1920 the three of them returned to Hera's native France. Things did not go too well with the marriage, not least on account of the mutual infidelities of both Bessarabo and Hera. And so, with a little help from her daughter, Madame made herself a widow once again, stuffing her husband's dead body into a trunk and depositing it at Nancy station. The smell of Bessarabo's corpse putrefying in the left-luggage office ensured the arrest of Hera and Paule Bessarabo and both were put on trial charged with murder. Madame shielded behind a preposterous defence which involved some mysterious and menacing South American secret agent; but in a momentary lapse of filial duty, Paule gave evidence against her mother, thus securing her own acquittal and a long prison sentence for Madame.

The corpse of Charles Bessarabo as it was taken from the trunk

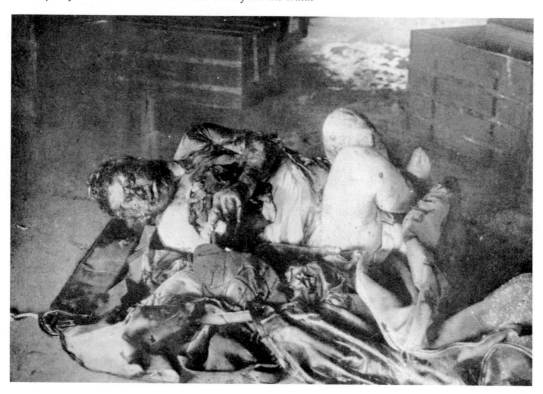

1921

George Arthur Bailey

Softness, Sentimentality, and a Lack of Logic. *Bailey's trial at Aylesbury Assizes for the poisoning of his wife was the first in Britain in which women were allowed to sit on the jury. Despite fears of 'feminine softness', Bailey was found guilty by a unanimous verdict.*

The crime itself had been prosaic enough, the kind of sordid incident that rarely enters the field of vision of the criminologist. Bailey had been charged at the Aylesbury Assizes with the murder of his wife by poisoning; in his defence Bailey claimed that his wife had threatened suicide and then swallowed an eggcupful of prussic acid, a common compound of cyanide.

However, for historians of the law, the Bailey case formed a landmark – it was the first murder trial at which women sat on the jury. There were three of them, and the self-conscious manner in which these ladies were accommodated by the court was at times almost burlesque. For a start the judge, Mr Justice McCardie, insisted that the court rise each afternoon during the four-day trial in order that the jury might partake of a refreshing cup of tea. Counsel, probably for the first time since they were called to the Bar, found themselves tongue-tied in their efforts to translate unpalatable facts in terms delicate enough for a lady's sensibilities. Even the judge was constrained to instruct counsel not to be so 'mealy-mouthed'.

It must be added, however, that in his own summing-up, Mr Justice McCardie charged the jury 'to arrive at your verdict without flinching, and to deliver it with unswerving firmness'. The implication, as Spencer Shew remarked in his *Companion to Murder*, was that he 'feared the male members of the jury were likely to succumb altogether to feminine softness, sentimentality and lack of logic'. The good judge had no need to worry, for this first mixed jury brought in a unanimous verdict of guilty. As for George Bailey, he was sentenced to death and hanged on 2 March 1921.

'The First Scientific Murderer'

The first murder by bacteria poisoning is said to have been committed by the fraudulent French financier Henri Girard. In 1910 Girard took out an insurance policy on Monsieur Louis Perotte for the sum of 300,000 francs; two years later Perotte, his wife and two children became ill with what appeared to be typhoid. Coincidentally, Girard had not long before taken delivery of some cultures of that same bacteria from a Parisian laboratory supplier. In the end it was only Louis who perished, despite the frequent injections of 'camphorated camomile' administered by his old friend Girard.

After insuring their lives for worthwhile sums of money, Henri Girard's next potential victims were fed *Amanita phaloides*, a variety of poisonous fungus. Both were very ill, as might be expected, but to Girard's great disappointment they proved hardy enough to recover their

Downfall of a Fat Man

One of the best known and best loved comedians in the world, Roscoe 'Fatty' Arbuckle's popularity was exceeded only by that of Charlie Chaplin. That is to say, it was until the weekend of Labour Day, 1921, when Arbuckle and some studio friends decided to celebrate with a lavish party at the Saint Francis Hotel, San Francisco. Despite Prohibition the liquor flowed freely; and so did the sexual favours. The tragic result was that a young bit-part actress named Virginia Rapp was taken sick in a bedroom booked by Arbuckle, and a few days later died in hospital. Virginia's lover, a comedy-film director, accused Roscoe Arbuckle of causing her death by rape. Despite the volume of false evidence, and a judge never far from perjury, two juries failed to agree and a third acquitted Arbuckle – with a full apology for the distress that he had suffered. But Hollywood had its own special form of rough justice, and the once-feted comedian's face disappeared overnight from the cinema screens. His close friends found him a little work as a director (using the jolly soubriquet 'Will B. Goodrich'), and Arbuckle attempted an acting comeback early in 1933; but the high life had taken its toll of a great performing talent, and everybody's favourite Keystone Cop died suddenly in a hotel room in New York in June 1933.

Roscoe 'Fatty' Arbuckle

health. Which was more than poor Madame Monin could do when it fell her turn to strengthen Henri Girard's bank balance. In April 1918 the unfortunate widow succumbed to an aperitif poisoned with bacteria – and Girard collected her insurance. By now the insurance companies had become suspicious that so many of the people on whom Girard had taken out policies were falling sick – even dying – so soon afterwards. He was arrested in August 1918, and while in custody made a number of statements which almost amounted to confessions, though Girard concluded that he was, underneath, a good man 'with a very warm heart'. The jury of his peers had no opportunity to make up their own minds; before his case came to trial Henri Girard took his own life – by swallowing germ cultures.

1922

Frederick Bywaters and Edith Thompson

A Court of Morals. *One of the century's most notorious Crimes of Passion, Bywaters and Thompson conspired to murder Edith's husband Percy. Most of the trial evidence centred on Edith's letters which were a mixture of endearments and hints about taking Percy's life. Both were convicted and executed.*

A CONVENTIONAL UPBRINGING AND A RESPECTABLE MARRIAGE

Edith Graydon was born on Christmas Day, 1893, and brought up in Manor Park, near Ilford. At school she proved both intelligent and charming, if a little deceitful, and was able on leaving to obtain a respectable post as a secretary at Carlton and Prior, a wholesale milliners at 168 Aldersgate Street, in the City of London. She remained with the same employer throughout her working life, impressing with her ability and responsibility to the degree that she was promoted, first to bookkeeper, and later to manageress. Indeed, throughout her married life she was earning a higher wage than her husband, Percy Thompson, a shipping clerk with another firm in London's 'Square Mile' whom she met while travelling to Liverpool Street station each morning. They were married on 15 January 1915, when she was 22 and her new husband 26. In 1916, Thompson

enlisted in the London Scottish Regiment, but was soon discharged because of heart trouble and returned to his former job. In July 1920 the Thompsons bought their own terraced house at 41 Kensington Gardens, Ilford; the previous owner, Mrs Lester, continued to live in the house as a lodger.

The Thompsons had settled to living the sort of respectable and unexciting existence typical of couples of their age and station. Spending most of the week separated by their employment in London, their social life consisted of dinner with friends and the occasional visit to a West End show or a local fête or garden party. Edith was left to satisfy the more frivolous and romantic aspects of her nature by harmlessly flirting with Percy's men friends and retreating into her own colourful imagination, fuelled by a voracious appetite for romantic novels. What is clear is that married life, and Percy Thompson in particular, was a great disappointment to her. She yearned for the adventure she read about; stolid, prosaic Percy hardly fitted her notion of the perfect partner for life. He wouldn't even have a good row when she occasionally tried to express her dissatisfaction with things, becoming moody and uncommunicative. Edith Thompson was becoming stifled beyond endurance.

A STORY-BOOK LOVER

In June 1921 the Thompsons spent their annual summer holiday at Shanklin on the Isle of Wight. Avis Graydon, Edith's younger sister, was invited along and in order to even up the numbers Percy extended the invitation to include a young friend of the Graydon family, Freddie Bywaters; Bywaters was just eighteen years old. He had been brought up in Manor

Park and played regularly with the younger Graydon children. His father had died in the Great War and the family had been forced to move away to Westow Road in Norwood. In 1918, at the age of sixteen, he had joined the Merchant Navy as a clerk, though he later became a steward. He had just returned from a trip to Australia aboard the *Orvieto* when he joined the holiday party. For Edith Thompson it was a perfect holiday. She was free of all the normal restraints and could join in with the youngsters swimming, playing tennis and having a generally good time. But it was more than that, because dashing young Freddie, with his tales of foreign parts, had turned his attentions from the younger Avis towards Edith.

> One year ago today we went for that memorable ride round the island in the charabanc do you remember? – that was the first time you kissed me.
>
> (Letter from Mrs Thompson to Bywaters, 14 June 1922)

The thought of a secret lover must have been irresistible to Edith. The mutual attraction must have been fairly obvious, but all that complacent Percy Thompson noticed was that his wife seemed happier and that Freddie seemed a pleasant young fellow. He needed little persuading that it was a good idea that Freddie Bywaters should come and stay as a lodger at Kensington Gardens on the pretext that he would be handy for seeing Avis at the Graydons' home in Shakespeare Crescent at nearby Manor Park. Such close proximity created the right climate for Edith's affair to go further.

> It's Friday now darlint ... I am wondering if you remember what your answer was to me in reply to my question 'What's the matter?' tonight of last year. I remember quite well – 'You know what's the matter, I love you.
>
> (Mrs Thompson to Bywaters, 20 June 1922)

> I do remember you coming to me in the little room and I think I understand what it cost you – a lot more darlint than it could ever now. When I think about that I think how nearly we came to be parted for ever. If you had not forfeited your pride darlint I don't think there would ever have been yesterday or tomorrow.
>
> (Bywaters to Mrs Thompson, 1 October 1922)

The relationship seems to have been regular-

Frederick Bywaters

ised when Freddie and Edith met secretly at lunchtime at the Holborn Restaurant on Monday, 27 June 1921, to celebrate Freddie's nineteenth birthday.

> Mrs Thompson told me she was unhappy, and I said: 'Let me be a pal to you – let me help you if I can' ... Mrs Thompson and I had been having an argument, and she suddenly burst into tears, and I advised her to wait, not to give up hope, and not commit suicide ... I extracted a promise from her to wait five years, so that she should not commit suicide.
>
> (Evidence of Bywaters in court)

It was only a matter of time before even unobservant Percy Thompson began to notice what was going on in his own house between his wife and the young lodger. The inevitable happened on Monday, 1 August.

I had some trouble with my husband that day. I think it originated over a pin. But eventually it was brought to a head by my sister not appearing at tea when she said she would. I wanted to wait for her, but my husband objected, and said a lot of things to me about my family that I resented. He then struck me several times, and eventually threw me across the room. Bywaters was in the garden ... He came into the room and stopped my husband. Later on that day there was a discussion about a separation ... I wanted a separation and Bywaters entreated my husband to separate from me. But he said what he usually said, that he would not. At first he said he would, and then I said to him. 'You always tell me that ... and later, you refuse to grant it to me.'

(Evidence of Mrs Thompson in court)

Freddie Bywaters was, not unnaturally, asked to find alternative accommodation and did so four days later, returning to his mother's house in Norwood.

A LIFE OF SECRECY

The separation of the two lovers did nothing to dampen the ardour of their affair. They met whenever possible, snatched lunchtime meetings in restaurants, and more regularly when Edith went to see her family on Fridays and Bywaters would be there on the pretext of visiting Avis. Bywaters was also away at sea on the SS *Morea* five times in the next year for periods of between six weeks and two months. The progress of the lovers' relationship was charted through a succession of rambling love letters. Edith wrote more than eighty in just over a year and Bywaters was little less prolific. At first Bywaters sent his correspondence to Edith at her work address, but later she arranged a *post restante* address at Aldersgate Post Office under the name 'Miss P. Fisher'. The style of Edith's letters moved effortlessly between affection, reflection, conspiracy and anecdote.

Darlingest – Will you please take these letters [letters from a previous girlfriend in Australia] back now. I have nowhere to keep them, except a small cash box I have just bought and I want that for my letters only and I feel scared to death in case anybody else should read them.

(Mrs Thompson to Bywaters, 11 August 1921)

For all the secrecy, Percy Thompson was sporadically aware that something was still going on.

Come and see me Monday lunchtime, please darlint. He suspects. Peidi.

(Mrs Thompson to Bywaters, 20 August 1921)

After the first of his sea voyages, Freddie Bywaters, always the man of action, determined to have it out with Percy Thompson and visited the house in Kensington Gardens on 5 November with that in mind.

I had taken Mrs Thompson out previously. Apparently he [Percy Thompson] had been waiting at the station for her and he had seen the two of us together. He made a statement to Mrs Thompson – 'He is not a man or else he would ask my permission to take you out' – and she reported that statement to me the following day. In consequence of that I went and saw Mr Thompson ... I said: 'Why don't you come to an amicable agreement? Either have a separation or you can get a divorce.' And he hummed and hawed about it. He said: 'Yes – No – I don't see it concerns you.' I said: 'You are making Edie's life a hell. You know she isn't happy with you.' He replied: 'Well, I've got her, and I will keep her.'

(Evidence of Bywaters in court)

And so the matter remained unresolved. When Bywaters went away to sea again on 11 November Edith was soon writing to him again.

At night in bed the subject – or the object, the usual one – came up and I resisted, because I didn't want him to touch me for a month from Nov 3rd ... He asked me why I wasn't happy now – what caused the unhappiness and I said I didn't feel unhappy – just indifferent, and he said I used to feel happy once. Well, I suppose I did ... but that was before I knew what real happiness could be like, before I loved you darlint ... I told him I didn't love him but that I would do my share and make him happy ... I was feeling awful.

(Mrs Thompson to Bywaters, 16–20 November 1921)

I gave way this week (to him I mean) it's the first time since you have been gone. Why do I tell you this? ... We had – was it a row – anyway a heated argument again last night (Sunday). It started through the usual source. I resisted – and he wanted to know why since you went in August I was different – 'Had I transferred my affections from him to you.' Darlint it's a great temptation to say 'yes' but I did not. He said we were cunning, the pair of us ...

He said 'Has he written to you since he has been away,' and when I said 'No' he said 'That's another lie.'

(Mrs Thompson to Bywaters, 21 or 28 November 1921)

Darlint, I've surrendered to him unconditionally now – do you understand me? I think it's the best way to disarm any suspicion, in fact he has several times asked me if I am happy now and I've said 'Yes, quite' . . . Darlint, you are a bad bad correspondent really darlint I absolutely refuse to talk to you all next trip, if you don't mend your ways. Darlint, are you frightened at this – just laugh at me.

(Mrs Thompson to Bywaters, 3 January 1922)

It may be wondered why Mrs Thompson didn't just leave her husband for Freddie Bywaters. After all, she had the security of her own job and was earning a good wage. But in that very different age a hint of scandal would have been sufficient to get her dismissed and lose any chance of gaining such respectable, well-paid employment in the future. Already, Percy had caused some fuss at her place of employment when he learned that Bywaters had been sending letters there. Edith Thompson might have been romantic, but she didn't much fancy the privations of poverty.

I'd love to be able to say 'I'm going to see my lover tonight.' If I did he would prevent me – there would be scenes and he would come to 168 [Aldersgate St] and interfere and I couldn't bear that . . . Darlint it's funds that are our stumbling block – until we have those we can do nothing. Darlingest find me a job abroad. I'll go tomorrow.

(Mrs Thompson to Bywaters, 2 October 1922)

Besides this, one suspects that Edith quite liked the idea of having two men fighting over her favours. She was careful to avoid letting her husband completely lose hope of a reconciliation and seems to have gone out of her way to arouse the jealousy of one man for the other. In early 1922, a predictable complication of her affair had to be dealt with.

About 10.30 or 11 a.m I felt awfully ill – I had terrible pains come all over me – the sort of pains that I usually have – but have not had lately – do you understand . . . About 7 something awful happened,

darlint I don't know for certain what it was, but I can guess, can you, write and tell me.'

(Mrs Thompson to Bywaters, 24 January 1922)

In 1922 to procure an abortion was an illegal act with serious consequences. Mrs Thompson was sufficiently afraid of motherhood both to risk dangerous medical measures and the possibility of imprisonment if it were discovered. The same problem arose four months later.

About these fainting fits darlint . . . I'm beginning to think its the same as before . . . What shall I do about it darlint, if it is the same this month . . . I still have the herbs.

(Mrs Thompson to Bywaters, 1 May 1922)

Throughout this period Edith was growing increasingly concerned over Bywaters's continued devotion to her during his prolonged trips at sea. She began to weave a fantasy to bind her lover to her, the fantasy which was eventually to put a noose around her neck.

You must do something this time . . . opportunities come and go by – they have to – because I'm helpless and I think and think and think . . . It would be so easy darlint – if I had things – I do hope I shall . . . Have enclosed cuttings of Dr Wallis's case. It might prove interesting. [The letter contained two newspaper cuttings, one headed 'Mystery of Curate's Death', the other 'Poisoned Chocolates for University Chief. Deadly Powder posted to Oxford Chancellor. Ground Glass in Box'.]

(Mrs Thompson to Bywaters, 10 February 1922)

He puts great stress on the fact of the tea tasting bitter, 'as if something had been put in it' he says. Now I think whatever else I try it in again will still taste bitter – he will recognise it and be more suspicious still . . . I wish we had not got electric light – it would be so easy. I'm going to try the glass again occasionally – when it is safe. I've got an electric light globe this time.

(Mrs Thompson to Bywaters, 1 April 1922)

I used the 'light bulb' three times but the third time – he found a piece – so I've given up – until you come home.

(Mrs Thompson to Bywaters, 24 April 1922)

None of this actually occurred, as Percy Thompson's apparent perfect health and later medical evidence was to indicate. This seems to have been perfectly understood by Bywaters, who pandered to Edith's little fiction but avoided anything which resembled action. Nevertheless, it did increase the desperate and fevered atmosphere which was beginning to engulf the hopeless affair.

WHEN FICTION BECOMES REALITY

On Saturday, 23 September Bywaters arrived back in Tilbury for the last time. He was now resolved to settle matters once and for all. He would 'have it out' with Percy Thompson and be done with it. Over the next weekend the lovers met several times.

On Friday the 29th I met Mrs Thompson about midday and took her to lunch, and then she went back to her business. I went to Fuller's tea shop between three and four . . . Later on Mrs Thompson came in. I left her in Ilford that evening about quarter to seven, and then I went home to my mother's. On Saturday morning, about nine o'clock, I took her for a walk in Wanstead Park.

(Evidence of Bywaters in court)

On the Monday they met for lunch, and met again at Fuller's in the early evening. The same pattern was followed on the next day, Tuesday, 3 October, but from Fuller's Mrs Thompson went off to meet her husband at Aldersgate Street Station. They had arranged to go with some friends to see Hermione Gingold and Binnie Hale in Ben Travers's *The Dippers* at the Criterion Theatre. Meanwhile, Freddie Bywaters went over to Manor Park to visit the Graydons for the evening. He left them at about 11 p.m.

I thought, I don't want to go home; I feel too miserable – I want to see Mrs Thompson . . . I walked in the direction of Ilford. I knew Mr and Mrs Thompson would be together, and I thought perhaps if I were to see them I might be able to make things a bit better . . . I went to see Thompson to come to an amicable understanding for a separation or divorce . . . it kind of came across me all of a sudden.

(Evidence of Bywaters in court)

At midnight the Thompsons arrived back at Ilford Station from London. As they walked along Belgrave Road, on their way to 41 Kensington Gardens, Freddie Bywaters rushed up to them from behind and, pushing Mrs Thompson aside so that she fell to the ground, confronted her husband. Mrs Thompson cried out pitifully, 'Oh, don't! Oh, don't!' as Bywaters and Percy Thompson struggled.

I pushed Mrs Thompson with my right hand, like that. With my left I held Thompson and caught him by the back of his coat and pushed him along the street, swinging him round . . . I said to him: 'Why don't you get a divorce or separation, you cad?' . . . He said: 'I know that's what you want. But I'm not going to give it to you. It would make it too pleasant for both of you.' I said: 'You take a delight in making Edie's life hell.' Then he said: 'I've got her – I'll keep her – and I'll shoot you' . . . going at the same time like that with his right hand – as if to draw a gun from his pocket. As he said that he pushed me in the chest with his left fist, and I said: 'Oh, will you?' and drew a knife and put it in his arm . . . I had the knife in my left hand. All the time struggling, I thought he was going to kill me . . . and I tried to stop him.

(Evidence of Bywaters in court)

I said to him: 'You've got to separate from your wife.' He said: 'No.' I said: 'You'll have to.' We struggled. I took my knife from my pocket and we fought and he got the worst of it . . . I didn't intend to kill him. I only meant to injure him.

(Statement by Bywaters to the police, 5 October 1922)

Bywaters then ran off down Seymour Gardens, eventually arriving back at his mother's house in Norwood by taxi at three in the morning.

Percy Thompson had received four superficial cuts beneath the ribs on his left side. There were two on his chin and two deeper ones on his lower jaw. He had a stab wound on his right forearm and there were two stab wounds in the back of his neck, one of which had severed the carotid artery and caused his death some minutes later. Meanwhile Mrs Thompson had got to her feet.

When I came to my senses, I looked round for my husband and I saw him some distance down the road. He seemed to be scuffling with someone . . . I saw somebody running away, and I recognised the coat and hat.

(Evidence of Mrs Thompson in court)

She then hurried over to her husband;

He fell against me and said 'O-er' ... I helped him along by the side of the wall, and I think he slid down the wall onto the pavement ... I went to get a doctor.

(Evidence of Mrs Thompson in court)

A little way down the road she came upon a couple walking back from the station. She was hysterical, but managed to blurt out 'Oh, my God! Will you help me? My husband is ill – he's bleeding!' She was then taken to a local doctor, but hurried back to kneel beside her husband's body. A doctor arrived a little later, followed at 1 a.m. by Police Sergeant Mew. Percy's body was removed and Mrs Thompson escorted the 50 yards or so to her home. She confided to Mew: 'They'll blame me for this.'

On the evening of the next day, Freddie Bywaters was arrested at the Graydons' house in Shakespeare Crescent. Edith Thompson was taken into custody later that night. Bywaters made a statement saying that he had returned straight home from the Graydons the previous evening, and the next morning Mrs Thompson said that her husband had been attacked by a 'mystery assailant'. Soon afterwards, she was allowed to glimpse Bywaters in the police station, and exclaimed: 'Oh, God! Oh, God! What can I do? Why did he do it? I didn't want him to do it! I must tell the truth.' She then made a statement admitting that Bywaters had been Percy Thompson's attacker. That evening Bywaters was informed that Mrs Thompson would be charged with her husband's murder. 'Why her? Mrs Thompson was not aware of my movements,' he replied. He then made a full admission of his actions on the evening of 3 October.

The next few days were spent by the police in checking the background to the case and routinely searching the possessions of the accused. Two of Bywaters's letters to Mrs Thompson were found in her desk at Carlton and Prior. Then a week after the crime they discovered a large cache of letters that Mrs Thompson had written to Bywaters in his sea chest aboard the SS *Morea* at Tilbury. They made interesting reading. The charges of conspiring to murder, attempting to murder and inciting to murder were added to the basic charge against Mrs Thompson.

THE COURT OF MORALS

When the trial of Edith Thompson and Frederick Bywaters opened at the Old Bailey on Wednesday, 6 December 1922, large crowds collected outside the courtroom to witness the spectacle. The Solicitor General, Sir Thomas Inskip KC, led for the prosecution. Cecil Whiteley KC defended Bywaters. Sir Henry Curtis-Bennett represented Mrs Thompson. The judge was Mr Justice Shearman.

Curtis-Bennett immediately rose to ask the judge that the bundle of 62 letters that the prosecution wished to use be declared inadmissible. This was curtly refused and Curtis-Bennett had to fall back on an agreement that had already been reached with the prosecution that only limited extracts would be read out. This had the advantage of excluding references to Mrs Thompson's attempts at self-abortion which, it was felt, would put the jury implacably against her. The disadvantage, however, was that editing out the large gossipy and inconsequential bulk of the letters failed to reveal their fantastic and highly romanticised character. The references to poisoning seemed far more sinister in this bare context.

The second disaster for the defence was Mrs Thompson's insistence on going into the witness box. She was sure that the jury would understand the full tragedy of her 'great love'

Sir Thomas Inskip   *Sir Henry Curtis Bennett KC*

1922

95

Mr Justice Shearman

her husband was killed. . . . My client is no ordinary woman . . . She reads a book and imagines herself one of the characters in the book. She is always living an extraordinary life of novels . . . Thank God, this is not a Court of Morals, because if everybody immoral was brought here I should never be out of it, nor would you. Whatever name you give it, it was certainly a great love that existed between these two people.

In his summing up, however, Mr Justice Shearman adopted the tones of an Old Testament prophet:

The charge really is – I am not saying whether it is proved – a common or ordinary charge of a wife and an adulterer murdering the husband . . . You are told this is a case of great love. Take one of the letters as a test – 'He has the right by law to all that you have a right to by nature and by love.' If that means anything, it means that the love of a husband for his wife is something improper because marriage is acknowledged by law, and that the love of a woman for her lover, illicit and clandestine, is something great and noble. I am certain that you, like any other right-minded person, will be filled with disgust at such a notion.

The jury retired on Monday, 11 December. It took them just over two hours to reach a verdict of guilty against both defendants. When sentenced to death, Bywaters stated 'I say the verdict of the jury is wrong. Edith Thompson is not guilty. I am no murderer. I am not an assassin.' Mrs Thompson sobbed, 'I'm not guilty! Oh, God, I'm not guilty!' as she was led from the dock.

While some sections of public opinion were smugly satisfied by the verdict, others were horrified. To many, Edith Thompson had been sentenced to hang for adultery. It was also fifteen years since a woman had been hanged and it seemed now a primitive act of vengeance. A petition for a reprieve was raised, and collected several thousand signatures. Three days before the sentence was to be carried out Freddie Bywaters made a final attempt on his mistress's behalf. A statement by him was hurried to the Home Secretary.

I killed him and I must pay for it. The judge's summing-up was just, if you like, but it was cruel. It never gave me a chance. I did it, though, and I can't

but in the shaken and pallid state she presented to the world during the trial she was frequently confused and made to appear to lie under cross-examination. Freddie Bywaters was already reconciled to his fate, and sought only to exonerate his lover from any blame for his actions.

The greatest disadvantage that Edith Thompson faced, however, was the stifling tone of moral rectitude with which the prosecution attempted to envelop the trial, an attitude which the judge seemed to endorse. The love affair was painted as a sordid, secretive piece of adultery leading inevitably to a grubby crime committed by two deceitful and amoral people. Curtis-Bennett tried his eloquent best to counteract this impression in his summing up to the jury:

The letters provide the only evidence upon which the charge of murder is framed against Mrs Thompson. Everything that was done and said by her on that night shows as strongly as it can that not only did she not know the murder was going to be committed, but that she was horrified when she found complain . . . I swear she is completely innocent. She never knew that I was going to meet them that night . . . For her to be hanged as a criminal is too awful. She didn't commit the murder. I did. She never planned it. She never knew about it. She is innocent, absolutely innocent. I can't believe that they will hang her.

The Home Secretary was unmoved. At 9 a.m. on 9 January 1923, Edith Thompson was carried, barely conscious, from her cell in Holloway Prison and hanged by the executioner John Ellis. At the same moment Frederick Bywaters was hanged in Pentonville Prison by Thomas Pierrepoint.

Sir Henry Curtis-Bennett commented later on the case:

She spoiled her chances by her evidence and demeanour . . . I had a perfect answer to everything, which I am sure would have won an acquittal if she had not been a witness. She was a vain woman and an obstinate one. Also her imagination was highly developed, but it failed to show her the mistake she was making . . . In short, Mrs Thompson was hanged for immorality.

Most modern observers would also add that two murders resulted from the tragic love affair between Freddie Bywaters and Edith Thompson; the fatal stabbing of Percy Thompson in the darkness of Belgrave Road and the judicial hanging of Edith Thompson in the crisp morning air of Holloway Prison. There were also two murderers: young Freddie Bywaters and the English judicial system.

1922

FRANCE

The French Bluebeard

The notorious 'Bluebeard of France', Henri Desiré Landru, made use of the newspaper matrimonial advertisements to become acquainted with some several hundred eligible women whose financial prospects he carefully recorded in a notebook. Many of these unlucky women Landru simply deceived into believing his good intentions until he had plundered their money and possessions; others, the more stubborn, required him to resort to sterner methods. In short, between May 1915 and January 1919 he murdered ten of these women and incinerated their remains in a kitchen stove. Despite the overwhelming evidence against him – including the notebook and the incinerator full of charred human bones which was brought into court – Landru continued to protest his innocence. It did him no good at all, and 'Bluebeard' was put to the guillotine on 25 February 1922.

Landru's victims

97

1923

The Dot King Mystery

Although the murder of chorus-girl Dot King remains officially unsolved, there was heavy suspicion at the time of her death that her gangster boyfriend was implicated. One of the most characteristic crimes of the 'Roaring Twenties'.

As murder mysteries go, it would have defied the talents of the finest crime-fiction writer to invent.

Anna Marie Keenan was born in New York in 1894, the fourth child of a recent Irish immigrant family. By her late teens Anna had developed into a most extraordinarily beautiful young woman, with fair hair, skin like silk and clear blue eyes, and in 1912 she became Mrs Eugene Oppel. Sadly for her chauffeur husband, Anna was just not the marrying kind; life, she instinctively knew, had so much more to offer than babies and a kitchen stove. Inside two years the couple separated and Anna entered the more glamorous world of fashion modelling as $25 a week. In no time at all, her employers recognised that their new model was wasted on the cat-walk, and soon Anna was engaged in the more exotic activity of entertaining the fashion house's visiting buyers. Treated to the best that Broadway could offer, the kid from Amsterdam Avenue was on her way *up*.

It was at about this time, while she was living in New York's Great Northern Hotel, that Anna met Marie. We have no other name for her, but Marie whoever-she-was became a powerful driving influence in the young woman's life. It was Marie who changed Anna's name to Dot King; it was Marie who introduced her to Jack Lannigan – and it was Jack who introduced her to life in the fast lane. He ran a string of night clubs and other 'entertainments', first legally, and then, under Prohibition, illegally – it was all the same to Dot, who got to milk the wealthy male customers anyway. In fact Dot was having the time of her life.

It was in the early part of 1922 that Dot met 50-year-old John Marshall (real name: J. Kearsley Mitchell), a wealthy Boston manufacturer in New York on business, or so he said. They had so much fun on that first date, that when they woke up the next morning in Dot's room at the Great Northern, Marshall decided that things should be put on a more permanent, and certainly more discreet, footing. And to this end he set Dot up in a little love-nest at the top of 144 West 57th Street. John Marshall only paid infrequent visits to the apartment, and then they were brief, always made – for the sake of appearance – with his secretary John Wilson, who was obliged to wait outside the door of the flat. (It should be stated for the record that John Wilson was not really John Wilson any more than John Marshall was John Marshall; Wilson was John H. Jackson, and he wasn't Marshall's secretary but a prominent New York lawyer who acted as Marshall's attorney.) However, the infrequent visits certainly didn't mean that Dot was left lonely – in fact the arrangement suited her just fine. After all, she had other fish to fry – big fish like Draper Daugherty, son of President Harding's Attorney-General; and Albert Guimares, a Puerto Rican gigolo with whom Dot was apparently so infatuated that she didn't even mind him beating her up, let alone plundering her jewellery and money. And for comfort she had Hilda Ferguson, a blonde showgirl who for a period shared the West 57th Street apartment.

One memorable evening, Dot, Marshall and 'secretary' Wilson were seated at supper in the Brevoort Hotel when a page walked through the dining room calling: 'Mr Mitchell. Telegram for Mr. J. Kearsley Mitchell.' In one simple, unguarded moment, a couple of cats were suddenly let out of a couple of bags. 'Here boy,' beckoned Marshall. Now Dot was no Einstein, but even she knew the difference between 'J. Kearsley Mitchell' and 'John Marshall'. And so it was revealed that the one was in reality the other, a hugely wealthy and hugely influential businessman and stockholder with interests in Philadelphia, Boston, New York, Newport and Palm Beach, married to the daughter of international financier Edward B. Strotesbury of Philadelphia, and father of three fine children. And Wilson, as we know, was Jackson.

On brief acquaintance you might have put Dot down as being a mite greedy, but underneath all the glitz and bravado she was a good girl at heart, and it is unlikely that she would ever have spread round this potentially explosive piece of scandal. But she did tell her one close confidante, her black maid Ella Bradford, called, for some unexplained reason, 'Billy'. And Billy almost certainly told the rascally Guimares. Anyway, Dot was soon being threatened into blackmailing her lover.

On 14 March 1923, Mitchell, shadowed as ever by John Jackson, arrived in New York for a date with Dot. Jackson left the couple at noon as they enjoyed an intimate luncheon, after which Mitchell left the apartment, arranging to call back later that evening to escort Dot to dinner. No sooner had the door closed behind him than Dot made a telephone call to Guimares.

At 7.30 p.m. Mitchell and Jackson returned to 144 West 57th Street and went up to the top-floor apartment in the lift. Shortly afterwards they came down again in company with Dot King. The trio returned at midnight, and Jackson departed not long after, leaving Dot and Mitchell in the apartment. It was 11.30 on the following morning that Billy Bradford let herself in as usual with her own key. In the hallway lay two fur coats; in the bedroom she found the grotesquely twisted body of Dot King. She was dead.

A terrified Billy ran down into the street to grab a cop, and together they returned to the apartment where patrolman Kelleher called for an ambulance and some senior officers. On the floor lay Dot King's final words: 'In case anything should happen to me . . .' It was her last will and testament.

At six in the evening Captain Arthur Carey of Homicide arrived, followed by the District Attorney and the Chief Medical Examiner. A closer search of the bedroom revealed an empty chloroform bottle and a cotton gauze pad. The state of the room indicated that a fierce struggle had taken place, and Dot's body showed a number of minor abrasions as well as blisters on her face and around her mouth consistent with chloroform burns.

As for clues, there were rather few on the face of it – a man's pocket-comb lay beside the chloroform bottle, and in the rack of the small lobby was a man's umbrella to which were adhering some cotton fibres similar to those from the chloroform pad. A pair of Mitchell's yellow silk pyjamas were recovered from under the sofa where the ever-discreet Billy Bradford had hidden them. On the obvious evidence the motive appeared to be robbery; Dot's jewellery, valued at $15,000, was missing, as were a number of expensive gowns and furs. More significant, though, Dot's personal correspondence with her 'companions' had also been taken – all except one letter from Mitchell arranging their last date. Only Dot and Billy had keys, so, as there were no telltale break-in signs, it must have been Dot herself who let her killer into the flat. The lift boy confirmed that Mitchell, Jackson and Miss King had gone up to the apartment on the previous night, and only Jackson had come down. Dot was dead and Mitchell was missing.

'Marshall's our man,' insisted Captain Carey (he was still unaware of 'Marshall's' real identity). 'Find him and you've found the killer.' But it was not going to be as simple as that!

In the meantime Carey thought he might pay a bit of attention to the next suspect in line – Albert Guimares. As it turned out, the Puerto Rican seemed to have a watertight alibi for the night of the murder; at least that is what he told the police. It was less impressive when it was checked out; and the hotel staff that Guimares claimed saw him denied to a man that they had clapped eyes on him in at least the previous 24 hours. As for the obviously recent bite marks on Guimares' hand, he had received them in a fight with someone, somewhere. And no, he couldn't remember who or where, he must have been drunk.

As nobody could find the elusive John Marshall, attention began to focus more strongly on Guimares – for both murder and potential blackmail. In fact the future was beginning to look decidedly bleak for the Puerto Rican, when out of the blue the Assistant District Attorney received a telephone call from Marshall's attorney. Marshall, it seems, had heard of the interest being shown in Guimares and was a little worried because he himself had been with Dot only a couple of hours before she must have been killed. Marshall agreed to travel to New York and make a statement as long as there was no chance of his real identity being revealed. Assistant DA Ferdinand Pecora agreed and a meeting was convened attended by Marshall, Pecora, Captain Carey and District Attorney Banton. It was Marshall's story that when Wilson (also being kept incognito) had left them on the night of 14 March, he and Dot had quaffed a bottle of champagne, and then . . . Anyway, he left at about 2 a.m., went down in the lift, tipped the elevator boy $2, and returned to his hotel. John Thomas remained emphatic that Marshall had not used his lift before he went off duty at seven in the morning. On 24 March a New York newspaper published 'Marshall's' true identity, and J. Kearsley Mitchell took his family to Europe while the fuss died down.

The press had also caught up with Mr Draper M. Daugherty – remember him? – one of Dot King's wealthy playmates from way back. It turned out that the bottle of chloroform found beside Dot's body was more distinctive than anybody could have guessed. It was one of a special batch manufactured exclusively for use by the US Army. And the manufacturer was none other than Draper's father Harry M. Daugherty! What's more, boy Daugherty had served in France during the Great War in a unit where that chloroform was used. Coincidence? Probably, but at least the media attention took some of the heat off J. Kearsley Mitchell and his besieged family.

What about Albert Guimares? He remained in the frame for a while, but eventually they had to release him for lack of evidence – liar and bully he may have been, but did that make him a killer? The law did catch up with him in the end, and as the result of some crooked deal he was invited to be a guest of the Atlanta prison service for a while.

So who killed Dot King? Who was it broke the wings of the girl they called the Broadway Butterfly? If I *had* to make a bet, my money would go on Guimares.

Marie-Marguerite Fahmy

The Oriental Underneath. *Edward Marshall Hall's defence of Madame Fahmy on the charge of shooting her playboy husband is reckoned to be among his very finest, earning acquittal for his client and the approbation of the nation for himself.*

Within the personalities and the lifestyles of the Fahmy case two leading characters lay all the ingredients that together make either a great Romance, or a great Crime of Passion. It was to be the meeting of two quite alien cultures that set this runaway train of emotions hurtling towards the latter course.

He was Prince Ali Kamel Fahmy Bey, a volatile young Eygptian playboy, holding a nominal diplomatic post with his Government's embassy in Paris, and heir to his father's immense fortune. She was a beautiful, sophisticated Parisienne ten years his senior.

When they met in Paris in 1922 Fahmy instantly fell in love with the beautiful Marie-Marguerite Laurent, a recent divorcée, and pursued her relentlessly and passionately. He followed her to Deauville, where they became lovers, and in December Marguerite was converted to the Muslim faith and the couple married, embarking on a life that revolved around the fashionable high spots of Egypt and Paris. Subsequent events were to illuminate the dark recesses that lay behind this outwardly bright and carefree extravagance.

The beginning of July found the Fahmys ensconced in a luxury suite at London's famous Savoy Hotel. On the evening of 9 July the couple fell into bitter disagreement over an operation that Marguerite wished to have performed in Paris, but her husband insisted be carried out in London – or he would not provide the money to pay for it. The quarrel accompanied them to supper in the hotel restaurant, where Madame Fahmy was overheard threatening to crack a bottle over Prince Ali's head.

Later on, as part of his customary courtesy, the leader of the restaurant's small orchestra approached the Fahmys' table to ask Madame if there was any particular tune that she would like them to play. 'I don't want any music,' she replied. 'My husband has threatened to kill me tonight.' With a polite bow the conductor made a tactical withdrawal with the words, 'I hope you will still be here tomorrow, Madame.'

Twice during that tense evening Fahmy asked his wife to dance with him; twice she refused; twice she accepted the same invitation from his personal secretary, Said Ernani. They returned to their fourth-floor suite at about 1.30 a.m., the squabbling clearly continuing to escalate. John Beattie, a luggage porter, going on his business past the Fahmy rooms, was startled to see the door fly open, and the Prince launch himself into the corridor complaining, 'Look at my face; look what she has done.' The porter recollected seeing nothing more alarming than

Madame Fahmy

a small red blemish on the Egyptian's face, and before he could gather himself for a response Madame Fahmy came out of the room talking loudly, excitedly and in French. With what must be considered great tact, Beattie persuaded the warring couple to return to their room and stop making a public nuisance of themselves. Turning his head as he resumed his way along the corridor, the porter caught a glimpse of Fahmy, still outside his room, crouched down whistling and snapping his fingers at a small dog. Before he had reached the end of the passage, three sharp, loud noises obliged him to hastily retread his steps. The sound was from a gun, Madame Fahmy's gun; and when Beattie arrived back at the entrance to their suite it was Marguerite Fahmy herself holding it. Her husband lay on the floor, bleeding from the head.

Ali Fahmy was to die shortly after admission to hospital; at about the same time Madame

A cartoon captioned 'The Captive Soul of Fahmy'. The characters are, from right to left, Prince Ali Kamel Fahmy Bey, his secretary Said Enani, and Enani's secretary – known as 'the light, the shadow of the light, and the shadow of the shadow of the light'

Fahmy was being charged with his murder. By the opening of the trial at the Central Criminal Court on 10 September 1923, sufficient information was already publicly available to ensure that the case was a sensation even before the first witness took the stand.

That first witness (for the prosecution), under the expert cross-examination of popular defender Sir Edward Marshall Hall, began to reveal the grim story of repression, mental cruelty and physical abuse which had led poor Marguerite to her most desperate method of escape. The witness was Fahmy's secretary, Said Ernani, and he agreed that the couple were always in dispute because of his master's strong views on the position of women; that having wooed her with sugar-coated promises and elegant flattery, Fahmy forced her to become a Muslim before their wedding as it was a condition on which a large legacy from his mother depended. Despite Fahmy's prom-

ise that a clause would be entered into the marriage contract allowing Marguerite the right to initiate a divorce if things became intolerable, he had this agreement struck out of the document so that only he could annul the marriage. As to the physical side of things, Said Ernani denied that Fahmy had sworn on the Koran to kill his wife, but reluctantly admitted a series of lesser bodily attacks – once occasioning Marguerite a dislocated jaw. Warming to his defence, Marshall Hall read out to the court a letter written by Fahmy to Marguerite's younger sister: 'Just now I am engaged in training her. Yesterday, to begin with I did not come in to lunch nor to dinner and also I left her at the theatre. This will teach her, I hope, to respect my wishes. With women one must act with energy and be severe – no bad habits. We still lead the same life of which you are aware – the opera, theatre, disputes, high words, perverseness.' Sir Edward then touched on the bizarre (certainly in the eyes of 1923) sexual appetites of the Prince, and in particular the homosexual relationships which he enjoyed with (among others) the witness himself – a liaison which had become popular gossip in Egypt. Referring to Fahmy's sexual use of his wife, the defender elicited such information as to suggest that the very complaint for which she wished to attend a Paris clinic, and which had initiated the quarrel on the night of the murder, almost certainly arose from complications associated with persistent anal intercourse.

Marshall Hall's closing speech – as indeed his whole handling of the defence – has gone down as one of his most outstanding, relying as it did on emphasising the fatal consequences of intermarriage between the sons and daughters of East and West:

She made one great mistake, [he told the jury] possibly the greatest mistake a woman of the West can make. She married an Oriental. I dare say the Egyptian civilisation is, and may be, one of the oldest and most wonderful civilisations in the world. But if you strip off the external civilisation of the Oriental, you get the real Oriental underneath. It is common knowledge that the Oriental's treatment of women does not fit in with the way the Western woman considers she should be treated by her husband . . .

The curse of this case is the atmosphere which we cannot understand – the Eastern feeling of possession of the woman, the Turk in his harem, this man who was entitled to have four wives if he liked for chattels, which to us Western people with our ideas of women is almost unintelligible, something we cannot deal with.

He then came to the night of the murder, and in one of those moments of dramatic brilliance which illuminated his career, Marshall Hall took up the pistol which had shot Fahmy dead. He crouched in imitation of Ali Fahmy, stealthily advancing towards his wife, about to spring like a wild animal upon her. 'She turned the pistol and put it to his face, and to her horror the thing went off': the jury found themselves momentarily looking down the barrel of that same gun. Then, as his words died in the silence, he dropped the weapon with a deafening clatter on to the courtroom floor.

'I do not ask you for a verdict,' he told the jury. 'I demand a verdict at your hands.'

Mr Justice Swift, at the time the youngest judge sitting on a High Court Bench, followed with his summing-up. It concluded: 'A person who honestly believes that his life is in danger is entitled to kill his assailant if that is the only way he honestly and reasonably believes he can protect himself. But he must be in real danger, and it must be the only way out of it.'

Quite clearly the jury found this the perfect description of Madame Fahmy's predicament; at any rate it took them a little over an hour to return a verdict of not guilty. Those two words were all but drowned by the outburst of cheers from the court, and taken up by the huge crowd outside, all awaiting just such a result.

For Marshall Hall was the undying gratitude of a beautiful woman, and the unstinting respect of his peers. Only the Egyptian Govern-

Madame Fahmy's gun passed into the collection of her defence counsel, Sir Edward Marshall Hall, and was sold at auction in 1987

ment was less than impressed, and cabled the Attorney-General, complaining bitterly about the derogatory remarks made about Orientals. For Marie-Marguerite Fahmy was the love and admiration of a nation; and now, the freedom to 'be forgotten by everybody except my own friends'.

1924

Jean-Pierre Vaquier

Mr Jones's Liquid Breakfast *A classic case of the fatal triangle in which the mysteries of radio provide the access to strychnine and an arrogant Frenchman puts his own head in the noose.*

Vaquier was a French Basque, born in Niort in the Départment of Aude, and displaying all the striking features of temperament and dark good looks of that most aristocratic race. At the time he met Mabel Theresa Jones he was 45 years old and using his expertise with the newly invented radio – or 'wireless' – to keep in working order the set proudly installed in the Hotel Victoria, Biarritz, for the entertainment of its guests. The Frenchman cut a most dashing figure in his elegant dress and his immaculately shaped beard and moustaches combed flamboyantly outwards.

Mabel Jones was very much the English rose. Married with two children she was nevertheless of an independent spirit, and having money of her own she had indulged in a string of business ventures with no very conspicuous success. It is characteristic of 'Mabs' Jones that her prophylactic for impending bankruptcy was to seek the comfort and luxury of the Victoria Hotel, Biarritz.

Here they met. Vaquier had no English, Mabel no French, but through the intermediary of a French-English dictionary they conducted an affair whose passion would have been the

envy of any linguist. That the situation was not without humour was shown at Vaquier's subsequent trial. Mrs Jones described to the court how she and her lover had been interrupted by the chambermaid in his hotel bedroom on their return to England:

> 'I told him [Vaquier] he had put me in a nice plight.'
> *Judge:* 'Did you say that in English?'
> 'Yes.'
> 'By that time he was understanding?'
> 'No; he simply got the dictionary.'

However the dream was broken by Mabel's husband insisting she return home. Mabel's husband, about whose early history we know very little, was Alfred Poynter Jones, aged 37, who married Mabel in 1906. As is usual in the eternal triangle, the husband was as different as possible from the lover. He had purchased the Blue Anchor hotel in Byfleet, Surrey (with his wife's money, it is said), which must have been a great convenience – for Alfred liked nothing better than to spend his days drinking. In fact he did very little else, and life became a monotonous cycle of heavy drinking, deep alcoholic slumbers, and monstrous hangovers.

When Mabel Jones returned from France at the beginning of February she did so in a very leisurely way via Bordeaux and Paris, with Vaquier as her devoted travelling companion. On England's shore the Frenchman booked himself into the Russell Hotel in London while Mrs Jones made her way to Surrey. Within a week Vaquier had booked himself into the Blue Anchor Hotel at Byfleet as an unpaying guest of the landlord's wife. Whether Jones knew or even cared about the liaison is uncertain; he may well have approved of Mabel's 'distraction' as a way of giving himself more drinking time. Certainly Jean-Pierre at the end of six weeks had become as familiar to him as the hotel's beer pumps.

On the evening of 28 March 1924 the Blue Anchor was host to a big party at which there was a great deal of drinking done, not least by Alfred Jones, and it was past midnight before the drunken landlord lurched unsteadily to his bed.

Despite a massive hangover (which anyway must by now have become part of life's grey pattern for Jones) he was up and slouching about the bar before nine the next morning. There in the bar parlour sat Jean-Pierre Vaquier, always an early riser, sipping his coffee. There on the mantelshelf sat Mr Jones's invariable aperitif to the day – a bottle of bromo-salts. Closely watched by Vaquier, Jones staggered to the bar, mixed his seltzer and downed it in one long gulp. 'My God,'he shouted, 'that's bitter!' It was one of the last coherent things he uttered; by the time Dr Carle arrived the unhappy man was already going home; lying in fearful agonised convulsions on his bed, he was dead by 11.30 a.m.

The doctor was in no doubt that Alfred Jones had been poisoned, and from his experience a poison not unlike strychnine was the cause. After establishing that the victim had breakfasted solely on bromo-salts he sought out the bottle, which he observed with mounting suspicion had been thoroughly washed out and dried. The cover-up was by no means thorough enough to deter Carle, however, and from the sediment in the glass from which Jones had drunk the fatal draught and from some crystals scraped from the floor of the bar parlour, the doctor was able to salvage sufficient to enable him to establish beyond doubt that the poison in Alfred Jones's stomach and small intestine originated in the glass which had contained a cocktail of bromo-salts and strychnine.

The police investigation was already under way, though it was to be three weeks before Superintendent Boshier of the Woking force felt confident enough to arrest Vaquier and his mistress. On his apprehension Vaquier claimed: 'I will make known tomorrow who administered the poison.' In fact the disclosure was not made until the Frenchman stood in the dock at Guildford Assizes six weeks later charged with Jones's murder. In the meantime Jean-Pierre had been busy exposing his enormous conceit to the hungry lenses of the press photographers – as it turned out, very much to his disadvantage. For on 16 April the photograph of Vaquier in one of the newspapers caught the eye of a man named Bland. And Mr Bland had a most interesting story to tell.

During the early part of March, Vaquier, who had returned to London for a few days, had cultivated the goodwill of a neighbouring pharmacist – Mr Bland – who happened to speak fluent French. Vaquier had paid several visits to Bland's shop to purchase small amounts of various innocuous chemicals which he claimed to require for experiments into a new type of radio receiver. So Mr Bland was less surprised than he might have been when his French customer's next shopping list included twenty grammes of perchloride of mercury and .12 of a gramme of strychnine hydrochloride. Though both were deadly poisons, and Bland had never heard of their use in connection with radio, who was he to dispute the word of this international expert? Vaquier signed the poisons register with the name 'J. Wanker' (pronounced 'Vanker') and was not seen by the pharmacist again until he identified him in court as one and the same as Jean-Pierre Vaquier.

The trial opened at Surrey's Summer Assizes at Guildford on 2 July 1924 before Mr Justice Avory. For the Crown, as is the custom in all poisoning cases, the Attorney-General (on this occasion Sir Patrick Hastings KC) led, assisted – in an unfamiliar prosecution role – by Sir Edward Marshall Hall KC. Vaquier's defence was in the capable hands of Sir Henry Curtis-Bennett KC.

Vaquier, quite naturally, was his own star witness – a role which he accepted with enthusiasm. Now was the time to make known who administered the poison – or at least who had ordered its purchase. (Vaquier had reluctantly accepted the futility of denying that it was he who bought the strychnine, and had devised a story implicating Mabel Jones's solicitor who, he insisted, needed it to put down a dog!) The following extract from the Attorney-General's cross-examination of the prisoner reveals more than a trace of eccentricity:

Sir Patrick Hastings: Do you know what strychnine is? – *Vaquier:* I knew it was a deadly poison.

Has anybody ever asked you before to buy dangerous poisons for them? – Nobody.

Was it only the second time that you had seen the solicitor of Mrs Jones that he asked you to buy strychnine? – Yes.

So the person who asked you to buy the strychnine was somebody to whom you had never spoken before? – I had never spoken to him before.

Did you know of any reason why he could not buy the poison for himself? – He told me he was very busy and had not time to buy it.

He gave you a sovereign for the purchase? – A pound note.

Did that strike you as a large sum of money to buy enough strychnine for one dog? – Perhaps he had no change.

Did you ever give him the change you must have got from buying the strychnine? – No, he never asked me.

[The prisoner is shown the poison-book signed by him]

Is that your usual signature? – No.

What is the name you have written there? – Wanker.

You knew, then, that you were putting a false name to the poison-book? Why did you not put your real name? – Because I had been told that when you buy poison you never sign your own name.

Who told you that? – The solicitor.

Did the gentleman who asked you to buy the poison tell you to sign a false name? – Yes.

Did it strike you as odd that a complete stranger who wanted to poison a dog was telling you to sign a false name? – No.

In the end, Vaquier fooled nobody. The court had listened with commendable patience to his rambling defence translated in to and out of French by the court interpreter and had taken against him. The jury, after an absence of two hours, brought in the anticipated verdict of guilty; it was not a popular one with Jean-Pierre Vaquier, whose abusive oaths it was not necessary to translate. His appeal dismissed, the flamboyant Frenchman gave his swan song at Wandsworth Prison on 12 August 1924.

There is an interesting observation on Vaquier's demeanour in court to be found in Sir Patrick Hastings' own account of the trial (in *Cases in Court*, Heinemann, 1949): 'The most curious feature of the trial was the attitude of the prisoner himself. His overweening vanity

was self-evident, but his knowledge of criminal procedure came entirely from the French courts. He expected to be bullied, not only by the prosecuting counsel, but by the judge himself. He expected to be shouted at and called an assassin. The studied courtesy and impartiality with which he was treated appeared not only to take him by surprise, but to raise in his mind an entirely erroneous belief as to the course the trial was taking. As nobody shouted at him he thought they liked him; as nobody called him an assassin he seemed to think that nobody thought he was one. From first to last he appeared to be under the belief that the case was proceeding in an atmosphere of kindness which could only end in a triumphant success.'

Nathan Leopold and Richard Loeb

Far Short of Perfection. *The case that gripped America. Rich, highly intelligent, but bored, teenagers Leopold and Loeb planned to commit the perfect murder, but were betrayed by Leopold's spectacles left carelessly at the scene of the crime. At their trial, Leopold and Loeb were saved from the death sentence only by the impassioned pleading of the country's leading defence attorney Clarence Darrow.*

In Chicago in the summer of 1924 two boys, seventeen-year-old Richard Loeb and eighteen-year-old Nathan Leopold, were indicted for murder. Apart from the youth of the two killers, and the apparent pointlessness of their crime, the case shot to prominence in large part because of the wealth and social standing of the families involved.

The victim, fourteen-year-old Robert Franks,

had not returned home from school; nor did he return later that night, causing his parents understandable distress. Early on the following morning Jacob Franks received a letter stating that his son was safe and would be released in exchange for a ransom of $10,000. The letter also contained detailed instructions how the money should be handed over. Mr Franks was to wrap it in a parcel and stand on the rear platform of a specified train out of Chicago at four o'clock that same afternoon. The money was to be thrown off the train at a spot close to a grain elevator south of Englewood. However, before Franks could set out on his journey, the early afternoon papers led with the discovery of a dead body lying naked in a culvert under a railway crossing twenty miles south of the city. It was that of young Bobbie Franks.

A number of suspects passed through police custody over the next few days, and were released after routine questioning. Meanwhile, an examination of the spot where the body was found revealed a pair of spectacles. The optician who sold them was traced and he identified his customer as Nathan Leopold, a graduate of the University of Chicago and at the time a second-year law student at the same institution. The State Attorney sent for Leopold and questioned him about his movements on the night that Robert Franks was slain; Leopold claimed that he had been driving round town with his buddy Dick Loeb. Nobody *really* thought Leopold was involved in such a sordid matter, but for prudence' sake it was thought best to hold him for further questioning. Next day officers sent for Richard Loeb and asked him about the same evening. He wasn't certain, but he thought he and Nate were just driving around town. It now occurred to one of the detectives to check with Leopold's chauffeur, and that gentleman clearly recalled the car was in for repairs and could not have been driven on the night in question. After two days the boys broke down and confessed to murder. The motive, bizarre as it was, was that Loeb had decided to commit the perfect crime, which would involve kidnapping, murder and extortion. He had confided his plans to Leopold because he needed another pair of hands to help carry them out. In fact Nathan Leopold

was not at all happy about the exploit, but as would be emphasised later at their trial, he was the weaker character, and much under his friend's influence. When their plans were completed, the couple wrote a ransom letter; it was addressed 'Dear Sir' because at the time they had no idea who their victim would be. Then they hired a car under false names and drove over to a private school which Loeb had formerly attended, arriving just as afternoon classes were over and the boys were coming out. The random pointer of fate now swung in the direction of poor Robert Franks. He was invited into the car for a ride and ten minutes later he was stunned by a blow on the head with a chisel wielded by Richard Loeb. So severe was the wound that young Bobbie quickly bled to death. The car was then driven to the spot where the body was dumped. Once back in town the assassins took the ransom note and addressed it to Mr Jacob Franks. Seemingly unperturbed by their grisly act, the boys popped into a restaurant for a hearty meal before bed. On the following morning Loeb arrived at Leopold's home and they took the blood-stained rental car to a garage and washed it as best they could before returning it.

The trial of Leopold and Loeb opened on 21 July 1924 before Judge John Robert Caverly, Chief Justice of the Criminal Court of Cook County. As well as their own confessions, the defendants had provided the District Attorney's office with incontestable clues in the form of Nate Leopold's spectacles, carelessly dropped at the scene of the disposal, and Dick Loeb's typewriter, which had been proved beyond any doubt to be the machine on which the ransom demand was written.

But if things were beginning to look black for the young men in the dock, they at least had consolation in their legal representative – Clarence Darrow, the defence attorney who had become a legend in his own lifetime, and had been persuaded out of retirement to take on the case. If it was a foregone conclusion that Leopold and Loeb would be found guilty, there was just a slim hope that they might be spared the ultimate punishment for their crime; and if anybody could save them from the death pen-

Dear Sir:

    Proceed immediately to the back platform of the train. Watch the east side of the track. Have your package ready. Look for the first LARGE, RED, BRICK factory situated immediately adjoining the tracks on the east. On top of this factory is a large, black watertower with the word CHAMPION written on it. Wait until you have COMPLETELY passed the south end of the factory – count five very rapidly and then IMMEDIATELY throw the package as far east as you can.

    Remember that this is your only chance to recover your son.

                    Yours truly,
                    GEORGE JOHNSON

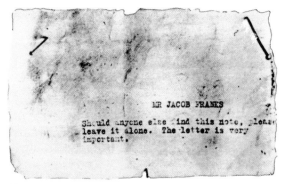

MR JACOB FRANKS

Should anyone else find this note, please leave it alone. The letter is very important.

The ransom note proved to have been written on a typewriter in Nathan Leopold's possession

alty it was Clarence Darrow. Darrow claimed in his autobiography*: 'No client of mine had ever been put to death, and I felt that it would almost, if not quite, kill me if it should ever happen. I have never been able to read a story of an execution. I always left town if possible on the day of a hanging. I am strongly – call it morbidly, who will – against killing.' With this case, however, Darrow knew that he would lose whichever way the sentence went. As a champion of the poor and oppressed he was loved and venerated as America's Great Defender; if he saved his clients from what was popularly regarded as their just deserts for the

*The Story of My Life, Clarence Darrow. Charles Scribner's Sons, New York, 1932.

heinous, cynical assassination of a child, then Darrow would earn the disapprobation of the nation. If Leopold and Loeb were to go to their deaths without him lifting a finger to help, Darrow would be unable to live with his own conscience. In the end he courageously followed the only path he knew.

It was obvious that Darrow could not sustain a defence of insanity – his clients' confessions alone were testament to the careful planning and careful covering up that shouted 'premeditation' at the jury. On the other hand, neither their activities nor their motive could be considered 'sane' even by the most liberal observer. In a modern court of law this problem might easily be overcome by resorting to a defence plea of 'diminished responsibility', with its automatic reduction of the charge to the non-capital manslaughter (or 'culpable homicide'); but this was 1924. What Clarence Darrow was able to do, however, was introduce this element of temporary insanity as a mitigation not of the charge, but of the sentence.

As he rose to sum up his case in mitigation, there was not a single other sound throughout the court, not a movement, there was only one focus of everybody's attention:

Your Honour, if in this court a boy of eighteen and a boy of nineteen should be hanged on a plea of guilty, in violation of every precedent in the past, in violation of the policy of the law to take care of the young, in violation of all the progress that has been made and of the humanity that has been shown in the care of the young; in violation of the law which places boys in reformatories rather than prisons – if Your Honour in violation of all that and in face of all the past, should stand here in Chicago alone to hang a boy on a plea of guilty, then we are turning our faces backwards towards the barbarism which once possessed the world. If Your Honour can hang a boy at eighteen, some other judge can hang him at seventeen, or sixteen, or fourteen. Some day men would look back upon this as a barbarous age which deliberately set itself in the way of progress, humanity, and sympathy, and committed an unforgivable act... I am pleading for the future; I am pleading for a time when hatred and cruelty will not control the hearts of men. When we can learn by reason and judgement and understanding and faith that all life is worth saving, and that mercy is the highest act of man.

America's legendary defence counsel Clarence Darrow between his clients Leopold (left) and Loeb

It is recorded that a deathly silence locked the court for two minutes after Darrow had resumed his seat. America's Great Defender had saved two more lives from an untimely appointment with the Grim Reaper.

Nathan Leopold and Richard Loeb were both sentenced to life imprisonment for murder and 99 years for kidnapping. Richard Loeb was killed in prison in 1936 when he became involved in a homosexual brawl. Nathan Leopold served 33 years of his sentence, during which time he wrote his autobiography; he was released in 1958, married in 1961, and died ten years later.

AUSTRALIA

Better than the Workhouse

In 1924 Edward Williams killed his three young daughters because he could no longer afford to look after them and feared that they would be confined to an institution: 'The majority of prostitutes are women who were raised in institutions such as my girls would have been sent to ...' he claimed. Despite enormous public sympathy, the Australian Minister for Justice, Thomas Ley, refused to commute Williams's death sentence and he was duly hanged. Ironically, Thomas Ley was himself convicted of murder in England in 1946, and committed to Broadmoor.

1925

Lock Ah Tam

A Case of Diminished Responsibility. *Respected leader of Liverpool's Chinese community, Lock Ah Tam killed his family while in the grip of what we now recognise as epileptic automatism. There was no provision at the time for a defence of diminished responsibility, that came only with the 1957 Homicide Act.*

Like all the world's great ports, Liverpool has long had a firmly established Chinese community; in England it developed in those years that brought Victoria's reign to a close, when the ships in our docks were Britain's lifeline to the world, and their crews came from all the races and all the places that could be imagined.

One of these sailors from a foreign land was Lock Ah Tam. Born in Canton in 1872, he arrived in England on board ship in 1895, quickly exchanging the ocean's wide horizons for the terra firma of Liverpool's dockland, and a job as a clerk in the Shipping Office.

Tam's command of the English language, and his naturally industrious approach to his work, endeared him as much to his employers as his generous, honest personality endeared him to the hearts of the Merseyside Chinese Community. In both these areas of his life, Tam's prestige grew. It was a mark of the respect accorded him that he was appointed European representative of the powerful Chinese stevedores organisation, the Jack Ah Tai, and shortly afterwards became the trusted superintendent of Chinese labour to three major steamship companies. And Tam had not left his politics

back in Canton when he embarked; now he was the English spokesman for the great revolutionary leader Sun Yat-sen, of whose Koch Mai Tong organisation he became president.

Above everything else, Tam was a family man; his integration into the country of his adoption was completed by his Welsh-born wife, the former Catherine Morgan. With Catherine, his two daughters Doris and Cecilia, and his son Lock Ling he lived and entertained his friends in a comfortable home at 122 Price Street, in Birkenhead. All in all, he was reaping the rewards of his virtue.

One of Tam's most characteristic virtues was his generosity to the Chinese community around him, and for them he founded the Chinese Progress Club, where seamen far from home could be among their own people, to feel safe from suspicious and not always friendly Western eyes. It was this final act of kindness that was indirectly responsible for the tragedy that was to overtake Tam and his family.

On a February night in 1918 Tam had peace-

Typical vessel of the times in Liverpool docks

110

Lock Ah Tam

fully settled into the Club for a couple of well-earned drinks and a game of snooker with friends. Without warning the door was broken down by a gang of drunken Russian sailors, and in the brawl that followed Tam was dealt a skull-cracking blow with a billiard cue. When the police arrived Tam was still bleeding profusely from his injury, and rather unsteady on his feet, but well up to the task of identifying his assailant.

In fact, the attack seemed for a while to have done no lasting damage. However, those close to the gentle Tam began to be aware of increasingly disturbing shifts in his once balanced personality. For one thing he had begun to drink heavily; and while he was never an abstemious man, the Chinaman was now on the way to becoming a chronic alcoholic. Consequent on these bouts of drinking (and later without them), Lock Ah Tam stated to display uncontrollable paroxysms of manic rage, during which he would stamp his feet and foam at the mouth, bloodshot eyes almost popping from

his swollen red face. And more than once he had attacked his own colleagues and friends over some imagined provocation.

Inevitably Tam's business suffered, and he never recovered from the crippling loss of more than £10,000 when a shipping venture failed in 1922. In 1924 Lock Ah Tam suffered the final humiliation of bankruptcy.

It was quite apparent now that Tam's brain had been severely unsettled by the blow that it had suffered during the fight at the Progress Club. He had become a sad, broken wreck, but none could have predicted the final outcome of his tragedy.

On 31 November 1925 Lock Ling Tam had only recently returned to Liverpool after nine years at school in China, and to celebrate this homecoming and to mark the boy's twentieth birthday the family gave a small party, inviting a select group of friends and relations to drink to Lock Ling's health and future happiness. Everything seemed uncannily normal; it was as though the calendar had dropped back seven years, with Tam acting the genial host of old – affectionate to his family, charming and attentive to his guests, while the festivities wound their merry way through to the early hours of the next morning.

The last of the guests had departed, and the household had retired exhausted but happy to their beds. Through encroaching sleep young Lock Ling was aware of an enraged shouting. Startled into wakefulness he left his room and met his two sisters, who had also been brought from their beds by the sounds of fighting, now coming audibly from their parents' bedroom. Fearing for his mother's continued safety, Lock Ling suggested she spend what remained of the night next door with her friends the Chins. As Mrs Lock expressed reluctance, young Lock shunted his mother and sisters into the sitting-room, and went alone next door to secure the help of Mr Chin, lest his father should again become violent.

Meanwhile the three women trembled to hear Tam shouting to Margaret Sing, a young woman who occupied the double role as maid and part-time companion to Mrs Lock. Wisely, she had kept to her room during the nocturnal quarrelling; but now Tam was demanding his

111

boots, demanding that Margaret get them for him. With more fear than devotion she took Tam's boots to his room, where she found him red-faced and foaming at the mouth, with a revolver in his hand. Margaret fled to the safety of the sitting-room and the comfort of her mistress, and between them the four women made a hasty job of barricading the door against the approaching sound of Tam's fury. Barely had they thus secured themselves than the full weight of Tam's body battered against the resisting door. Temporarily repulsed, the aggressor slunk back to his lair.

By this time Lock Ling had returned with Mrs Chin, and the company retired to the downstairs kitchen while the son went out to find a policeman. Without warning there was a deafening explosion from the kitchen doorway, drowning what sound Mrs Lock may have made as she slumped to the floor; a second explosion felled Cecilia, and Doris had just enough time to see the spectre of madness standing before her, a gun in each hand, before she too was blasted to heaven.

When the telephone rang at Birkenhead Central police station the voice on the other end of the line requested simply: 'Send your folks, please. I have killed my wife and children.'

On 5 February 1926 Lock Ah Tam stood at the Chester Assizes charged with the murder of his wife and two daughters; on the bench sat Mr Justice (later Lord Justice) Mackinnon.

For Lock Ah Tam the Chinese community who could never forget his past goodness contributed to retain the formidable defender Sir Edward Marshall Hall. Hall's often moving defence pivoted on the injury suffered by Tam eight years previously, and with the expert witness of a specialist in psychiatric disorders, he sought to prove that Tam had been, at the time of the killing, a victim of 'epileptic automatism', in which condition he would appear conscious but have no knowledge of or control over what he was saying and doing. Sadly for Lock Ah Tam it was to take another thirty years and the introduction of the Homicide Act before a defence on such grounds could be successfully advanced; and under the archaic McNaghten Rules he was clearly not, in the eyes of the law, 'insane' – the fact that he had telephoned the police and confessed was adequate proof that not only was he conscious of what he had done, but aware that it was wrong.

After a retirement of only twelve minutes, the jury found Lock Ah Tam guilty of murder. It was said by observers that in a courtroom full of Tam's sobbing friends, before a judge so moved he could scarcely speak the words of the death sentence, only Tam remained apparently calm – an inscrutable peace that stayed with him until the drop opened beneath his feet, and the rope tightened around his neck.

FRANCE

The Corpse in the Cupboard

In March 1925 Dr Pierre Bougrat murdered his wartime friend Jacques Rumebe and robbed him of a 25,000-franc payroll. Unable to find an opportunity to properly dispose of the corpse, Bougrat was obliged to leave it sealed in a cupboard in his flat. By and by, the thoroughly unscrupulous Bougrat was arrested on a charge of uttering false cheques, and a routine search was made of his home; it was in great part the awful stench of decomposing flesh that gave away the corpse's hiding place. At his trial Bougrat insisted that his friend had committed suicide in his surgery after having been attacked and robbed elsewhere. No, the jury didn't believe it either, and Dr Bougrat was sentenced to a lifetime's hard labour on Devil's Island; he subsequently escaped, however, and made his way to Venezuela where he died in 1962 at the age of 75.

1926

The Murder of Edwin Creed

Described by the coroner, H. R. Oswald, as 'the perfect crime', the bludgeoning to death of cheesemonger Edwin Creed in his London shop remains one of the great unsolved mysteries.

On 28 July 1926 Edwin Austin Creed, by all accounts a kindly man, remained behind in his specialist cheese shop to clear up and wash his hands after packing his young assistants off home to their suppers. So far it was a familiar pattern, but this evening was to end up horribly different.

Later that evening, after dark, PC Watts was patrolling his regular beat around Bayswater when he passed Mr Creed's cheesemongering business on the corner of Craven Hill Gardens and Leinster Terrace. Wafting up from the grating over the cellar beneath the shop the policeman caught a strong smell of gas. Puzzled, Officer Watts shone his torch-beam down into the cellar. There, on the stairway leading up to the shop he could just make out a man's foot. The foot, it turned out, was attached to Edwin Creed, late cheesemonger of Bayswater. Lying on his back on the stairs, Creed's head was covered in blood from a savage bludgeoning with some heavy blunt object. From the fact that his sleeves were rolled up, and that a hand towel was draped over the staircase banister, it was deduced that Creed had been about to rinse his hands in the cellar wash-basin when his killer knocked at the shop door. The shopkeeper draped the towel over the banister as he went up to the shop – it was quite characteristic of his obliging nature to open up for late customers if he was still about the premises.

Fire! Fire!

Petrus Hauptfleisch was what you would call a heavy drinker. In the end it put paid to his marriage, and unable to bear the thought of looking after himself, he went to live with his mother. On 13 January 1925, Hauptfleisch was seen running out of the front door yelling to the neighbours to come help – his mother was on fire! And when help arrived it was as he had said; the unfortunate Mrs Hauptfleisch was lying beside the kitchen stove dead, her face and body severely burned. The forensic evidence in the trial of Petrus Stephanus Francois Hauptfleisch successfully destroyed the entirely false account that he had given of his mother trying to clean the kitchen chimney by burning it out with petrol, and he was found guilty of murder and hanged shortly before Christmas 1926.

113

From the trail of blood it was obvious that Edwin Creed had been battered to death in the shop, and his body dragged across the saw-dust-covered floor and thrown down the cellar stairs. For a reason never explained, three gas jets had been turned on in the basement but not lit – it was the smell from these that had first attracted PC Watts's attention.

The motive for the crime became clear when it was discovered that £40 had been plundered from the shop safe. Clues, however, were few. In fact the only object of interest connected with the scene of the murder was a left-hand wash-leather glove which had been left on the floor of the shop, presumably by the killer. However, this led nowhere, and the coroner's inquest into Edwin Creed's death had already begun when the police were sent their next clues in the form of two letters. Both had been penned by the same hand, and inscribed 'Important. Urgent', and both had been posted from the Notting Hill district of London. The letters had been written anonymously, and indicated that their author could solve the mystery of Creed's untimely death. However, despite pleas by the police, the coroner and the press, nothing further was heard from the mysterious corres-pondent. And nothing further materialised to help the police or the court to get any closer to the truth of the enigma. The coroner's jury were left with only one possible verdict: 'Wilful murder against some person or persons unknown.'

1927

Frederick Guy Browne and William Henry Kennedy

Bullets have their own fingerprints. *The shooting of Police Constable Gutteridge by Browne and Kennedy provided ballistics expert Robert Churchill with the triumph of his career, and was the first time that such evidence was heard in an English court of law.*

On 27 September 1927 the body of Police Constable George Gutteridge was found in a quiet country lane between Romford and Ongar in the county of Essex; he had been shot four times, twice through the left side of his face and once through each eye. The fact that PC Gutteridge was still clutching his pencil, and his report book lay by his side, indicated that he was in the middle of making inquiries when he was killed – probably by a motorist whom he had stopped. Time of death was esti-mated at between 4 and 5 a.m.

Local records showed that a car had been stolen at around 2.30 a.m. from the garage of Dr Edward Lovell at London Road, Billericay, ten miles from the spot where the policeman was killed. The car was later found abandoned in Foxley Road, Brixton, in south London. For-

TO CHIPPING ONGAR

P. C. GUTTERIDGE
FELL HERE

TO ROMFORD

Detectives at the scene of PC Gutteridge's murder

ensic examination revealed bloodstains on the car's running-board and a spent cartridge case under one of the seats.

It was not until some months later that there was any further progress in the Gutteridge murder, and then it was by way of good luck. The incident occurred at Sheffield when another car was stolen and driven in such an erratic manner as to force a fellow motorist off the road, damaging his vehicle. The driver had noted down the offending car's registration number and reported the incident to the police. Although the number plate proved to be false, it did provide the police with the first of a series of clues which led to the Globe Garage, a business carried on at Clapham Junction by Frederick Guy Browne. Browne was known as a small-time crook specialising in car theft; he was also known to be possessed of a violent temper and an unreasoning dislike of the police. It was during one of Browne's regular

periods of imprisonment – this time at Dartmoor – that he had met and teamed up with Scottish-born William Henry Kennedy. When Kennedy was released from prison in 1928 he made immediately for London and joined Browne at the Globe Garage. Three months later, when stopped driving a recently stolen car, they shot dead George Gutteridge. At the time of the murder Browne was 47 years old, Kennedy 36.

It was during the early part of January 1928 that police lay in wait at Browne's garage waiting for his return. They were not disappointed – Browne arrived driving yet another stolen car. He was arrested and charged with car theft, and while he was in custody Detective Inspector Barker ordered a thorough search of the garage premises and of Frederick Browne's home off London's Lavender Hill. The result of the search was a veritable arsenal of hand-guns and ammunition. In all the police found four

Frederick Guy Browne
William Henry Kennedy

weapons, including a Webley revolver loaded with bullets of the same type as those which had robbed PC Gutteridge of his life. The armoury was subsequently handed over to Robert Churchill, the forensic gun expert, in whose hands the science of ballistics became a powerful tool in the fight against crime.

Meanwhile, Kennedy had been apprehended in Liverpool where he had fled with his wife. In custody, he wisely chose to make a confession, while at the same time putting the whole blame for murder on to Browne's shoulders. According to Kennedy, on the evening of 27 September the previous year they had stolen a car, a Morris Cowley, from Dr Lovell's garage at Billericay and were driving it to London via the quiet back lanes when a policeman signalled with his lantern for them to stop. Browne, who was driving, ignored the instruction and PC Gutteridge took out and blew his police whistle. The car stopped. The constable approached, taking out his notebook and pencil as he was walking. When he drew level with the vehicle, Browne raised the revolver and shot the officer twice in the head. He got out of the car, walked over to his victim and shot at close range through each of his eyes. A legend has grown up since the case that Frederick Browne's purpose in doing this was connected with an old superstition that the last image a dying person sees is photographed on to his eyes. A more likely explanation is that Browne was a vicious thug with a reputation for hating policemen, and was having a bit of revenge.

The two men drove south to London and dumped the Morris at Brixton before taking a train to Clapham. Browne, it is only fair to add, insisted that Kennedy's story was a pack of 'wilful or imaginative lies', and claimed that he had been at home fast asleep in bed at the time PC Gutteridge was being murdered.

The trial opened before Mr Justice Avory at the Old Bailey on 23 April 1928. Although Mr E. F. Lever and Mr F. J. Powell advanced spirited defences for Browne and Kennedy respectively, the balance of evidence was tipped irreversibly in favour of the prosecution by the expert testimony of Robert Churchill. Churchill had carried out test firings with the gun and ammunition suspected of being used in the killing, and a close examination with a comparison microscope of the slugs taken from the body and those fired in the tests showed the same identical rifling marks. Similarly the spent cartridge case recovered from the floor of the car and those test-fired bore identical breech and firing-pin marks. As if this were not damning enough, the powder discoloration, or tattooing, of the victim's skin around the entry wounds matched the black powder used in the cartridges in Browne's possession. Both Browne and Kennedy were convicted of the murder of PC George Gutteridge and executed on 31 May 1928, Frederick Browne at Pentonville Prison and William Kennedy at Wandsworth.

Doubt was cast on the outcome of the Gutteridge murder in a study published in 1993.* In it, the authors conclude: 'According to Kennedy's solicitor, Browne was never at the scene of the crime, and the police knew it. A detailed analysis of the trial and hitherto unrevealed evidence shows that the evidence on which Kennedy was convicted was dubious in the extreme and obtained by questionable tactics, and that Browne's conviction and execution was a tragic miscarriage of justice in which the police colluded.'

*The Long Drop, Christopher Berry-Dee and Robin Odell. True Crime, London, 1993.

SOUTH AFRICA

A Desperate Solution

Just one of the many individuals whose ambitions outstrip their slender purses, Huibrecht De Leeuw was disgraced not by his lack of funds, but by the unworthy means by which he sought to increase his portion. Town clerk of Dewetsdorp, in the Orange Free State, the young man had for some time been attempting to juggle the cash kept in the exchequer safe and the record kept in the accounts books to his own financial advantage. Clearly not a state of affairs that could pass unnoticed for ever, and time was already running out; the books were in a mess, and the fact had *not* passed unnoticed. Now the Mayor himself was demanding that a tally be made. When the deadline came and passed, and De Leeuw had aroused no tangible gesture of sympathy from his already borrowed-dry friends, he turned – as no few had done before him – to more desperate solutions.

On 8 April 1927, Mayor P. J. von Maltitz, accompanied by two representatives of the town's finance committee, arrived to conduct their own inspection of the accounts. As they pored with increasing anxiety over the columns of incomplete figures, a tremendous explosion ripped through the building, tearing off the roof and setting the fabric ablaze. During the conflagration the Mayor perished, and his financial advisers received fatal injuries. An arrest followed closely upon evidence given by a local tradesman from whom the improvident De Leeuw had been obliged to borrow a match to ignite his home-made bomb.

Offered the choice, De Leeuw elected that his fate should be decided not by a 'jury of his peers', but by a judge and two assessors. It probably made no difference; found guilty of murder, De Leeuw could at least comfort himself with the conviction that 'I am prepared to meet my Creator'. And perhaps he did, on 30 September 1927.

1928

The Death of Harry Pace

Arsenic in the Sheep Dip. *A landmark in the English judicial process; Pace's wife Beatrice was named by the coroner as Harry's killer, though at her subsequent trial the judge instructed the jury to return a formal verdict of not guilty against Mrs Pace. A Bill was later passed by Parliament debarring coroners from naming suspected persons in their verdicts.*

The facts of the matter were these. Harry Pace, quarry-man and part-time sheep rearer, living at Fetterhill Farm, in Coleford on the edge of the Forest of Dean, had been taken ill while dipping sheep in the early summer of 1927. Pace was clearly suffering so acutely from stomach pains and a burning sensation in his throat that it was thought prudent to confine him to the Gloucester Royal Infirmary for observation. He was discharged in October, but in December was stricken with a similar attack. On 10 January 1928 Harry Pace died.

Harry had been an unsavoury, withdrawn man, given to fits of violent rage, most of which was directed at his long-suffering wife Beatrice Annie. In a statement given to the police later, Mrs Pace described some of the brutal indignities that her husband had inflicted on her: 'My husband and I had a very unhappy life, and I left him on several occasions. He started to be cruel to me about two months after our marriage. He tied me to a bedstead with a rope, apparently for nothing, and left me all day, untying me when he came home from work. That same night I ran away from home after he was asleep. When we went to bed he took up a small pistol and put it under his pillow. He followed me to my father's house at about two o'clock in the morning. My brother spoke to him out of the window; he said: "Tell her to put her head out and she shall have the contents of this." He had a shotgun with him. He has always been cruel to me. On one occasion he got the blankets off the bed, put some paraffin on them and set them on fire. This was at night. My little girl and I had to sleep out. He also dug a hole in the garden and buried my baby's clothes, and we had to sleep on the straw in the pigsty. He repeatedly threatened me with a razor, and one day he forced my head on the table and struck at me with a hatchet; I managed to get my head out of the way, but the dent is still in the table.' Mrs Pace concluded: 'My husband has been a very peculiar man. At times for years I have often thought that he was not in his right senses.'

And now Harry was dead, and Beatrice Pace would not have been normal herself if she had not given at least a sigh of relief. Little did she guess that Harry had not finished with her yet; he still had a few more tricks up his sleeve from beyond the grave.

The funeral was arranged for 15 January, and would have proceeded without interruption had it not been for the suspicions of Harry's brother Elton, who obtained an order from the coroner, Mr Maurice Carter, to stop the funeral and conduct a post-mortem examination. In many respects it is comforting to be reminded of the degree of power that still rests in the hands of the ordinary citizen to effect this kind of dramatic action. In the case of Harry Pace things would probably have been best left alone. Nevertheless, Harry's mortal remains were subjected to close medical scrutiny, and in his evidence to the inquest Professor Walker Hall testified that he could discover no signs of natural disease in the body's organs, but that the appearance of the stomach lining suggested the presence of a strongly irritant poison; furthermore, changes in the liver, heart and kidneys pointed to arsenic, the last dose of which must have been taken between six and 48 hours before death, but that the poison must have been present in the body at least three weeks before death; the total amount of arsenic found was 9.42 grains. Asked if it would have been possible for Pace to have absorbed the arsenic – which was a major active constituent of sheep-dip – through the skin, Professor Hall excluded the possibility of infiltration to the extent found, unless there was a cut.

During the inquest, which was to span an incredible 22 hearings between 16 January and the end of May, Sir William Willcox, a senior medical adviser to the Home Office, was summoned to comment on the post-mortem findings, and submitted his report on 23 March. The symptoms, he confirmed, were indicative and typical of arsenical poisoning, the analyses showing the substance to be present far in excess of a fatal dose. In addition, Willcox felt that the previous illness – in July 1927 – also suggested arsenical poisoning. Other symptoms exhibited by the late Mr Pace – pigmentation of the skin, slight jaundice, inflamed throat, and the retardation of putrefaction in a sample of blood – were all suggestive of the same conclusion.

Dr Ellis gave evidence on the analysis of various preparations of sheep-dip found about the farm, and advanced several theories to the coroner's jury as to how the potentially lethal substance could have been secretly administered.

After the briefest of summations, the coroner emphasised that in his opinion there was no evidence to support the suggestion that Harry Pace had been accidentally poisoned. After an hour's retirement the jury's foreman was able to state that in the opinion of his colleagues and himself, 'Harry Pace met his death by arsenical poisoning administered by some person or per-

Mrs Beatrice Annie Pace (Syndication International)

sons other than himself, and in our view the case calls for further investigation.'

In a move that was subsequently to be heavily criticised (and quite rightly so), the coroner declined to accept this verdict: 'Only the committal of a person after a coroner's inquiry can bring about an investigation, which cannot take place unless there is some person named. It is necessary for you to name a person if a person is to be charged.' The jury retired for a further 25 minutes before returning with the amended verdict 'that Harry Pace met his death by arsenical poisoning administered by Beatrice Pace'.

Within minutes Mrs Pace, sitting distraught in the body of the court, was arrested on the coroner's warrant. With cries of 'I didn't do it! I didn't do it!' her pathetic figure was assisted to the cells.

Beatrice Pace was committed for trial at the Gloucester Assizes on 2 July 1928. Mr Justice Horridge presided, and the case for the prosecution, as is traditional in poisoning cases, was led by one of the Law Officers of the Crown – in this instance the Solicitor-General, Sir Frank Boyd Merriman KC. Such was the strength of sympathy for the plight of Mrs Pace that a public subscription was sufficient to enable her solicitors, Wellington and Mathews, to retain the services of no less an advocate than Mr Norman (later Lord) Birkett KC; it was, incidentally, the first poison case to be defended by Birkett.

In his opening address, the Solicitor-General observed that there was no dispute whatever as to the cause of Harry Pace's untimely decease – he had died from a massive nine and a half grains of arsenic, more than four times the lethal dose. The sheep-dip – purchased, he emphasised, by Mrs Pace – contained at least 2,800 grains in a single packet! Mrs Pace, he reminded the court, had made two significant statements to the police: 'I don't think it possible for any person who had visited him to have given him any poison to take'; and 'It is my view, and I am convinced, that my husband poisoned himself and I don't think anyone else could have done it. If they had, I should have known.' In all, Sir Frank Merriman called seventeen witnesses, fairly equally divided between medical experts and relatives of the deceased. Of the latter, Leslie, the eleven-year-old son of the Paces, had some of the most damaging evidence to relate. He described the day on which his father, lying on his sick bed, had asked for a box in which he kept his sheep-dipping materials to be brought to him. After checking the contents he instructed the boy to lock the box away in a chest of drawers in the room. The implication was clear: Harry Pace already suspected that he was being slowly poisoned and was keeping the source under lock and key.

Pace's mother recalled how, two days before his death, her son had complained of the bitterness of the water that was given to him to drink, and asked her to bring a fresh glass from the tap. And then came Elton, whose suspicions had initiated this elaborate legal ritual. He

claimed that he had heard – 'with his own ears' – Mrs Pace wishing 'the old bastard' was dead, wishing she could poison him. On one of his visits, Elton maintained, he found Beatrice Pace leaning across his brother murmuring, 'Harry, you're dying – we shan't see you much longer.'

The medical witnesses in the main reiterated what they had presented to the coroner's court. It was Sir William Willcox that Norman Birkett met in cross-examination:

Birkett: Arsenic may find its way into the body through the mouth? – *Wilcox*: Yes.
Sometimes through the skin? – If the skin is broken.
You have from time to time referred to cases of accidental poisoning from certain preparations such as sheep-dip, which contain arsenic? – Yes.
Also, that there is a danger of suicidal death from this preparation? – Yes, there is, of course, a risk.
There is a risk of chronic arsenical poisoning to those who carry out sheep-dipping? – Yes.
If the most perfect methods of cleanliness were not followed during the process, some of the arsenic might be absorbed when taking food? – Yes, if the person did not wash his hands, or if there were rashes on the hands.

As the case for the prosecution closed, the court rose for the lunch recess. When it reconvened, Norman Birkett rose to take one of the biggest and most successful gambles in the whole of his long career at the bar: 'The Solicitor-General in opening,' he said, 'stated that the duty upon him was that he must prove by evidence that the dead man was poisoned by arsenic obtained by sheep-dip administered by the prisoner with intent to murder. I submit there is no evidence of administration by the prisoner.' Mr Birkett continued: 'The scientific evidence is consistent with administration by the deceased as much as with any other theory. The fact that there was arsenic in the body, the quantity found, the effect upon the organs, all these are consistent with self-administration. The burden on the Crown is that they must exclude it, and that, in my submission, they have not done. Of the Crown evidence there is a very considerable body of positive evidence against it. Dr Du Pre said that on every opportunity he had of observing the prisoner she exhibited the demeanour of a devoted wife and nurse. That is the evidence for the Crown. Upon the vital point, Who did it? the Crown were completely silent. There was no evidence whatever . . . The evidence of the Crown is that possession of sheep-dip in 1927 was precisely the same possession which had operated in 1922, 1923, 1924, 1925, and 1926. There had been purchased identical or similar sheep-dip in all six years. The only evidence of possession given by the Crown is evidence of that in the "sheep-box" known to the deceased but unknown at the time to the prisoner.'

Amid general surprise, the judge responded: 'My opinion is that it would not be safe to ask the jury to proceed further with it.' He therefore instructed them to return a formal verdict of not guilty, and to evident public approbation Mrs Pace was acquitted.

There remained the disgraceful, and allegedly illegal, behaviour of the coroner at the original inquest into the death of Harry Pace, and his insistence that the jury name a suspect in the case. In the wake of Beatrice Pace's acquittal, the *Law Journal* commented: 'The cor-oner's jury returned, as we suggest with no jurisdiction whatever, a verdict of murder against Mrs Pace.' A few months latter, amid loud cheers in the House of Commons, Mr (later Sir) Rhys Hopkin Morris introduced a Bill to limit the duty of a coroner to finding the cause of death and to debar him from naming guilty persons in his verdict. Despite being given a second reading, the Bill failed to become law. That did not happen until 1976, when the Broderick Committee reported its recommendations on 'Death Certification and Coroners'. It had been convened to examine, among other more medical issues, the role of the coroner in making observations as to the guilt of a particular party, and his power to commit that person for trial. The Committee recommended that a coroner should have no such power. The still-fugitive Richard Bingham, Lord Lucan, was the last person to be named as a killer by a coroner, following the inquest into the death of the Lucans' nanny, Sandra Rivett, in June 1975.

1929

Eva Rablen

Death of a Dutiful Husband. *Although the autopsy found no trace of poison in Carroll Rablen's stomach, his wife Eva was identified as having purchased strychnine. So great was the public interest in this typically Jazz Age crime that Mrs Rablen's trial was held in a huge open-air dance pavilion.*

Described variously as 'a gin-guzzling flapper' or 'a fun-loving wife', the real Eva Rablen probably fell between the two; the one thing you *could* say about Eva was that she liked to enjoy herself – which made her choice of Carroll Rablen for a husband most puzzling. Older than his wife, Rablen was also profoundly deaf as a result of injuries suffered during the First World War; furthermore, a retiring nature excluded him from most of his wife's activities. And Eva was certainly the very epitome of the 'bright young thing' of the Jazz Age – never happier than when she was dancing and

Eva Rablen (indicated with an arrow) at her open-air trial

drinking. In the end the Rablens developed the rather eccentric solution of Carroll driving Eva to the dance-hall or speakeasy (remember, this is the Prohibition era) and then sitting patiently in the car outside until she had finished enjoying herself, and driving her home to sleep off the booze.

Presumably this docile, dutiful man would have continued to minister to his wife's Bacchanalian needs until he (or probably she) dropped. But Eva was getting restless – and greedy. On the evening of 26 April 1929, it was a Friday, Carroll Rablen had chauffeured his wife to the weekly dance held at the Tuttleton school-house in Tuolumne County, California. As usual he waited outside while Eva stretched her legs on the latest dance craze, the Charleston. At midnight Mrs Rablen bought her husband a cup of coffee which he drank gratefully. He was less thankful when the first convulsion shot like lightning through his body, and as he screamed in agony the disturbance brought Rablen's father and uncle out of the dance and to Carroll's side. They were just in time to hear him complain about 'bitter coffee' before death released him from further suffering.

Ironically, the investigation which followed

such a sudden and inexplicable death revealed no indication of foul play. An autopsy did not find any trace of poison in Rablen's stomach, and a search of the school-house and surrounding area failed to turn up anything like a poison bottle. Fortunately for the principles of justice, Carroll Rablen's father, who had never been keen on his son's choice of wife, insisted that Eva had killed him to get her hands on the $3,000 insurance. A new search was made at the school, and this time a small empty bottle which had contained strychnine was discovered hidden under a staircase. The bottle was traced to the Bigelow drug store in nearby Tuolumne, where the pharmacist identified Eva Rablen as the 'Mrs Williams' who had purchased strychnine in the form of rat killer. The shopkeeper's evidence was later corroborated by a comparison between Eva's known handwriting and the signature in the pharmacist's poisons register. District Attorney Grayson now had sufficient reason for suspecting Mrs Rablen to call on the expertise of the forensic chemist Dr Edward Heinrich. A second post-mortem performed by Heinrich found traces of strychnine in the stomach, and in the cup from which Carroll Rablen drank the 'bitter' coffee. Traces were also found in coffee stains on the upholstery of Rablen's car seat.

Eva Rablen, through her attorney C. H. Vance, strongly denied killing her husband, and by the time of the preliminary hearing the case had become a local sensation. Indeed, so great was the interest that Judge Pitts transferred the preliminaries from his courtroom to an open-air dance pavilion in the middle of town, where the proceedings were watched by hundreds of thrill-seekers from miles around.

When the case came to the superior court the process was entirely more sombre, and entirely in keeping with the dignity of the law. On 17 May 1929 Eva Rablen stood before Judge Warne in Sonora, California, and pleaded not guilty to murder. She was given a trial date of 10 June, but in the meantime Eva's attorney had become so alarmed on reading Dr Heinrich's damning report that he persuaded his client to change her plea to one of guilty. Eva Rablen was committed to life imprisonment to be served at San Quentin Prison.

The St Valentine's Day Massacre

Quintessential Prohibition gangland massacre instigated by Al Capone against rival bootlegger 'Bugs' Moran.

One of the most characteristic crime issues in America during the twenties and thirties was the emergence of the gangster and the birth of organised crime. In this context we should draw the distinction between the 'gang' and the 'Gang'; that is, between a group of villains who have banded together in a 'gang' for the purpose of carrying out any one of several types of crime for personal gain, and the 'Gangs' – highly organised territorial groups based on the systematic corrupting of legal authority, the control of vast financial empires

and the manipulation of power that such control bestows.

Unlike the 'gang', whose range temporally and geographically is boundless, the 'Gang' can be placed very definitely in the twentieth century; indeed we can even pinpoint the date and location of the Gangsters' rise to power – the United States of America, 16 January 1920. On this date Congress passed the Eighteenth Amendment to the Constitution, which made America 'dry' – the beginning of Prohibition.

Only briefly popular, this new restriction soon fell into such ridicule and disrepute as to make it virtually unworkable. People who had rarely drunk before started to demand liquor in protest for their rights; those who already drank drank more; for every formerly legal bar two speakeasys opened up – undercover drinking clubs selling alcohol kept in steady supply by the convoys of the newly-emerged 'bootleggers'. Overnight, it seemed, the country's mobsters – taken mostly from the dregs of the Irish and Italian immigrant communities – had found themselves an open gold-

'Membership cards' for New York speakeasies

The Saint Valentine's Day Massacre (Popperfoto)

mine. Foreign ships brought cargoes of spirits from England, France, Bermuda and other sources; they unloaded their wares just outside the three-mile limit in International waters into fast 'rumrunners' which did frequent battle with the US Coast Guard, their machine-guns blazing, in order to land the liquid gold. A case of whisky bought for $15 would resell at $80; a $3 barrel of beer retailed for $60. Overland a continuous stream of alcoholic beverages

UNITED KINGDOM

Curse of the Beast

Gifted psychic and dabbler in the occult, Norah Farnario had become inextricably involved in that brand of magic represented by the Order of the Golden Dawn and its infamous leader Aleister Crowley, 'The Great Beast'. On the morning of 19 November 1929, when Norah did not return to her lodging on the island of Iona, off the rugged west coast of Scotland, a search was made which eventually found her body spreadeagled on a bleak heather moor, naked but for the magical robe of her Order, a ritual dagger in her hand, and a grimace of stark terror on her face. There was only one explanation, however irrational it may have seemed to the level-headed Scots police – Norah Farnario had been the victim of a vicious psychic murder. Whatever had attacked her on that freezing November night it was no earthly presence, nor any Heavenly phenomenon – poor Norah had looked straight into the jaws of Hell . . .

The Body in the Green Opel

Kurt Erich Tetzner was convinced that there must be more to life than working; so he decided to die. No, seriously. As Erich saw it, the plan was foolproof: all he needed to do was insure his life for a huge sum of money, persuade people that he was dead, and collect. Having planned with his wife that a blazing-car fatality would be the most convincing, Tetzner addressed himself to the problem of finding a substitute body for his own. On 25 November 1929, he picked up a young hitch-hiker in his green Opel car, strangled him, crashed the car and set it on fire. It was a tearful Frau Tetzner who identified the charred remains by the few fragments of clothing that remained unburned.

But insurance companies are bad losers, and suspicious too; in this case they called in Germany's leading forensic pathologist and the one, coincidentally, who was the acknowledged specialist in fire deaths. Within hours, Professor Richard Köckel had established that the corpse was certainly not that of Tetzner. As a consequence a tap was put on Annie Tetzner's telephone, and the mysterious 'Herr Stranelli', who was a frequent caller, was finally identified as none other than Herr Tetzner. Tetzner confessed to murder when he was arrested, retracted his confession in court, and confessed again just before he was executed at Regensburg on 2 May 1931.

---

reached America across the Canadian border.

Territories of operation were divided up and jealously fought over; inter-gang warfare resulted in an unprecedented wave of street violence and killing. The overall homicide rate in 1926 had reached a staggering 12,000 a year, and in the Chicago area alone during the two years 1924–26 there were 92 gangland murders – 90 per cent of them unsolved.

Chicago – never a 'clean' city – had become the prototype of Gangland, harbouring some of the country's most ruthless and vicious criminals. Criminals like Alphonse 'Scarface' Capone, Frank Nitti, Dutch Schulz, Jimmy Blue Eyes, Frank Costello, Jack 'Legs' Diamond, Joe Adonis, Big Jim Colosimo . . .

Among Big Al Capone's few effective rivals during those profitable days of Prohibition bootlegging was the audaciously successful George 'Bugs' Moran. Certainly the Moran gang's hijacking of the Big Man's liquor shipments, their blowing-up of his speakeasies, and the sniping at his lieutenants were costing Capone plenty of dollars; what was worse, his pride was hurting. Then Capone laid the plans

for a brutal and most ingenious revenge. On 13 February 1929, Moran received a telephone call from one of his own bootleg suppliers – a haul of cheap whisky was waiting to be delivered to Bugsy's warehouse. Arrangements were made for 10.30 a.m. on the following morning – 14 February, St Valentine's Day. While seven of Moran's gang were waiting in the warehouse, a police car screamed to a stop outside and out jumped two uniformed cops and three plain-clothes men. They relieved the gangsters of their weapons, lined them up against the wall, and strafed back and forth with their machine guns – stomach, chest, head. The seven dropped into a lake of their own blood. So, with a squad of his men masquerading as policemen, Capone had the last laugh. Or did he? Miraculously, George Moran was late for that 10.30 a.m. appointment with death, arriving only when the real police had got to the scene of the butchery, and in fact outlived Capone by many years, succumbing in the end not to an assassin's bullet but to cancer of the lung.

1930

The Murder of Margery Wren

The extraordinary case of an elderly shopkeeper who obviously knew the identity of the man who fatally bludgeoned her, but refused to name him; indeed, in the days before she succumbed to her injuries she did all she could to hinder the police inquiry.

On the evening of Saturday, 20 September 1930, 82-year-old Miss Margery Wren was found alive but with fatal bludgeon wounds, on the floor of her Ramsgate shop. During the subsequent five days before she succumbed to her injuries Miss Wren made it quite clear that she knew the identity of the person responsible for the attack, but was unwilling to name him.

Despite a number of seemingly relevant clues, and the services of one of Scotland Yard's most experienced detectives, the assailant was never brought to trial. The police had, it is true, a short-list of suspects – not uncommon in such a case – but what has given this crime its enduring mystery, and rarity, is the reluctance of the victim, even in the face of death, to co-operate in the apprehension of her attacker.

In his autobiography* Superintendent Hambrook states categorically: 'Owing to the fact that nobody had seen the murderer near the shop at the crucial time, I was unable to lay my hands on him; nor could I penetrate the

strange mystery of why Miss Wren was so apparently anxious to shield him.' But does this mean that he had no idea of who the killer was or, as Browne and Tullett point out enigmatically in their biography of Sir Bernard Spilsbury** 'Superintendent Hambrook says that there were six suspects of whom A, B, and C were able to clear themselves [at the inquest]. One of the remaining three, D, E, or F, was the murderer. Miss Wren knew which, and the police may know too. But it has never been possible to pin the crime on him.'

The following notes present all available details. The reader's deductions and conclusion are as good as anyone else's – the Case File is open.

THE ATTACK

Despite the conflicting accounts given by Miss Wren herself, it was fairly early established that a brutal attack had been made on the old lady's person. The accident explanation at first given by the victim ('I came over giddy and down I went') was, however, not entirely discounted until the pathologist had submitted his report; support for the theory rested on the testimony of a widowed cousin who recollected that Miss Wren's rather old-fashioned habit of wearing long skirts had often led to her tripping up. In addition Margery Wren had fallen over some six months previously while trying to reach some boxes on a shelf in the shop; on that occasion she had quite badly injured her face.

When Sir Bernard Spilsbury performed his post-mortem he listed seven lacerations to the top of the head, and a further eight wounds

---

Hambrook of the Yard, Walter Hambrook; Hale, London, 1937.

**Bernard Spilsbury – His Life and Cases*, Browne and Tullett; Harrap, London, 1951.

and bruises on the face, consistent with having been inflicted by a pair of fire-tongs (such as were found close to Miss Wren's battered body) which anyway were found to have blood and hair from the victim's head stuck to them. There had, additionally, been an attempt at strangulation. There is good reason to believe, apart from Miss Wren's suggestions, that her assailant was familiar with his victim and her habits, and was no stranger to the layout of the premises (this was indicated by the methodical way in which the building had been searched by the killer). He appears to have left by the back entrance, through the yard.

The Chief Constable of Ramsgate, Mr S. F. Butler, issued the following statement:

The police are now convinced beyond all doubt that Miss Margery Wren was the victim of a brutal and savage murder. This disposes of any theory that may still exist in the minds of the public to the effect that Miss Wren may have met her death by accident. I earnestly appeal to any person entering or leaving the shop between the hours of 2 p.m. and 6 p.m. on Saturday last, or to anyone who saw any person in the vicinity of the shop or entering or leaving the premises between these hours, to communicate with me at once.

THE MOTIVE

Motive was always the controversial question; unlike most similar crimes there did not appear to have been a robbery associated with the attack. Of course, the assailant could have been disturbed before he had a chance to steal – but why, then, was the house methodically searched but nothing of value taken from it? The signs pointed to the fact that the intruder had a definite plan in mind. For example, drawers had been removed from cupboards and examined – carefully. To what purpose? What was more important than the money and valuables . . . and important enough to kill for? Perhaps, as Hargrave Lee Adam* suggests, it was a search for a document – but if so, what sort of document? That the killer was not a criminal by 'profession' is at least partly justified by the fact that of the many fingerprints

*Murder Most Mysterious, Hargrave Lee Adam; Sampson, Low, Marston, London, 1932.

Miss Margery Wren, and her shop

found where the murderer had been, none could be matched to existing criminal files.

It might be useful here to consider the financial position of Miss Wren.

For about fifty years, until two years before the murder, Margery Wren had lived in and run the little shop in Church Road, Ramsgate, with her maiden sister Jane. When the latter died she left property valued at £921 12s 7d. She appointed Mr Stewart Watson Oldershaw, solicitor of Lincoln's Inn, London, and Mr Harry Jarralt of Picton Road, Ramsgate, to act as executors and trustees. Her furniture and personal effects she left to Margery; she also provided that her freehold shop and cottage, together with the goodwill of the business, should be held in trust, the income to be paid to Margery Wren. On Margery's death it was to pass to a cousin, Richard Archibald, of Chapel Place, Ramsgate.

In her own will, Margery Wren bequeathed most of her property to a cousin (probably a Mrs Cook). In the meantime she lived frugally – not entirely of necessity, as she had made it known that she had some £1,000 invested in Government bonds, as well as various sums of money in tin boxes hidden about the house (these last had not been looted by the attacker, despite his having found them). As with many elderly retiring eccentrics (she would, for example, plead poverty in order to get a free bowl of broth from a nearby soup kitchen) Miss Wren attracted a reputation as a miser who was hoarding a fabulous wealth. Did this play a part in the crime?

THE INVESTIGATION

When Chief Inspector Hambrook and Detective Sergeant Carson arrived from Scotland Yard on

UNITED STATES

Blow Up

Lawyer Arthur D. Payne chose 1930 to blow up his wife and son with a car bomb; Mrs Payne died, but miraculously the nine-year-old boy survived. Although police were reluctant to launch an investigation given the position of the bereaved husband and his recent tragic loss, an alert reporter on the *Amarillo News* set up his own private inquiry into the incident which directly resulted in Arthur Payne's trial and eventual conviction for murder. Awaiting execution, Paine detonated a small explosive device strapped to his chest, thereby cheating the executioner.

24 September they found themselves faced with the unusual problem that not only was the victim unwilling to co-operate in the identification of her attacker but proved herself to be capable of deliberately misleading the inquiry by giving the names of several quite respectable and totally innocent local people. All these bogus clues had to be investigated as a matter of routine, and so aggravated an already difficult situation.

Aside from Miss Wren's own contribution to the confusion, the police had to deal with varying degrees of frustration as the result of other red herrings. One of these was a small linen handkerchief which was found in the shop and thought to hold the key to the assailant's identity. The handkerchief bore a name in one corner, which eventually proved to belong to a ten-year-old pupil from St George's, the local school; it transpired that a set of half a dozen of them were given by an aunt to the boy and his brother, and to avoid squabbles over ownership their mother had marked the corners with their respective names. The object in question was almost certainly dropped by the lad on one of his after-school trips to the Wren tuck-shop.

Another deliberate attempt to mislead the police was made by a young man who said that on the day of the murder he had taken a train from London that arrived at Ramsgate at about four o'clock in the afternoon; and he claimed that he had alighted at Dumpton Park station. He was subsequently forced to admit that fear of suspicion had led him to fabricate the story of getting off the train before Ramsgate. He had in fact travelled as far as that station, walking home past Miss Wren's shop in Church Road.

The coroner's inquest was unable to be more definite in their investigation. The coroner, summing up, reported: 'The fullest inquiries have been made into the circumstances, and if any real evidence had resulted from the inquiries it would have been brought before you.' A verdict was returned of murder 'by person or persons unknown'.

1931

Alphonse Capone

The Self-Made Man. *Unquestionably the gangster's gangster, Al Capone's violent career became a Hollywood legend. Ironically, the only serious trouble he had with the law was a conviction for tax evasion, and though there were many Gangland attempts on his life he eventually succumbed to pneumonia.*

All in all 1931 was a momentous year for the world's most famous gangster; at the beginning of the year Al Capone was honoured by his contemporaries who elected him to the National Crime Syndicate, and later by the forces of law and order who finally caught up with him. Alphonse Capone was the fourth of nine children born in the tough district of Brooklyn on 17 January 1899 to Neapolitan immigrant parents. From an early age Capone ran with the Five Points Gang, led by a young hoodlum named Johnny Torrio, and it was at about this time that Capone acquired the 'Scarface' nickname. Despite his later claims that the three jagged scars were battle mementoes from his military service in France, they in fact originated in a fight with Frank Galluccio when Capone was a bouncer at a Brooklyn brothel. Scarface Al's associate, Johnny Torrio, had been called to Chicago in 1910 to help out the organisation of 'Diamond' Jim Colosimo's empire, and in 1919 Capone was also summoned. By the following year Torrio and Colosimo had disagreed violently over the future of the Chicago operation, and Capone's expertise at killing people was in demand. He shot Colos-

imo to death on 11 May 1920. Torrio then took control of the empire for just five years before a serious attempt on his life forced a strategic withdrawal to Italy, leaving Chicago in the hands of Al Capone. Capone immediately set about enlarging his share of the Gangland action; Dion O'Bannion had already been assassinated in 1924, and in 1926 O'Bannion's lieutenant, Hymie Weiss, was gunned down. Rival bootlegger 'Bugs' Moran was the next obstacle to be removed, and seven of his gang were machine-gunned to death in the notorious St Valentine's Day Massacre of 1929. Moran, by a quirk of mistiming, avoided death but went into hiding.

'Big Al', as he liked to see himself

129

Capone faces the Federal Grand Jury (Topham)

Capone was the supreme underworld boss of Chicago at last – ten years and more than 1,000 deaths after his arrival in the Windy City. In 1931 'Scarface' was elected to the National Crime Syndicate, and in the same year he suffered the humiliation of an eleven-year prison sentence – not as a gangster, but as a tax evader. Released in 1939, Big Al, half-insane, retreated to his Florida estate to live on the memory of his former glory. He died of pneumonia in 1947.

UNITED KINGDOM

Who Killed Julia Wallace?

One of the most enduring mysteries of British criminal history began in 1931. Following his trial at the Liverpool Assizes in April of that year, William Herbert Wallace had been convicted of the murder of his wife Julia, though that verdict was subsequently overturned by the Court of Criminal Appeal and Wallace was released. On the evening of 19 January Wallace turned up for his regular game at the Liverpool Central Chess Club, but before he arrived a telephone call was received at the club from a man calling himself Qualtrough, and asking that a message be left for Mr Wallace to meet him on the following evening at an address in Mossley Hill. Obedient as always to the call of business – though he had never heard of Qualtrough – Wallace set out for the appointment as directed. After searching for two hours he realised that the address simply did not exist. When Wallace arrived back at his home, it was to find his wife lying dead on the floor, her head battered with an iron fire poker. Despite the ultimate clearing of his name, William Wallace was nevertheless subjected to malicious rumour and gossip which ultimately damaged his health and led to an untimely death from kidney failure in 1933. As with all celebrated unsolved murders, there has been no shortage of 'final solutions'.

1932

The Case of Elvira Barney

Murder among London's 'bright young set', the case was confused by the effects of fashionable alcohol abuse. Although Elvira Barney was acquitted of murdering her lover there is some reason to suspect the safety of that verdict.

In the early hours of the morning of 31 May 1932 the persistent ringing of a telephone beside the doctor's bed dragged him into consciousness; it was 4.45 and a hysterical woman was yelling down the line: 'Come quickly. There has been a terrible accident.'

When he arrived at 21 Williams Mews, the doctor found Mrs Elvira Barney, somewhat the worse for drink, sitting sobbing hysterically, and Mr Michael Scott Stephen, her lover, somewhat the worse for a bullet through his lung, lying at the top of the stairs. He had been shot in the chest at close range and was dead inside ten minutes. It was not long before the police, led by Detective Inspector Winter, had arrived at the Knightsbridge house and found the .32 Smith and Wesson revolver which had ended Stephen's life lying on the floor; two of its chambers were empty.

Mrs Elvira Dolores Barney, whose case was so soon to become a *cause célèbre*, was 27 at the time she shot to prominence, but due to the ravages wrought by the gin bottle looked some years older. She had been born into a wealthy family of good breeding, and her father, Sir

John Mullins, was a government broker. Elvira had married an American cabaret singer, but the couple soon tired of each other and Mr Barney returned to the United States and was never seen or heard from again. Mrs Barney

Elvira Barney and her lover, Michael Stephen

was what used to be described as a 'socialite', though in the worst possible interpretation of that word – in short, she was rich, spoilt, and hopelessly addicted to alcohol and men. Michael Scott Stephen was one of those men. Twenty-four-year-old Stephen was described in court by Sir Patrick Hastings, Mrs Barney's attorney, as being 'as worthless as she herself had become; he had no money and no occupation, although it is said that he was once engaged to a dress designer, and he was apparently quite content to exist upon such funds as Mrs Barney was prepared to provide for him'. It was an uneasy kind of partnership and, inflamed by drink, the couple frequently fell to loud quarrelling.

On the night of 30 May 1932 Elvira had given a party at her home, attended by the usual rag-bag of idlers, ne'er-do-wells and hangers-on; when this gathering broke up she and Michael transferred their drinking first to the bar of the Café de Paris, and then to the Blue Angel Club in London's Soho. The couple left the Blue Angel at around midnight while they were still just able to stand, and returned to Williams Mews where, according to custom, they continued drinking and squabbling loudly. Neighbours subsequently recalled hearing the quarrel, and a woman's voice screaming: 'I will shoot you.' One might have thought that the fact that this was followed by a couple of shots would have prompted neighbours to call the police; but they had heard it all before – too many times. The shouting, the abuse, the threats; Mrs Barney had even taken pot-shots at Stephen from the window on one occasion. So what really happened that morning? Michael Stephen was certainly never going to give his version of the events, and on 3 June Elvira Barney was arrested and charged with his murder.

Quite how things would have turned out for Mrs Barney had she not secured the services of Sir Patrick Hastings to present her defence it is difficult to say; certainly he was the strongest card in her hand. According to her own story, Mrs Barney had told the police that Stephen had, during their 'disagreement', threatened to leave her; she then, in a histrionic gesture, threatened to kill herself with the revolver she

kept beside the bed (it should be added that they were in bed at the time, though Mrs Barney did not mention it in her early statements). There followed a brief struggle during which Stephen tried to wrestle the gun from his lover's hand, and it suddenly went off with tragic results.

The trial of Elvira Barney opened at the Old Bailey in July and was presided over by Mr Justice Humphreys. Patrick Hastings was opposed by Sir Percival Clarke acting for the Crown. The prosecution had no shortage of ammunition in its armoury – not least the medical brilliance of Bernard Spilsbury and the ballistics brilliance of gunsmith Robert Churchill. It was Spilsbury who gave Patrick Hastings the greatest cause for concern; indeed it was this concern that resulted in the case giving British legal process a 'first'. In his autobiography, Hastings wrote: 'Sir Bernard had become recognised as an almost inevitable witness in a prosecution for murder, and I had cross-examined him on many previous occasions. He was an absolutely fair witness, and a most knowledgeable and skilful medical man, but unfortunately there had grown up a practice among some prosecuting counsel to treat him almost as an expert on murder. He was invariably permitted to sit in Court throughout the trial, and a question of this sort was not infrequently put to him by the prosecution: "Sir Bernard, you have been in Court and you have heard the suggested defence put forward on behalf of the prisoner. In your opinion, is that defence consistent with the results of your examination?" To which Sir Bernard could only reply "No". In my opinion this was a most unfortunate question. If Sir Bernard was not cross-examined, his opinion remained unchallenged; if he was, he was entitled, indeed bound, to give reasons for that opinion, and those reasons given with all the weight of his skill and experience must be most deadly for the defence. I spent much anxious thought in deciding upon the best method of avoiding this particular danger in the case of Mrs Barney.'

The result was that Sir Patrick made a request of the judge that Spilsbury should not be allowed to sit in the court during the trial except when called as an expert witness.

Although it was the first time such a request had ever been made, Travers Humphreys ruled that the request was proper, and Sir Bernard was asked to leave the court. Thus the defender's worst fears could not be realised. And it is in great part due to this fastidious attention to all aspects of his brief that made Patrick Hastings one of the most formidable advocates of his day.

Robert Churchill's evidence indicated that the gun in question was one of the safest types manufactured, and due to the fact that it could not be cocked by hand and required an especially long pull on the trigger to activate the internal hammer, it was unlikely to be fired by mistake. Spilsbury built on this by adding that the direction of the wound (horizontal) and the lack of scorch marks on Stephen's clothes around the entry point of the bullet suggested that the gun had been fired from a greater distance than would have been the case in an intimate struggle for possession of the weapon.

On the afternoon of the second day of the trial Patrick Hastings put his client into the witness box. First she related incidents from her unsatisfactory life with a brutal husband, helping to create an atmosphere of sympathy. She went on to describe her deep love for Stephen, and the cruel and careless way in which he treated her generous and affectionate nature. On one occasion, she recalled: 'I was so unhappy I thought I would make him think I was going to commit suicide. So when he was outside I fired the pistol at random in the [bed]-room. I thought that if he really believed I'd killed myself he'd go and fetch people . . .'

In his closing speech to the jury, Patrick Hastings concluded: 'I claim that on evidence that has been put before you, Mrs Barney is entitled – as a right – to a verdict in her favour. I ask you, as a matter of justice, that you should set her free.'

After a retirement of one hour and 50 minutes, the jury did exactly that, and as she left the court, a large crowd of well-wishers cheered Mrs Barney in the street. She went to France shortly afterwards, and after four more years abusing her body with alcohol, she died in Paris.

UNITED STATES

The Lindbergh Baby Kidnapping

It became one of the world's most controversial crimes, epitomising as it did the triumphs and the tragedies of the Jazz Age. The twenty-month-old baby son of famous pioneer aviator Charles A. Lindbergh was kidnapped on 1 March 1932; a ransom note left nearby demanded $50,000. Following several abortive attempts the money was eventually passed over, but on 12 May the child's dead body was found hidden not far from the Lindbergh house. Identified when he tried to spend some of the ransom money, Bruno Hauptmann, an illegal German immigrant, was arrested and tried for the baby's murder. Found guilty, Hauptmann was sent to the electric chair. The case still arouses strong feelings today, and not all commentators are convinced of Bruno Hauptmann's guilt.

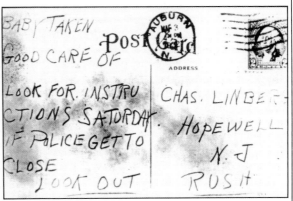

First communication from the kidnapper of little Charlie Lindbergh

1933

Samuel James Furnace

Goodbye to all ... *An unsuccessful attempt by Furnace to pass off the killing of his victim as his own suicide. In fact Furnace did commit suicide, but not until he was taken into custody and charged with murder!*

The history of crime is punctuated by the cases of those individuals who, for reasons of need or greed, seek to 'disappear', and in doing so leave behind an unrecognisable corpse in the hope that it will be taken for their own. The best known case is probably that of Alfred Arthur Rouse – the notorious 'Blazing Car Murder' of 1930. Rouse had got himself into so much trouble with mistresses and illegitimate children that it was prudent to start a new life. To this end he picked up a vagrant in his car, and after parking in a country lane outside the village of Hardingstone, doused the vehicle in petrol and set fire to it with the man inside. Rouse was easily discovered in his wickedness and eventually hanged. An almost identical murder – this time for the insurance money – had been committed by Kurt Erich Tetzner in Germany in 1929. In 1931, he too was executed.

Two years later, in January 1933, Samuel James Furnace was also making plans for his own 'death'. Furnace was a former ship's steward with honourable service in the Black and Tans during the 'troubles' in Ireland, and at the time in question was working as a builder and decorator. He was also in deep financial difficulty.

On 3 January 1933 the owner of 30 Hawley Crescent, in London's Kentish Town district, looked out of his window and saw that the shed at the back of the house, which he rented to Samuel Furnace for his business, was on fire. The fire brigade was summoned, and when officers got the flames under control they found the charred body of a man. A brief note was also found, written in what was later proved to be Furnace's handwriting: 'Good-bye all. No work. No money. Sam J. Furnace.' Despite this elaborate charade, the option of suicide was quickly rejected in favour of homicide when the bullet wound was found in the charred remains, which could not possibly have been self-inflicted. The theory was confirmed when lack of soot in the body's lungs and lack of carbon monoxide in the blood proved that death had taken place *before* burning.

An examination of what was left of the clothing covering the body produced a clue which would result in a positive identification of the corpse. In one of the pockets was what remained, after being burnt by the fire and soaked by the hoses, of a Post Office savings book; it bore the name Walter Spatchett. Medical evidence later confirmed the identity of Spatchett, a rent collector with the same firm of estate agents which had employed Samuel Furnace. Spatchett had last been seen at around 5 p.m. on Monday, 2 January 1933.

So where was Furnace? It seemed that even if he had 'died' unsuccessfully, he had disappeared most convincingly. Indeed it was claimed at one stage that half the police forces

(Right) Scotland Yard's 'wanted' notice

METROPOLITAN POLICE.

MURDER

WANTED

For the wilful murder of **Walter Spatchett**, whose dead body was found on the 3rd January, 1933, in a shed at the rear of 30, Hawley Crescent, Camden Town, London, occupied as an office by the wanted man.

SAMUEL JAMES FURNACE, born 1890, about 6 feet, well built and set up, complexion fair, hair fair (thin in front), eyes hazel, full face, square jaw, gunshot wounds on left leg and both arms, long scar on right bicep shewing marks of 13 stitches, 1 tooth missing in front upper jaw which may be replaced by false tooth. When last seen on the 7th January, 1933, was wearing a brown suit, black shoes, light trench coat with sliding belt, brown and red check lining edged with brown leatherette binding. He has also a brown overcoat, a grey soft felt hat and a bluish coloured cap. Possesses a fair sum of money. In possession of a revolver. He has passed in the name of Raymond Rogers but might assume any other name.

He might seek employment in the building and decorating trade as a foreman or workman, or in the mercantile marine as a steward or seaman and may take lodgings at a boarding house, apartment house, coffee house, cottage, or any place taking male lodgers.

A warrant for his arrest has been issued and extradition will be applied for.

Any person having knowledge of his whereabouts is requested to inform the nearest Police Station at once.

Metropolitan Police Office
New Scotland Yard S.W.1.
9th January 193..

TRENCHARD,

The Commissioner of Police of the Metropolis.

Printed by the Receiver for the Metropolitan Police District, New Scotland Yard, London, S.W.1. 13 22923/1600 in the country were mobilised into the hunt, one of the most extensive and complex ever mounted. As is frequently the case, it was the fugitive's own ineptitude that proved his downfall. Just short of a fortnight after the fire in Kentish Town, Mr Charles Tuckfield received a rather curious letter, dated 14 January:

Just a line to you in hope that I shall be able to see a friend before I end it all . . . I am at Southend, quite near the station, making out I have been ill with the 'flu. So have been able to stay in all the week. I am far from well through want of sleep. I don't think I have slept an hour since the accident happened. Now what I want you to do is not for me but for May and the kiddies. My days are numbered. I want you to come down Sunday, on your own please. Catch the 10.35 from Harringay Park, that gets you down in Southend at 12.08. Come out of the station, walk straight across the road and down the opposite road. Walk down on the left side. I will see you. I am not giving my address in case you are followed. Just walk slowly down. If you come will you bring me fifteen and a half shirt and two collars, any colour will do. Also one pair of socks, dark ones, and one comb. I think that is all now.

Best of luck. Mine is gone.

The letter was from Tuckfield's brother-in-law, Sam Furnace.

By the time the investigation was put in the hands of Scotland Yard's Superintendent George Cornish and Inspector Yandell, Mr Tuckfield had wisely taken his correspondence to the police and agreed to carry out all Furnace's requests. As he walked down the road opposite the station – Whitegate Road – the curtain of the ground-floor room of Number 11 twitched open; inside was Samuel Furnace. Before Charles Tuckfield had set one foot over the threshold, surveillance police had entered the house by a back door and taken the fugitive into custody.

Back at Kentish Town police station, Samuel Furnace made a statement about the tragic events of the night of 2 January: 'I was showing [Spatchett] through the door, with the gun in my left hand, and as he was going through the door the gun went off and shot him. He fell to the ground groaning. I realised my position and lost my head. I went out. When I got back I found he was dead . . . The idea struck me to

destroy the body by burning it, making out the body was mine . . . The idea at first seemed too terrible, but no other way seemed possible.' It is often only when a case comes to trial, and all the sensitive evidence which has been suppressed in the interests of an impartial hearing is finally presented that the public becomes privy to the details underlying a case. In the matter of Sam J. Furnace even that was denied us. At seven o'clock on the morning after Furnace made his statement, a police officer on routine inspection looked into his cell just in time to see Furnace lift a small bottle to his mouth. The phial contained hydrochloric acid, and despite emergency treatment at nearby St Pancras Hospital Samuel Furnace died the following day. A subsequent coroner's jury, however, felt justified in declaring Furnace guilty, not of manslaughter as he was clearly indicating in his statement, but of the murder of Walter Spatchett.

AUSTRALIA

Eric Roland Craig

The Man Whose Luck Ran Out. *A rare early case of an Australian serial killer, and a case which clearly confused a succession of juries.*

Craig faced trial for murder on four separate occasions in Australia in 1933, resulting in one verdict of manslaughter, two jury disagreements, and eventually a conviction for murder.

On 9 December 1932, Craig picked up 30-year-old prostitute May Miller in a car that he had earlier stolen from Sydney city centre. The woman directed him to a 'lovers' lane' near to Centennial Park in the suburb of Paddington, where she demanded five shillings and started to take her clothes off. Craig, unemployed at the time, replied that he did not have five shillings, and Miss Miller, after a spirited bout of cursing, attacked him. In response Craig picked up the broken branch of a fig tree lying nearby, and beat her head to a pulp. He then stripped the body and dragged it into the bushes before gathering up the victim's clothes and knotting them together in a bundle and dumping them on the roadside.

Five days later Eric Craig stole another car and picked up sixteen-year-old Bessie O'Connor, a well-known New South Wales swimming champion, and drove her to the Sydney National Park. The next morning Bessie was found naked and almost dead from a series of terrible head wounds, thought to have been inflicted with an axe. As in the case of May Miller, her clothing was later found knotted together in a clump of bushes close to the scene of the crime. Bessie O'Connor died in hospital without regaining consciousness, and a special murder squad was assembled. An observant detective on the team noticed that in tying up the clothes the knot used was the same as that in the May Miller case; it was a knot familiar to artillerymen. The first obvious step was to make a check of serving soldiers at the large barracks in Victoria district, close to where the two stolen cars had been abandoned. When these inquiries proved negative, the search was widened to include former soldiers, and then witnesses identified Eric Craig as the man seen with the victims shortly before the killings.

Under interrogation, Craig admitted the murder of May Miller, but denied responsibility for the death of Bessie O'Connor. He was tried first for the Miller murder, found guilty on the lesser charge of manslaughter on grounds of provocation, and sentenced to twenty years. Craig then faced three further trials, all arising from the killing of Bessie O'Connor. Twice the jury failed to agree on a verdict, and on the third occasion Eric Craig was found guilty and sentenced to death. On 19 September 1933, the capital sentence was commuted to life imprisonment without possibility of remission.

Although he never admitted any crime other than the murder of May Miller, police recalled that in 1932 another prostitute named Hilda White had been found dead in a park in Paddington; she had been strangled and stripped, and some of her clothing had been tied together with a now familiar knot . . .

Fit as a Fiddle and Ready to Hang

Twenty-five-year-old Kenneth Neu, a night-club singer with some talent and a history of mental instability, was picked up in New York's Times Square by wealthy theatre-owner Lawrence Shead on 2 September 1933. Neu, so he said, thought the older man was interested in giving him a job, and when they got back to Shead's hotel room and it was obvious the man was looking for sex, Neu strangled him. He also stole his watch, money, and one of his suits. Two weeks later, Kenneth Neu killed and robbed store-keeper Sheffield Clark; subsequently he was arrested driving Clark's car and wearing Shead's suit. Neu admitted the murders, and despite conclusive proof that he was suffering brain damage resulting from neuro-syphilis, Kenneth Neu was convicted of murder and spent the last few days before his execution composing his swan song, 'I'm Fit as a Fiddle and Ready to Hang'. He did, on 1 February 1935.

1934

The Story of Bonnie and Clyde

America's best-known criminal duo met their end in a hail of bullets during a Texas Rangers ambush; Bonnie died with a half-eaten sandwich in her mouth, Clyde with his boots off.

Arguably the world's most famous killer couple, Bonnie Parker and Clyde Barrow have much to thank Hollywood for in whitewashing their memory and transforming a pair of ruthless thieves and vicious killers into a daring and glamorous couple of Robin Hoods. The truth of the matter was closer to the description given by America's Public Enemy Number One, John Dillinger: 'They were kill-crazy punks and clodhoppers; they were bad news to decent bank robbers – gave us a bad name.'

Clyde Chestnut Barrow, a latent homosexual with a fanatical passion for cars and guns, had been torturing small animals since childhood. He met Bonnie Parker in January 1930 when he was not quite 21; Bonnie was eighteen months younger and had already been through one broken marriage. She was to lose Clyde, too, for a couple of years – he was arrested and imprisoned for robbery the day after they met.

Within weeks of Clyde Barrow's release in February 1932, the 'Barrow Gang' (including at various times Bonnie, Clyde and his brother Buck Barrow, Buck's wife Blanche, Ray Hamilton, W. D. Jones and a few others) embarked on a series of armed robberies and murders that would terrorise the southwestern states for two years. They started in Texas, where the first killing was that of jeweller John Bucher of Hillsboro, whom they shot dead and robbed of just $40. This was followed by the senseless murder of Sheriff Maxwell and his deputy at Atoka, Oklahoma. Robbing and killing their way through Michigan, Kansas and Missouri, it is impossible to calculate the total number of crimes committed by the gang over the follow-

Bonnie Parker in characteristic pose, gun in hand, cigar between teeth, standing by a stolen car

ing year. Occasionally they came close to capture, but usually a combination of police bungling and Barrow's reckless driving kept the couple just this side of the prison bars. But even Bonnie was once moved to say: 'It can't be long now before they get us.'

In January 1934 Bonnie Parker and Clyde Barrow broke their old partner-in-crime Ray Hamilton out of Huntsville Prison, and with another convict, Henry Methven, began a new series of bank heists. Among the killings during the next few months were three more policemen. The end came towards the end of May, and it has been suggested that it was Methven's father who alerted police to the gang's movements in an attempt to win immunity for Henry. At any rate, on 23 January six heavily armed officers waited in ambush along the highway just outside Gibsland, Louisiana. Just after nine in the morning a tan-coloured Ford V–8 came into sight, driven by Clyde Barrow, with Bonnie beside him eating a sandwich. In all upwards of 150 shots were fired into the car, fifty of them ripping into the bodies of Bonnie and Clyde. One of the officers said later: 'We just shot the hell out of them ... they were just a smear of wet rags.'

This poem, idealising their exploits, was written by Bonnie Parker:

The Story of Bonnie and Clyde

You've read the story of Jesse James –
Of how he lived and died;
*   If you're still in need*
*   Of something to read,*
Here's the story of Bonnie and Clyde.

Now Bonnie and Clyde are the Barrow gang,
I'm sure you all have read
*   How they rob and steal*
*   And those who squeal*
Are usually found dying or dead.

There's lots of untruths to these write-ups;
They're not so ruthless as that;
*   Their nature is raw;*
*   They hate all the law,*
The stool pigeons, spotters and rats.

AUSTRALIA

The 'Pyjama Girl' Case

On 1 September 1934 the body of a young woman dressed in pyjamas was discovered in a culvert near Albury, between Melbourne and Sydney; she had been bludgeoned and shot, and an attempt had been made to burn her body. Although a number of well-meaning people identified the corpse as that of a missing woman named Coots, and somebody suggested that she might be Linda Agostini, there was no definitive proof of identity and the body was preserved in formalin at Sydney University's pathology lab. And there it remained for the next ten years. In 1944 New South Wales elected a 'new broom' in the person of Mr W. J. Mackay, and this new Commissioner of Police determined to solve the 'Pyjama Girl' case and give her a decent burial. And so the now wrinkled body was taken out of its preserving tank and dolled up with make-up and a decent hair-do, and a new photograph was circulated. Again the name Linda Agostini came up. Antonio Agostini, an Italian restaurant worker, was contacted in connection with the disappearance of his wife. According to his statement, Linda had been a dangerous alcoholic who on an evening in 1934 had begun to wave a gun around in a threatening manner; during the struggle for possession of the weapon, Mrs Agostini had accidentally been shot. Agostini had panicked and hidden the body. Despite the fact that it was proved that Linda Agostini had died of bludgeoning to the head, not a bullet, her husband was convicted only on a manslaughter charge. He served six years' hard labour in Australia before being deported to his native Italy.

Appreciative letter sent by Clyde Barrow to Henry Ford in 1934, praising his 'dandy' cars

They call them cold-blooded killers;
They say they are heartless and mean;
   But I say this with pride,
    That I once knew Clyde
When he was honest and upright and clean.

But the law's fooled around
Kept taking him down
   And locking him up in a cell,
    Till he said to me,
'I'll never be free, So I'll meet a few of them in hell.'

The road was so dimly lighted;
There were no highway signs to guide;
   But they made up their minds
    If all roads were blind,
They wouldn't give up till they died.

The road gets dimmer and dimmer;
Sometimes you can hardly see;
   But it's fight man to man
    And do all you can,
For they know they can never be free.

From heartbreak some people have suffered;
From weariness some people have died;
   But take it all in all,
    Our troubles are small
Till we get like Bonnie and Clyde.

If a policeman is killed in Dallas
And they have no clue or guide;
   If they can't find a fiend,
    They just wipe their slate clean
And hang it on Bonnie and Clyde.

There's two crimes committed in America
Not accredited to the Barrow mob;
   They had no hand
    In the kidnap demand,
Nor the Kansas City depot job.

A newsboy once said to his buddy;
'I wish old Clyde would get jumped;
   In these awful hard times
    We'd make a few dimes
If five or six cops would get bumped'.

The police haven't got the report yet,
But Clyde called me up today;
   He said, 'Don't start any fights –
    We aren't working nights –
We're joining the NRA.'

From Irving to West Dallas viaduct
Is known as the Great Divide
   Where the women are kin,
    And the men are men,
And they don't 'stool' on Bonnie and Clyde.

If they try to act like citizens
And rent them a nice little flat,
   About the third night
    They're invited to fight
By a sub-gun's rat-tat-tat.

They don't think they're too tough or desperate,
They know that the law always wins;
   They've been shot at before,
    But they do not ignore
That death is the wages of sin.

Some day they'll go down together;
And they'll bury them side by side;
   To few it'll be grief –
    To the law a relief –
But it's death for Bonnie and Clyde.

The Brighton Trunk Murders

On 17 June 1934, a human female torso was found in a trunk at the left-luggage office of Brighton railway station. The remains were never identified, and her murderer never caught. What is more extraordinary is that on 15 July – barely one month later – another corpse was found in another trunk in a Brighton lodging house. This time the victim *was* identi-

fied, as ex-dancer and prostitute Violette Kaye. Her lover, a petty crook who called himself Tony Mancini, was charged with Violette's murder, but thanks mainly to the remarkable efforts of Mr Norman Birkett, his defence attorney, Mancini was acquitted at trial. In 1976, in an interview with the *News of the World* headed 'I've Got Away With Murder', he confessed his guilt.

The second Brighton trunk victim, Violette Kaye

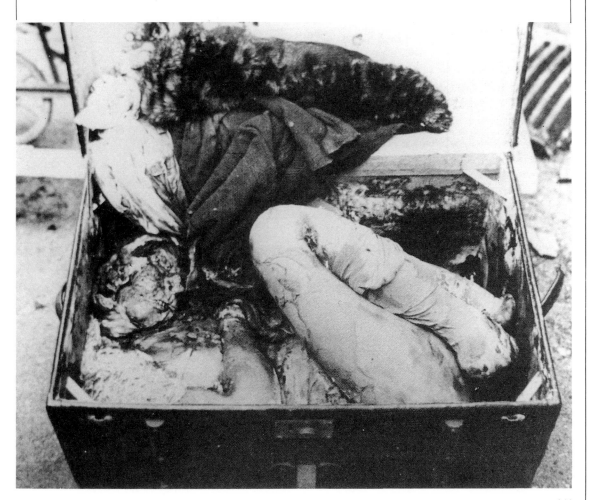

1935

Alma Rattenbury and George Percy Stoner

Murder at the Villa Madeira. *Another of the sensational crimes of passion of the 1920s and 1930s. At trial both Alma Rattenbury and her young lover claimed sole responsibility for the death of Francis Rattenbury; Alma was acquitted, Percy Stoner was sentenced to death. Three days later Mrs Rattenbury committed suicide.*

The facts were these. In 1935, 68-year-old retired architect Francis Mawson Rattenbury was living with his already twice-divorced wife Alma at the Villa Madeira in the refined English south-coast resort of Bournemouth. The ménage was completed by an eighteen-year-old handyman/chauffeur named George Stoner, whom Alma had seduced first at an Oxford hotel and had subsequently taken as a permanent lover. If Rattenbury knew of the affair (and he could hardly have avoided it), it seems not to have bothered him as long as he had his hand firmly on the real love in his life – the whisky decanter. In the small hours of 25 March Alma, so she claimed, found her husband lying on the drawing-room carpet; his head was beaten in, but he was still breathing. When the doctor and the police arrived, summoned by a startled maid, they found Alma Rattenbury apparently much the worse for

drink, gibbering hysterically and making what appeared to be a confession: 'I did it with a mallet . . . He's lived too long . . .' and so on. It was just the first of several admissions of guilt, most of which were aimed at protecting her beloved Percy. Percy himself had begun to make statements, too, the essence of which were that *he* was the guilty party and Mrs Rattenbury had nothing to do with the dreadful

Alma Rattenbury

incident. By this time Francis Rattenbury had succumbed to his injuries, breathing his last at the Strathallen Nursing Home, and Alma and Percy – still confessing like mad – were facing a murder charge. The trial opened on 27 May 1935 at the Old Bailey before Mr Justice Humphreys. By now, Alma Rattenbury had been persuaded by her counsel to stop protecting Percy Stoner, and reluctantly she did so. Percy, with a show of dignity beyond his years, upheld his confession (though he uttered not one single word throughout the trial). Despite attempts by the prosecuting counsel and the judge himself to implicate Mrs Rattenbury in 'leading Stoner astray', she was acquitted. On 31 May, Percy Stoner was convicted of murder and sentenced to death.

Heartbroken, Alma Rattenbury committed suicide three days later. Then Percy began to talk; giving notice of appeal he claimed that he had been innocent all along, that it had been Mrs Rattenbury who killed her husband. Stoner was reprieved and served just seven years of a life sentence before being released in 1942 to join the armed forces fighting the Second World War. Percy survived the war, married, and settled down to a quiet life in the town one might have thought he wanted to forget – Bournemouth.

This quintessentially English *crime passionel* has received periodic attention over the succeeding 45 years, with the debate continuing over who *really* killed Francis Rattenbury. Despite his continuing health and longevity, Percy Stoner has remained silent on the matter. On 28 September 1990, newspapers reported that Percy Stoner, now 73 years old, had appeared before the Bournemouth magistrates. He pleaded guilty to a sexual attack on a twelve-year-old boy in public lavatories near his home. Stoner had been arrested after police found him in the conveniences wearing only a hat, shoes and socks; he was put on probation for two years.

UNITED STATES

Death of the Ice-Cream Blonde

Leading lady in numerous Hal Roach comedy two-reelers, Thelma Todd – the 'Ice-Cream Blonde' – played opposite such giants of the silver screen as Stan Laurel and Oliver Hardy and the Marx Brothers. On 16 December 1935, Thelma was found dead in a car in the garage of the house she shared with movie director Rowland West; the car engine was still running. It was suggested at the time – and it may well be true – that she had committed suicide by inhaling the vehicle's exhaust fumes; but if that was so, where was the customary suicide note, and more important, how had her false teeth come to be knocked out and her face and clothes spattered with blood? One possibility was that Rowland West himself had engineered the death in response to Thelma's predilection for the company of other men. But more sinister motives were also being explored. It was well known that Thelma Todd, as proprietor of 'Thelma Todd's Roadside Rest' restaurant, had been made a lucrative offer by no less an entrepreneur than Salvatore 'Lucky' Luciano – whose celebrity as a gangster far eclipsed Thelma's as an actress. Thelma had turned down this 'golden opportunity' to turn her restaurant into one of the Mob's illegal gambling dens, and she had turned it down very loudly and publicly. Was it possible that 'Lucky' had taught her a lesson *pour encourager les autres*? Theories, just theories – the kind of theories so beloved of Tinsel Town. But the police and pathologists had come up with a suggestion of their own. What if Thelma Todd had come home that cold winter night, found herself locked out of the house, and while she waited to be rescued, got into the garage, sat in the car and turned the engine on for warmth? It would be unusual if Thelma had not been drinking heavily, making it likely that she fell asleep and was poisoned by carbon monoxide from the car's exhaust. Anyway, it was the hypothesis most favoured by the coroner's jury when they returned a verdict of 'accidental death'.

1936

Death of Thelma Mareo

The Expert Who Died Too Soon. *Mareo was tried and convicted of the murder of his wife and although he was almost certainly innocent spent many years in prison. A great* cause célèbre, *it is one of the few blemishes on the reputation of New Zealand's legal machine.*

When Eric Mareo set sail for Australia in 1931, he must have been looking forward to a far brighter future than the one he was leaving behind as the badly paid orchestra conductor of a mediocre theatrical company. But if he had known then what his new life had in store for him, Eric Mareo would certainly have made the best of what he already had – and been very grateful for it.

Things did not go too badly at first – Eric found work, and better still, two years after his arrival in Australia he met and fell in love with Thelma, an actress whom he had met through their mutual involvement in the performing arts. The couple travelled on to New Zealand, and there they married and settled in so well that Eric Mareo was able to send for his two children by a previous marriage. But disaster, as it sometimes does, lurked just around the corner.

Work prospects became less certain and the inevitable domestic friction escalated as alcohol and barbiturate drugs filled the empty spaces between quarrels. It is difficult at this distance to know whether it was the drugs that caused the problems or whether the drugs simply numbed the emotional pain. Thelma became increasingly neurotic, and began to exhibit lesbian tendencies, falling into a suicidal hysteria when it was thought she might be pregnant. Both Thelma and Eric Mareo were by now heavily dependent on the effects of the barbituric acid veronal, and she was moving closer and closer to mental collapse. In March 1935, Thelma Mareo was examined by a doctor who reported finding her 'shaking and trembling and likely to commit suicide'. By April she was worse, and a friend staying at the house recalled periodic attempts to rescue Thelma from the veronal haze with sal volatile. On Monday 15 April, Thelma Mareo was dead.

All the clinical and post-mortem findings on the death of Mrs Mareo were consistent with a self-administered fatal dose of veronal accelerated, quite unwittingly, by the friend's administration of sal volatile which had the effect of hastening the body's absorption of the drug. However, despite the strength of this evidence, in 1936 Eric Mareo was charged with the murder of his wife by barbiturate poisoning, tried, convicted and sentenced to death. The ultimate penalty of the law was eventually commuted to life imprisonment and for Eric Mareo the twelve-year nightmare of proving his innocence began.

His case attracted many influential supporters. Most active among these were Mareo's defending counsel, Mr Humphrey O'Leary KC, and the notable New Zealand surgeon Sir James Elliott. In 1939, Sir James was on business in London, during which time he paid a visit to Sir William Willcox, at the time England's leading toxicologist, and among the top three in the world. Sir James offered Willcox his opinion that the medical evidence presented at Mareo's trial had received less attention than its importance merited, and in particular evidence based on Willcox's own published studies – that 'once a person wakens after having taken a dose of veronal he will not again relapse into coma without a further dose', an important finding in the light of the Mareo case. Sir William was happy to confirm this clinical fact, adding that a large dose of the drug would induce a coma with no return to consciousness, whereas a small dose would result in a coma followed by a confused state of mind during which the victim might well take further doses without remembering or knowing what he was doing.

Disquiet over the case continued, although nothing concrete was achieved until May 1941, when Eric Mareo's 'defence committee' retained the services of a solicitor, Mr Maurice Smith, for the purpose of consulting Sir William Willcox further, and asking him to undertake a detailed review of the medical evidence. If his conclusions were favourable to Mareo, Willcox would be asked to sign an affidavit to that effect.

As expected, Sir William advised Smith that in his own mind there was not the slightest doubt that the medical evidence supported Eric Mareo's innocence, and agreed to sign any papers necessary as soon as they had been prepared according to the requirements of a court. Tragically, before the affidavit could be prepared, Sir William Willcox died, and Maurice Smith was obliged to return empty-handed to New Zealand. Had Sir William survived just a few days longer, there is every reason to suppose that Eric Mareo would have been spared a further seven years languishing in gaol.

As it was, by 1946 Mareo's champions had raised sufficient finance to re-open his case before the Court of Appeal at Wellington. Although this first appeal was dismissed, a further two years of legal wrangling finally won Eric Mareo's release in 1948. He had spent a total of twelve years in prison, and died shortly after his release.

Albert Fish

The Cannibal. *After one of the most sensational trials of the decade, cannibal, necrophile and murderer, Fish was executed in the electric chair at Sing Sing. He went to his death claiming: 'What a thrill it will be, the only one I haven't tried.'*

Although Albert Fish was a rather meek, retiring man, he was known to be a good Christian and a good family man who adored his six children. Despite an unhappy childhood, there was little early warning of the monster into which he would develop, and his sexual perversions remained comparatively latent until 1917 when Albert's 'eccentricities' were trig-

Albert Fish (Press Association)

Part of the Budd family showing young Grace on the right

gered by his wife's desertion. From this point, according to Dr Fredric Wertham, 'There was no known perversion which he did not practice and practice frequently'. Obsessed with the religious concept of atonement through self-punishment, Fish abused his own body as cruelly as ever he did his victims, engaging in savage bouts of self-flagellation, burning, and the insertion of needles into the pubic areas of his body. When he was finally taken into custody, an X-ray disclosed no less than 29 metallic foreign bodies in his flesh; some had been there for so long that they had begun to erode. Nobody had the slightest idea of the scale of

146

Albert Fish's activities as a torturer, murderer, necrophile and cannibal.

On 3 June 1928, Fish, calling himself 'Frank Howard', arrived on the doorstep of the Budd apartment in New York City. He was there in reply to young Paul Budd's advertisement in the newspaper; Paul was looking for a job, and 'Howard' had come to offer him one on his fictional Long Island farm. The kindly, generous old man then remembered that his 'sister' was holding a children's party that very day, and suggested that while he was waiting for Paul to pack his grip, he could take the Budds' twelve-year-old daughter Grace to the party. It was the last time that Mr and Mrs Budd saw her – alive or dead.

Then in November 1934, Mrs Budd received an unexpected letter:

Dear Mrs Budd
Some years ago a friend of mine, Captain John Davis, shipped from California to Hong Kong, China, where at that time there was a great famine. It was dangerous for children under the age of twelve to be on the streets, as the custom was for them to be seized, cut up, and their meat sold for food. On his return to New York, my friend seized two boys, one six the other eleven, killed, cooked and ate them. So it was that I came to your house on 3 June 1928, and under the pretence of taking your daughter Grace to a party at my sister's I took her up to Westchester County, Worthington, to an empty house up there, and I choked her to death, I cut her up and ate part of her flesh. I didn't fuck with her. She died a virgin.

From an imperfectly erased address on the back of the envelope in which this letter was sent, police were led to 66-year-old Albert Fish's seedy room in a New York boarding house. For Fish it was the end of a criminal career that acknowledged the violent assault of more than 100 young girls and the murder of twelve of them.

On 12 March 1935, Fish was brought to trial at White Plains, New York, charged with the murder of Grace Budd, to whose pathetic remains Fish had led police. Although his defence attorney made a genuine and convincing case for Fish's insanity, the jury found him guilty of murder; one of the jury later confided: 'I thought he was insane, but he deserved to be electrocuted anyway.' And he was, on 16 January 1936.

A Human Jigsaw Puzzle

On 29 September 1935 Susan Haines Johnson saw part of a human arm pointing out of some wrapping in a gully beneath a bridge over the Gardenholme Linn on the Edinburgh-to-Carlisle road just outside Moffat, Scotland. It was to be the first of 70 pieces of two bodies recovered from the area over the next six weeks. With unbelievable skill and patience a team of forensic pathologists from Glasgow and Edinburgh Universities not only pieced the bodies together, but were subsequently able to positively identify Mrs Isabella Ruxton and her maid Mary Jane Rogerson. All roads led back to Dr Buck Ruxton – not least because his wife and maid were missing from the family home in Lancaster, and his house was spattered from top to bottom with human blood. Ruxton was tried, convicted, and, on 12 May 1936, hanged at Strangeways Prison, Manchester.

The two heads found in Gardenholme Linn, later identified as those of Mrs Ruxton and Mary Rogerson

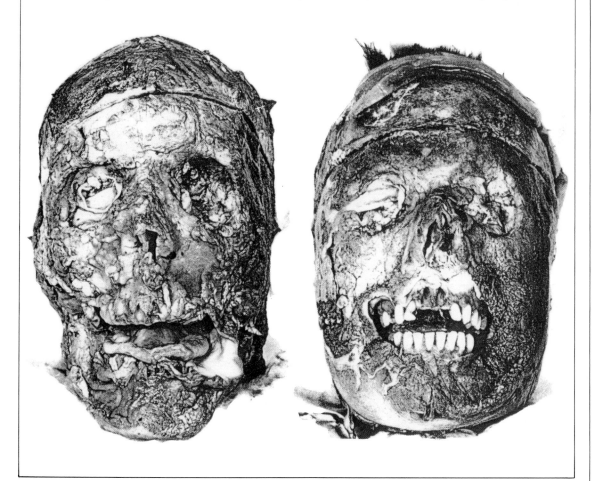

1937

Anna Marie Hahn

For Services Rendered. *After her arrest for the murder of several of her elderly patients, Mrs Hahn declared: 'I have been an angel of mercy to them.' She was rewarded by being the first woman in Ohio to die in the electric chair.*

With her husband Philip and young son Oscar, Anna Hahn emigrated from her native Germany, arriving in Cincinnati in 1929. Like so many immigrants before them, the Hahns made their home among their compatriots. They settled into the city's well-established German quarter, and very soon Anna, with her ready smile and cheery manner, became accepted as the unofficial (and certainly unqualified) 'nurse' to the elderly gentlemen in the German community; or, as Anna described herself, an 'angel of mercy'.

The wealthier these *alterer Herren* were, the more accommodating Anna was. And if their attentions sometimes passed beyond the merely paternal, then who was Anna to deny these harmless grandfathers their last geriatric fling? And if they felt that the best way to reward these 'services' was by a small gift or bequest, then who was Anna to deny them the pleasures of giving?

Herr Ernst Köhler, for example, died in 1933 leaving Anna his large house. On 1 June 1937, Jacob Wagner was taken on as a patient only to pass away on the following day; later that same week another patient, 70-year-old Georg Opendorfer, also died suddenly.

But Anna Hahn's extravagant lifestyle was also beginning to attract envious gossip, and there were wagging tongues a-plenty to remark on how both Herr Wagner and Herr Opendorfer died only after suffering acute stomach pains and vomiting. Soon the city police were

Justice Delayed

In January 1937 ten-year-old Mona Tinsley disappeared from her home in Newark, Nottinghamshire; she was last seen in the company of her 'uncle' Frederick Nodder who had collected Mona from school. Mona Tinsley's body had still not been found when Nodder was put on trial at Birmingham Assizes charged with her abduction. On 6 June, while Nodder was serving his prison sentence, his victim's remains were recovered from the River Idle. This time Fred Nodder faced his accusers at the Nottingham Assize Court, and despite his fierce denials was found guilty of murder. Before sentencing Nodder to death, Mr Justice McNaghten told him: 'Justice has slowly but surely overtaken you.'

interested enough in the tittle-tattle to secure exhumation orders on a number of 'nurse' Hahn's deceased patients. In each instance the autopsy revealed that death had been accelerated by various poisons, most often a mixture of croton oil (a strong purgative) and arsenic. Unfortunately for her, Anna's home was also found to be well stocked with poisons, and so the 'angel of mercy' found herself in custody.

Anna Hahn's defence that she was merely embezzling the old gentlemen, not killing them, suffered a setback when Philip Hahn testified that his wife had on several occasions tried to persuade him to insure his life for large sums. When he refused, he unaccountably began to suffer stomach cramps and vomiting. Anna's future began to look very bleak indeed.

Convicted and sentenced to death, Anna Marie Hahn perished in the electric chair on 7 December 1938.

1938

James Boyd Kirkwood

The Man Who Confessed. *A case emphasising the difference between English and Scottish law in the matter of diminished responsibility pleas prior to the 1957 Homicide Act. Had Kirkwood been tried in England he would almost certainly have hanged.*

Police officers, by both training and experience, are on the whole a broad-minded bunch of individuals – there's nothing much, tragic or comic, that they haven't seen or heard after a few years on the beat. This is especially true in a busy city like Edinburgh. However, the good copper also knows that there is always a surprise or two waiting just round the corner.

It was 10.45 on the bright summer morning of 7 August 1938 when the desk officer at Edinburgh's West End police station in Torphichen Place got one of those surprises. He couldn't quite take it in the first time, so he asked the big man standing in front of the desk to say it again. 'I killed a woman last night at "Ormelie" in the Corstorphine Road. The body's in the grounds.' That's what the desk sergeant thought he'd said.

Ormelie was the mansion owned by the former Lord Provost of Edinburgh, Sir William Thomson; at the time Sir William was holidaying with his family and the house was unoccupied. From a potato patch in the grounds to the rear of the building the police unearthed, as they were told they would, the naked body of a woman. She had suffered severe injuries to the head, presumably inflicted with the heavy bloodstained hammer found inside the house, and she had been subjected to a brutal sexual attack, probably carried out with the shaft of the same weapon. Death, according to the pathologist, occurred about 21 hours before the body was found – the same time the man giving his name as James Kirkwood claimed to have killed her. Subsequent identification showed the victim to be 35-year-old Jean Powell, an assistant at a local dairy. Needless to say, Kirkwood, who turned out to be employed by the Thomsons as a gardener at Ormelie, was immediately placed under arrest and charged with murder.

The trial of James Boyd Kirkwood was acted out before the sombre backdrop of the Edinburgh High Court of Justiciary. Presiding was the Lord Chief Justice Clerk, Lord Aitchison. Craigie Mason Aitchison had been Labour MP for Kilmarnock and Lord Advocate in Ramsay McDonald's second administration. He took silk in 1923, and was involved in many of Scotland's major murder trials – Oscar Slater (see 1908), Jeannie Donald, and John Donald Merrett. Lord Aitchison was appointed Lord Chief Justice Clerk in 1933.

Kirkwood was in many ways one of life's unfortunates. He was 30 years old, and despite a strong, almost powerful build, infantile paralysis had left him with a crippled arm, and from his late teenage years he had suffered periodic epileptic fits. In Kirkwood's defence, a noted psychiatrist of the time explained to the court how such debilitating attacks over a long period of time would result in deterioration of the patient's mental capability. He would, the doctor declared, 'be likely to be irritable and emotionally unstable, moody and morbid in outlook, and might act in an irresponsible manner'. In other words, Kirkwood's attorney was building up a plea of diminished responsibility and, luckily for his client, the trial was being held in Scotland, at that time the only place in Britain where such a defence was possible. England and Wales would have to wait until the Homicide Act of 1957 – twenty years later – before temporary mental disturbance such as that caused by epilepsy would be accepted as a mitigation resulting in the lesser charge of manslaughter.

Thus in 1938 the Edinburgh court was able to accept a guilty plea to the offence of 'culpable homicide' (the Scottish equivalent of manslaughter). James Kirkwood was sentenced to life imprisonment, but he did appeal through his legal representatives against a sentence 'of such appalling severity'. The eleven judges comprising the appeal panel fully debated the issue of appropriate sentences for those suffering from epilepsy. In the end it was decided that the sentence was sound, and the appeal was dismissed.

AUSTRIA

An Obsessive Greed

Martha Marek was, by any standard of wickedness, in a class of her own. She worked up to the 'ultimate crime' via a most grotesque insurance fraud. Martha had taken out a policy on her husband's safety against accident; she then chopped away at one of his legs with an axe (*and* with his agreement!) before putting in her claim. The surgeon treating Emil Marek's leg injuries was suspicious that the angles of the cuts were not entirely consistent with his account of the story, and the couple were charged with fraud. Martha later tried to bribe the hospital staff but without succeeding in anything other than lengthening her prison sentence. Martha had obviously learned one lesson while in prison – keep it simple. On her release, Martha went on to poison her husband, her children, the old lady to whom she had become companion, and a couple of lodgers – all of whose lives had been comfortably insured in Martha's favour. And Martha? She was eventually executed by beheading with an axe.

1939

The Murder of Pamela Coventry

A severe test of the practice of identification through body secretions. A cigarette end found at the scene of the murder was saliva-matched with a suspect's cigarette; unfortunately the man proved to be a 'non-secretor', one of only fourteen per cent of the population whose blood type cannot be revealed by their other body secretions.

The case started, as so many of its kind do, with a missing child report. After lunch on 18 February 1939, eleven-year-old Pamela Coventry set off from her home in Coronation Drive, Hornchurch, to meet some friends on their way to a dancing class. The friends hung around until 1.30 and then went on without her. When Pamela failed to return home that night Mrs Coventry reported her missing, and a police search was launched. However, it was not the police team which found Pamela's body, but a passer-by. She had been stripped but for a petticoat pulled up round her neck, and her legs had been trussed up with electrical flex and string. It fell to Sir Bernard Spilsbury to examine the girl's body, and the experienced eye of the pathologist was soon able to provide Scotland Yard with further valuable clues. Pamela had been sexually assaulted, and the cause of death was manual strangulation. The process of digestion indicated that death had occurred within an hour of Pamela eating her last meal; as she had disappeared shortly after eating lunch, that set the time of her murder at between 1.20 and 1.45 p.m., and so she must have been killed close to home. When the victim's legs had been untied, a cigarette-end of the hand-rolled variety was found caught between the thigh and the abdomen. Part of the flex used to tie the legs up to the chest was of a distinctive seven-strand 600-ohm type not manufactured in the previous seven years; the rest was of a common type, as was the green garden twine. Several days after the discovery of the body a number of significant articles were found wrapped up in a copy of the *News Chronicle* dated 11 January: a school badge, some buttons, and a length of flex similar to that used to tie the victim's legs.

The nature of the crime and the discovery of the body on an airfield so close to the child's home suggested to detectives that the killer was a local man, and with information gathered around the district, investigating officers were able to target 28-year-old Leonard Richardson, who lived in Coronation Drive, not far from the Coventry family. At the time of the murder Richardson's wife had been in hospital giving birth to their child, and he was alone in the house, a routine search of which turned up a number of pieces of evidence which were later examined by forensic specialists. For a start there was some garden twine and some flex of the common type used to tie the body; there was also a sequence of copies of the *News Chronicle* from which one issue was missing – that of 11 January. A raincoat hanging in Richardson's hallway bore small spots of human blood on the inside of the sleeve and pocket. Finally, it did not go unnoticed that the bottom of Richardson's garden bordered the airfield; what was more, the wire fence separat-

Sir Bernard Spilsbury at work in his laboratory   (Inset) *Pamela Coventry* (Syndication International)

ing them had been pressed down, as though somebody had climbed over at that point.

Mr Richardson, understandably, denied having anything to do with Pamela Coventry's death; he was, he claimed, at his sister-in-law's house at 1.30 on the afternoon in question, and at work before and after that. Both his relative and his employer supported Richardson's alibi. However, other witnesses were found who claimed to have seen him at his house at 1.15 p.m. Unbelievably, as he sat talking to detectives, Leonard Richardson rolled himself a cigarette.

This, then, was the tangible evidence available to the prosecution when the case came up for committal at the Romford Magistrates' Court, where Leonard Richardson was ordered to stand his trial at the Central Criminal Court. The process opened in March 1939 and

Richardson, as we shall see, was most fortunate in his defence team, led by Mr (later Lord Justice) Winn. He was lucky, because a skilful defence all but annihilated what at first seemed to be evidence – albeit circumstantial – of the most damning kind.

It is worth following an acknowledged master in the field along his own analysis of the evidence. Although he was not directly involved in the case, the redoubtable pathologist Professor Francis Camps subsequently presented a lucid discussion of the evidence in the Richardson case,* from which the following arguments emerge:

The green flex and garden twine: The defence rightly pointed out that although these articles

The Investigation of Murder, F. E. Camps and Richard Barber. Michael Joseph, London, 1966.

152

were deemed 'similar' to those used to tie the body of Pamela Coventry, they were in such common use that as scientific evidence it was little better than useless. Indeed, the judge himself felt obliged to question why the eminent Home Office Analyst, Dr Roche Lynch, had been called to present evidence on matters which might more reliably be assessed by experts from the manufacturing industry. Of the special, rarer type of wire used on the body, none was ever found in association with the defendant.

Bloodstains on the raincoat: Again it was Roche Lynch who dealt with this piece of evidence, and again it proved to be rather a red herring – though it must be added that this was not the analyst's fault. Richardson claimed that the stains resulted from a minor injury to his hand, and that could well have been so. If this blood had been the same group as that of the victim, and different from Richardson's, it could be a very damaging clue indeed. The fact was that Sir Bernard Spilsbury had omitted to take a blood sample during autopsy, so Pamela Coventry's group was not known.

The cigarette-end: 'Experts' from the tobacco world had already ponderously pronounced that the material found on the body and that rolled up by Leonard Richardson were 'identical'; however, in those days when scientific chemical tests such as neutron activation analysis were a way off, the methods were crude to the extent of, as it was described, 'smell after ignition'. In other words, the burning tobaccos smelt alike. What the defence were able to do was find an expert to demolish the evidence that the cigarette paper around the suspect butt was identical to those in the packet used by Richardson. It was simply not even *possible*, the defence expert insisted; the method of cutting and packing the papers ruled that out. Besides, a random sample of cigarette-ends of the home-made variety were picked up from a factory floor, and despite their different origin all were similar to each other and similar to the cigarette made by Leonard Richardson.

The pressed-down fence: It was undeniable that the fence at the end of Richardson's garden had been pressed down in the centre – just as if a heavy load had been carried over it. What nobody but the defence solicitors bothered to check were the fences of the properties on either side of the Richardsons. Both had been pressed down; both had been pressed down even lower than the Richardsons'. Yet another red herring.

Most of this information came out during the cross-examination of Crown witnesses, and when it came Mr Winn's turn to present the defence he opened by submitting that the prosecution had not proved its case, and there was, therefore, no case to answer. The judge was not prepared to go quite as far as he was entitled – that is, to instruct the jury to return a formal verdict of not guilty; but he did allow the jury to retire and decide for themselves

Murder by Request

In a case, so he claimed, of 'murder by request', Rodney Greig repeatedly stabbed and then cut the throat of girlfriend Leona Vlught. He subsequently explained to arresting officers that Miss Vlught could see no future for herself and had asked Greig to put her out of her misery.

Unwilling to let a good story go ungilded, newsmen reporting the case added that Rodney Greig had also drunk his victim's blood – an accusation which he vigorously denied. Greig was put in the gas chamber at the end of 1939.

whether the case should proceed. After deliberation, they returned to court to announce that, on the evidence presented, they would not be able to arrive at a verdict. The case was consequently dismissed and Leonard Richardson released. The murder of Pamela Coventry remains an open case.

1940

Assassination of Leon Trotsky

By order of Josef Stalin, the exiled Russian revolutionary was tracked to his fortress villa in Mexico and killed by a blow to the head with an ice-pick.

While Leon Trotsky, the Russian revolutionary leader exiled by Stalin, was taking refuge in an ostensibly siege-proof villa at Coyoacan, outside Mexico City, he fell victim to the one type of assassin against whom it is all but impossible to guard – a treacherous friend. There had already been one serious attempt on Trotsky's life on 24 May 1940, when a gang of assassins led by the Mexican artist and Stalinist agent David Siqueiros gained entry to the fortress by wearing police uniforms. They strafed the bedroom with machine-gun fire, but miraculously Trotsky and his wife Natalie, who had been hiding under the bed, were unhurt. Prophetically, Trotsky commented: 'Fate granted me a reprieve. It will be of short duration.' On 20 August 1940 Frank Jackson, a trusted comrade, arrived at the villa to discuss revisions before the publication of a new article by Trotsky. While the two men were alone in the study Jackson drove an ice-pick through Trotsky's skull. When he was taken into custody Jackson was revealed to be Moscow-trained agent Jacques Mornard.

Some years later, Mornard's fingerprints finally proved his real identity as a Spanish Communist activist named Jaime Ramon Mercader; the assassination had, predictably, / been ordered by Josef Stalin. Jackson/ Mornard/Mercader served twenty years in solitary confinement before being released in 1960. He was given a Czech passport and returned to oblivion behind the 'Iron Curtain', where he worked as a radio mechanic.

1941

Antonio 'Babe' Mancini

Chicago Comes to London. *An unsavoury gangland murder which results in Mancini taking his case first to the Court of Appeal and then to the House of Lords where it becomes a legal* cause *célèbre.*

It is surprising how many complex legal arguments arise out of sordid backstreet crimes which would otherwise go unremarked by public and criminologist alike. Never was this more apparent than in the case of Mancini. It occurred at the time when Britain, along with much of the rest of the world, was allied in its fight against fascism; it was a period when America's recent gangland experiences with Prohibition and beyond had eventually found its way around the globe via the Hollywood movie boom. US-style gangsters were popping up the world over, and London's share centred around the night clubs, bars and strip joints of Soho. One of these seedy drinking clubs, in Wardour Street, was managed by an equally seedy character named Antonio 'Babe' Mancini (they mostly affected these preposterous nicknames in emulation of their gangster heroes across the Atlantic – perhaps Mancini had wanted to be 'Baby Face' Nelson. Who knows?). In the early hours of the morning of 1 May 1941 'Babe' Mancini got into a disagreement with a fellow Gangland bit-part player

named Harry Distleman (though he preferred 'Scarface' Distleman – no doubt after Big Al Capone). The upshot of the argument was that 'Babe' stabbed 'Scarface' to death.

At his Old Bailey trial before Mr Justice McNaghten, Mancini pleaded self-defence, but the jury convicted him of murder. And that was about as far as such cases usually got. However, Mancini's attorney took the case to the Court of Criminal Appeal where he argued that by not giving full emphasis to the point in his summing-up, Mr Justice McNaghten had deprived the jury of the option to find a verdict of manslaughter, and consequently deprived Mancini of the possibility of conviction on a non-capital charge. The appeal was dismissed.

Mr Hector Hughes KC, defending Mancini, then took the unusual step of applying to the Attorney-General, Sir Donald Somervell, for leave to appeal to the highest court in the land, the House of Lords. In an even more unusual step, Sir Donald granted his fiat to be heard in the Lords. On 2 and 3 October 1941 the evidence was presented to the panel of law lords comprising the Lord Chancellor Viscount Simon, Lord Sankey, Lord Russell of Killowen, Lord Wright and Lord Porter. This time around they considered the defence's complaint that Mr Justice McNaghten had not adequately instructed the jury on the matter of *provocation*. Mr Hughes argued that the judge should have made it clear that if the jury felt that the defendant was provoked, or if there was any reasonable doubt about the provocation) then he should be acquitted of the charge of murder. For the Crown, Sir Donald Somervell countered that it was not incumbent upon a judge to advance information on a possible charge of manslaughter unless the evidence before him either raised the issue directly, or left open a

155

possibility of doubt – which did not apply in the case of Mancini.

After a retirement to consider the evidence, the Lord Chancellor delivered their Lordships' judgment on 16 October. Viscount Simon was of the opinion that although Mancini had advanced the defence at his trial that he was obliged to use the knife in self-defence, it was the duty of the judge in his charge to the jury to adequately state any other view of the facts which might reasonably arise out of the evidence presented, and which would reduce the offence to manslaughter. The fact that Mancini's counsel did not stress the alternative case to the jury – which he might feel it difficult to do without prejudicing his main line of defence – did not absolve the judge from the duty to direct the jury to consider the alternative, 'if there were material which would justify such a direction'. The argument that there was lack of direction on the matter of provocation depended entirely on whether there was evidence in front of the jury which might, if they chose to believe it, be regarded as amounting to *sufficient provocation*. And this is where Mancini's case failed. In order to reduce murder to manslaughter, the provocation would need to have been such as to deprive the person provoked of the power of self-control. The test that had to be applied was what would the effect of that provocation be on a 'reasonable' man. His Lordship declared that if the evidence before a jury at the close of a case did not contain material on which a reasonable man could find a verdict of manslaughter rather than murder, it was not a defect in the summing-up that manslaughter was not dealt with. Therefore there was no error of law in Mr Justice McNaghten's summing-up.

It was a creditable example of the way in which the intrinsic fairness of the English legal system permitted such lengthy and painstaking deliberations to be conducted on behalf of one of society's less upright citizens. Shortly afterwards, however, all avenues of appeal having been explored, 'Babe' Mancini kept his appointment with the hangman. [See also 1944, the case of Leonard Holmes.]

UNITED STATES

The Man in the Attic

Theodore Coneys was a 59-year-old vagrant who broke into the home of Philip Peters intending to commit a burglary and instead secretly took up residence in the attic, creeping down for food when Peters was sleeping or out of the house. Coneys had been living in the loft for almost a year when, on one of his forays for sustenance, he woke Peters from his bed and felt obliged to kill him before retreating to his hideaway. It was a puzzled police force that tried to solve the ultimate in 'locked room' mysteries. Months later, Theodore Coneys was spotted disappearing into the roof by police officers set to watch the 'empty' house after neighbours had reported disturbances. The 'Spiderman of Denver', as he became known, was taken into custody and later imprisoned for the murder of Philip Peters.

1942

Harry Dobkin

Another Victim of the Blitz. *Professor Keith Simpson's early triumph with forensic dentistry was responsible for identifying the near-skeletal remains of Mrs Rachel Dobkin.*

On 17 July 1942 a workman helping to demolish the badly bomb-damaged Vauxhall Baptist Chapel in Vauxhall Road, Kennington (now Kennington Lane), prised up a stone slab and found beneath it a mummified body. The immediate assumption was that the remains were either of an air-raid victim or had come from the old burial ground underneath the church, which had ceased to be used some fifty years before. When the church had been bombed on 15 October 1940 more than a hundred people had been killed in the conflagration and the area around the chapel had been the target of a number of Luftwaffe raids between that time and March of 1941. Nor was this the first body that the workers had come upon while demolishing the chapel. Nevertheless, routine was followed, and the police were called in, arriving in the persons of Detective Inspectors Hatton and Keeling, and the bones were removed to Southwark Mortuary for examination by the pathologist, Dr Keith Simpson.

Simpson immediately suspected foul play. In trying to raise the bones, the skull had become detached, and Simpson realised that the head had already been cut from the body. In addition to this, the limbs had been severed at the elbows and knees, flesh had been removed from the face, the lower jaw was missing and the bones were partially burnt. It was obvious that an attempt had been made to disguise the

The decomposed and charred body of Mrs Rachel Dobkin

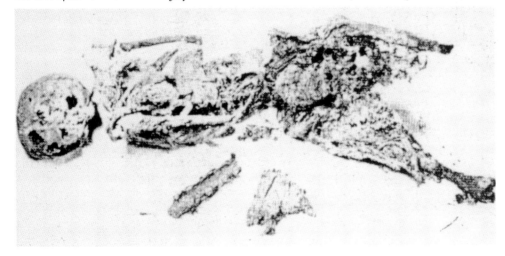

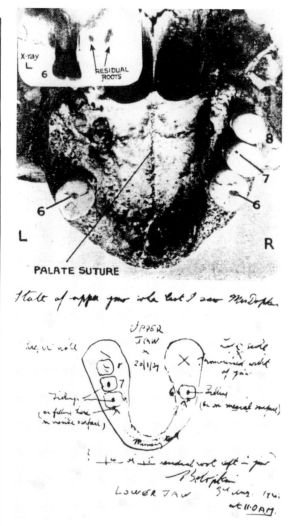

Mrs Dobkin's dental record as drawn by her dentist and matched with the skull of the body in the crypt

identity of the corpse. Dr Simpson obtained the permission of the coroner to take the remains back to his laboratory at Guy's Hospital for a more detailed inspection. Returning to the crypt of the church in a vain attempt to find the missing limbs, Simpson noticed a yellowish deposit in the earth, subsequently analysed as slaked lime. This had been used to suppress the smell of putrefaction, but it also had the effect of preventing maggots from destroying the body. Examining the throat and voice box, Simpson detected a blood clot,

strongly indicating death due to strangulation.

The next task was to discover the identity of the victim. The body was that of a woman aged between 40 and 50, with dark greying hair, was five feet one inch tall, and had suffered from a fibroid tumour. Time of death was estimated at between twelve and fifteen months prior to discovery. Meanwhile the police had been checking the lists of missing persons, and noted that, fifteen months previously, Mrs Rachel Dobkin, estranged wife of Harry Dobkin, the fire-watcher at the firm of solicitors next door to the Baptist Chapel at 302 Vauxhall Road, had disappeared. An interview with her sister elicited the information that she was about the right age, with dark greying hair, was about five feet one tall, and had a fibroid tumour. She also gave police the name of Mrs Dobkin's dentist, Barnett Kopkin of Stoke Newington, who kept meticulous records and was able to describe exactly the residual roots and fillings in her mouth. They matched the upper jaw of the skull. Finally, Miss Mary Newman, the head of the Photography Department at Guy's, superimposed a photograph of the skull on to a photograph of Rachel Dobkin, a technique first used six years earlier in the Buck Ruxton case. The fit was uncanny. The bones found in the crypt were the mortal remains of Mrs Rachel Dobkin.

Rachel Dubinski had married Harry Dobkin in September 1920, through the traditional Jewish custom of a marriage broker. Within three days they had separated, but unhappily nine months later a baby boy was born. In 1923 Mrs Dobkin obtained a maintenance order obliging her husband to pay for the upkeep of their child. Dobkin was always a spasmodic payer, and over the years had been imprisoned several times for defaulting. In addition, Mrs Dobkin had unsuccessfully summonsed him four times for assault. However, it must be said in mitigation of Dobkin's actions that she habitually pestered him in the street to get her money, and it should be remembered that she was still demanding cash in 1941 when the 'child' was twenty years old and hardly a dependent. Dobkin was to hint later that she was also blackmailing him over some undisclosed indiscretion at work.

On Good Friday, 11 April 1941, Dobkin and his wife had met in a café in Kingsland Road, Shoreditch, near to where he lived in Navarino Road, Dalston. They left at 6.30 p.m. and she was never seen alive again, though he claimed that she had boarded a number 22 bus to visit her mother. The next day Rachel's sister reported her missing to the police, implicating Harry Dobkin in the process. Because of the priorities of war, Dobkin was not interviewed about the disappearance until 16 April. On the night of the 14th a small fire had broken out in the ruined cellar of the Baptist Church. This was peculiar, because there had been no air raids and the blaze was only noticed at 3.23 a.m. by a passing policeman. When the fire brigade arrived Harry Dobkin was there, pretending to put it out. He told the constable that the fire had started at 1.30 a.m. and that he hadn't bothered to inform the authorities because there was little danger of the fire spreading. There was a serious air raid on the next night, so the incident was quickly forgotten. Dobkin was interviewed twice more about his wife's disappearance and a description and

photograph were circulated by the police, but no further action was taken.

In May 1942, before the body was found, Dobkin had ceased to be a fire-watcher and was back in Navarino Road. Three weeks later he was observed by a local policeman entering the Baptist Church in Kennington at 6 a.m. On 26 August, Dobkin was interviewed for the first time by Chief Inspector Hatton, and escorted to the church cellar, where he vehemently denied any involvement in his wife's death. He was then arrested for her murder.

The trial of Harry Dobkin opened at the Old Bailey on 17 November 1942, with Mr Justice Wrottesley presiding and Mr L. A. Byrne prosecuting. Dobkin's counsel, Mr F. H. Lawton, spent most of his efforts trying vainly to challenge the identification evidence. The prisoner's appearance in the witness box left the jury unimpressed, and it took them only twenty minutes to arrive at a verdict of guilty. Before his execution Dobkin confessed to his wife's murder, claiming that she was always pestering him for money and he wanted to be rid of her for good. On 7 January 1943 Harry Dobkin was hanged in Wandsworth Prison.

AUSTRALIA

'I'm a Dr Jekyll and Mr Hyde . . .'

The third death was on 28 May 1942. Gladys Hosking had followed Ivy McLeod and Pauline Thompson in the succession of strangled corpses to be found where they had fallen on the streets around Melbourne. It was also to be the last death, thanks to an observant sentry at the local US Army base who remembered challenging a shaken and dishevelled GI coming into camp late on the night of the murder. The description happened to match that of a young soldier reported for threatening violence to a young woman only a couple of days before; both these descriptions fitted Edward Joseph Leonski, a big Texan who had recently confided to a camp buddy the alarming news that 'I'm a

Dr Jekyll and Mr Hyde! I killed! I killed!' There was not a lot of need to search for incriminating evidence; Leonski provided his own. Sure he had killed these ladies: 'It was to get their voices!' He recalled with particular affection that Pauline Thompson had sung to him as he walked her to her home, a soft, sweet voice: 'I could feel myself going mad about it.' Nutty as a fruit-cake? The court-martial didn't think so, despite the prisoner's own best efforts and a long family history of insanity. The 'Singing Strangler', the 'Melbourne Jack the Ripper', was hanged on 19 November 1942, at Pentridge Gaol; it is said that in the hours before execution he sat in his cell singing softly to himself.

1943

Dennis Edmund Leckey

The Right to Silence. *In which a single, basic blunder by the judge allows a brutal sex-killer to walk free.*

English law has built into it – and quite rightly so – certain safeguards for the protection of persons accused of committing a crime. One of these fundamental rights – and one currently under threat – is to remain silent; in other words, a suspect is not obliged to say anything that may incriminate him until he has the benefit of legal advice. An extension of this is the right of an accused not to give evidence at his own trial. And it must not be inferred from a prisoner's silence in either of these circumstances that he is making an admission of guilt; and it must certainly never be suggested, either from the Bench or by counsel. Indeed, so strictly is this basic rule applied that any deviation could represent grounds for the verdict being overturned. The case of Dennis Leckey was one such rare example.

In 1943 Caroline Trayler was just eighteen years old, but already a bride of six months, with a husband on active service with the British Forces in North Africa. And like many lively youngsters in her peer group, Caroline was bored; the war which had disrupted English

life since 1939 had been going on just too long. She had a part-time job as a cinema usherette, which gave her a small financial independence, but there was little enough in those days of austerity on which to spend her hard-earned wages.

It might have been just another familiar Sunday evening spent with her mother behind the black curtains which kept their modest private lives from the searching eyes of the Luftwaffe's bombers. But this was Whit Sunday, and Caroline Trayler was determined to get some pleasure out of the holiday. As it was she ended up drinking at the Mechanic's Arms, Folkestone. At closing time she left, a little the worse for drink, on the arm of an off-duty soldier. The darkness swallowed them up; Caroline never returned from it.

When her anxious mother reported Caroline's disappearance, the police moved into a now-familiar wartime routine – first search the considerable area of the town's bomb-damaged buildings. Caroline Trayler's body was found four days later in a blitzed shop, and a cursory glance at the body indicated strangulation compounded with violent sexual assault.

The medical examination was undertaken, as it was in so many cases during those war years, by pathologist Dr Keith Simpson. Simpson's reconstruction suggested that the 'rape' almost certainly began with Caroline Trayler's consent – the dirtied state of her calves was consistent with her lying with her legs wide apart and flat on the floor. Whether she changed her mind or found herself in the hands of a sexual sadist we will never know. The bruising around Caroline's throat indicated her killer had tried unsuccessfully to strangle her from the front, then turned her over and completed the job

160

from behind. The pathologist then began the gruesome task of scavenging such clues as the body could offer to the identity of the attacker. Simpson found a half-dozen dark body hairs stuck to Caroline Trayler's thighs; they contrasted sharply with her own auburn colouring and almost certainly came from her killer. The girl's fingernails had become torn and broken during the struggle, and scrapings from the nails contained rusty-brown fibres, in all likelihood from the assailant's clothing. All that was needed now was a suspect to match the clues.

If Dennis Leckey, a serving Artillery gunner, had not gone absent on the day that Caroline's body was found, it is possible that the trail would never have led to him. As it was, the Folkestone police issued a nationwide description and a request for his apprehension. Gunner Leckey was picked up in London ten days later. Formally arrested, Leckey was required to surrender samples of his body hairs which Professor Simpson confirmed matched those left behind during the assault on his victim. Furthermore, the couple had 'exchanged' hairs, one of Caroline's being found on Leckey's uniform trousers. The fibre taken from beneath Caroline Trayler's fingernails matched those of his uniform shirt. Not conclusive proof, perhaps, but strong enough evidence with which to bring Dennis Leckey to trial, for the jury to return a verdict of guilty, and for Mr Justice Singleton to pronounce sentence of death.

At the conclusion of the Leckey trial, in a legal error that was as damaging to the prosecution case as it was inexplicable from so experienced a judge, Sir John Singleton not once but three times in his summing-up gave utterance to the sentiment that the prisoner's reluctance to make a statement to the police at the time of his arrest could be seen as an indication of guilt: 'Of course, he is not bound to say anything – but what would you conclude?' he asked the jury. Anyway, it was enough to force the Court of Appeal to overturn the conviction, and allow Dennis Leckey – without dispute the brutal killer of poor Caroline Trayler – to walk free; society had, on this thankfully rare occasion, become victim to its own impeccably fair legal system.

Jarvis Catoe

The Case of the Scapegoat. *Jarvis Catoe murdered eight women; for one of these killings an innocent man was jailed for life. Under arrest, Catoe claimed that a diet of pornography and crime books brought on his 'spells'.*

Savage killer Jarvis Catoe managed to elude detection long enough to murder seven women in Washington and one in New York City; he escaped detection altogether in the case of his first victim, Florence Dancy, when a man named James Smith was wrongly convicted of her murder and jailed for life in 1935.

The regularity of Catoe's killings accelerated after he raped and strangled Josephine Robinson on 1 December 1939. Between September 1940 and January 1941, he killed three more women, all in Washington. Still gathering momentum, on 8 March 1941 25-year-old Rose Simons Abramowitz asked Catoe if he would wax her kitchen floor. Once inside her apartment, Catoe raped and murdered her. Three months later he picked up Jessie Strieff by posing as a cab driver. He drove her to a nearby garage where he raped and killed her, and then dumped the body in another garage several blocks away. Despite an extensive state police presence, and support from the FBI, no arrest was made.

In August 1941, Jarvis Catoe transferred his attentions to New York City where, on the morning of the 4th, he offered 26-year-old Evelyn Anderson a lift in his car, and then strangled her. But by this time his luck had run out, and the wrist watch which Catoe had stolen from Evelyn Anderson finally came into police possession. Catoe had given the watch to his girlfriend as a present, and she in turn had asked her uncle to pawn it.

When Catoe returned to Washington a warrant for his arrest was waiting. Under interrogation, he finally admitted the Strieff and Abramowitz murders and by way of explanation claimed that he suffered from what he called 'spells' after reading crime stories and pornography. Catoe later confessed to ten rapes and six other murders, including the killing in 1935 of Florence Dancy.

Both Washington and New York laid claim to Jarvis Catoe – New York for the murder of Evelyn Anderson, and Washington for the murder of Rose Abramowitz. In the end he was tried in Washington, though by this time he had retracted his confession, claiming that it had been coerced from him under torture and duress. He was, nevertheless, found guilty and sentenced to death. Jarvis Catoe was executed in January 1943, chanting a hymn as he walked to the death chamber.

1944

Leonard Holmes

The Case of the Unfaithful Wife. *It was wartime infidelity that forced Holmes to murder his wife, a common enough motive for marital violence during the Second World War, and one which led to the rationalisation of the defence of Provocation.*

Leonard Holmes represents a sad, if by no means uncommon phenomenon of wartime conditions the world over. He was demobilised from the Army in October 1944 after serving King and Country in the still-effervescent Second World War. When he returned to his home in New Ollerton, Nottinghamshire, Holmes discovered that his absence, far from making his wife's heart grow fonder, had given Peggy Ann the opportunity to spread her affections farther afield. It was, therefore, an uneasy homecoming, and matters did not improve over the succeeding weeks. On 19 November the couple were spending the evening drinking at a local public house when, inflamed by drink, Holmes got it into his head that his wife was being too familiar by half with a bunch of RAF men standing at the bar. Once ignited, the flames of the subsequent quarrel continued to rage throughout the evening and on the journey home. When they arrived, Mrs Holmes, also somewhat the worse for drink, unwisely decided to confess: 'If it eases your mind, I *have* been unfaithful to you.' There was a brief pause, a silence, before Holmes picked up a hammer and smashed it down on his wife's head; then for good measure he strangled her.

It was, we have observed, a common domestic murder with a common motive – sexual jealousy. Leonard Holmes faced trial and was convicted and sentenced to death at the Nottingham Assizes in February 1945. And there, one might think, the matter would end, with just two more tragic victims of a war that was claiming millions. However, Leonard Holmes was about to become a minor *cause célèbre*.

In the time allotted to him after sentence, Holmes's attorney made application to the Court of Criminal Appeal to overturn the sentence on the grounds that Mr Justice Charles had instructed the jury that it was not open to them to return a verdict of manslaughter. Presenting their Lordships' judgment, Mr (later Lord) Justice Wrottesley declared:

It cannot be too widely known that a person who, after absence for some reason such as service, either suspects already, or discovers on his return, that his wife has been unfaithful during his absence, is not, on that account, a person who may use lethal weapons upon his wife, and, if violence should result in her death, can claim to have suffered such provocation as would reduce the crime from murder to manslaughter.

Clearly the provocation factor was of great importance in a case such as this. As the law stood (and for that matter still stands), in the general run of criminal cases provocation is entitled to be taken into account only in *mitigation* – that is, once a verdict has been reached, the judge, in deciding sentence, is entitled to consider the degree of provocation and adjust the severity of sentence accordingly. However, in charges of murder, provocation amounts to a *legal defence*; it is unlikely to secure a defendant's release, but it could be successful in reducing the charge to manslaughter. This was especially beneficial in days when the death sentence for murder was *mandatory*.

Bearing this in mind, the then Attorney-General, Sir Hartley Shawcross KC, granted permission for Leonard Holmes's case to be referred for appeal before the House of Lords. The matter was argued before Lords Simon, Porter, Simonds and du Parq, with Holmes's counsel contending that provocation by adultery was a matter for the jury to consider, and the Crown submitting that words could never amount to good enough justification for the taking of life – it would be unfortunate, Sir Frank Soskice suggested, if a confession to adultery should be seen as a licence to kill. It was a sentiment endorsed by the Bench, and Lord Simon reiterated that only very rarely could provocation be applied in cases where there was *an intention to kill*. His Lordship then underlined the court's judgment with reference to the Bard: 'Even if Iago's insinuations against Desdemona's virtue had been true, Othello's crime was murder and nothing else.' So the final appeal was lost; words alone were not, by and large, sufficient to reduce a crime. (However, the discovery of a partner *in the act of adultery* was deemed sufficient provocation to reduce murder to manslaughter.)

The legal battle for Leonard Holmes's life was over, and on 28 May 1945 he was hanged.

UNITED STATES

Person or Persons Unknown

Hearing that there was oil beneath the farmland worked by black minister Revd Isaac Simmons, a white mob rounded up Simmons and his son and drove them to a remote spot where the clergyman was tortured and shot, and young Eldridge Simmons was savagely beaten up and run out of the county. Although Eldridge Simmons later identified his father's killers, the local coroner's inquest returned a verdict of death at the hands of 'a person or persons unknown'.

1945

Karl Gustav Hulten and Elizabeth Marina Jones

The Wartime Bonnie and Clyde. *An American army deserter and a London prostitute join forces to live out their Hollywood gangster fantasies.*

It was a late afternoon in the October of 1944, towards the end of the Second World War, when the man who liked to call himself Second Lieutenant Richard Allen, of the 501 Parachute Infantry Regiment, US Army, walked into a small café in Queen Caroline Street on London's Hammersmith Broadway. Coincidence was about to cross his path with that of a young woman; between them they would commit one of the most cold-blooded, senseless killings of the twentieth century.

Karl Gustav Hulten, who for no honest reason was masquerading under the sobriquet 'Ricky Allen', recalled the meeting at his subsequent trial, 'I saw Len Bexley [an acquaintance] sitting there with a young lady. I took another seat, but he asked me to come over and join them, which I did.' Bexley introduced 'Ricky' to Elizabeth ('Betty') Jones, an eighteen-year-old stripper who worked under the name Georgina Grayson; under this latter name she rented a room at 311 King Street, not far from

where they now sat. Born and brought up in South Wales, Betty had been married when she was only sixteen to a soldier, a man ten years her senior with a quick temper and a brutish manner. When he punched her on their wedding day it was for the last time; she walked out on him then and there, making her way up to London and a succession of seedy, unfulfilling jobs – waitress, barmaid, cinema usherette, and striptease dancer at the Blue Lagoon Club, an occupation from which she had recently emerged unemployed.

Hulten further remembered, 'We were there a while in the cafeteria, and afterwards we all got up and left together. Mrs Jones and I walked towards the Broadway. I asked her if she would care to come out later on.'

At 11.30 that same evening – Friday, 13 October 1944 – Betty Jones was just about to give up her wait outside the Broadway Cinema, when a two-and-a-half-ton ten-wheeled US Army truck pulled up in front of her with Hulten in the driver's seat. Betty was soon sitting up beside him in an appropriately bizarre start to an affair which was to destroy them both.

In a sense they were still children, still locked in the world of celluloid fantasy that comprised wartime entertainment. We know from subsequent statements that the conversation on that first date was not the normal run of boy-girl talk. 'Ricky' opened by telling his new friend that the truck was stolen, and that he was a lieutenant in the US paratroops (in fact Private Hulten was a deserter). This obviously appealed to Betty's sense of the romantic, and she responded that she had always wanted to do something exciting 'like becoming a gun moll like they do in the States'. Hulten then boasted, quite untruthfully, that he had 'carried

164

a gun for the Mob' in Chicago, and started to brandish a stolen pistol.

Perhaps the point of no return had already been reached, with both now committed to act out the roles they had chosen for themselves, and admired in each other. At any rate, a sequence of events that would not stop short of murder had been put into motion.

Past midnight on the road outside Reading, Berkshire, the truck overtook a lone girl on a bicycle. Stopping the vehicle, Hulten stepped down and waited for the girl to pass and as she did, pushed her off her machine and grabbed the handbag which had been slung over the handlebars. Before their startled victim could regain her feet, these modern highwaymen were speeding back to London, the proceeds of their crime just a couple of shillings and some clothing coupons. At 5 a.m. Betty Jones was tucked up in bed at King Street, Hulten in a nearby car-park in the truck.

On Thursday, 5 October the wartime Bonnie and Clyde climbed once more into the cab of the ten-wheeler. Robbery was once more on their minds. Their first decision, to 'do' a pub, was abandoned. Betty suggested robbing a taxi-cab; Ricky forced one to stop, and with a gun at the driver's head, ordered him to 'Let me have all your money.' Luckily – as future events would show – the cabbie had a passenger, whose evident alarm panicked Hulten, and this robbery too was abandoned in an undignified scramble to escape. Driving back into London's blackout along the Edgware Road, at Jones's suggestion the pair picked up a young woman making her way to Bristol via Paddington station; Hulten offered to drive her out as far as Reading (which seemed to have some magnetic attraction for him), and the girl climbed gratefully into the truck between them. Hulten later recollected, 'When we were almost through Runnymede Park going towards Windsor I stopped the truck off the road. I told the girl we had a flat tyre. We all got out . . . I hit the girl over the head with an iron bar.' While Hulten held her face down on the ground, Jones rifled the girl's pockets. 'By this time the girl had ceased struggling. I picked up her shoulders and Georgina [Jones] picked up her feet. We carried her over and dumped her

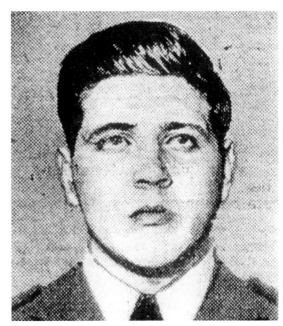

Contemporary newspaper photograph of Karl Hulten
Elizabeth Marina Jones

about three feet from the edge of a stream.' Proceeds of this crime? Less than five shillings. The victim, thankfully, survived.

The next day, Friday, Hulten once again called for Jones at King Street, and in the early hours of the following morning they decided to try another taxi robbery.

By 2 a.m. they were approaching the Chiswick Roundabout in the back of George Heath's hired car, a grey Ford V-8 saloon, registration number RD 8955.

'We'll get out here.'

Heath pulled into the kerb. According to betty Jones. 'As Heath was leaning over [to open the door for Jones] I saw a flash and heard a bang . . . Heath moaned slightly and turned a little towards the front. Ricky said, "Move over or I'll give you another dose of the same." I heard [Heath] breathing very heavily and his head was slumped on his chest.'

Hulten now replaced Heath behind the wheel of the saloon, and while he drove off towards Staines his companion systematically emptied the dying man's pockets. Heath struggled to keep hold of his life for just fifteen more minutes before succumbing to a massive internal haemorrhage. His corpse was unceremoniously cast into a ditch by Knowle Green, just outside Staines. The couple arrived back in home territory at 4 a.m., and after wiping the car of fingerprints, dumped it in the cinema car-park behind Hammersmith Broadway. After a quick snack in the Black and White café, they went back to Jones's room to look over the loot.

Six hours after it had been discarded, George Heath's body was discovered in its resting place by auxiliary fireman Robert Balding. Heath's less immediately useful possessions, such as his chequebook and driver's licence, lay where they had been thrown out on to the Great Southwest Road by Betty Jones the night before; they were found by John Jones, an apprentice electrician. This gave a possible identity to the recently found corpse, and a

The Man Who Killed Redheads

Joe Medley was a professional criminal whose previous convictions included armed robbery, for which, had he not escaped, he would have served a sentence of from 30 to 60 years. When he did escape, for no discernible reason he took exception to redheaded women and built a new career on killing them. After prison, Medley went to New Orleans where he met Laura Fischer, a 28-year-old redhead. On Christmas Eve 1944, Laura's body was found drowned in the hotel bathtub, though the subsequent autopsy could find no marks of violence that might have indicated foul play. By this time Medley was headed for Chicago, where he registered at a hotel with another redhead, Blanche Zimmerman. Blanche was found on 17 February 1945, dead, as Laura Fischer had been, in a tub of water in the hotel bathroom. The fact that her body contained no small quantity of alcohol and drugs at the time contributed to a coroner's jury returning a verdict of accidental death. In Washington, Medley next became acquainted with 50-year-old redhead Nancy Boyer. No baths this time; Nancy was found shot dead on the floor of the kitchen in her apartment. It was March 1945, and Jor Medley would soon be no further threat to redheads. The FBI had traced Medley to St Louis where he was arrested in possession of some of Mrs Boyer's belongings. Extradited back to Washington, he was charged with her first-degree murder, and on 7 June 1945, he was sentenced to death. On the morning of 3 April 1946, still waiting on Death Row at Washington State Prison, Medley and a fellow prisoner, Earl McFarland, escaped. Medley was recaptured eight hours later still close to the prison; McFarland was picked up a week later in time to meet his execution date. Joe Medley died in the electric chair on 20 December 1946.

description of George Heath and his car was circulated to all police units.

In the meantime the gunman and his moll had been disposing of their victim's marketable possessions: his fountain pen and propelling pencil were snapped up by Len Bexley; a wristwatch went to Hulten's hairdresser, Morris Levene. They passed the afternoon spending the proceeds at the White City greyhound track, and in the evening they watched Deanna Durbin in the film *Christmas Holiday*. But bravado had become the new name of their dangerous game, and on the night of Sunday, 8 October the couple were openly driving around in George Heath's V-8. After spending the next morning in bed at King Street, Hulten again climbed behind the wheel and took a trip to Newbury, to his old army camp; in the evening he returned to London and the arms of another girlfriend, Joyce Cook.

Patrolling his customary beat on this Monday night, PC William Walters spotted a Ford saloon parked in Lurgan Avenue, off the Fulham Road. The car's number was RD 8955.

In response to his call, Walters was soon joined by Inspector Read and a sergeant, who set watch on the car. At about 9 p.m. Hulten left Joyce's house and got into the stolen V-8.

'Is this your car, sir?' inquired PC Walters.

Back at Hammersmith police station, Hulten introduced himself as Second Lieutenant Richard Allen, 501 Parachute Regiment. In his hip pocket had been found a Remington automatic and a handful of ammunition. 'Allen' claimed that he had found the car abandoned out at Newbury. In the early hours of Tuesday morning Lt Robert Earl de Mott of the American CID took Hulten to their headquarters in Piccadilly. This was in perfect accord with war-time protocol, which recognized the 'sovereignty' of American servicemen while stationed in Britain, and did not permit them to be tried in a British court. The Americans, however, in an almost unprecedented act of disdain for Hulten, waived this right and returned him to the ministrations of British law and justice.

Meanwhile Hulten had given the police Jones's address at King Street, and she had been interviewed at Hammersmith police station, where she made a statement and was released. Clearly haunted by her part in what had become known as 'The Cleft-Chin Murder' (descriptive of George Heath), and prompted by a chance meeting with an old friend, Henry Kimbelly (who, coincidentally, was a War Reserve police constable), Elizabeth Jones made a full confession of her part in the crime, albeit laying much emphasis on Hulten's dominant role. She later enlarged the point by claiming that she was afraid of Hulten and terrified by his threats of violence. Karl Hulten gave as good as he got, and blamed Betty for egging him on to the final deed: 'If it hadn't been for her, I would never have shot Heath.'

Six months before VE day, Hulten and Jones appeared at the Old Bailey before Mr Justice Charles. Six days later, on 21 January 1945, sentence of death was pronounced on them both. Appeals were dismissed in February.

For Karl Hulten, the last reel of the third-rate gangster movie he had made of his life came to an end on 8 March 1945, a week after his 23rd birthday, at the end of a rope. His co-star, too, had made her last appearance. Reprieved just two days before her execution date, Betty Jones spent the next ten years in gaol, and was released on licence in 1954.

1946

Otto Steven Wilson

An Unnatural Urge. *For no better reason than 'an urge to kill and destroy women', Otto Wilson destroyed two lives before being taken into custody.*

In the early afternoon of 15 November the body of Virginia Lee Griffin, the 25-year-old wife of a truck driver, had been found by a chambermaid, stuffed into the closet of a run-down Skid Row hotel room; she had been choked to death and mutilated with a knife. Almost immediately after, the body of Mrs Lilian Johnson was discovered in a hotel room only a few blocks away; she too had been choked to death and hideously mutilated.

Before nightfall, a manhunt was under way, centring on the bars and hotels of Skid Row. Police patrolmen were issued with the description of a man who had booked into the rooms where the victims had been found.

Patrolman Harold Donlan of the city police recalled that he had seen a man answering this description drinking around the local bars, and made a particular point of diverting his route around the liquor dives. At 5.30 p.m. he found Otto Wilson, just about to buy a drink for a new girl he had met. 'I walked over and put the handcuffs on him,' Donlan said later. And in doing so he probably saved Wilson's companion from being his third victim.

By 7.30 p.m., Wilson had confessed to both murders, pleading that he was searching for love, but had always been mentally unstable and had lost control of himself. The psychiatrists were not quite so benevolent in their assessment of Otto Wilson: 'He has an urge to kill and destroy women. He may be considered

The Wartime Enterprise of Dr Petiot

A practising physician and one-time mayor of the town of Villeneuve, Dr Marcel Petiot had a long history of criminal involvement (notably drug trafficking) before the Second World War broke on Europe's doorstep, providing him with the lucrative diversion of robbing and then killing wealthy Jews whom he had promised to help escape from the excesses of the Germans. Death in most cases was by lethal injection. The authorities finally caught up with the deadly

doctor when the chimney of his Paris surgery caught fire during a mass corpse-burning session, and Petiot confessed to a total of sixty-three murders. He also claimed, in mitigation, that he was a member of the French Resistance and was simply executing Nazi collaborators. Dr Petiot was eventually charged with the murders of the 27 people whose remains were found in the basement incinerator at his surgery; he was put to the guillotine on 26 May 1946.

a sexual psychopath and degenerate. His hatred of womankind has unquestionably been built up for years and increased by alcoholic stimulation. If he had not been apprehended, there is no telling how many other victims of his lust and passion there might have been.'

Wilson's trial commenced on 18 June 1945, and he pleaded not guilty by reason of insanity; on 28 June, a jury found him sane and guilty of murder. Otto Wilson was given a capital sentence, and died in the gas chamber on 20 September 1946.

UNITED KINGDOM

The Sadist

Neville George Clevely Heath was a sexual sadist who indulged in extreme forms of flagellation and bondage. On 20 June 1946, these practices developed into murder when staff at the Pembridge Court Hotel, where Heath had booked in with Miss Margery Gardner, found her mutilated body:

Margery Gardner's naked body lay on its back, the feet tied together with a handkerchief; her wrists, judging by the marks, had also been bound, though the ligature had been removed. Her face had been severely bruised consistent with having been punched repeatedly. There were no fewer than seventeen vicious slash marks on various parts of her body – marks with a distinctive criss-cross pattern. In addition the breasts had been bitten, the nipples almost bitten off. Finally some rough object had been

Neville George Clevely Heath

Characteristic pattern of skin marks found on Margery Gardner with the whip used to inflict them

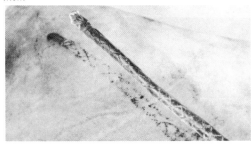

forced into her vagina causing excessive bleeding. The unspeakable savagery of the injuries were compounded by the fact that Margery Gardner had been alive when they were inflicted; death came later, from suffocation.

Heath killed once more before his arrest, this time in Bournemouth where he murdered and mutilated Doreen Marshall. It is characteristic of his cynical attitude that before succumbing to the hangman, Heath is said to have asked the prison governor for a whisky, adding: 'You might as well make that a double.'

1947

The 'Black Dahlia' Case

A tarnished tale of Tinsel Town, the 'Black Dahlia' was found dead on a Los Angeles vacant lot, the letters BD hacked into her thigh with a knife. Despite a huge investigation, the case remains one of America's unsolved classics.

Over the decades since it became the world's movie Mecca, Hollywood has acquired a reputation for ruining thousands of young lives – mostly those of country and small-town girls attracted by the razzle-dazzle and the promise of fame and fortune as a 'star'. Few ever made it. Some got as far as occasional extra-work, fewer still made 'starlet' grade; most went home disillusioned and penniless. Those that hung around drifted into the less glamorous worlds of waitressing, barmaiding and prostitution.

Elizabeth Short *might* have been one of those girls, but she wasn't. The truth is, Beth was into all kinds of trouble long before she hit the streets of Tinsel Town, and in many ways her end was as predictable as if it had been etched in stone. Elizabeth was born in Medford, Massachusetts. In 1942 she left home for Miami where she worked as a waitress. With America's involvement in the Second World War, the country was beginning to fill up with handsome young men in uniform, which was fine by Beth – and they seemed to enjoy her company too. 1943 found Beth in California where

she continued waitressing, 'modelling', and entertaining the troops. She was doing just that in a Santa Monica bar on an evening in September; and while the bunch of sailors getting merry on booze and Beth's company were entitled to be there, at nineteen Beth wasn't. She was picked up in a police raid and sent back to her mother in Medford. Within days Beth was back in Santa Monica with a new job working in the stores at Camp Cooke, the local army base. Never happier than when she was among servicemen, it didn't take Beth long to make 'Camp Cutie of the Week', and soon afterwards she moved in with a sergeant. Not exclusively of course – after all, Miss Short had a lot of charms to spread around.

One of the other 'friends' was a young Air Force Major, Matthew Gordon, to whom Beth became engaged. It may even have been true love – we will never know – because not long after they met, Gordon was posted, and in the summer of 1946 he was killed in an air crash. It would be convenient to think that it was this tragedy that pushed Elizabeth Short on to a one-way track of self-destruction, but she had already climbed on to that roller-coaster years before.

Beth had by now decided to swop 'Camp Cutie' for a more promising future as 'Screen Cutie', and had hit the road to Hollywood. Here she set about reinventing herself as the enigmatic 'Black Dahlia', emphasising her naturally black hair by never wearing any other colour clothes, from her underwear outwards. She was much more successful, by most accounts, at getting into producers' beds than into their films, and while she was waiting to be plucked off the sidewalk and turned into a star the Black Dahlia could always use her natural charms to make ends meet. At this time

170

she was staying with a friend named Dot French, a cinema usherette with a home out at Pacific Beach. Beth Short stayed here over the December of 1946, and on 8 January she called a manfriend named 'Red' to pick her up from the house and drive her to the Biltmore Hotel in Los Angeles; she said she was going to meet her sister. Over the next few days Beth was seen around town but no significant information ever came out of these vague sightings.

On the morning of 15 January 1947 the body of a young woman was discovered on waste ground in a suburb of Los Angeles. She had been crudely cut in two at the waist, and the remains had been horribly mutilated; on one of her thighs the letters BD had been carved with a knife. Subsequent post-mortem examination revealed that the victim had died not long before her corpse had been found, and a fingerprint check proved the woman's name was Elizabeth Ann Short – the Black Dahlia. As days passed during which detectives pieced together the tawdry life and loves of the failed starlet, the wackos queued up for the privilege of confessing to her murder. All major homicides attract their share of cranks eager for the limelight, but the death of the Black Dahlia seemed to bring them crawling out of the

Curious note received with a package of Elizabeth Short's personal belongings; no letter followed

woodwork; some were women claiming that they had killed Beth for stealing their man. Ten days after the discovery of the murder the *Los Angeles Examiner* received an envelope on which was pasted a message in cut-out letters promising: 'Here is Dahlia's belongings. Letter to follow.' The belongings turned out to be Elizabeth Short's birth certificate, social security card and other oddments such as snapshots and newspaper clippings; there was also an address book with one page torn out – presum-

Funeral service for the 'Black Dahlia' (Popperfoto)

ably the page on which the name of the sender was written. Fingerprints on the envelope were too smudged for matching with FBI records. The promised letter proved to be an anticlimax. Like the previous communication the words were collaged letters cut from newspapers; it read simply: 'Have changed my mind. You would not give me a square deal. Dahlia killing was justified.'

Elizabeth Short, the Black Dahlia, was quietly buried on Saturday, 25 January 1947 in the Mountain View Cemetery at Oakland, California. To date, nothing more has emerged to help close the file on her murder.

ABOARD SHIP

The Trial Without a Body

In October 1947 ship's steward James Camb raped and murdered actress Gay Gibson aboard the *Durban Castle* out of South Africa. Although Camb disposed of his luckless victim out of one of the liner's portholes and the body was never found, fresh scratches on the suspect's arms and back indicated his involvement in a fierce struggle. Blood-flecked saliva on the pillow cover of Miss Gibson's bed was consistent with manual strangulation, and in situations of abject fear such as that Gay Gibson must have felt at the hands of her attacker, it is common for the bladder to empty – which accounted for the

extensive urine staining on the bed. In March 1948, after the ship had docked in Southampton, Camb was tried, convicted and sentenced to death; however, he did have one stroke of luck. At the time his execution was scheduled to take place, Parliament was debating the abolition of capital punishment, and the Home Secretary thought it only fair to suspend executions until the matter was resolved. As it turned out James Camb was especially fortunate, because the clause was finally deleted from the Bill and hanging recommenced.

James Camb

Detectives examining the port-hole

1948

Peter Griffiths

Marks of Cain. *In the search for the brutal killer of three-year-old June Devaney, the head of Lancashire's Fingerprint Bureau masterminded the country's first exercise in mass-fingerprinting.*

At twenty minutes past midnight on 15 May 1948 staff nurse Gwendoline Humphreys was making her routine round of CH3, a children's ward in the Queen's Park Hospital outside Blackburn. Of the twelve cots only six had occupants, and the oldest of these small sleeping figures was June Anne Devaney, not yet four. June had been admitted to the ward ten days before with mild pneumonia, had made a good recovery and had been looking forward to being collected by her parents later in the day.

Ten minutes later Nurse Humphreys heard a sound like a child's voice calling and looked out of the window on to the grounds, then put her head round the door of CH3; finding everything as it should be, she returned to the kitchen. At 1.20 a.m. she felt the draught from an open porch door giving access to the hospital grounds; the catch of the door had been faulty for some time so she closed it and thought no more of it.

While she was on her feet, Nurse Humphreys put her head round the door of the children's ward to make sure all her charges were tucked up safely. As she looked down into the empty cot where June Devaney had been sleeping an hour before, the nurse's heart skipped a beat.

The drop side of the cot was still in place, which could only mean the girl had been bodily lifted and taken out. With the help of the night sister, Gwen Humphreys made a search of the immediate area, noticing as she did a large 'Winchester' bottle beneath June's bed. The last time the nurse had seen it had been on her 12.20 round, when it was in its proper place on an instrument trolley at the end of the ward. She also noticed some footprints on the highly waxed floor.

Having failed to locate the child, the hospital authorities alerted the local police, and officers began to carry out a systematic search of the extensive hospital grounds. At 3.17 a.m. the body of June Anne Devaney was found by a police constable close to the boundary wall; she had suffered terrible injuries to the head, and first indications suggested sexual interference.

Mr C. G. Looms, Blackburn's Chief Constable, Detective Superintendent Woodmansey, and a police surgeon arrived within the hour. Detective Chief Inspector John Capstick and Detective Sergeant John Stoneman from Scotland Yard were met off the morning Preston train by a police car which sped them to Blackburn.

On that bleak afternoon of Saturday 15 May, the Yard officers waited in the drizzling rain as the waterproof sheeting was peeled back revealing the tragic body of June Devaney. Jack Capstick recalled that first glimpse later: 'I am not ashamed to say that I saw it through a mist of tears. Years of detective service had hardened me to many terrible things; but this tiny pathetic body, in its nightdress soaked in blood and mud, was something no man could see unmoved, and it haunts me to this day.'

Detective Chief Inspector Colin Campbell, head of the Lancashire Fingerprint Bureau, had been at the hospital since 5 a.m. and had already assembled a catalogue of potentially vital clues. These included a vast number of fingerprints, among them those on the Winchester bottle. There were also the footprints which had been seen by Nurse Humphreys. Colin Campbell ordered photographs to be taken of the prints, and then the wax beneath the prints was carefully scraped off for further forensic tests for microscopic fibres and particles.

It became the task of a team of detectives to trace and fingerprint every person who in the past two years could have had a legitimate reason to have been in the children's ward; there were 642 of them. When all the prints but one set on the Winchester bottle had been eliminated, DCI Campbell could state with confidence that these were the marks of June Devaney's killer. However, fingerprints are of use only if there is a suspect whose prints can be compared with them, or if a matching set can be found in one of the police fingerprint bureaux. In this case there was no suspect, and there were no matching prints on file – the person who killed June Anne Devaney had no criminal record.

Knowing their killer was just a fingerprint away the Yard men, in consultation with local forces, decided to take the unprecedented step of fingerprinting every male over the age of

sixteen who was in Blackburn on 14 and 15 May. Using twenty officers and the electoral register, Inspector William Barton began a two-month trawl of more than 35,000 homes, and Chief Inspector Campbell designed a special compact card for the convenience of the 'mobile' fingerprint squad. Towards the end of July the fingerprinting had been all but completed, but without success. It began to look as though June Devaney's killer had slipped through the net. Then a procedure was tried that would not be possible today. In the immediate post-war years, rationing persisted, and records were kept of the issue of ration books and the Registration Number by which they and their owners were identified. It was a simple, if time-consuming, operation to check the local registration officer's file against the National Registration numbers on the fingerprint cards to see who had been missed. One of those numbers belonged to Peter Griffiths, a 22-year-old former soldier then living in Blackburn. At 3 p.m. on Thursday, 12 August, Chief Inspector Colin Campbell confirmed that Griffiths was the owner of the prints on the Winchester bottle.

When Griffiths left home for work on the night shift at a local flour mill he was intercepted and arrested. After a half-hearted attempt at denial, Griffiths made a full confession, adding by way of defence that he was

Track of the killer's footprints through the children's ward

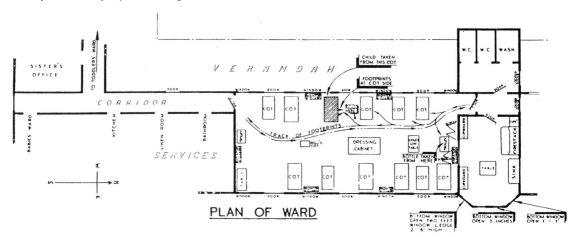

PLAN OF WARD

drunk at the time: 'I picked the girl up out of the cot and took her outside by the same door. I carried her in my right arm and she put her arms round my neck and I walked with her down the hospital field. I put her down on the grass. She started crying again and I tried to stop her from crying, but she wouldn't do, like, she wouldn't stop crying. I just lost my temper then and you know what happened then.'

On Friday, 15 October 1948, Griffiths' trial opened before Mr Justice Oliver at the Lancaster Assizes; by now the prosecution had considerably more than a confession and a fingerprint to offer the jury. After retrieving the prisoner's suit from a pawn shop the police forensic laboratory had uncovered two further damning pieces of evidence: fibres taken from Griffiths' clothing proved a perfect match for the fibres adhering to the victim's body and those found on the window ledge where the killer had entered the hospital. Human bloodstains were found in several places on both the suit jacket and trousers – blood group A, the same group as June Devaney's.

Such was the solid weight of indisputable scientific evidence that Griffiths' defence of insanity stood little chance of influencing the decision of the jury; they retired for a bare 23 minutes before returning to empower Mr Justice Oliver to pass the only sentence that the law then allowed in the case of murder: death. On Friday morning 19 November, the sentence was carried out at Liverpool Prison.

On 3 November the police had honoured their pledge to the citizens of Blackburn; about 500 people took up the option of having their

The Winchester bottle　　*Peter Griffiths*

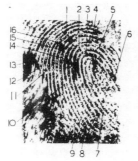

Left, the print found on the Winchester bottle; right, Peter Griffiths' fingerprint

fingerprint record returned to them, while the remaining 46,500 were ceremoniously pulped at a local paper mill observed by the Mayor and a coterie of journalists, photographers and newsreel cameramen.

Mass Murder in Tokyo

Japan's most famous murderer and its longest serving prisoner, Sadamichi Hirasawa, was convicted of the killing of twelve bank employees. On 26 January 1948 Hirasawa entered the Imperial Bank of Tokyo building posing as an official from the Health Department and announced that due to an outbreak of dysentery all employees must be given a dose of preventive medicine. Within seconds of drinking the cyanide liquid, bank staff began to drop dead on the spot; Hirasawa fled with 180,000 yen. After nearly 40 years' incarceration, Sadamichi Hirasawa died in prison in 1987.

John George Haigh

The Acid-Bath Murders. *Haigh's misunderstanding of the term* corpus delicti *led to his overconfident confession to the killing of Mrs Olive Durand-Deacon, and his arrest. Haigh's trial was enlivened by his ludicrous attempt to establish a defence of insanity by claiming to have drunk his victims' blood!*

John George Haigh first saw the light of day on 24 July 1909; less than 24 hours later Louis Bleriot made history by crossing the English Channel for the first time in an aeroplane. John Haigh would also make history one day – history of a very different kind.

Among his schoolfellows Haigh, who was known as 'Ching' because of his almond-shaped, almost oriental eyes, presented something of an enigma. The carefully scrubbed and slickly groomed exterior belied a lazy brain and a dishonest temperament incapable of telling the truth. While Ching's problem undoubtedly arose in part from his parents' refusal to allow him any social intercourse with his peers outside school, a heavy burden of responsibility must rest within Haigh's own personality, and his uncontrollable urge towards spitefulness, malice and dishonesty. He particularly delighted in punching and tweaking little girls and anybody else younger and weaker than himself; and if there were no human playmates to torment, then little Ching was content to torture insects and small animals.

Academically, Haigh was perceived as a dullard as well as an idler, and to nobody's surprise he left school at seventeen quite without distinction or qualification – unless one counts a certain *savoir-faire*, a sort of affable cunning. The pattern of John Haigh's personality was summed up in an uncannily perceptive description given by his first employer: 'He was lazy; he was always late. But he had charm. I had to like him.'

The dapper Mr Haigh

Haigh's Crawley 'workshop'

By the age of 22, Haigh had started his own estate, insurance and advertising agency, though this must have seemed too much like hard work, because he later became a car sales-man. Not that there is anything intrinsically dishonourable about that calling – the problem in Haigh's case was that the cars were just not his to sell. Through the simple deception of using fictitious letter-headings to obtain money on hire-purchase agreements, John Haigh became prosperous. On 6 July 1934, at Bridling-ton, Haigh married Miss Beatrice Hamer. Four months later he was imprisoned and Mrs Haigh left, never to communicate with him again. On his release fifteen months later, Haigh transferred his dishonesties to Glasgow, where he earned himself a four-year stretch for fraud.

Released once more on to the streets, and clearly undismayed by recent setbacks, Haigh's prospects went from strength to strength as he drifted from fraud to fraud. In the summer of 1944 he renewed the acquaintance of a man he had first met in 1936. The man's name was William Donald McSwan, and their meeting proved to be the turning point in Haigh's life of crime – the point at which Haigh the swindler, Haigh the blackguard, became Haigh the Acid-Bath Murderer.

In his later confession, Haigh recalled:

We met at the Goat public house in Kensington High Street, and from there we went to number 79 Gloucester Road, where in the basement I had rented I hit him on the head with a cosh, withdrew a glass of blood from his throat and drank it. He was dead within five minutes or so. I put him in a 40-gallon tank and disposed of him with acid, washing the

177

Detectives searching the yard of Haigh's 'workshop' for the remains of Mrs Durand-Deacon

sludge down a manhole in the basement. I had known this McSwan and his mother and father for some time, and on seeing the mother and father I explained that he had gone off to avoid his 'Call up'. I wrote a number of letters in due course to his parents purporting to come from him and posted, I think, in Glasgow and Edinburgh, explaining various details of the disposition of properties, which were to follow. In the following year I took separately to the same basement the father Donald and the mother Amy, disposing of them in exactly the same way as the son . . .

. . . I met the Hendersons by answering an advertisement offering for sale their property at 22 Ladbroke Square. I did not purchase. They sold it and moved to 16 Dawes Road, Fulham. This runs in a period from November 1947 to February 1948. In February 1948, the Hendersons were staying at Kingsgate Castle, Kent. I visited them there and went with them to Brighton, where they stayed at the Metropole. From here I took Dr Henderson to Crawley and disposed of him in a store room at Leopold Road by shooting him in the head with his own revolver. I put him in a tank of acid as in the other cases. This was in the morning and I went back to Brighton and brought up Mrs Henderson on the pretext that her husband was ill. I shot her in the store room and put her in another tank and disposed of her with acid. In each of the last four cases I had my glass of blood as before.

In February 1949, Haigh was living at the Onslow Court Hotel, west London, and had become friendly with fellow resident Mrs Olive Durand-Deacon, a widow of independent means whose modest fortune Haigh had already earmarked for his own use. On the pretence of assisting Mrs Durand-Deacon in a scheme for marketing false fingernails, Haigh lured her down to his 'workshop' outside Crawley, Sussex. Here he shot the unsuspecting woman through the neck, and having stripped it of any valuables, steeped her body in a 40-gallon oil drum of sulphuric acid.

In the course of the subsequent inquiry into the disappearance of Mrs Durand-Deacon, police interviewed Haigh on several occasions and formed a very poor opinion of his oily, ingratiating manner. A visit to his Crawley workshop revealed significant enough clues – not least a recently fired .38 Webley revolver and traces of blood – to place Haigh under arrest. Under questioning, Haigh made this startling announcement: 'Mrs Durand-Deacon no longer exists. I've destroyed her with acid. You can't prove murder without a body.' Of course Haigh was quite wrong; a number of significant cases *have* been proved without a corpse. But he was also wrong about Mrs Durand-Deacon no longer existing. It was true that the acid had succeeded in its grisly task of reducing Mrs Durand-Deacon's flesh and bones to a greasy sludge – but what Haigh had not taken account of was the longer time needed to destroy plastics. A set of acrylic dentures, custom-made for Mrs Durand-Deacon, were positively identified by her dentist, and her red

Death in the Air

With two other people, Albert Guay blew up a Quebec Airways DC–3, killing all 23 passengers and crew. While they were checking the passenger lists the police came to the name of Rita Guay, whose husband was a known crook and at the time involved in a romantic liaison with a woman named Pitre; Pitre was identified as having delivered a package to be transported aboard the fatal flight. Albert Guay was arrested and made a confession implicating his accomplices; all three were tried, found guilty of murder and, in 1951, hanged.

plastic handbag, with many of its contents, was positively identified by her friends.

Haigh's extravagant claim that he was a vampire who drank the blood of his victims was seen for what it was – a rather unsophisticated ruse to establish a defence of insanity and exchange Broadmoor for the noose. As it was, John George Haigh kept his appointment with the hangman at Wandsworth Prison on 10 August 1949.

'I'd have killed a thousand . . .'

In the space of just twelve minutes, Howard Unruh shot thirteen people dead on the streets of Camden, New Jersey. He would certainly have claimed many more lives and provided a lot more work for the local medical services if he had not simply run out of ammunition; 'I'd have killed a thousand,' he told a psychiatrist, 'if I'd had bullets enough.' The shootings took place on 5 September 1949, but the problem had started years before that. A withdrawn, almost hermetic man, Unruh just hated his neighbours. Of course, they were really no worse than anybody else's neighbours – it was Howard that had the problems. The folks in the next street

wouldn't dream of persecuting him – Howard just thought they did, and had begun to keep a careful note in his diary of all these imagined grievances, and at the same time set about perfecting the marksmanship skills he had acquired on army service. Unruh was 28 years old at the time he made the headlines, and the inevitable crack might not have appeared for some time if the security gate he had fitted to the house to keep the neighbours out had not been stolen. Perhaps Howard Unruh found the seclusion he so desired in the Trenton State Hospital for the insane.

1950

Ernest Ingenito

A Family At War. *A criminal since his youth, Ingenito married Theresa Mazzoli and the couple went to live with her family, where Theresa's mother nagged Ernie mercilessly. The marriage began to disintegrate and before long Ingenito had been thrown out of the family home for infidelity. He returned armed, and in one night of terror left seven people dead.*

Ernie was born in 1924 into a poor rural Pennsylvanian family, and did not benefit overly from an early education – save that kind of *ad hoc* training in cunning absorbed through running with the local street gangs. At fifteen the boy was arrested during the course of a burglary – not his first crime, just the first he was arrested for – and put away in the Pennsylvania State Reformatory. In 1941 Ernie's much-loved mother died, and with her passing the last restraint on his criminous career was severed. Like so many of his kind Ingenito drifted into the US Army having failed to appreciate that the services necessarily run on discipline; after a brief undistinguished career, he served two years in the stockade for assaulting an officer before being dishonourably discharged.

In 1947 Ernest Ingenito married Theresa Mazzoli and went to live with the Mazzoli family in Gloucester County where, over the course of the next few years, he fathered two sons. The domestic arrangements were not ideal – for a start Theresa's mother, Pearl, took against Ernie, and had a tendency to nag him.

And Mike Mazzoli didn't seem to understand his son-in-law's fondness for drink and other women. It was this that finally led Mazzoli to throw Ernie out on his ear and forbid him to see his daughter again; Theresa in her turn forbade him to see the children again. On 17 November 1950 Ernie Ingenito was told by his lawyer that he would only get access to his sons through a court order; it was the final straw. Ernie returned to the lodging-house where he had taken a room and selected a .32 carbine and two pistols from his collection of guns. Then he went visiting.

When he knocked on the front door of the Mazzoli house Ernie came face to face with Mike Mazzoli, who told him in plain language to push off. They were the last words he uttered before his son-in-law gunned him down. Next on the hit-list was Teresa, though mercifully she later recovered from her wounds in hospital. When the shooting had started, Pearl Mazzoli fled to her parents' home nearby, but nothing was going to stop Ernie now – he was going to track down every last damn member of the Mazzoli family. After shooting Pearl, he rampaged through the house slaughtering Pearl's mother Theresa Pioppi, her sister-in-law Marion, brother Gino and Gino's nine-year-old daughter, and finally brother John. Ernie had just one more murderous trip to make – out to Mineola where Michael Mazzoli's parents lived; there he massacred Frank and Hilda Mazzoli. By midnight it was all over, and Ernie Ingenito had wreaked his insane revenge. He had also, not surprisingly, attracted the attention of the police.

Before armed officers took him into custody, Ernie made a half-hearted attempt to take his own life, but he was patched up in time for his trial in January 1951. He was indicted on a sample charge of murdering Mrs Pearl Mazzoli and sentenced to life imprisonment, and as Ernie was clearly as mad as a hatter his sentence was ordered to be served in the New Jersey State Hospital for the Insane at Trenton. It was, to be sure, a rather more benign punishment than the one suggested by Ernie's wife from her hospital bed: 'I wish they would hang Ernie,' she said. But for good measure Ernest Ingenito was put on trial again in 1956; charged with a further four counts of murder, he was convicted and handed down a life sentence for each.

1951

Herbert Leonard Mills

Ode to Death. *Mills telephoned the* News of the World *claiming to have found the body of a woman in a wood; he then attempted to sell the newspaper his confession to her murder. It transpired that Mills, like others before him, was trying to commit the perfect murder. Like others before him, he failed.*

It is not often that a national newspaper gets the chance of a scoop, of a totally exclusive murder story, so it must have seemed as though Christmas had come in August when a voice came through on the *News of the World*'s newsroom telephone: 'I've just found a woman's body. It looks like murder.'

Of course it was more than the fragile co-operation between police and journalist could have withstood to have kept the law in ignorance of such a dramatic revelation; so, having ascertained the location of the public booth from which the informant had telephoned, and its number, the reporter asked the young man to wait by the box for a return call. In the meantime the Nottingham police force were alerted that there was a possible murder in their area. The *News of the World* had barely time to resume telephone contact before the police had arrived at the call box.

The caller, it was discovered at the police station, was nineteen-year-old Herbert Leonard Mills, of Mansfield Street, Nottingham. The youth had certainly not been lying about finding a woman's body; it was there in a secluded part of the woods near Sherwood Vale, and judging by the marks of strangulation and bludgeoning, he had been right about murder. The victim was later identified as Mrs Mabel Tattershaw, aged 48, who had lived at Longmead Drive.

Mills also had possession of a broken bead necklace which he claimed to have picked up at the scene of the crime, and he gave a rather hazy description of a man with a limp whom he had seen in the neighbourhood of the body.

After giving blood samples and fingernail parings, Leonard Mills was released to the eagerly waiting *News of the World* where he seemed in his element. He expounded to crime reporter Norman Rae how he had had this idea for a sonnet – Mills had great, though as yet unfulfilled, literary ambitions – and sought romantic inspiration in the leafy glades of Sherwood. Then he found the woman's body, 'very white and pale', and had taken up Shelley's *Ode to Death* to read; he had then telephoned the newspaper. There was an obvious feyness to the story, but it seemed at least credible. In return for cash, Mills was to make several more increasingly elaborate statements to Rae.

Meanwhile the police had been probing into the background of Mabel Tattershaw, trying to find a motive for what on the face of it seemed to be a senseless murder. Mrs Tattershaw was married to a man who worked away from home more often than not, and by him she had two daughters, one living in Nottingham and a fourteen-year-old still at home with her mother. To make her meagre ends meet, Mrs Tattershaw took in lodgers. Poverty had been unkind to Mabel; it had aged her beyond her middle years and had taken its toll of what physical attraction she may once have claimed. Like a shabby spectre on life's periphery, she came and went, unremarked, about her humdrum existence. Who, detectives wondered, even *noticed* poor Mabel Tattershaw, let alone felt compelled to kill her?

Norman Rae, a detective of a different kind, was finding it difficult to stop Leonard Mills making statements to his newspaper, each a little more explicit than the last, and each accompanied by a similar exaggerated demand for payment. On 24 August they met again at a hotel in Nottingham, where in an episode that must be unique in British criminal history, Mills was to write for a newspaper journalist (on hotel notepaper) his complete confession to the killing of Mrs Mabel Tattershaw. With the scrupulous correctness that dignified the best of his profession, Norman Rae cautioned Mills that he must acknowledge that he made the statement of his own volition, and that 'I have warned you, if it contains information material to the murder, I will take your statement and yourself to City police headquarters.' For the next hour Mills wrote in silence; on the following morning Rae accompanied him to Nottingham and handed over the document to Superintendent Ellington.

At the beginning the statement contained Mills's motive – 'I had always considered the possibility of a perfect murder' – and at the end, his confession: 'I now confess I murdered Mrs Tattershaw'; between the two was the story of a cold-blooded, pointless killing.

On 2 August 1951 Mabel Tattershaw had gone to the Roxy Cinema in Nottingham; seated next to her was Herbert Leonard Mills. We do not know what he used as an opening gambit, but before long they were whispering together in the dark like old friends. We do know what was in the young man's mind: 'Seeing the possibility of putting my theory into practice, I consented to meeting her on the morrow.' To be noticed, and by a young man at that, must have thrilled Mabel for the first time in many dull years. Little surprise, then,

FRANCE

Un Crime Passionnel

Yvonne Chevallier was the wife of Dr Pierre Chevallier, member of the French Cabinet and former mayor of the town of Orléans, where the couple lived with their four-year-old son Matthieu. In 1951 Madame Chevallier fired five bullets into her husband's body in what she claimed was a fit of jealous rage over his affair with Madame Jeanette Perreau. Although public disapprobation had been so strong as to have necessitated the removal of the trial from Orléans to Rheims in the hope of finding an impartial jury, no sooner did the court find out that it had a mistress to hiss at than Madame Chevallier was restored to popularity and, amid tumultuous cheers in court, she was acquitted.

that she kept the assignation; little surprise that she was willing to follow wherever her escort might lead. He led her into the seclusion of the woods, and then 'She took off her coat and laid down . . . she said she was cold, I covered her with her own coat, and then my coat . . . I put on a pair of gloves . . .'

That he was happy with the result of his 'experiment' is clear from Mills's statement: 'I was rather pleased. I think I did rather well. The strangling itself was quite easily accomplished.'

But this formed only part of the evidence carefully collected and assessed by police officers in preparation for Leonard Mills's trial; there was also the medical testimony. Professor Webster, pathologist with the Home Office Laboratory in Birmingham, detailed the many other bludgeoning injuries committed on Mrs Tattershaw's body, both before and after strangulation. Further forensic evidence linked Mills with the murder by identifying hairs from

his head on the victim's clothing, while fibres from under Mabel's fingernails came from the blue suit that he had worn on the afternoon of the murder.

All this made it very difficult for Mr Elwes KC to construct any kind of adequate defence at the Nottingham Assizes in November 1951. It was Mr Elwes's contention – on behalf of his client, for it is difficult to see how so able a counsel could have taken his brief with anything approaching optimism – that Mills had come across the woman's body in the wood and, in an attempt to gain notoriety and money, had *invented* a sequence of stories which he told to the Press.

But for the jury Mills's story was just too good to be false; they concluded that it was he who had killed Mabel Tattershaw, leaving it to Mr Justice Byrne to condemn him to death. And so in December the brief moment of fame ended for Leonard Mills on the drop at Winson Green Prison.

1952

Gaston Dominici

A Very French Affair. *The Drummond family were on a camping holiday in France when they were shot dead. The finger of suspicion pointed at the Dominicis who owned a farm close by – and in particular old Gaston Dominici. Gaston confessed several times, and retracted his confessions; he attempted suicide during the police reconstruction of the crime. Finally he was tried, convicted, sentenced to death and then reprieved.*

In the summer of 1952, 61-year-old Sir Jack Drummond, a distinguished English biochemist, took his wife Ann and eleven-year-old daughter on a camping holiday to southern France. On the night of 4 August, Sir Jack brought the Hillman station wagon to a halt at a picturesque spot by the river just outside the Provençal village of Lurs.

Early the following morning local police were alerted by Gustave Dominici, a 33-year-old farmer who had come across the dead bodies of the Drummond family at their campsite. Sir Jack and his wife had been shot, Elizabeth had been bludgeoned to death.

The nearest habitation to the scene of the

The discovery of Lady Drummond's body (Popperfoto)

murders was a farm named Grand'Terre, some 150 yards away, owned by 75-year-old Gaston Dominici and worked by his sons, one of whom was Gustave. Despite their deep suspicion that the Dominici family were involved in the killings, a search of Grand'Terre revealed nothing incriminating. It was not until several weeks had passed that investigating officers received their first promising lead. A railway worker told detectives that Gustave Dominici had admitted to him that young Elizabeth Drummond had still been alive when he found her. It wasn't much, but sufficient to have Gustave charged with the offence of failing to help a person in danger of dying. But still the police could not penetrate the smoke-screen of lies and deceits thrown up by the machinations of

the unscrupulous Dominicis. Eventually the seriousness of the crime and the eminence of the victims resulted in no less an official than Commissaire Edmond Sebeille, Superintendent of the Marseilles police, being given charge of the inquiry.

For almost a year Commissaire Sebeille and his team worked away trying to undermine the resistance of the Dominicis, until finally Gustave and his 49-year-old brother Clovis admitted that they knew the identity of the killer: it was their father Gaston. Despite his loud accusations of treachery, old Gaston eventually made a confession. He had been on a nocturnal prowl around the area of the farm, carrying his rifle as always, when he stumbled upon the Drummonds' camp. As it was obvious that Sir

Jack and his wife were undressing for bed the old farmer decided to hang around and watch. Unfortunately for them all, Jack Drummond caught Dominici at it, and during the ensuing struggle was shot dead. Fearing identification, Dominici then shot Ann Drummond and, as she tried to run away, bludgeoned Elizabeth about the head with the butt of his gun. Or so he said then. Because over the course of the next several weeks Gaston Dominici retracted and confessed again with monotonous regularity. At one point he accused Gustave of the murders, which resulted in Gustave retracting his accusation of Gaston in favour of another assassin. The whole bizarre situation was crowned when, during one of those reconstructions of the crime so beloved of the French authorities, Gaston broke free from the police and tried to kill himself by jumping off a railway bridge.

Gaston Dominici was put on trial at the Digne Assizes in November 1954; after an eleven-day hearing he was found guilty of murder. His advancing years saved Dominici from the guillotine, and he served only a brief period in prison before being released in 1960; he died in 1965 at the age of 83.

1952

Postcard sent by Elizabeth to her schoolchum from holiday

Gaston Dominici, handcuffed and under heavy police guard (Popperfoto)

1953

Christopher Craig and Derek Bentley

For the Sake of Example. *One of Britain's most infamous cases, and one of its most celebrated miscarriages of justice. The execution of Bentley for the murder of PC Miles led to increased pressure for the abolition of capital punishment. In 1991 the case was referred back to the Court of Appeal and it is to be hoped that at last Derek Bentley will receive a long-overdue posthumous pardon.*

The early 1950s witnessed the emergence of the Teddy Boys, Britain's first modern youth cult. They were popularly caricatured with their drape coats and drainpipe trousers, their crepe-soled blue-suede shoes; and with flick-knife, bicycle chain and knuckle-duster as accessories an otherwise harmless cult of adolescent fashion was manipulated into the bogey and scapegoat of post-war apprehension. 'Teenagers' were discovered, and their 'delinquency' came to be seen as a social problem. The authorities, notably the police, were quite unprepared for this development. It was in any case difficult enough to comprehend or control, but Press and public were demanding action. The police were determined to use the heaviest of heavy-handed tactics in order to combat disruptive behaviour, and in those cases that came before a court the judges were equally enthusiastic in handing out exemplary sentences to all

young tearaways. This background – which has become more familiar over successive decades and successive cults – is essential to an understanding of the controversial trial of Christopher Craig and Derek Bentley.

THE ACCUSED

Christopher Craig came from a 'good' home. His father was chief cashier at a bank, and had been a captain in the London Scottish Regiment during the First World War. The family lived in a comfortable house, 9 Norbury Court Road, Norbury, in southwest London; Chris was born on 19 May 1936 and attended Norbury Secondary School until the age of fifteen. He suffered from dyslexia – a condition which was little understood at that time – and left school barely able to read or write. To counteract this potential embarrassment, young Chris Craig affected the outward image of the hard man, using as his role model the American gangsters of the 1930s. This included acquiring guns, which were then, so soon after a war, easy to get hold of; the final collection numbered 40, which he used to take to school to impress his friends and enhance his playground credibility. The second unfortunate influence on Craig was his brother Niven, ten years his senior and already embarked on a serious criminal career. He had been involved in an unsuccessful armed robbery at Waltham Abbey with four other men, and when arrested at a flat in Kensington was in possession of a loaded revolver. On Thursday, 30 October 1952, Niven Craig was convicted at the Old Bailey of robbery with violence and resisting arrest, and was sentenced to two concurrent terms of twelve years' imprisonment. Christopher Craig, sixteen

Christopher Craig (Syndication International)

Derek Bentley

years of age, was an admiring onlooker at the trial.

Derek Bentley had been born on 30 June 1933, and lived at 1 Fairview Road, Norbury, not far from Craig. His father owned an electrical business and the family had been bombed out twice during the Blitz. Young Derek had received head injuries on one of these occasions and to this was attributed his below-average intelligence. When he left school he was for most practical purposes illiterate, and took occasional jobs as a dustman and a removal man; but his ruling passion in life was body-building. He was soon convicted of shop-breaking and sent to Approved School. On returning to Norbury he took up with Christopher Craig, whom he hero-worshipped. Together they carried out a number of small-scale burglaries, but on at least one occasion Bentley refused to accompany Craig because he was carrying a gun. In November 1952 Bentley was nineteen years old.

THE CRIME

In the late afternoon of Sunday, 2 November 1952, Chris Craig went to the pictures with his girlfriend. He saw *My Death Is a Mockery*, a B-picture in which a policeman is shot and the hero hanged after being captured in a shootout. Craig then went home for tea and was out on the streets again by 8.30 p.m. He called round to the Bentleys' house, where Mrs Bentley said Derek was out. Actually Derek was in – watching television – but his parents had an instinctive mistrust of Craig and worried about his influence on their son. A little later two other friends, Norman Parsley and Frank Fazey, came round for Bentley and he followed them out, where they found Craig, hanging about on the street. After a bit of chatting the other two went off and Craig and Bentley decided to catch a 109 bus into Croydon. Craig was armed with a revolver with a sawn-off barrel, a knuckle-duster and a sheath-knife;

Bentley had a smaller knife. On the bus, Craig passed the knuckle-duster over to Bentley.

The two young men got off the bus at West Croydon Station and walked down the length of Tamworth Road to Reeves Corner; then they walked back up the other side of the street, stopping about twenty yards up to look in the window of a sweet shop. Craig then shinned over the six-foot iron gate of Barlow and Parker, wholesale confectioners, to be followed a few moments later by Bentley.

Across the road a woman, putting her child to bed, saw all of this activity out of the window and telephoned the police. It was 9.15 p.m. Immediately a police van and a police car from Z division set out to investigate the call. In the van were DC Frederick Fairfax, PC Norman Harrison, PC Budgen and PC Pain. The car contained PC Sidney Miles and PC James McDonald, in all a very formidable show of strength for a suspected break-in. They arrived at Tamworth Road at 9.25 p.m.

PC Sidney Miles (Syndication International)

Meanwhile Craig and Bentley had climbed a drainpipe on to the flat roof of the building. Thinking they had seen a light in the garden below, they hid for some minutes behind the winding-shed of a lift, from where they heard the arrival of the police. DC Fairfax climbed the iron gate and, seeing a footprint on the window sill beyond, climbed on to the roof by way of the drainpipe. Vaguely aware of the figures behind the lift housing, he approached across the roof.

Fairfax: I'm a police officer! Come out from behind that stack!

Craig: If you want us, fucking well come and get us!

Fairfax: Alright.

With this the officer rushed forward and grabbed Bentley. Still holding him, Fairfax then tried to approach Craig, but Bentley broke free.

Bentley: Let him have it, Chris!

Craig then shot at the policeman from a distance of six feet, grazing him on the shoulder. Fairfax stumbled, got up and chased the nearest figure, who happened to be Bentley, and floored him with a punch. Using Bentley as a shield, he then ducked behind a roof light and began to frisk the lad, relieving him of the knuckle-duster and his small knife.

Bentley: That's all I've got, guv'nor. I haven't got a gun.

DC Fairfax next manoeuvred Bentley behind the head of a staircase on one side of the roof, while Craig retreated to behind the lift housing at the opposite end. Fairfax then let go of Bentley in order to help PC McDonald on to the roof beside him.

Fairfax: He got me in the shoulder.

Bentley: I told the silly bugger not to use it.

As PC Harrison also tried to climb on to the roof to the right, two shots rang out and Harrison ducked behind a chimney stack.

Harrison (To Fairfax): What sort of gun has he got, Fairy?

Bentley: He's got a .45 Colt and plenty of bloody ammunition, too.

By this time more police had arrived outside the building, along with at least six officially issued .32 calibre police guns. PC Miles had originally gone off in search of the confectioners' manager and now returned with the keys to the building. He and PC Harrison entered the building and went up the internal staircase. As the two policemen emerged through the roof door a shot was fired and PC Miles fell dead, shot through the forehead, just above the left eyebrow. As another shot rang out in the direction of DC Fairfax and PC McDonald, the latter dragged the body of PC Miles behind the stairhead, leaving Bentley temporarily unattended. At the same time PC Robert Jaggs was climbing the drainpipe to join his colleagues and further shots rang out.

Craig: Come on, you brave coppers! Think of your wives!

Bentley (to Jaggs): You want to look out. He'll blow your head off.

PC Harrison then proceeded to throw his truncheon, an empty milk bottle and a piece of wood at Craig.

Craig: I'm Craig! You've just given my brother twelve years! Come on, you coppers! I'm only sixteen!

Harrison next dashed out of the stairhead door to join the other policemen on the roof. PC Lowe Stewart also climbed the drainpipe, but, seeing the body of PC Miles, he climbed down again and positioned himself in a small yard to the west of the building, immediately beneath where Craig was hiding.

Craig: It's a Colt .45 – Are you hiding behind a shield? Is it bullet-proof? Are we going to have a shooting match? It's just what I like ... Have they hurt you, Derek?

Fairfax, McDonald and Jaggs then began to push Bentley round the stairhead and down the stairs.

Bentley: Look out, Chris! They're taking me down!

When Bentley was safely down the stairs DC Fairfax then returned to the roof, armed with a .32 automatic.

Fairfax: Drop your gun – I also have a gun!

Craig: Come on, copper – let's have it out!

Fairfax then ran out of the stairhead and, as a shot came in his direction, returned it with two of his own. He then manoeuvred around the roof lights towards Craig. Four times an empty click came from Craig's gun.

Craig: See – it's empty.

Craig climbed over the railings at the side of the roof and stood poised on the edge.

Craig: Well, here we go. Give my love to Pam.

With this he hurled himself from the roof, a drop of 25 feet, hitting on the way (according to the police) the edge of an old greenhouse. PC Lowe Stewart, waiting below, came up to him as he lay on the ground.

Craig: I wish I was fucking dead! I hope I've killed the fucking lot.

In fact he had almost killed himself; he had fractured his spine and broken his breastbone and forearm. At 10.45 p.m. Craig was taken to Croydon General Hospital in the same ambulance as DC Fairfax.

THE TRIAL

At 11.45 p.m., Christopher Craig was charged with the murder of PC Sidney Miles by Detective Chief Inspector John Smith, while lying in the cubicle next to Fairfax in hospital. At 1.15 a.m., DCI Smith and DS Shepherd visited Craig's home, where they discovered a .45 bullet in his bed-clothing and a box containing 137 rounds of ammunition in the attic.

Meanwhile Derek Bentley had been taken by police car to Croydon police station. He was claimed to have said, 'I knew he had a gun, but I didn't think he'd use it. He's done one of your blokes in.' At the station, however, he made a statement which denied this, 'I did not have a gun and I did not know that Chris had one until he shot.' He was then also charged with the murder of PC Miles.

The trial of Christopher Craig and Derek Bentley opened at the Old Bailey on Tuesday, 9 December 1952. The judge was the Lord Chief Justice, Lord Goddard. Mr Christmas Humphreys prosecuted, Mr John Parris, a Leeds lawyer, represented Craig, and Mr F. H. Cassels undertook Bentley's defence. The whole atmosphere was highly prejudicial to the defendants; even Cassels openly stated his belief that 'both the little bastards ought to swing'. It was realised early on that Craig, on account of his age, could not be sentenced to death, and much attention was paid to the question whether Bentley could have been an accomplice in the murder, as well as the attempted robbery, when he was already in police custody?

Craig appeared in the dock on crutches; his lawyer had received the brief only three days before the trial opened. Several of the police witnesses contradicted each other as to the sequence of events on the roof, how many shots were fired and what exactly was said. The bullet which shot PC Miles was never produced in court, and evidence was brought of callous and boastful remarks made by Craig in hospital, which seemed highly dubious in view of his seriously injured and often comatose state. The prosecution's case as to Bentley's culpability in the crime was strongly supported by the judge, who seemed to take great pleasure in wielding Bentley's knuckle-duster during his summing up. The trial lasted three days and it took the jury only 75 minutes to find both defendants guilty, though they added a recommendation for mercy on Bentley's behalf.

Craig, because of his age, was ordered to be detained during Her Majesty's pleasure. Bentley was sentenced to death.

THE ANGER AND THE DOUBTS

On 6 January 1953 Detective Sergeant Fairfax, as he now was, was awarded the George Cross, PCs Harrison and McDonald received the George Medal, and PC Jaggs the British Empire Medal. This was all before Derek Bentley's appeal had been heard on 13 January and could hardly have created a calm and unbiased atmosphere in which to consider Bentley's fate. The appeal was quickly dismissed.

The Press was largely in support of the verdict, liberally airing their prejudices about teenage delinquency; nevertheless, there was an audible volume of protest from the growing

Derek Bentley hides his face after being remanded in custody (Syndication International)

lobby of citizens opposed to capital punishment. There was a justifiable feeling that Bentley was to hang simply because they couldn't hang Craig. He had been largely convicted on the famous phrase 'Let him have it, Chris', yet at the trial no mention had been made of the possible opposite meaning to that phrase: 'Let him have the gun.' Even from the police version of events, his subsequent words seemed to support this interpretation. In any case, the phrase referred to the injuring of DC Fairfax and not the shooting of PC Miles which occurred some time later. Yet beyond all of this lay the undeniable fact that it seemed to defy natural justice that a man, already in police custody, should hang when the actual perpetrator of the crime did not.

Derek Bentley was hanged in Wandsworth Gaol at 9 a.m. on Wednesday, 28 January 1953, by the official executioner, Albert Pierrepoint. Before he died Bentley asked his parents, 'I didn't kill anyone. So why are they killing me?' Outside the prison gates a crowd of some 5,000 people shouted 'Murder!' and sang *Abide with Me* as nine o'clock arrived. The notice of Bentley's execution was ripped from the prison gates and angrily destroyed.

The ultimate sanction, death by hanging, was not revoked for another twelve years, but the case of Derek Bentley, along with those of Timothy Evans, Ruth Ellis and James Hanratty, provided the most eloquent evidence in the campaign to change the law.

The Bentley family never thought Derek would be executed; since his death the rest of the family, notably Derek's father William and sister Iris, have fought tirelessly for a posthumous pardon. William Bentley died in 1974; Iris continues the battle on her brother's behalf to this day (Popperfoto)

It should be remembered, though, that Christopher Craig did not hang. He served just ten and a half years in prison and was released in May 1963. He moved to Buckinghamshire, where he was not known, became an engineer and married in 1965.

CANADA

Too Honest for His Own Good

In June 1953 the shot bodies of three American hunters were found in a remote area of Quebec province. Wilbert Coffin, a gold prospector, told police he had met the men and helped them fix their broken-down car. For his honesty Coffin was arrested and charged with the hunters' murders. During his confinement Coffin remembered that he had seen another jeep at the same time, carrying two Americans, but vital information was ignored. Instead, Wilbert Coffin was convicted of the killings and sentenced to death. In 1955 he escaped from jail using a fake gun carved out of soap, but on the advice of a lawyer gave himself up; he was executed in February 1956. In 1958 a man confessed to the murder of the three hunters and implicated a second man – theirs, he said, was the other jeep that had been seen by the late Wilbert Coffin.

1954

John Donald Merrett

'Mother has shot herself . . .' Acquitted in 1926 of murdering his mother, Merrett changed his name to Chesney and married Vera Bonner. In 1954 he drowned his wife and strangled his mother-in-law, and then before the police could catch up with him, committed suicide. Fibre traces on Chesney's clothing confirmed his guilt.

It didn't take young Merrett long to get into serious trouble – eighteen years to be exact. In 1927 he stood before judge and jury at Edinburgh's High Court of Justiciary charged with the murder of his own mother.

Donald was born in New Zealand in 1908, the only child of John and Bertha Merrett. In 1924 Mr Merrett abandoned Mrs Merrett and went his own way, leaving Bertha to return to her native England with the boy, then sixteen years of age and with the promise of a fine future. He attended the prestigious Malvern College for a year before passing on to Edinburgh University in 1926. Sadly, for all his academic promise, Donald was not comfortable soaking up the wisdom of academe, and it was barely a month before he took to walking out of the house in the morning with the pretence of going to study, and then getting up to whoever knows what illicit pastimes. Mrs Merrett was deceived at the other end of the day as well. In the evenings, when Donald took to his room 'to pursue his studies' she fretted that he might

be overdoing things in his quest for knowledge. Not a bit of it; he had slipped out of the house by the back way and was pursuing the knowledge of such things as his worthy mother would never have imagined – mostly at the Palais de Danse in Dunedin's Picardy Place. Nor did poor innocent Bertha Merrett realise that her treasured 'Donnie' was also plundering her bank account by the simple means of forging her signature on cheques. It was a state of affairs that could not go unnoticed for long; sooner or later Mrs Merrett would receive a bank statement . . .

On the morning of 17 March 1926, Mrs Merrett and her son were in the drawing room, she writing a letter, he reading a book. A little after 9.30 the maid, who was at her duties in the kitchen, heard a shot; moments later 'Donnie' rushed in, crying, 'Rita, Rita, my mother has shot herself.' When they got back to the drawing room, there was Mrs Merrett lying on the floor, barely alive, and with blood draining from a bullet wound through her right ear.

Bertha Merrett was rushed to the Edinburgh Royal Infirmary where she was treated as a suicide case. When she had recovered sufficiently Mrs Merrett told the doctor: 'I was sitting down writing letters; my son Donald was

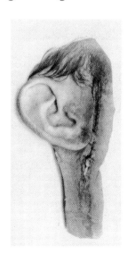

Mrs Merrett's ear bearing the wound from a bullet that 'Donnie' was accused of shooting at her; it featured as an exhibit in the case against him

192

standing beside me and I said "go away, Donnie, don't annoy me," and then I heard a kind of explosion. I do not remember anything after that.' On 27 March Bertha Merrett drifted into a coma and four days later she died. Donald, meanwhile, had continued to lead a life filled with pleasure, and continued to finance it with his mother's money – in fact by the time she passed beyond caring, her Donnie had reduced the bank balance to just four pounds and a couple of shillings. But in the face of such success, Donald seems to have become careless, and soon both the Midland Bank and the local police were taking an interest in his activities.

In November 1926 John Donald Merrett was arrested and charged with the murder of his mother, and on the first day of February the following year he was arraigned before the Lord Justice Clerk, Lord Alness, at the High Court of Justiciary in Edinburgh. In one of his rare appearances for the defence Sir Bernard Spilsbury gave his expert medical opinion that the trajectory and distance from which the bullet had been fired was entirely consistent with Mrs Merrett having shot herself. The jury was clearly swayed by this evidence, and although Merrett was convicted on several counts of forgery the jury, by a majority, found the charge of matricide against Donald Merrett 'not proven'. Merrett served eight of a twelve-month sentence and on his release re-entered the world he knew best – the criminal under-world. And for this purpose he became John Ronald Chesney.

As Chesney, he married Vera Bonner the following year, and towards the end of 1929 inherited £50,000 – a great fortune in those days. Generous with his new-found wealth, Chesney put £8,400 of the windfall in trust for his wife; she was to enjoy the interest on this capital until her death, when it reverted to Chesney. The next twenty-odd years were busy ones for Ronald Chesney – busy spending his inheritance, busy making more money (mainly as an ocean-going smuggler), busy spending that . . . By 1953 he had separated from his wife and was penniless. How he wished he had not been quite so generous to Vera all those years ago; how he wished he could get his hands on

John Ronald Chesney – Lieutenant-Commander turned smuggler

that £8,400 again! There was only one thing for it.

At the time Chesney was living in Germany, though we know that he visited England on 3 February 1954, and during that time he and his estranged wife went to the cinema together. He also made a second trip, this time on a passport in the name of 'Leslie Chown'. Vera was now living with her mother, a rather eccentric woman who insisted on calling herself 'Lady' Menzies; between them they managed a small home for the elderly at Montpelier Road, Ealing. It was at this address that Chesney arrived at about 10.30 p.m. on 10 February bearing two bottles of gin. Having rendered his wife unconscious through drink, Chesney lifted her into the bath, part-filled it with water, and pushed her under until the unfortunate woman

drowned. It was, in many ways, a perfect plan; he had slipped unobserved into the house, had fabricated a terrible but believable accident, and was about to slip out again and travel back to Germany as Leslie Chown.

But few plans are entirely perfect, and this one reckoned without an unexpected encounter with 'Lady' Menzies in the hallway. Having battered and strangled his mother-in-law to death, Chesney tried to hide her body under some cushions in an unused back room. But by this time events were quite beyond his control – a tragic death caused by falling drunkenly into a tub was one thing, but the hastily concealed, bloody corpse of an elderly woman was bound to arouse suspicion.

Chesney got back to Germany, but he knew it was only a matter of time before the police caught up with him. And so it was. Ronald Chesney had already got away with murder once, and he knew there would be no 'not proven' verdict this time. When the British police arived on 16 February, Chesney's body had already been found in a wood outside Cologne. He had shot himself through the head.

(left) Mrs Bonnar, alias 'Lady Menzies', at her marriage to 'Lord Menzies' (Syndication International)

FRANCE

The Price of Love

When Denise Labbé's two-and-a-half-year-old bastard child drowned in a wash-basin at Blois in November 1954 people couldn't help recalling the two previous occasions on which the unfortunate infant had almost met a similiarly watery end while in its mother's care. The result of the combined wagging of tongues was that 28-year-old Denise was taken in for questioning at the gendarmerie and thence before the examining magistrate; here she confessed to what she enigmatically described as 'a ritual murder' of her daughter. She had, it transpired, fallen under the spell of Second Lieutenant Jacques Algarron of the St Cyr military school; he in turn had fallen under the spell of Friedrich Nietzsche and arrogantly supposed himself to be a representative of that philosopher's breed of 'Supermen'. At any rate, he exerted an unhealthy and total control over Denise Labbé, who was informed on 1 May 1954 that 'The price of our love must be the death of your daughter . . . an innocent victim must be sacrificed.' The idea seemed to be that only through suffering could their union become strong. Exactly one year after the 'monstrous act', Labbé and Algarron stood their trial, she receiving a lifetime of penal servitude, he collecting twenty years' hard labour.

1955

Ruth Ellis

The Last Woman to Hang. *Convicted of shooting her unfaithful lover, Ruth Ellis was the last woman to be hanged in Britain; her controversial execution led in great part to the eventual abolition of the death penalty.*

Ruth was the unremarkable, rather brassy night-club hostess-turned-manageress of The Little Club, a tawdry late-night drinking establishment in London's West End. Her life so far had not been entirely a bed of roses, having been born in 1926 into a large impoverished family, been made pregnant by a married French-Canadian soldier at the age of sixteen, and then left to bring up her son alone. To pay the bills, Ruth took up modelling for a camera club until, at nineteen, she was taken on as a Mayfair club hostess by one Morris Conley, a man much involved in the leisure industries of drinking, gambling and prostitution. Then Ruth married a violent alcoholic named George Ellis, a Southampton dentist. She gave birth to his daughter, Georgina, just before Ellis filed for divorce – it was almost a year to the day after their wedding. Ruth returned to London and willingly into the clutches of Morris Conley again. She briefly hopped back up on her bar stool at Conley's Carroll's club, before being offered the job as his manageress at The Little Club in 1953. Not a bed of roses by any means

Ruth Ellis (right), with David Blakely and a friend at the race circuit

The Magdala Tavern as it looks now, unchanged from that fateful day in 1955

– so if Ruth drank just a bit too much and enjoyed the loud company that gravitated to the club, who could deny her these modest pleasures?

David Blakely was a member of The Little Club, and Ruth was later to claim that he was the first customer she served there. However that may be, there was instant sexual attraction; a good-looking, if somewhat degenerate youth, with a generous manner, a romantic occupation – he was a racing driver – and an above average appetite for drink, Blakely was probably just what Ruth needed at the time.

The romance lasted for about a year, during which time Ruth became pregnant and had an abortion, and seemed to be going about as well as such a match might reasonably be expected to go. And then things began, some said inevitably, to sour. Blakely had started seeing other women, Ruth had started to object, Blakely began to make his escape.

Nevertheless, he and Ruth still saw each other, and despite the fact that she had started living with a man named Desmond Cussen, seemed to be getting on well together. They arranged to meet on Good Friday, 8 April 1955, and David was to pick Ruth up and take her back for drinks at Tanza Road, Hampstead, where his friends Anthony and Carole Linklater lived. In the end, Blakely decided not to collect Ruth, and went back to Tanza Road with Linklater alone. At about 9.30 p.m. Ruth telephoned and was told by Anthony Linklater that David wasn't there. At midnight she presented herself on the doorstep, ringing furiously on the bell; nobody answered. So Ruth attacked Blakely's van parked outside. It wasn't long before the police were advising Mrs Ellis to go home and stop making a nuisance of herself. She did go, but not before pushing in a couple more of the van's windows.

Early the following morning, 9 April, Ruth telephoned the Tanza Road number and whoever answered just hung up. On the 10th, Easter Sunday, she made an early morning telephone call which was answered by 'Ant' Linklater. Ruth just had enough time to blurt out 'I hope you're having an enjoyable holiday . . .' before he put the receiver down. She was going to add 'because you've ruined mine.' That evening, after a day spent with the Linklaters and their new baby on Hampstead Heath, David Blakely, his hosts and a friend named Clive Gunnell were having an impromptu party back at Tanza Road when they ran out of beer. David and Clive Gunnell obligingly drove down to the local, a pub called the Magdala, to stock up, and while they were there took the opportunity to have a quick one for the road back. When they came out of the pub at around 9.20 p.m., they saw Ruth standing there. Ignoring her, Blakely walked to the driver's door of his car. As Ruth followed him

(opposite) The hanging controversy begins (Syndication International)

Daily Mirror

THURS
JULY 14
1955

1½d FORWARD WITH THE PEOPLE
No. 18,046

Millions of people are worried about the fate of RUTH ELLIS. Today we ask our readers—

SHOULD HANGING BE STOPPED?

RUTH ELLIS . . . HER EXECUTION HAS SET THE WHOLE WORLD TALKING.

YESTERDAY was not a happy day in Britain. The sun shone but the nation was upset.

At 9 a.m. in Holloway Gaol a woman of twenty-eight suffered death by hanging. Her body was later buried within the precincts of the prison.

Mrs. Ruth Ellis was not a virtuous woman. She admitted shooting one of her two lovers because she thought he was unfaithful. This was the gruesome end to a sordid affair.

Yet who in Britain yesterday felt happy that this mother of two children should lose her life —even though she herself had taken life?

Do the people of Britain believe that the punishment for murder should be CAPITAL PUNISHMENT?

M.P.s would not go past the prison

Are Members of Parliament satisfied that hanging is the expression of the public will?

Some M.P.s were NOT happy yesterday. Some who were to drive past Holloway Gaol on their way to the House of Commons took a different route to avoid the prison.

Five months ago M.P.s debated capital punishment. On a free vote they decided against a suggestion that the death penalty should be suspended FOR AN EXPERIMENTAL PERIOD OF FIVE YEARS and replaced by life imprisonment.

But did this vote mean that the majority of M.P.s were in favour of hanging? They voted against its suspension — not against its abolition.

One man had to decide her fate

How would they have voted on the straight question: Should we abolish the death penalty for good?

How would they vote today?

Because there is a death sentence, one man has a terrible responsibility. In court the witnesses give evidence, the jury return a verdict, the judge passes sentence. They all represent the public conscience. All did their duty at the trial of Ruth Ellis.

But one man—a professional politician who happens to be Home Secretary—had to decide whether this woman should be reprieved.

What an unenviable task.

While this young woman waited in her prison cell, one man had to decide whether there should be visited on her the retribution prescribed in a pitiless Biblical phrase:

"And thine eye shall not pity; but life shall go for life, eye for eye, tooth for tooth, hand for hand, foot for foot."

These words from the Old Testament Book of Deuteronomy were written probably 2,500 years ago, before the birth of Christ, by an unknown Jewish scribe.

And the enlightened British nation today still follows the teaching of all those centuries ago.

It is understandable why people in

Britain felt uneasy yesterday. In the rush of life the particular case of Ruth Ellis will be forgotten. But the problem of capital punishment remains.

Some murderers attract much public sympathy. There has been more talk about the fate of PRETTY YOUNG Ruth Ellis than there was about the similar fate of UGLY Mrs. Christofi, aged fifty-three, who strangled her daughter-in-law.

But is it unnatural if the execution of a pretty young mother causes public distress?

One fact remains:

Whether a murderess is pretty or ugly.

Whether a murderer is young or old.

Whether a killer attracts public sympathy or not—the lawful penalty is death by hanging.

Time for a change in the Law?

What the Ruth Ellis case has done is to focus attention on the whole problem of capital punishment.

People are asking:

Is hanging degrading to a civilised nation? Has the time come for hanging to be abolished in Britain?

or—

Should hanging be retained as the just penalty for taking life?

The "Mirror" believes that the public should be able to voice its views.

Today we ask readers to give their verdict. There is a voting form in the Back Page.

Please express your opinion on the voting form in the Back Page

she pulled a revolver from her handbag and shot at him. Blakely ran, then fell, and Ruth stood over him and emptied the chamber into his back.

Ruth made no attempt to escape, and by an irony an off-duty policeman had witnessed the whole scene. Later at the police station, Ruth

UNITED STATES

The Death of Flight 629

Jack Gilbert Graham insured his mother's life for $37,000 and then planted a bomb on United Airlines Flight 629 which she boarded at Denver. The device exploded just ten minutes after take-off, killing all 44 passengers and crew. Graham, who had nurtured a hatred of his mother ever since she placed him in an orphanage for the first eight years of his life, readily confessed and was sent to the Colorado Penitentiary gas chamber in January 1957 (see also 1949).

Jack Gilbert Graham (Topham)

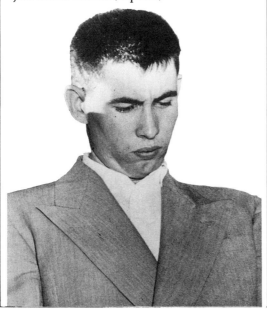

admitted that 'I intended to find David and shoot him.' She was just as co-operative at her Old Bailey trial, though in deference to her legal advisers Ruth formally entered a plea of not guilty. In reality, there was not much in legal terms that could be said in Ruth Ellis's defence; she had been clearly seen by witnesses to shoot Blakely, she had admitted to the police that she killed him, and any plea of provocation would have been futile because of Ruth's premeditation and planning.

It is almost certain that if Ruth Ellis were to be put on trial today, charged with the same offence, she would advance a plea of 'diminished responsibility'. This defence was made possible by the Homicide Act of 1957, which states that 'Where a person kills or is a party to the killing of another, he shall not be convicted of murder if he was suffering from such abnormality of mind (whether arising from a condition of arrested or retarded development of mind or any inherent causes or induced by disease or injury) as substantially impaired his mental responsibility for his acts or omissions in doing or being party to the killing'.

In practical terms this converts the murder charge into one of manslaughter, a considerable advantage in the barbarous days when a capital sentence was mandatory for murder. The plea of diminished responsibility puts the burden of proof on the defence and, as in the case of insanity pleas, the proof need not be 'beyond reasonable doubt' but 'on a balance of probabilities'. Medical evidence must obviously be presented on the defendant's behalf as to their state of mind, but it is for the *jury* and not expert witnesses to decide, on the basis of the evidence offered, whether the 'abnormality' amounts to diminished responsibility.

As it was, Ruth Ellis was predictably found guilty of murder and, according to the law of the time, sentenced to death. Ruth rejected all attempts to persuade her to appeal, and despite petitions galore calling for commutation of the sentence she was hanged at Holloway Prison in London at 9 a.m. on Wednesday, 13 July 1955. Among her last words, on being told of

The official post-mortem report on Ruth Ellis after her execution

POST-MORTEM EXAMINATION.

Name ELLIS, Ruth   **Apparent Age** 28 years

At H.M. Prison, Holloway   **Date** July 13 1955

EXTERNAL EXAMINATION	
Nourishment	Well nourished.
Marks of Violence,	Evidence of proper care and attention.
	Height – 5ft. 2ins. Weight – 103 lbs.
Identification, etc. ...	DEEP IMPRESSIONS AROUND NECK of noose with suspension point about 1 inch in front of the angle of the L.lower jaw. Vital changes locally and in the tissues beneath as a consequence of sudden constriction. No ecchymoses in the face – or, indeed, elsewhere. No marks of restraint.
How long dead	1 hour.
INTERNAL EXAMINATION	
Skull	Fracture-dislocation of the spine at C.2 with a 2 inch gap
Brain Meninges	and transverse separation of the spinal cord at the same level.
Mouth, Tongue, Oesophagus	Fractures of both wings of the hyoid and the R.wing of the thyroid cartilage. Larynx also fractured.
Larynx, Trachea, Lungs ...	Air passages clear and lungs quite free from disease or other change. No engorgement. No asphyxial changes.
Pericardium, Heart and Blood Vessels	No organic disease. No petechiae or other evidence of asphyxial change.
Stomach and Contents ...	Small food residue, and odour of brandy. No disease.
Peritoneum, Intestines, Etc.	Normal.
Liver and Gall Bladder ...	Terminal congestion only.
Spleen	Normal.
Kidneys and Ureters	Slight terminal congestion only.
Bladder, Etc.	Lower abdominal operation scar for ectopic pregnancy operation
Generative Organs ...	in L.tube, now healed. No pregnancy.
Other Remarks	Deceased was a healthy subject at the time of death. Mark of suspension normally situated and injuries from judicial hanging – to the spinal columnand cord – such as must have caused instant death.
CAUSE OF DEATH ...	Injuries to the central nervous system consequent upon judicial hanging.

Signed

M.D. Lond.

146, Harley St , W 1, and Guy's Hospital (Pathologist) Reader in Forensic Medicine, London University.

the people petitioning on her behalf, were: 'I am very grateful to them. But I am quite happy to die.'

For what consolation it may have been to her, Ruth's execution had finally sickened politicians and public alike of the capital sentence. Ruth Ellis was the last woman to be hanged in Britain, and a decade later, with the double execution of Peter Allen and Gwynne Evans in 1965, hanging effectively ceased.

1956

The Fatal Triangle

One of history's most curious examples of the fatal love triangle, solved to the satisfaction of a jury by a recreation of the murder by forensic serologists.

The Albert Goozee story, at least in as far as it concerns the criminologist, began in January 1955, when the ex-merchant seaman took lodgings with the Leakey family at their home in Poole, Dorset. The family comprised Thomas Leakey, a World War I veteran who had lost a leg in the service of his country and now operated a wood-lathe in a local factory, his 53-year-old wife Lydia Margaret and their twelve-year-old daughter Norma. The Leakeys had two more children, but they had grown up and left home. Goozee, somewhere in his early thirties, was, in the parlance of the day, a 'ladies' man'. During his stay with the Leakeys he ran through a number of mundane service jobs – bus conductor, roundsman, that sort of thing – and was usually dismissed for over-familiarity with female customers. He was also becoming decidedly familiar with Margaret Leakey, though it is fair to say that she never complained.

Norma Leakey's thirteenth birthday fell on 4 February 1955, and 'uncle' Albert was the life and soul – he even managed to win a kiss in the dark from Mrs Leakey during the game of Postman's Knock. That night, according to Goozee, Margaret Leakey crept uninvited into his bed, followed shortly afterwards by Norma; Albert Goozee must have thought all his Christmases had come at once. However, it was not a situation guaranteed to result in marital harmony, and after some months the long-suffering Thomas Leakey took himself off to Andover.

Leakey obviously thought better of his move, because at the beginning of June 1956 he returned to Poole and threw Goozee out instead. And while Albert Goozee might then have been happy to leave well alone, he was pestered by notes from Margaret Leakey asking him to 'come back home, and I will be a mother to you', or words to that effect. He continued to see the matronly Mrs Leakey, but by no means exclusively. On 15 June, a Friday, Albert Goozee and two friends visited the theatre in Bournemouth. Outside they encountered a woman and her teenaged daughter trying to get in to see the show. Generously, or so the woman thought, Goozee offered a spare ticket to the fourteen-year-old while her mother was found a place at the rear of the stalls. However, Albert's motives proved far from altruistic, and before the entertainment had reached the first interval he was hauled into the manager's office and thence to the police station where he was charged with indecently assaulting the girl. Two days later, on Sunday afternoon, Albert Goozee collected Margaret and Norma Leakey from their home and ferried them in his car to a picnic at Bignell Wood, in the New Forest.

What followed we have only Albert Goozee's word for; his companions never lived to tell the tale. According to Goozee, then, it was Mrs Leakey's intention to make a wood fire on which to boil the picnic kettle, and accordingly she went equipped with an axe! 'Mrs Leakey suggested we take one of the smaller paths into the forest, which we did. We started to get a fire going. She then told Norma to go for a walk while the kettle was boiling to see if she could find some bluebells. I had an idea that this was only a blind. Norma walked away and left us . . . Next thing I knew Norma was standing over her mother, screaming "You beast, why don't you leave Albert alone?" I did not realise she had the axe in her hand . . . She struck her mother across the head with the axe; she hit her once and went into hysterics. I hit Norma a couple of times in the face with my fist and she stopped screaming.'

As Goozee pushed Norma into the back of the car Mrs Leakey was struggling to get into the front passenger seat, ending up slumped half in and half out of the vehicle with a knife in her hand. Goozee, according to his own narrative, tried to take the knife, but accidentally slipped and fell, and in doing so became impaled on the blade: 'I thought my life was finished, so I jabbed the knife in her. Norma came out of the car and came at me screaming "What have you done to my mother; why don't you do the same to me?" After that my mind must have gone blank. I don't remember stabbing Norma. I passed out. I came to about an hour later and they were both lying there. They were both dead so I got in the car and drove down in the direction I could hear the traffic.'

The strain of driving became too much for Albert, and he stopped at some point along the Cadnam–Brook Road where a passing motorist found him staggering about, bleeding and rambling that 'There has been a murder in the forest'; adding, 'I did it; I've got a knife in me; get the police'. And so Albert Goozee came to the attention of the police for the second time in a weekend.

When his bloodstained car was searched, detectives found a letter addressed to the Chief Constable of Bournemouth, and a knife with a six-and-a-half-inch blade which proved to be the weapon which had stabbed Mrs Leakey, her daughter, and Goozee himself. The distinctly odd letter read, in part: 'I was told to leave the house. I did, but Mrs Leakey still comes after me so I have come to the only possible way out before I go after another young girl. Please do not put too much trouble on my brother because he knows how Mrs Leakey and Norma went after me. I went into the Army to get away from it all [in fact his service lasted just two weeks before he bought himself out]; but once you have messed about with a young girl there is not much you can do for yourself . . .'

'*The only possible way out.*' Was that the truth of it? Did Albert Goozee deliberately set out to kill his lover and her daughter? Was it Goozee who had packed the axe, with a far more sinister plan in mind than chopping wood? Was it Goozee who finished the job off with a vicious blade, and then stabbed himself for effect?

As it turned out, the forensic serologists were able to cast light on the sequence of events. Albert Goozee had claimed that, despite his mind having 'gone blank', he stabbed his two victims *after* he had fallen on the knife himself. If this were true, then the blood of the Leakeys should have been predominant on the blade. Laboratory tests showed, however, that most of the blood was Group O – Goozee's group – while the only Group A blood, which the two women shared, was found around the hilt. The inevitable conclusion was that 'the knife had first been used on the women, and only then plunged into Goozee'.

It certainly convinced the jury at Winchester Assizes, and Albert William Goozee was convicted and sentenced to death, though this was later commuted to life imprisonment. The ironic thing was that despite all Goozee's self-recrimination about having sexual relations with Norma Leakey, it was just a fantasy – the post-mortem examination revealed that Norma was still a virgin when she died.

1957

The Case of Dr Adams

One of the most disgraceful examples of 'trial by newspaper' in modern criminal history. From the time he was charged, Adams was pilloried by the Press, with the exception of veteran crime reporter Percy Hoskins – whose faith was rewarded when Dr Adams was acquitted of murder.

John Bodkin Adams was born on 21 January 1899 at Randalstown, County Antrim, the son of a prosperous watchmaker. He first attended school at Coleraine, where the family had moved, and later studied medicine at Queen's University, Belfast. In 1921 Adams graduated with a fairly good degree and, after a year on the wards of a hospital in Bristol, went into general practice in Eastbourne. It was his first acquaintance with a town in which he would spend the rest of his life. The early years were good to Dr Adams, and if he was not a brilliant doctor, he was an attentive one who quickly made a secure reputation for himself, his portly figure atop a motorcycle becoming a familiar sight in the resort. The doctor made a particular point of cultivating patients among the wealthier 'county' set and minor gentry, and within a decade had enlarged his practice and become the most fashionable medic in Eastbourne. Adams's particular joy was his collection of motor cars, among which he numbered two Rolls-Royces. There was also another side to Dr

Adams – the man who worshipped regularly with the Plymouth Brethren and taught Bible class on Sundays. In short, he was nobody's idea of a serial killer.

In July 1956 Mrs Gertrude Hullett, widow of a Lloyd's underwriter and a patient of Adams's, fell seriously ill. Adams had already been treating her for nervous collapse, and as a result of regular prescriptions of barbiturate drugs the unfortunate woman had become addicted to them. Although his patient was still alive, if unconscious, Dr Adams felt for some reason that he should alert the coroner to this 'peculiar' case and advise a post-mortem. On 23 July Mrs Hullett died, and Adams certified the cause as cerebral haemhorrage. However, the autopsy revealed this to be a *very* 'peculiar' case, because when Dr Francis Camps performed the autopsy he declared cause of death as barbiturate poisoning. At the inquest on Mrs Hullett the coroner, Dr Sommerville, found that she had committed suicide; he also added in summing up that Dr Adams had been guilty of 'an extraordinary degree of careless treatment'.

It was also discovered that Mrs Hullett had left her Rolls-Royce to Adams in her will. Now the tongues began to wag; now the memories began to be jogged. And by the time Scotland Yard had completed their report it was known that over the previous ten years Dr Adams had been a beneficiary in the wills of more than 100 patients, and had received numerous expensive gifts, including another Rolls-Royce. Some were constrained to joke blackly that Adams made his rounds with a bottle of morphine in one hand and a blank will in the other.

It was the case of Mrs Edith Alice Morrell that the police decided to prosecute. Mrs Morrell, the widow of a wealthy businessman, had arrived in Eastbourne from Liverpool in 1949, where Dr Adams had treated her for severe arthritis and partial paralysis. Adams's treatment consisted, as it often did, mainly of heroin and morphine. As might be excused in a person of her age and infirmity (as well as her intake of heroin and morphine), Mrs Morrell tended to be a little eccentric and unpredictable. She made half a dozen or more wills, one of which bequeathed *everything* to her dear, understanding doctor; then she made another in which he received not a brass farthing. Next she promised him a car and a chest of silver – then she denied it. Greedy as he certainly was, Adams even went to the sick woman's solicitor and asked him to add a codicil mentioning the gift; the solicitor, quite rightly, refused to do any such thing. In August 1950 Mrs Morrell made her last will, this time relenting and leaving the silver and the car to Adams; but capricious to the last, Edith Morrell made a codicil just two months before her death on 13 November 1950, withdrawing the gift. In fact it was Mrs Morrell's son Arthur who gave Dr Adams not only the box of silver and the Rolls-Royce, but also an antique cupboard he had long admired. Dr Adams was treating his patient right up to her last breath, and when that had been taken he certified death as being due to cerebral thrombosis.

During the trial of Dr Adams for the murder of Mrs Morrell, the Old Bailey jury heard a great deal of evidence from the nurses attending the deceased as to the medication administered by Adams – barbiturates, secomid, morphine, heroin . . . all in increasing quantities. The implication was clear: the doctor had been slowly killing his patient. Unfortunately it was quite impossible to verify the amounts of drugs in the body at death because Dr Adams had given immediate authorisation for cremation, making exhumation for autopsy impossible. The court also heard from Detective Superintendent Hannam, who had interviewed Dr Adams and recalled that in response to questions about Mrs Morrell's death, the doctor claimed: 'Easing the passing of a dying person is not all that wicked. She wanted to die – that cannot be murder. It is impossible to accuse a doctor.' He was wrong.

Unsurprisingly a scandal such as this – a doctor killing off his elderly patients for a share of the estate – attracted the world's Press like vultures to carrion; and whether they believed Adams's guilt or not, most journalists *hoped* it was true. It has been said, quite fairly in retrospect, that John Bodkin Adams was tried and almost convicted by the newspapers. As always there are distinguished exceptions, in this case the redoubtable crime reporter Percy Hoskins who, against the odds, persuaded his newspaper, the *Daily Express*, to follow his own belief that Adams was innocent.* In fact, all that Percy Hoskins had done was the same as Geoffrey Lawrence QC, Adams's defence counsel – he had carefully looked at the case, and realised that for all their braggadocio the Crown had a very weak case. For a start the supposedly damaging testimony of the nurses who gave evidence of apparently reckless drug administrations was quite at variance with the written records contained in the medical log books. Furthermore, Adams had absolutely no personal motive for terminating Mrs Morrell's life – he stood to gain nothing from the will, and he knew it. However, it was perhaps fortuitous that the doctor was charged only with the one murder – it ensured that suspicious-looking details of other patients' deaths could not be introduced as evidence.

On 10 April 1957 Dr Adams was declared not guilty. Although he resigned from the National Health Service, he courageously returned to Eastbourne where he took on a few loyal private patients. Adams was subsequently struck off the Medical Register, but reinstated in 1961 when he resumed general practice. He died in 1983 at the age of 84.

Controversy still surrounds the Adams case; some remain convinced he was a murderer, others that he practised euthanasia. The truth of the matter is probably that Dr Adams was simply a sloppy doctor with an ingratiating manner and an eye to personal advancement.

*When Adams was found not guilty, Lord Beaverbrook, proprietor of the *Express*, who had always been sceptical of his stance telephoned Percy Hoskins in Eastbourne with the message: 'Two men have been acquitted today – Adams and Hoskins.'

1958

Killing of Johnny Stompanato

Celebrated Hollywood 'murder', in which Cheryl Crane, the fourteen-year-old daughter of star Lana Turner, stabbed to death her mother's gangster lover. In the end a sympathetic jury returned a verdict of justifiable homicide.

Ranking high among the tawdry scandals of Hollywood was the killing of actress Lana Turner's gangster boyfriend Johnny Stompanato. Johnny had his finger in so many crooked pies that his assassination did not come as much of a surprise; what caused the sensation was that his killer should be the screen star's fourteen-year-old daughter Cheryl Crane.

Lana (born Julia) Turner's life had already been touched by similar tragedy when she was barely a teenager and her stevedore father was murdered by robbers in a San Francisco alleyway. Her introduction to the silver screen has become one of Tinsel Town's most enduring legends. It is said that at the age of just fifteen, Julia Turner was strutting down Sunset Avenue wearing the skintight sweater and stiletto heels so beloved of aspiring starlets when she was seen by journalist Billy Wilkerson. In true Hollywood style he asked her if she'd like to be in the movies – really! And for a change somebody meant what they said. With Wilkerson's encouragement Julia got herself an agent, and, through him, a small part in the very unmemorable *They Won't Forget* and a new name – Lana.

At the age of nineteen, Lana Turner entered into the first of what would be a long succession of less than ideal marriages. Within two months of the ceremony she had parted from bandleader Artie Shaw and later they divorced. Lana's second husband was businessman Stephen Crane; they met at a nightclub, danced together, and were married the following week. Unfortunately, Crane was not yet divorced from his previous wife and the marriage to Lana was temporarily annulled; by this time she was pregnant. Lana and Crane finally married and baby Cheryl was born five months later. When this marriage also collapsed Lana Turner became Mrs Henry 'Bob' Topping, and millionaire Topping was succeeded by one of the screen's most famous Tarzans, Lex Barker. The relationship with Barker came to an acrimonious end provoked, it is said, by Cheryl's jealousy, and Lana married in fairly quick succession Fred May, Robert Eaton and Ronald Danse. Cheryl was now a confused and insecure ten-year-old with no very high opinion of her mother or her mother's morals. Just how seriously the relationship had deteriorated was illustrated by an incident at one of her many expensive boarding schools. Told by a teacher that if she did not write a letter to her mother she would go to bed without supper, Cheryl wrote: 'Dear Mother, this is not a letter, it is a meal ticket . . .'

Lana, meanwhile, had fallen for the smooth patter of part-time gigolo, part-time crook Johnny Stompanato. Johnny, some say, had telephoned the star for a bet, and invited her out on a blind date. Lana, more impulsive than discriminating, became obsessively fond of her new lover and, it has to be said, he of her. In fact this was what fuelled the fires of tragedy that would end in his untimely and brutal

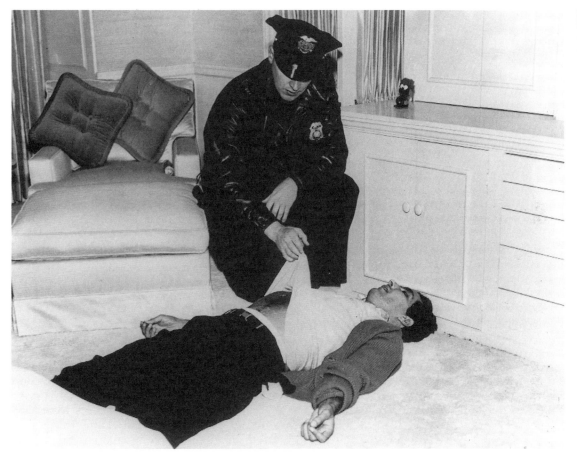

Johnny Stompanato lies dead from a stab wound (AP/
Topham)

death. Johnny became violently and irrationally
jealous, and when Lana was obliged to travel
to England to film *Another Time, Another Place*,
he followed her out of jealousy of her co-star
Sean Connery. It is recalled that Stompanato
once burst on to the film set and threatened
Connery with a gun – an ill-considered move
that ended with the actor laying out the gangster with one swift blow to the chin. The
quarrels between Lana and Johnny became so
aggressive that the English police were finally
forced to deport Stompanato after he had tried
to strangle Lana. Still they clung desperately to
each other, and surprisingly the relationship
actually brought young Cheryl closer to her
mother than she had been for a long time; of

all her mother's husbands and lovers Johnny
was the one Cheryl seemed to take to.

By now Cheryl's enforced independence had
given her a maturity and approach to life far
in advance of her fourteen years. During the
school holidays at Easter 1958, Cheryl joined
her mother and Johnny Stompanato at their
home in North Bedford Drive, where there was
certainly no hint of the horror that was to come.
On the evening of 4 April, Good Friday, Cheryl,
Lana and Johnny were at home when one of
the frequent quarrels erupted, during which
Stompanato became his usual threatening,
bullying self and Cheryl slipped into the
kitchen and picked up a carving knife; she said
later that she was afraid Johnny would hurt

her mother. The row between Lana and Johnny was escalating, and according to Lana's later testimony, 'I would have to do everything he told me or he'd cut my face or cripple me... he would kill me, and my daughter, and my mother...'

Events were beginning to take on a menacing physical threat, with Stompanato flailing his fists around... but before he or Lana realised what was happening, Cheryl rushed up to Johnny and drove the nine-inch blade of the carving knife into his stomach. Although he was still alive when the doctor arrived, by the time the police got to the scene Johnny Stompanato was dead.

In the days between the killing and the inquest the sensation was kept burning by the publication of Lana Turner's letters to her lover which had inexplicably found their way from the dead man's apartment to the offices of the Los Angeles *Herald Examiner*. The coroner's inquest opened on 11 April and was broadcast live on national television. Lana Turner gave the performance of her life as the abused and terrified mother fearful for her own and her child's safety from a man insane with violent jealousy, and told how, in the end, that innocent child was forced by circumstance to commit an unspeakable act in defence of her mother's life. There was scarcely a dry eye in the court, and after a token retirement the jury returned a verdict of justifiable homicide; Cheryl Crane was released to the joy of all.

Johnny's remains were flown back to his native Illinois where he was given an extravagant funeral. One of his former employers, the

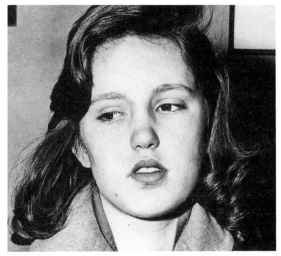

Cheryl during the inquest into Stompanato's death (Topham)

gambler and gangster Micky Cohen, said of Johnny: 'Look, this was a great guy.' When the fuss had died down a little Johnny Stompanato's brother sued Lana and Stephen Crane for $800,000 damages, alleging parental negligence; in the end he accepted an out-of-court settlement of just $20,000.

Unlike many stars whose careers were shattered by personal scandals, Lana Turner survived the Johnny Stompanato incident and many have observed that the sensation had actually revived a flagging career. Cheryl Crane became a successful businesswoman in the field of real estate, and later published her autobiography in which she restated her court testimony on the Stompanato case.

AUSTRALIA

Just Sign Here

Aborigine Rupert Max Stuart was picked up in 1958 in connection with the murder of nine-year-old Mary Hattam at Ceduna, South Australia, and according to the police made a full confession. Max Stuart later retracted the confession, claiming that police officers had written the document and forced him to sign his name. There was considerable support for this accusation in view of Stuart's poor grasp of the English language. Following a controversial trial and a long sequence of appeals against his death sentence, Max Stuart was imprisoned for life.

1959

Guenther Fritz Podola

Murdered on Duty *Podola shot a police officer while resisting arrest for burglary. In the scuffle to recapture him, Podola hit his head and later claimed memory loss as a defence at his trial.*

By the middle of July 1959 the Metropolitan police had begun to close in on yet another of the capital's seedier villains; this time it was a man calling himself Fisher, who had been engaged in the unpleasant pursuit of blackmailing a 30-year-old model named June Schiffman whom he had previously burgled. On the afternoon of the 13th the telephone rang in Mrs Schiffman's South Kensington apartment; she lifted the receiver and managed to keep the conversation going long enough for the call to be traced to a nearby telephone box. Waiting for just such a break Detective Sergeants John Sandford and Raymond Purdy sped to the call box on South Kensington underground station, dragged its inhabitant out and hustled him up the wide flight of steps to the exit. In the ensuing scuffle the blackmailer broke away and fled into a block of flats in Onslow Square; at the entrance the policemen separated, DS Sandford trying to rouse the block's caretaker. Suddenly the fugitive leapt out of hiding and shot Raymond Purdy through the heart before fleeing along Sydney Place.

Over the next two days the police mounted a massive manhunt for a man described as tall, slim, and speaking with an American accent. Although identifiable fingerprints had been left on a marble ledge at the flats, there was no matching set in the Fingerprint Department's records. On 16 July the manager of the Claremont House Hotel, Kensington, called to tell the police that one of his guests, a Mr Paul Camay, bad been acting oddly ever since the fatal shooting. By now police had traced the killer's fingerprints to a 30-year-old German immigrant named Guenther Podola; he had been deported from Canada the previous year following sentences for robbery. Podola, Fisher and Camay were evidently one and the same man. On the afternoon of 16 July a team of detectives arrested Podola in his hotel room where they also found the weapon which had robbed their colleague of his life. During the encounter it was said that Podola struck his head on a door, and when he arrived at the police station he was dazed and suffering a number of superficial injuries. It was felt expedient to transfer Podola to St Stephen's Hospital, where he was put under observation while hand-

Scene outside the Claremont House Hotel as police lead Podola away

207

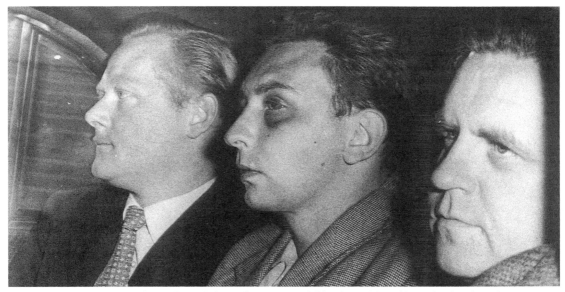

Podola on his way to remand in Brixton Prison; the controversial bruises still visible on his face (Syndication International)

cuffed to the bed. On 20 July he was charged with murder and remanded to Brixton Prison.

By the time his case reached the Old Bailey in September, Podola had taken advantage of the opportunity to elaborate his 'dazed' sen-

BERMUDA

'I Get Nasty . . .'

In March 1959 a 72-year-old woman was found dead in her home at Southlands beach, Bermuda; she had been raped and bludgeoned. A month later a second elderly woman was found in identical circumstances, and on 28 September a 29-year-old woman's body was found floating near a coral reef, mutilated by sharks but showing sufficient evidence of having been murdered. Wendell Willis Lightbourne first came to the attention of the police because he had been on the beach on the day of the last murder looking very agitated. Eventually the nineteen-year-old golf caddy broke down under questioning and confessed to the murder, concluding: 'I get nasty.' Lightbourne was convicted and sent to Britain to serve his sentence.

sations into a defence plea of total memory loss. Thus, before the trial could even begin, a jury had to be empanelled to decide whether Podola was fit to stand trial. Based on observations made in St Stephen's and at Brixton, four doctors supported the prisoner's claim that he was suffering amnesia, and two reported that in their view he was malingering. The jury also decided that Podola's memory loss was not genuine and he was put on trial on 24 September. The bulk of the Crown's case rested on the eye-witness account of the shooting and the events leading up to it by Detective Sergeant Sandford. Speaking from the dock in his own defence Podola stubbornly repeated that he had no recollection of the incident at all. After a retirement of just half an hour, the jury returned with a verdict of guilty and Podola was sentenced to death. Through his attorney, Podola applied to the Court of Criminal Appeal, but the application was turned down, their Lordships deciding that 'Even if the loss of memory had been a genuine loss of memory, that did not of itself render the appellant insane.'

Guenther Podola was hanged at Wandsworth Prison on 5 November 1959, the last person in Britain to be executed for killing a policeman.

1960

Michael Copeland

The Carbon-Copy Murders. *Copeland committed two murders – identical in every way – because he hated homosexuals. A third killing, in Germany, was committed for no reason at all.*

On Sunday, 12 June 1960 the body of 60-year-old William Arthur Elliott was found in isolated Clod Hill Lane, which crosses the moors near Baslow; he had been wearing no shoes. This was of great interest to the Chesterfield police who, on the previous day, had been called to Park Road where an Isetta 'bubble' car had been found crashed and stained with blood; inside was a pair of men's shoes. While police began a search of the desolate moorland for the weapon used to bludgeon Mr Elliott to death, detectives were making inquiries around his home at 9 Haddon Road, Bakewell, in an attempt to piece together the last hours of his life. In particular they wanted to talk to anybody who saw Elliott's ivory-coloured bubble car, registration number KLU 488, either before or after its accident.

As the search widened, the inquiry team, led by Detective Superintendent Leonard Stretton, learned of a bizarre incident that occurred about a week before William Elliott was killed. Fifty-one-year-old bus cleaner William Atkinson, of North Wingfield, claimed that he had been attacked in Boythorpe Road, which runs close to Park Road, in the same area the bubble car had been found. Mr Atkinson bore a remarkable physical likeness to the moors victim, and police had to allow the possibility that he may have been assaulted in mistake for Mr Elliott. What's more, the two men were known to each other, both being habitués of the Spread Eagle public house in Chesterfield.

Another much-needed clue was provided by Gladys Vickers of Sutton Spring Wood. Mrs Vickers told police that she thought she may have seen Mr Elliott attacked the night before his body was found; she knew Mr Elliott and said: 'I saw him being chased along an alley outside the Royal Oak public house. The man chasing him was dark-haired, swarthy, and with thin features, and he caught up with him. Then I heard someone say "Oh" and groan.' The possibility now arose that Elliott's bubble car had been used by his killer to transport the body up to the moor, and had then been abandoned back in Chesterfield.

Despite an investigation during the course of which more than 10,000 statements were taken, Superintendent Stretton's murder squad were reluctantly forced to concede that, for the time being anyway, the killer had slipped through their net. At the inquest into his death, the coroner declared that William Elliott had been murdered by 'person or persons unknown'.

Almost a year later, on Wednesday, 29 March 1961, an unidentified man was found dead from severe injuries in Clod Hill Lane, at almost the exact spot where William Elliott had been found murdered. The victim of the so-called 'Carbon-Copy Murder' was named as 40-year-old Chesterfield industrial chemist George Gerald Stobbs. The police were now working on the assumption that this was a 'carbon-copy' killing, and Detective Superintendent Stretton was given charge of the new investigation.

Later it was revealed that an abandoned car had been found in exactly the same spot in Park Road that Elliott's blood-stained bubble car had been left.

What happened next would tax the imagination of a crime-fiction writer. Police issued a statement on 1 April which revealed another dramatic similarity to the original 'bubble-car murder'. It appeared that a man named Gillespie, living near Stubbing Court, and bearing a great resemblance to the victim Gerald Stobbs, was attacked shortly before the latest killing. As in the case of the assault on William Atkinson before the Elliott murder, it was entirely reasonable that Dr Gillespie was mistaken for Stobbs. But already a firm link was being established between the two murders. An unbelievably coy local newspaper reported on 3 April 1961:

PROBE INTO DOUBLE LIVES OF VICTIMS
Undercover Man in Hunt for Killer

It was announced by officers investigating the 'Carbon-Copy Murders' that they are to give an 'undercover' man the task of infiltrating the circles in which both of the victims moved. Police now believe that both Mr Elliott and Mr Stobbs led double lives of which even their closest relatives were unaware. Both men had acquaintances in common and drank in the same public house – the Three Horseshoes at Chesterfield.

For 'double lives' read 'closet homosexuals'.

Despite this new revelation and the continued investigations by the Derbyshire constabulary, the case remained unsolved over the succeeding months. The only further dramatic incident was the death of 63-year-old Arthur Jenkinson shortly after he had been interviewed by the police. Although the coroner's jury returned a verdict of suicide, there was some persistent rumour that Mr Jenkinson had been murdered – had been overcome and had his head forced into the gas oven.

As month followed month the likelihood of getting to the bottom of the Carbon-Copy Mystery grew more remote. And so it might have remained but for the determination of the Chesterfield detectives.

During the investigation of the Elliott murder one of the suspects questioned was 21-year-old Michael Copeland. Copeland was on National Service in Germany, but at the time had been on leave and living at home in Chesterfield. He already had a police record, but it was not this that drew Copeland to the attention of the police. He had apparently boasted to his girlfriend that he was the killer and she, honest girl, had gone to the police. Apart from this piece of bravado there was nothing tangible to link Copeland with the crime, and he was released after questioning and resumed his tour of duty in Germany. But now Michael Copeland was back in Chesterfield; in fact he arrived back just a short time before the murder of George Stobbs. He was again taken into custody for questioning, and although he could not account for his whereabouts on the night of the murder there was no reason to suspect

A First for Forensic Botany

On 7 July 1960 eight-year-old Graeme Thorne – whose parents had recently won a large sum of money on the Sydney lottery – was abducted on his way to school; the kidnapper later demanded a ransom of A£25,000. On 16 August Graeme's body was found on a stretch of waste land ten miles from his home. Stephen Leslie Bradley was trapped by the ingenuity of forensic botanists who proved that fungus spores found in the victim's lungs came from a rare combination of trees found only in Bradley's garden.

Copeland more than anybody else without an alibi. Or was there?

It was Chief Inspector Thomas Peat who first made the connection. Both Elliott and Stobbs were homosexual. Suppose their killer was a homophobe – suppose Copeland was homophobic? And so, slowly, Peat began to cultivate the confidence of his suspect. As it turned out it was a short-lived exercise, because Copeland got into a drunken brawl and earned himself four months inside. However, on his release there was another policeman waiting to keep up the pressure. It took Inspector Bradshaw two years, but he managed to build up a strong relationship with Copeland, who began by revealing small confidences and ended confessing not only to the killing of Elliott and Stobbs because they were homosexuals ('It was something I really hated'), but also the quite inexplicable murder of a German boy while he was on service. In November 1960, Gunther Helm-brecht, sixteen years old, was stabbed to death while walking with a girl in the forest near the town of Verden in Germany. That same night Copeland staggered into the guard room at his barracks with a knife wound in his leg and explained that he had been attacked by two German civilians. An obvious suspect, Copeland was intensively questioned, but nothing concrete could be found to link him with the death of Helmbrecht. Until now.

At his trial in March 1965, Michael Copeland claimed that he had made the confessions only in order to force a trial so that he could establish his innocence and get the police off his back. The court did not believe a word of it, and Copeland was found guilty and sentenced to death. At the time the whole issue of capital punishment was under review in England, and his sentence was commuted to one of life imprisonment.

1961

Edwin Albert Bush

A Question of Identity. *This was the first successful use of the newly introduced Identikit system in identifying a killer. Bush stabbed Mrs Elsie Batten to death and was recognised by a patrolling policeman three days later.*

The Identikit system of identification was the culmination of research and development carried out by the Los Angeles Police Department, notably by Hugh McDonald. At its inception the 'kit' comprised a set of interchangeable transparencies of drawings. These depicted the variations on facial features – eyes, noses, ears, et cetera – which in a collaboration between the police operator and a witness could be assembled to give a composite picture of the wanted person. In theory it was possible to combine the components into thousands of millions of likenesses; in practice the system

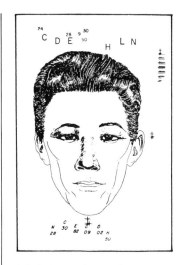

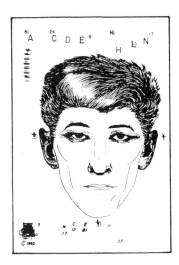

Edwin Bush, flanked by the two Identikit pictures which led to his arrest

Interior of Louis Meier's antiquities shop showing, centre right, the collection of swords

proved rudimentary and inaccurate – even, as in the case of the 'A6 Murder', a possible hindrance to the course of justice.

In 1959 the concept of Identikit was introduced to the investigating officers of Scotland Yard, but it was not until 1961 that the system was put to practical use. Britain's first Identikit Face was that of 21-year-old Edwin Albert Bush, author of a senseless and lacklustre crime in the heart of London's theatreland. Bush, obligingly enough for the launch of Identikit, was a fairly distinctive half-caste Indian who had walked into Louis Meier's antiquities shop in Cecil Court on 2 March 1961 – the day before the murder – and made inquiries as to the cost of a dress sword. He had been told £15, and then he went across the pedestrian court to the shop of a gunsmith named Roberts who replied to his question that, yes, he did occasionally buy swords, but would need to see it before agreeing a price.

On the following morning Edwin Bush returned to Louis Meier's shop, where he stabbed to death Meier's assistant, Mrs Elsie Batten, wife of Mark Batten, President of the Royal Society of Sculptors, and helped himself to a dress sword. At 10 a.m. he re-opened his transaction with the gunsmith, leaving the ill-gotten blade in the care of his son Paul Roberts, suggesting a price of, say, £10. He never returned to hear the gunsmith's verdict, but Bush (as prime suspect in the murder) could now be reliably identified by three people. This enabled a fairly accurate Identikit portrait to be made; accurate enough, anyway, for Police Constable John Cole to identify and arrest the subject while on patrol in Old Compton Street, Soho, on 8 March.

At Bow Street police station where he was interviewed by Detective Chief Superintendent John Bliss, Bush expressed the opinion that the Identikit looked like him, but denied any connection with the killing of Elsie Batten. However, it was not long before Edwin Bush was making his statement: 'I went to the back of the shop and started looking through the daggers, telling her I might want to buy one, but I picked one up and hit her in the back . . . I then lost my nerve and picked up a stone vase and hit her with it. I grabbed a knife and hit her once in the stomach and once in the neck.'

But aside from his confession, Edwin Bush's catalogue of carelessness had not ended at regularly showing his face in the area where he had committed murder; he had also left behind in the shop an identifiable footprint. There was blood on his clothing, and two fingerprints and a palm print on the sheet of paper he had used to wrap the sword.

Edwin Bush stood trial at the Old Bailey on 12 and 13 May. In his evidence he admitted going into Mr Meier's shop with the intention of stealing a ceremonial sword; he was then, he said, going to sell the sword to Mr Roberts in order to buy an engagement ring for his girlfriend. Bush then began to haggle over the price and: 'She let off about my colour and said, "You niggers are all the same. You come in and never buy anything", I lost my head . . .' He then repeated his previous account of the killing.

Bush had the benefit of Mr Christmas Humphreys QC as his defender, but at the end of the trial he was convicted, sentenced to death by Mr Justice Stevenson, and hanged. Of PC Cole's part in the apprehension of Mrs Batten's killer, the judge commented: 'You deserve the congratulations and gratitude of the community for the great efficiency you displayed in recognising Bush. You have been the direct instrument of his being brought to justice. Your vigilance deserves the highest praise, and I hope it will be clearly recognised by the highest authority.'

SOUTH AFRICA

Killer by name . . .

With much the greater part of his wealth deriving from the uncertain and dangerous illegal diamond trade, South African playboy Baron Dieter von Shauroth wisely took out substantial life insurance, and unwisely retained a young crook named Marthinus Rossouw as a bodyguard. When von Shauroth's corpse was found on 25 March 1961 it had two gunshot wounds in the head; he had clearly been robbed, and in his haste the assassin had spilled diamonds on the floor. When Rossouw – who affected the unfortunate *nom de guerre* 'Killer' – was interviewed he told police the extraordinary story that his employer had paid him 2300 Rand to kill him. Not surprisingly, the jury at his trial did not swallow this preposterous defence and convicted Rossouw of murder, for which he was later hanged. The insurance companies, however, eager as always for a loophole to avoid paying out, refused to honour the policies because of the suggestion of a 'murder-by-request' which would have nullified the insurance. It was only after lengthy legal negotiations that Mrs von Shauroth was awarded a compromise *ex gratia* payment.

1962

The A6 Murder

The hanging of James Hanratty for what became known as the A6 murder has been the source of endless controversy. Hanratty was accused of killing Michael Gregsten and the attempted murder of Valerie Storie; however, many informed commentators have laid the blame on another suspect in the case, Peter Louis Alphon.

At approximately 9.30 p.m. on the late summer evening of 22 August 1961, Michael Gregsten, a young married research scientist, and his girl-friend, Valerie Storie, were relaxing in his car at a lay-by outside the village of Dornley on the A6 road through Bedfordshire. It was an unlikely prelude to the five-and-a-half-hour nightmare that was to leave 36-year-old Gregsten dead and Valerie Storie crippled for the rest of her life. There in the quiet of the corn-field a man stepped from the darkness and tapped on the driver's side window; when Mike Gregsten wound the window down he found himself face to face with the barrel of a revolver. 'This is a hold-up.'

For two hours the gunman sat nervously in the back seat of the grey Morris Minor covering his prisoners with the weapon while relating a rambling and improbable story about his recent flight from the police. At 11.30 p.m. Gregsten was ordered to start his car for the first leg of a terrifying journey along the A6, traversing three counties and finally coming to an end at the prophetically named Deadman's Hill, where he was shot twice through the head at

point-blank range. After compounding his savage attack with the rape of Valerie Storie, the killer bundled her from the car and fired five bullets in quick succession into her body, causing injuries that robbed her for ever of the use of her legs, and almost of her life.

On 11 September, the manager of the Vienna Hotel in London's Maida Vale found two spent cartridge cases in a basement bedroom which had last been occupied three weeks before. These proved to match a gun which had recently been recovered from its hiding place beneath a seat cushion on the top deck of a number 36A bus; ballistics experts identified the weapon as that which killed Michael Gregsten. Checking the hotel's guest register for the time around the date of the murder, police discovered that Peter Louis Alphon, a 30-year-old drifter and petty crook, had booked in under a false name on the day after the shooting on Deadman's Hill. Although he resembled the description given by Valerie Storie of her attacker, when Alphon was paraded before her at Stoke Mandeville Hospital, Miss Storie failed to identify him; indeed she identified another man quite unconnected with the inquiry. Peter Alphon was released from custody.

By now the police had a second suspect, 24-year-old James Hanratty. Like Alphon he was a petty crook, and like Alphon he had booked into the Vienna Hotel under an alias. Hanratty had been the last occupant of the basement bedroom in which the cartridge cases had been found. The hunt was now on for James Hanratty who, on account of a number of outstanding burglaries, had gone to ground. However, it is significant that as soon as he became aware of police interest in him, Hanratty telephoned Chief Superintendent Bob Acott, then in charge of the enquiry, in order to protest his innocence and to tell Acott where his clothing could be found for forensic examination. On 11 October, Hanratty was traced to a café in Blackpool and arrested. Like Alphon before him, James Hanratty was put into an identification parade and this time Valerie Storie picked him out – though according to one witness it was not without difficulty. Hanratty was taken from the hospital and charged with murder, attempted murder and rape, and so began what was to become one of crime detection's most controversial decisions. It was Hanratty whose fate was to be the bewildering ordeal of the due process of law – the police stations and the magistrates' court, culminating in the trial at Bedford Assizes, and the then longest murder trial in British criminal history where, still protesting his innocence, James Hanratty was convicted and sentenced to hang.

The evidence against Hanratty was almost entirely based on identification – first by Valerie Storie, who was carried into the court on a stretcher, and then by witnesses who had seen the supposed killer driving Michael Gregsten's Morris Minor on the morning after the murder. In his defence Hanratty claimed that he left the Vienna Hotel on the evening of 22 August bound for Liverpool, where he anticipated selling some stolen jewellery. However, he could not remember either precisely where or with whom he had spent the night. This was clearly not satisfactory either to Hanratty's defence or to the Crown. And so Hanratty obligingly, if unwisely, changed his alibi and now maintained that he had not, after all, stayed in Liverpool but travelled west to the North Wales coastal resort of Rhyl. As it was, for all his protestations that this *was* the truth, Hanratty was not able to give an address or a name for the guest house in which he claimed to have spent the night. However, he could give a description, and was emphatic that there was a green bath in the attic room in which he stayed. While the trial progressed, the boarding houses in the town of Rhyl were searched for the green bath. The guest house called Ingledene, run by Mrs Grace Jones, was as Hanratty had described it; furthermore Mrs Jones recognised a photograph of Hanratty and agreed to

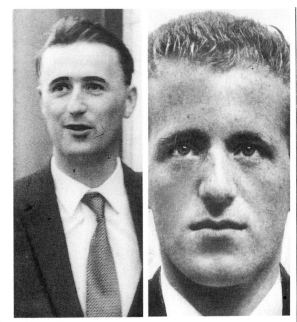

Alphon
(Hulton Deutsch)

Hanratty
(Syndication International)

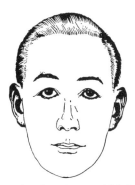 

Identikit picture which helped hang James Hanratty

come down to London to give evidence at his trial. Unfortunately, through a small lapse of protocol (Mrs Jones inadvertently spoke to another witness in the case and then denied it) her credibility as a witness was seriously undermined. As part of the Rhyl alibi, Hanratty also recounted going to visit an old acquaintance named Terry Jones. When he saw that Jones's taxi-cab was not outside the house (a sure sign that he was away from home) Hanratty left.

After 22 arduous days, Mr Justice Gorman sent the jury out to consider their verdict. They returned twice – once for further guidance from his Lordship, and a second time (much to his irritation) to ask for refreshments. After a retirement of ten hours, the jury finally delivered its verdict of guilty. On 3 April 1962, James Hanratty wrote a final letter to his parents:

... I have always loved you and Dad and all of my family and I don't think there is a son anywhere in the world that loves his Mum and Dad as much as I do at this stage. Though I will never see you again, through the fault of others, I will know in my own mind, as my love for you is very strong, your love

Jean Justice's Murder vs. Murder

216

for me will be just as strong ... I am sitting here Mum and you have been on my mind all evening. But I will be glad when morning does come ...

The following morning James Hanratty walked with dignity on to the scaffold at Bedford Gaol.

But already serious doubts were beginning to be expressed about the safety of Hanratty's conviction. In particular Jean Justice had already begun a campaign on Hanratty's behalf before the execution. On that November day in 1961, when Hanratty had stood in the dock of the magistrate's court at Ampthill, his unlikely champion sat just feet away in the public gallery. The 31-year-old son of a Belgian diplomat, Justice was about to embark upon a crusade which would last 30 years until his untimely death in July 1990. In particular, Jean Justice cultivated the acquaintance of the enigmatic Peter Alphon, one-time police suspect in the A6 case, and over the course of years encouraged Alphon to make various confessions. In one of his books on the case, Jean Justice recalled a phantasmagoric journey by car, in the company of barrister friend Jeremy Fox and Alphon, to the fatal cornfield at Dornley Reach:

... I was riding through the night with the A6 murderer. This time he was sitting where Valerie Storie had sat. As I studied his dark head against the windscreen, a gust of fear swept over me and I began trembling convulsively. I had suddenly realised what Peter's next move would be, for he would have only one name for what I now had to do: Betrayal ...

In a dramatic and unexpected telephone call to Jean Justice in March 1964, Peter Alphon revealed not only the real motive for the A6 murder, but also named the man (referred to subsequently as 'Mr X' to avoid libel suits) who paid him to 'separate' Michael Gregsten and Valerie Storie. In October of the same year Jean Justice's *Murder vs. Murder* was published in Paris by the Olympia Press. The book named Alphon as the A6 murderer and was produced abroad to evade Britain's prevailing libel laws.

Just under one year later, in December 1965, investigative journalist and veteran campaigner Paul Foot entered the arena with Justice and Fox, and six years later compiled his immensely persuasive summary of the case for Hanratty's innocence *Who Killed Hanratty?* (Jonathan Cape, London 1971). In the meantime the issue of *Queen* magazine for 14 September 1966 contained an article by Foot, naming Peter Alphon as the A6 killer for the first time in a British publication. Alphon countered with a denial on the BBC *Panorama* programme, and furthermore demanded that the Home Office compensate him over alleged persecution by Jean Justice. On the strength of evidence presented in the programme, Home Secretary Roy Jenkins decided that there was a case to answer in the matter of James Hanratty's alibi.

One of the most dramatic performances in the whole troubled case took place on 12 May 1967, when Peter Alphon called his 'World Press Conference' in the bar of the Hôtel du Louvre, Paris, for the sole purpose of confessing publicly to the A6 crimes: 'I shall also produce proof,' he claimed. In fact the proof turned out to be that he had received £5,000 into his account at Lloyds Bank – payment, he insisted,

for 'breaking up' the relationship between Michael Gregsten and Valerie Storie.

Five days after this charade, Peter Alphon repeated his confession on the ITN programme *Dateline*, and then three days later, on 21 May, while he was in Dublin, retracted his confessions in an interview with *People* newspaper crime reporter Ken Gardner. Alphon later telephoned Paul Foot to announce that the *People* retraction was a lie concocted by Ken Gardner. On 26 May, Foot and Jean Justice telephoned Alphon in Dublin, this time recording the calls, during which Peter Alphon once again confessed to murder, implicated 'Mr X' and confirmed this latest statement in a letter to Paul Foot. Alphon confessed several more times to the A6 murder: to Home Secretary Roy Jenkins on 28 September 1967; to Home Secretary James Callaghan on 15 December of the same year, and again in October of the following year.

And so the evidence collected by the then well-organised 'A6 Committee' founded by

John Lennon and Yoko Ono give their enthusiastic support to the A6 Committee (Popperfoto)

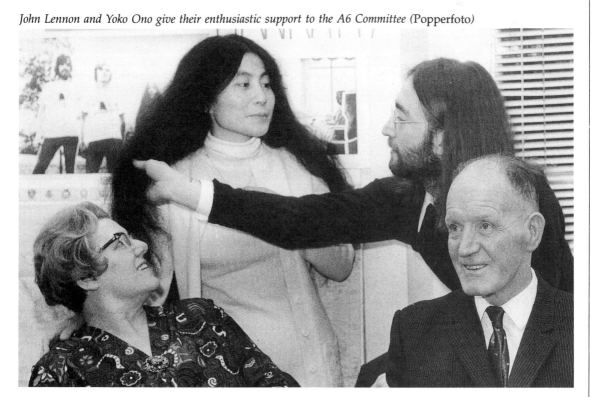

Justice, Fox, Foot, and by 1968 including the late John Lennon and his wife Yoko Ono, was painstakingly collated and woven into a powerful case which, they hoped, would persuade the new Home Secretary, Reginald Maudling, to institute an official enquiry; this was later undertaken by Lewis Hawser, a senior Queen's Counsel. Hawser reported, predictably, that in his opinion there was no reason to question the original verdict in the Hanratty case, and so the campaign went on, and on.

Jean Justice died in 1990, but as if to prove that old proverbs sometimes have a grain of truth, a silver lining appeared in the person of Bob Woffinden, himself no stranger to the crusade against miscarriages of justice. Woffinden was at the time working on a new film analysis of the A6 case, imaginatively sponsored by Channel 4 television, called *Hanratty – The Mystery of Deadman's Hill*.

As well as new evidence questioning the strength of Valerie Storie's identification of Hanratty, and further information on police interviews that cast shadows over Peter Alphon's evidence, the programme also introduced a most remarkable document in the form of a new, detailed, *written* confession by Alphon to the shootings on Deadman's Hill. Sadly, this information has also met with the customary blank-wall response from the British Home Office.

However, there is one possible solution, a solution never even dreamt of at the time of the A6 murder. It has been revealed that, because the crime involved sexual assault, there exists as part of the tangible evidence in police possession semen samples recovered from the victim's clothing. These biological samples could, with no difficulty, be subjected to DNA profiling in order to prove once and for all time whether or not James Hanratty was the attacker. Clearly Hanratty himself is unavailable to provide a control sample for comparison, but it is in the nature of DNA to carry unique hereditary factors which would enable another member of the same family to provide the sample – James's brother and tireless champion, Michael, has offered complete co-operation in any scientific tests. Professor Alex Jeffreys, the scientist responsible for the discovery and development of DNA profiling, has expressed his willingness to conduct the tests himself. Nevertheless, for reasons known only to themselves, Scotland Yard and the Home Office have refused the Hanratty family's solicitor, Mr Geoffrey Bindman, access to this vital evidence. It is difficult not to be deeply suspicious of this official refusal to pursue the truth. As Bob Woffinden observed, 'it is a classic Catch 22 situation' – Scotland Yard will not release the samples until the Home Office reopens the case, and the Home Office will not reopen the case without strong new evidence, such as a DNA profile.

AUSTRALIA

The Man Who 'Murdered' Himself

Between June 1961 and November 1962 the savagely emasculated corpses of four vagrants were found in various parts of Sydney. In one of the most bizarre episodes in Australian homicide, one of the bodies was identified as Allan Brennan – which came as a great surprise to those who knew Allan Brennan and regularly saw him, apparently alive and well, going about his business around the city. Police investigations, however, revealed that Brennan's real name was William McDonald, and that far from being a victim, McDonald was 'his own' murderer. What began as an entirely coincidental misidentification ultimately led to the arrest of a serial killer. The gross perversion of the killer's sexual mutilations was attributed by psychiatrists to an incident in McDonald's youth when he had been indecently assaulted by a corporal while serving in the Army.

1963

Assassination of President John F. Kennedy

The most famous assassination in modern world history, the incident has inspired more theories and counter-theories than any other crime.

> All my dreams of love are dim.
> I kill myself in killing him.
> I am of Satan, the expression
> Of evil will through my aggression.
> (Richard Eberhart, *The Killer*)*

Saturday, 23 November 1963†

KENNEDY ASSASSINATED

President Kennedy is dead. He was assassinated today when a sniper's bullet felled him as he rode slowly in an open-top car through a cheering Dallas crowd, his wife Jacqueline beside him. With the Kennedys in their car were Governor John Connally of Texas and Mrs Connally. The President was waving to the crowd lining the route. The crowd was cheering, even though Texas is an anti-Kennedy state. As the presidential convoy approached a huge underpass Mrs Kennedy waved and

*From *On Poetry and Power*, a collection of verses and texts on the assassination of President Kennedy. Basic Books, New York, 1964.
†This text is a composite derived from contemporary newspaper accounts of the assassination.

smiled too, saying: 'You can't say Dallas isn't friendly to you.' That was the same moment the gunman chose to open fire. The first bullet, fired from above, from a nearby warehouse, hit President Kennedy in the right temple and passed down to his neck. The second and third struck Governor Connally in the chest and wrist. President Kennedy slumped over in the back seat, face down; blood poured from his head. Mrs Kennedy cried out 'Oh, no!' and fell to her knees to cradle his head in her lap. Governor Connally remained half-seated, slumped to the left, there was blood on his forehead and face and blood was spattered over the limousine and over Mrs Kennedy's pink wool suit. At once everything was panic and turmoil.

President Kennedy's limp, unconscious form was still cradled in his wife's arms when, five minutes later, the limousine with an escort of police and Secret Service cars reached Dallas's Parklands Hospital. Then came the desperate half-hour while doctors struggled to do what they could. Surgeons, doctors and two priests were rushed to the hospital as the desperate battle for the President's life began. The White House physician Rear-Admiral George Burkley dashed to the hospital to set up the emergency operating theatre where the President was being given oxygen and transfusions of Type B blood. An operation was performed to relieve his breathing.

Father Oscar Hubert of Holy Trinity Church, Dallas, administered the Last Sacrament of the Roman Catholic Church to President Kennedy, and at 1 p.m. (7.30 p.m. British time) he was dead. Surgeons Dr Kemp Clark and Dr Malcolm Parry faced a stunned Press and described the 30-minute fight to save the President's life.

The Case of the Bad Loser

It is quite extraordinary how little some people are prepared to kill for. We have all become familiar with the tragic stories of desperate attackers preying on innocent strangers for the small change in their pockets or purses; but consider the case of Mark Fein. At the age of 32, New York businessman Fein was at least a millionaire, and a small part of that hard-earned fortune was devoted to financing his less certain speculations on horse racing, through the intermediary of Mr Rubin Markowitz, a bookmaker. In November 1963 Rubin, the betting man's friend, was dragged from the Harlem River, his bloated body the heavier for four .22 calibre slugs. As might be expected from a tale set against this backdrop of the twilight world of illegal gambling, there was the inevitable 'moll'

– in this case a redhead with a greedy nature and criminal inclinations named Gloria Kendall. Gloria confided to detectives investigating Rubin Markowitz's premature retirement from the turf that she had been in Mark Fein's apartment when the trunk containing Rubin's corpse had been collected for disposal; she also mentioned that Fein had owed him a gambling debt. With commendable impartiality, a jury preferred to believe Miss Kendall's version of the story to that concocted by the influential Mr Fein – resulting in the latter being sentenced to a prison term of thirty years to life. The question remains: why should so wealthy a man commit murder to avoid paying what turned out to be a very modest gambling debt? Was he just a bad loser?

'Red-headed Gloria'

Dr Parry said: 'We never had any hope of saving him. Immediate respiration methods were taken, but the President's condition did not allow complete resuscitation. He was critical and moribund . . . we inserted chest tubes, but the President lost his heart action.'

'Flash – Dallas. Kennedy seriously wounded. Perhaps fatally.' Now we know he has died in Jackie's arms. And the rest is silence. What is there to say? For Kennedy was of my generation. He fought my war. He endured our peace. All the songs he sang as he grew up, I sang too . . . And all his hopes for a better world, for his two young children, and mine, were my hopes.

(Bruce Rothwell, American columnist)

Once again an assassin's bullet had changed the course of American history.

SUSPECT

An hour after the President's death was announced from Parkland Hospital, as a vast manhunt for the killer got under way, there was a dramatic shootout in another part of Dallas. Police received a tip-off that a man suspected of being President Kennedy's killer was in the Texas Theatre, a cinema in the Oak Cliff area. Patrolmen John D. Tippit and M. N. Macdonald burst into the cinema, saw their quarry, and Officer Tippit opened fire. The man shot back and Tippit fell dead. Macdonald leaped on the gunman and in the struggle that followed the officer received a gash in his face. The fugitive was overpowered and arrested, and is reported to have said: 'Well, it's all over now.' A police statement issued later named the man as Lee Harvey Oswald, chief suspect in the killing of the President. Already the police had identified the window from which the fatal shot had been fired – on the fifth storey of a book depository. On the floor of the room detectives found a rifle – said to be a 7.65mm German Mauser – with one bullet in the chamber, and three empty cartridge cases on the floor. The gnawed remains of a fried chicken showed the killer had waited some time with his rifle beside him. Lee Harvey Oswald was employed as a stock clerk in the same building.

Something of Oswald's strange life history now began to emerge. He was an ex-US marine who had defected to Russia in 1959, but had defected back again, arriving in America with a Russian wife and baby daughter in May 1962. He turned up later in New Orleans where he became chairman of the pro-Castro committee 'Fair Play for Cuba'.

Monday, 25 November 1963

'I DID IT FOR HER'

The man accused of assassinating President Kennedy was himself shot dead today – in a Dallas police station. Fifty-year-old Jack Ruby, owner of the Carousel Lounge striptease club, was among a crowd surrounding armed police transferring Lee Harvey Oswald to a Texas jail when suddenly Ruby sprang forward and pushed a snub .38 revolver into Oswald's stomach and pulled the trigger. Oswald simply cried out 'Oh!' and fell to the ground. There was pandemonium; a police lieutenant jumped on Ruby and disarmed him as officers drew their guns and surrounded Oswald, half-pulling half-carrying him to the lift. A few hours later Lee Harvey Oswald died in Emergency Ward Two of Parkland Hospital; President Kennedy had died in Ward One two days before.

Taking the arrest of Jack Ruby on a murder charge as an opportunity to issue a statement, Police Captain Will Fritz announced: 'There's no doubt in my mind that Oswald was the man who killed the President. We have all the evidence. As far as I am concerned the case is closed.' One thing is certain – the disgrace of the Dallas police is now complete. They have already been criticised for their lack of precaution in the Kennedy shooting; now they have let Suspect No. 1 be shot down before their very eyes. As for Jack Ruby, he was revelling in his newfound celebrity. He told the Press: 'I did not want to be a hero, I did it for Mrs Jacqueline Kennedy. I wanted to spare her the grief and the agony of having to return to Dallas and testify in this man's trial.' His lawyer, Mr Tom Howard, said: 'Mr Ruby is a very fine man and was a great admirer of President Kennedy . . . there are many people here pitching for him.'

Meanwhile the Moscow morning newspapers were leading with the story 'Murderers of President Kennedy are trying to cover their traces; the police give no answers to justified questions'. In East Berlin similar reports were being fed to the people, claiming that Lee Harvey Oswald was 'a scapegoat for a Right-wing plot'.

And so before the late President's body had even been buried, the conspiracy stories were circulating. And in the thirty years since the tragic and untimely death of John F. Kennedy the plots have escalated in number and absurdity. Few groups have escaped blame for the 'plot' at one time or another. The Warren Commission was set up to investigate the evidence, and in 1964 submitted its report to President Johnson – in brief, it found that Lee Harvey Oswald was acting alone when he shot the President and they could find no evidence of a conspiracy. Inevitably, the Warren Commission was itself accused of perpetuating a conspiracy and of a cover-up. This accusation was formalised in the 1976 report of the House of Representatives Select Committee on Assassinations. This concluded that President Kennedy had 'probably been assassinated as the result of a conspiracy', suggesting that two gunmen were involved and, not for the first time, the Mafia were suggested as the culprits. And so the conspiracy theories multiplied and continue to multiply. Buried somewhere is the needle of truth, but it has been surrounded by an impossibly huge haystack of rumour, myth and, above all, secrecy.

AUSTRALIA

The Bogle-Chandler Mystery

One of Australia's most enduring mysteries of true crime involved the strange deaths of physicist Dr Gilbert Stanley Bogle and Mrs Margaret Chandler after a New Year's Eve party in Sydney in 1963. The two bodies were found the following morning, and although Bogle appeared to be dressed, his clothes had just been draped over him. Mrs Chandler's state of dress was rather more complete, but the position of her skirt indicated some sexual activity. Both bodies contained large quantities of alcohol, and it was assumed that this had some connection with their untimely departure from life. However, in spite of the most exhaustive forensic tests, no definite cause of death could be established. Dr Bogle's sensitive position as a Government scientist led to much wild speculation centring on international conspiracies to undermine the Australian defence programme, and in particular that Bogle had been engaged in the development of a death-ray weapon. A more prosaic explanation was offered by the fact that, when he was in party mood, Dr Bogle indulged in the hallucinogenic drug LSD, and, for what he supposed to be its aphrodisiac qualities, encouraged his paramours to do the same. One slightly sinister postscript is that although the case was considered closed in Australia, the United States Federal Bureau of Investigation kept an open file on the Bogle case for some years.

Dr Gilbert Bogle

1964

William Brittle

The Bugs and Beetles Case. *Although William Brittle provided an alibi for the time his alleged victim was killed, Professor Keith Simpson, with his unique knowledge of the breeding cycles of the insects that infest dead bodies, was able to disprove it.*

It was maggots that they were looking for on that June day in 1964; the two thirteen-year-olds scouted through Bracknell woods in the hope of finding a dead pigeon or squirrel, any dead meat that might be home to the fat white maggots that they needed for fishing bait. Then they found them; thousands of the things. The excitement ended as soon as the boys saw what the maggots were feeding on; as soon as they saw the arm. Terry King and Paul Fay, bright lads, went to the police: 'There's a dead body buried in the woods!'

For pathologist Keith Simpson the call-out was routine – a body discovered in suspicious circumstances. Beneath the covering of moss and leaves was the body of a man, lying on his back, his head wrapped in towelling. The corpse was too far decomposed for any normal time-of-death tests – in fact the police thought it might have been there for up to two months. But they had reckoned without a very special study that Keith Simpson had made his own. Simpson put the time of death as at least nine or ten *days* – 'but probably not more than twelve; its astonishing how quickly maggots will eat up flesh'.

The pathologist had routinely collected samples of the insect infestation and identified the maggots as those of the common blue-bottle (*Calliphora erythrocephalus*): 'The larvae I was looking at were mature, indeed elderly, fat, indolent, third-stage maggots, but they were not in pupa cases. Therefore I estimated that the eggs had been laid nine or ten days earlier. Adding a little more time to allow for the blue-bottles getting to the dead body, I reckoned death had occurred on 16 or 17 June.'*

Post-mortem examination revealed that the bones of the larynx had been crushed, and death had resulted from blood seeping into the windpipe. Identifiable features indicated that the victim was Peter Thomas, reported missing from his home at Lyndney on 16 June. It was also learned that Thomas had lent the sum of £2,000 to a man named Brittle. Under questioning William Brittle admitted that he had met Thomas at Lyndney on 16 June – in fact he had gone there specifically to repay the loan, or so he claimed.

Now it came to light that Brittle had been trained in unarmed combat while serving in the Army – information which was not lost on Professor Simpson, whose report on Thomas's throat injuries were entirely consistent with a blow such as a karate-chop. It was the firm belief of the police that Brittle *had* visited Peter Thomas on 16 June, not to repay the £2,000, but to dispose of his debt rather more decisively; he had then transported Thomas's body in the boot of a car to Bracknell woods. Unfortunately, the police had an independent witness who adamantly insisted that he had seen Peter

Forty Years of Murder, Professor Keith Simpson. Harrap, London, 1978.

223

The Beamish Controversy

During the first nine months of 1963 the inhabitants of Perth were put in fear by a spate of brutal and apparently pointless murders. Despite assistance from London's Scotland Yard and the United States Federal Bureau of Investigation, it was a piece of gratuitous luck that led to the apprehension of the assassin. A young couple had found a rifle hidden behind a rock, which forensic identification identified as the weapon used in the last of the killings. When Eric Cooke, a Perth truck-driver and burglar, went to retrieve his gun from its hiding place on 1 September he was arrested. Rejecting a defence plea of insanity, the jury found Cooke guilty of murder and he was sentenced to death. While awaiting execution, Cooke made a further confession and admitted to a murder for which a deaf mute named Beamish was already serving time. In one of the most controversial decisions in the history of Australian criminal law, the authorities decided not to accept Cooke's unsolicited admission of guilt, and Beamish remained in prison until he was paroled in 1971. Eric Edgar Cooke was hanged at Fremantle on 26 October 1964.

Thomas, alive and well, in Gloucester on 20 June.

In the end William Brittle was committed for trial and the main scientific evidence was offered by Professor Simpson. Simpson testified that he had found maggots of the common blue-bottle (*Calliphora erythrocephalus*) on the corpse, and that they had not yet pupated; this put the time since death at nine or ten days. Though he was appearing as an expert witness for the defence, the eminent entomologist Professor McKenny-Hughes corroborated Simpson's findings, and William Brittle was convicted of murder and sentenced to life imprisonment.

UNITED STATES

The Boy Who Couldn't Keep His Mouth Shut

An inadequate youth, Charles Schmid compensated by living in a world of make-believe and violent fantasy. In May 1964 he declared his intention to kill, and in company with two friends picked up fifteen-year-old Aleen Row, drove her out into the desert, and raped and killed her. He then began to boast of other murders – among them two girls who had recently been reported missing. In the end Schmid's friends became so terrified of him that they turned him in to the police. After a lengthy and complex trial, Charles Howard Schmid was sentenced to death, but narrowly escaped execution when the US Supreme Court temporarily suspended capital punishment. He died later in prison.

1965

'Jack the Stripper'

The first modern British crime to be recognised as 'serial murder'. Although it is officially unsolved, one police suspect in the case committed suicide after questioning.

The first victim of the killer who became known as 'Jack the Stripper' was Hannah Tailford, found strangled on the foreshore of the Thames near Hammersmith Bridge on 2 February 1964. She was naked but for a pair of stockings, and her underwear had been forced into her mouth. Nobody could have foretold that the death of one member of that vulnerable profession was the overture to one of London's most notorious cases of serial murder.

At first the death of Hannah Tailford could have been attributed to either murder or suicide. Dr Donald Teare, the pathologist called in to prepare the post-mortem report, found bruising around the jaw, but this could as easily have been sustained from a fall as from a deliberate blow. In the end the coroner, Mr Gavin Thurston, returned an open verdict.

Two months after the discovery of Hannah Tailford's body a second prostitute was found dead on the foreshore of the Thames at Duke's Meadows, Chiswick, about three hundred yards from where Hannah's remains had been found. The woman was later identified as Irene Lockwood, who also called herself Sandra Russell.

Investigating officers, then under Detective Superintendent Frank Davies, had entertained their share of the publicity seekers and lunatics who dog any such enquiry, including a believable 54-year-old bachelor caretaker who confessed to one of the murders while in custody on a theft charge; Kenneth Archibald was eventually found not guilty and set free after a trial lasting six days.

Twenty-two-year-old Helen Barthelemy was found sixteen days after the second victim, Irene Lockwood, on 24 March. Although she was naked, the pattern deviated in that the body had been dumped away from the river, in a driveway behind Swincombe Avenue, Brentford. Four of Mrs Barthelemy's teeth were missing, though there was no bruising consistent with this being the result of a blow. Helen, or 'Teddie' as she was called, had originally come from Scotland, reaching London via Liverpool and Blackpool's Golden Mile, where she

Hannah Tailford
(Hulton Deutsch)

Irene Lockwood
(Syndication International)

225

had worked as a striptease dancer and prostitute. It was becoming clear now that a single killer was responsible for this series of murders, and a marked atmosphere of panic was spreading among the capital's vice girls. In the meantime, Commander George Hatherill, head of CID at Scotland Yard, made a personal appeal to the city's prostitutes to put aside their time-

Helen Barthelemy

Margaret McGowan

Mary Fleming

Bridie O'Hara

226

honoured mistrust of the police and to come forward in strictest confidence if they had information about men who 'are odd or eccentric in their association with prostitutes, especially if they force them to strip naked'. The appeal certainly had an effect, and although in the end it did not advance the inquiry much, dozens of street girls reported to Shepherd's Bush police station. A new team consisting of women officers was attached to the murder team to pose as prostitutes in the hope of flushing 'Jack' from his lair. However, three months after his last attack, 'Jack the Stripper' claimed another victim.

In the early morning of 14 July 1964, George Heard, a chauffeur, found the naked body of a woman in a seated position at the entrance to a garage in Berrymead Road, Chiswick. Mary Fleming had arrived in the capital from Scotland, stopping off at Barrow-in-Furness to get married. However, at the time of her death she was living alone with her two young children in a room in Lancaster Gardens; she supported herself and her family on the proceeds of prostitution.

By now forensic tests on the body of 'Teddie' Barthelemy had revealed particles adhering to the skin which were identified under the microscope as flakes of the kind of paint used to spray cars; the laboratory also reported finding identical traces on the body of Mary Fleming.

The fifth victim, another prostitute from the Notting Hill district, went missing on 23 October. Margaret McGowan had been working her beat with a fellow prostitute the night she disappeared, but it was not until 25 November that her naked and decomposing body was found in a makeshift grave at Hornton Street, Kensington; she was identified by the tattoos on her left arm.

Then, on 16 February the following year Bridie O'Hara, the sixth of the 'Hammersmith Nudes' was found on a patch of waste land near the Thames at Acton. Dublin-born Bridie had last been seen on 11 February at the Shepherd's Bush Hotel; the cause of her death was asphyxiation after an unsuccessful attempt had been made to strangle her. Her front teeth were missing, and semen was found in the back of her throat.

Public concern over the apparent inability of the police to solve this spate of brutal murders now resulted in Scotland Yard's Assistant Commissioner summoning back from holiday Detective Chief Superintendent John du Rose, one of the Met's most experienced officers. Du Rose had already earned the nickname 'Four Day Johnnie' for the legendary speed with which he solved his cases; he was going to need every bit of that reputation now.

Du Rose immediately homed in on the most significant forensic clue – the paint traces – and organised a huge squad of searchers who made a sweep through no less than 24 square miles around the Thames at Hammersmith and Chiswick, minutely inspecting private and industrial buildings for evidence of painting activity.

After exhaustive searching, officers located the paint-spray shop where four of the bodies had been stored prior to disposal in or beside the river; furthermore, it was located close to where Bridie O'Hara's body had been found on the Heron Trading Estate.

The fact that the women were all abducted between the hours of 11 p.m. and 1 a.m., and dumped between 5 a.m. and 6 a.m., led police to make an educated guess that they were looking for a night-shift worker. A list of suspects was drawn up, but despite anticipation that an arrest was imminent, no charge was ever brought in the case. Nevertheless, a 45-year-old-man whose name has never been revealed killed himself during the investigation; his suicide note read, in part, that he was 'unable to stand it any longer'. When Superintendent du Rose ordered an inquiry into the man's back-

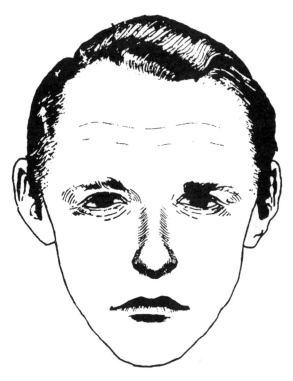

Identikit picture of 'Jack the Stripper' circulated to prostitutes throughout London's West End

ground it was discovered that he was a night security guard whose rounds included the paint shop on the Heron Trading Estate. Although there seemed to be no other evidence to incriminate the man, John du Rose wrote in his autobiography (*Murder Was My Business*): 'I know the identity of Jack the Stripper – but he cheated me of an arrest by committing suicide.'

1966

Jack Henry Abbott

In the Belly of the Beast. *Having already spent a total of 21 years in prison, Abbott stabbed a fellow prisoner to death and earned another fourteen. At about this time his cause was taken up by prominent American author Norman Mailer who succeeded in engineering his early parole. Once out, Jack Abbott killed again. He has written two best-selling accounts of his time in prison.*

When Jack Abbott first came to the attention of American author Norman Mailer he was 37 years old. Of those 37 years, he had spent more than 21 in prison – fourteen in solitary confinement. In 1966 he stabbed a fellow prisoner to death and was sentenced to an additional fourteen years. During this time Abbott engrossed himself in an intensive programme of self-education, becoming familiar with most of the major branches of philosophy and in the end choosing Marxism for himself. Mailer was at this time engaged on writing *The Executioner's Song*, an analysis of the life and crimes of convicted double-murderer Mark Gary Gilmore. When Abbott learned of the Gilmore project through a newspaper article, he wrote a letter to Mailer offering the benefit of his own experience of violence in prisons; it was his contention that only a person who has endured a decade or more of incarceration can fully appreciate the principle and practice of institutional violence.

The result was an extraordinary series of letters in which Mailer recognised 'an intellectual, a radical, a potential leader, a man obsessed with a vision of more elevated human relations in a better world that revolution could forge'. These letters were to constitute the basis of the best-selling autobiography *In the Belly of the Beast*. As a result of this success, and Mailer's conviction that he was 'a powerful and important American writer', Abbott was released on parole. He worked for a brief period as Norman Mailer's researcher, and enjoyed the attentions of the New York literati; but the years of institutionalisation had ill-equipped Jack Abbott for a life outside prison.

In the early hours of the morning of 18 July 1981, Abbott became involved in an argument with 22-year-old Richard Adan, an actor and playwright then working as a waiter at the Bini Bon diner on Second Avenue, New York. Abbott had taken strong exception to being told that the men's lavatory was for staff use only, and reacted in the only way that seemed natural to him – he stabbed Adan to death. After two months on the run, Abbott was arrested in Louisiana and sentenced to be confined in the maximum-security prison, at Marion, Illinois.

In 1981, shortly after Adan's death, his wife Ricci had begun the proceedings to extract financial compensation for the 'wrongful death' and 'pain and suffering' caused to Richard Adan by his killer. In 1983, Abbott had been found liable for monetary damages, but the motion had been legally blocked by him for seven years until this present jury was empanelled to determine the amount of those damages.

On 5 June 1990, Jack Abbott was back in court again. Now aged 45, neat in a brown

228

tweed sport jacket and jeans and wearing steel-rimmed spectacles, he declined the offer of legal aid and claimed instead his right to act as his own lawyer.

Under what has become known as the 'Son of Sam'* law, criminals are unable to profit financially from stories about their crimes. In Jack Abbott's case, the considerable income from *In the Belly of the Beast*, as well as a second book, *My Return*, and the subsequent film rights, was being held jointly by the New York County Sheriff and the New York State Crime Victims Board.

In *My Return*, Abbott discussed the Adan stabbing, and dismissed Mrs Adan's claim that her husband endured 'pain and suffering', commenting that far from it, he had benefited from a quick, painless death. Abbott also contended that because the whole argument only arose because of Richard Adan's apparent 'lack of respect', he was at least in part responsible for his own death. The confrontation the court had been waiting for took place at the end of the fifth day, when Jack Abbott questioned Mrs Ricci Adan.

'Are you under the impression I killed your husband?'
'You killed my husband. How could you do that?'
'What did I do?'
'I know you killed my husband with a knife. I know you thrust it into his chest and he died. He's dead.'

*During 1976–77 a wave of murders hit New York leaving six people dead and a further seven seriously wounded; the victims were all young couples sitting in parked cars. Ironically, the killer was traced through a traffic violation ticket issued to him on the night of his last murder; when police traced the car they found on the back seat a loaded .44 Bulldog revolver which had been used in previous killings. Thus the murderer who had written an arrogant note to the police some months before claiming: 'I am a monster. I am the Son of Sam', was identified as David Berkowitz.

Under arrest, Berkowitz claimed that mysterious voices had been ordering him to kill, and explained that his nickname had been taken from a neighbour, Sam Carr, whose black labrador dog kept him awake at night.

In August 1977, the Son of Sam was sentenced to 365 years' imprisonment, and his crimes attracted considerable media exploitation.

Jack Henry Abbott (Syndication International)

'I want somehow to convey to you what it means to be in prison for so long...'

IN THE BELLY OF THE BEAST

JACK HENRY ABBOTT

'Hell is now clear to behold'
NORMAN MAILER IN HIS INTRODUCTION
'Awesome, brilliant, perversely ingenuous'
NEW YORK TIMES BOOKS REVIEW
'Astonishing...a saga, an heroic story'
WASHINGTON POST

Blow-by-blow diagrams of Abbott's stabbing of Richard Adan

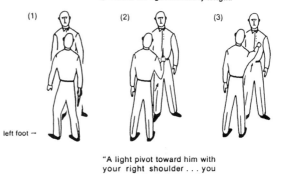

The killer moves his "left foot to the side, to step across his right-side body length."

(1) (2) (3)

left foot →

"A light pivot toward him with your right shoulder . . . you have sunk the knife in . . ."

'Does nothing else matter to you than that Richard Adan died at my hands?'

'Yes. Something has to be done. There has to be some kind of a balance, some retribution for what has happened to my husband. Some kind of payback. I don't know what.'

'Did you attend my trial?'

'No I did not. I was in shock. I didn't want to see it all. I didn't want to see you.'

'So you don't know what happened?'

'I don't know.'

'Do you care?'

'Objection!' yelled Mrs Adan's lawyer. 'You don't have to answer,' responded Acting Justice Arber.

Such overtly provocative questioning, including the suggestion that her late husband's life was 'not worth a dime,' soon reduced Mrs Adan to tears, a condition which Abbott berated with taunts like 'Could you answer the question without using a Kleenex?' At the same time he sneered quite regularly at Mrs Adan's continued attempts to secure financial compensation from Richard's untimely death.

On Friday, 15 June 1990, after six hours of deliberation and considerable use of an electronic calculator, the jury, to the apparent delight of everybody in court except Jack Abbott, awarded Mrs Ricci Adan $7.575 million damages ($5.575 million for loss of her husband's potential earnings and $2 million for the pain he suffered). Before he was returned to continue his sentence at Auburn state prison, Jack Abbott commented: 'It is a little excessive, your honour, I would say.'

UNITED KINGDOM

The Moors Murders

On 6 May 1966 two killers stood in the courtroom of the Chester Assizes and listened to sentence being passed on them. During the fifteen days that the trial had lasted, the nation had been paralysed with disbelief as they heard recounted a succession of horrors too awful to take in. In the two years since 1964, Ian Brady and his lover Myra Hindley had abducted a number of children, subjected them to unspeakable sexual degradation, then brutally killed them and buried their small bodies on the deserted moors outside Manchester. The court listened in tears to a tape recording made by Hindley of ten-year-old Lesley Ann Downey pleading to be allowed to go home; she never saw home again, only a shallow grave on the bleak Saddleworth Moor. Sentenced to life imprisonment, Brady and Hindley are still confined to jail, still regarded as the epitome of evil. In 1987 new interest was awakened in the so-called 'Moors Murders' when Myra Hindley confessed to a further two murders and both she and Brady assisted in a search for the bodies.

That of Pauline Reade was uncovered on the moors, the remains of Keith Bennett, aged twelve at the time of his death, could not be found.

Two of the modern world's most notorious killers, Ian Brady and Myra Hindley (Syndication International)

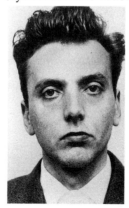

1967

Gordon Hay

Murder at Biggar. *The first case of murder solved by bite-mark comparison, when Gordon Hay left his teeth imprints on the breast of his victim as he sexually assaulted and strangled her.*

What was to become a landmark case in forensic dentistry began on 7 August 1967 with the discovery of the battered and strangled corpse of fifteen-year-old Linda Peacock in a cemetery in Biggar, a small town between Edinburgh and Glasgow. The girl had not been raped, though the clothing on the upper part of her body had been disarranged. An observant police photographer whose job it was to record the scene of the crime and the victim's position drew the police surgeon's attention to an oval bruise-type mark on one of the girl's breasts, consistent, he suggested, with a bite mark. This was quickly confirmed by the pathologist, and Scotland's foremost forensic dentistry expert, Dr Warren Harvey, was assigned to the team investigating Linda Peacock's murder.

Police officers had already eliminated the 3,000 people so far interviewed in the area. There remained a single group of 29 youths, all inmates of a local detention centre. Harvey suggested as a first step taking dental impressions of each of the men in an attempt to match a set of teeth to the distinctive bite mark on the victim's body. One mark in particular looked as though it might have come from an uncommonly sharp or jagged tooth.

Dr Harvey was now able, on observation, to reduce to five the number of impressions that could not yet be eliminated from suspicion. At this stage he consulted with Professor Simpson, another pioneer of forensic dentistry, and the two experts concentrated their attention on the 'jagged' tooth.

Of the five suspects, only one had a match. Investigations now centred on seventeen-year-old Gordon Hay, who was now known to have been missing from the Borstal dormitory at the time of Linda Peacock's murder; he had been seen returning just before 10.30 that night, dishevelled, breathless, and with mud on his clothes. Equally incriminating was the fact that Hay had met Linda at a local fair the previous day, and commented to a friend that he would like to have sex with her.

Hay willingly, almost eagerly, submitted to a further set of impressions being made of his teeth. From these the watertight evidence that would later convict him of murder was assembled. Closer examination by Warren Harvey revealed sharp-edged, clear-cut pits, like small craters on the tips of the upper and lower right canines – symptoms of a rare disorder called hypo-calcination. The upper pit was larger than the lower, and agreed with the bite mark on the victim's breast. Patient examination of no less than 342 sixteen- and seventeen-year-old boys produced only two with pits, one with a pit and hypo-calcination, and none with two pits.

In February 1968, Dr Warren Harvey spoke for a whole day from the witness box at Edinburgh's High Court of Justiciary. It was the first time that a Scottish jury had been required to consider bite-mark evidence, and clearly they were impressed. Gordon Hay was eventually convicted of the murder with which he was charged and, on account of his youth, sentenced to be detained 'during Her Majesty's pleasure'.

231

Massacre in Chicago

On the night of 14 July 1966 Corazon Amurao and five friends were at home in their Chicago nurses' residence. In response to a knock Corazon opened the front door and the six girls found themselves captives of Richard Speck who reeked of alcohol and waved a gun in one hand and a knife in the other. Speck then ordered the girls to lie on the floor and bound them with strips torn from a bed-sheet. It was at this point that he went on to assure himself of a place at the top of the list of the world's bloodiest mass murderers. At intervals of twenty minutes Speck dragged the girls one by one into another room and stabbed and strangled them. All, that is, except Corazon Amurao, who managed to wriggle under a bed and was miraculously overlooked by the killer. When Speck finally left, Miss Amurao raised the alarm and it was not long before the murderous Speck was identified by fingerprints left at the scene of his crime. After a brief trial Richard Speck was sentenced to die in the electric chair on 6 June 1967. However, the United States Supreme Court had suspended the death penalty and

Speck was resentenced to a term of 400 years' imprisonment. He maintained his innocence until 1978 when he made a full confession. Richard Speck died in prison in 1991.

Richard Speck (Syndication International)

Diagram showing the distribution of Speck's victims around their shared apartment

1968

Assassination of Dr Martin Luther King Jr

For an unbelievable second time in five years a major American politician is shot dead. Less than three months later this figure will increase when Senator Robert Kennedy is also felled by an assassin's bullet.

People have said that it was an assassination just waiting for the opportunity to happen. What is certain is that Dr Martin Luther King Jr was not enjoying the greatest of political popularity. On one side the great symbol of non-violent protest found himself assailed by a new wave of young black militants and, on the other, by the white authorities who had only recently witnessed the death of a teenager at a rally led by King.

Martin Luther King had arrived in Memphis, Tennessee, on 28 March 1968, to lead a march of striking dustmen; it had been a disaster, rioting erupted and a sixteen-year-old was shot and killed. Dr King had already received a lot of death threats over the years but that, as they say, comes with the territory. On 3 April Dr King was back in Memphis for meetings – prophetically, his flight was delayed by a bomb threat at the airport. During his stay King took room 306 at the Lorraine Motel. On the evening of 4 April, after a day of business appointments, he was in the motel room with Robert Aberna-

thy, an aide, awaiting the arrival of their dinner host Revd Samuel Kyles to collect them. Kyles arrived at 5.30 p.m., and while they were waiting for Abernathy to get ready, Dr King stepped on to the small balcony looking out on the back of the motel. At just after six o'clock a shot rang out across the open ground and Dr King was hurled backwards by the force of a bullet tearing into the right side of his face. Within seconds there was chaos – while Robert Abernathy went running on to the balcony to do what he could for his friend, Revd Kyles was yelling down the telephone for an ambulance; bystanders were running around helplessly, seeking any kind of cover in case the shooting continued. It did not; a single bullet from the assassin's gun had robbed the civil rights movement of its most charismatic leader. Martin Luther King Jr lived for less than an hour after being shot; he survived the ambu-

Dr King and the Revd Ralph Abernathy on the motel balcony where Dr King was later shot dead (Topham)

233

lance journey to St Joseph's Hospital but died at 7.05 p.m.

Back at the Lorraine Motel, police were already hunting the killer. Because of the tension of recent days in Memphis, and the previous threats to Dr King's life, a low-key police surveillance was being kept by detectives in the near vicinity. It proved to be a little too low-key in the event, but despite what had been learned from the assassination of President Kennedy only five years earlier it was still all but impossible to protect controversial public figures from attack by a lone sniper with a powerful long-range weapon.

The whole area around the motel had been sealed off, and police had begun to question bystanders. Inside ten minutes they had pieced together a broad scenario of the murder; the

The many faces of James Earl Ray (Popperfoto)

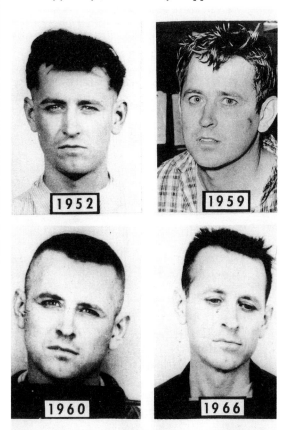

shots had been fired from a window opposite the motel, from the direction of South Main Street. After the shooting, witnesses had seen a man run from a rooming house at 418/422 South Main, dump a bundle in a doorway and drive off at speed in a white Ford Mustang with red and white registration plates. The man was described as being between 26 and 36 years old, white, average build and wearing a white shirt under a black suit. It took officers no time to locate the hastily discarded bundle – it contained a high-power rifle and binoculars.

In spite of an all-cars alert, the white Mustang and its driver had, for the moment, got away. However, given the number of clues the fleeing gunman had left behind him, it did not take the police long to come up with a name – James Earl Ray. The puzzling part was that assassinating political leaders was not exactly in Ray's usual line of business. Sure, he was a crook, but a very petty one, and very inept. After a succession of small-time robberies followed by brief terms of imprisonment, Ray earned himself twenty years in the Missouri State Penitentiary for a supermarket robbery in 1959. In 1967 he escaped, and it was while he was on the run that he shot and killed Martin Luther King Jr.

What the police did not know was that after the murder, Ray had sped to Atlanta, Georgia, where he left the Mustang and hopped on a bus to Detroit. From there he travelled to Canada, the location of several of his earlier misdemeanours. In Toronto, Ray applied for a passport in the name of Ramon Sneyd and flew to London; from there he departed for Portugal where he tried to sign on as a mercenary to fight in Africa. Failing in this quest, as he had failed in most of life's quests, James Earl Ray returned to London. By now the FBI had begun to follow his trail – Atlanta, Detroit, Toronto – and it seemed that Ray was doubling back to meet them halfway. Or almost. The FBI had alerted Scotland Yard to the true identity of Mr Sneyd, and when he tried to refill his rapidly emptying wallet by raiding a London bank, detectives found that the demand note was covered with Ray's fingerprints. Still trying to get a ringside seat for the fighting in Angola, Ray now booked a fare to Brussels where he heard they were recruiting mercenaries. It was another mistake. As he passed through airport security they found his unlicensed handgun; a quick check with Scotland Yard and Ray was arrested and flown, not to Brussels, but back to the welcoming arms of the FBI. The race was over and James Earl Ray, as usual, had lost.

As the result of a plea-bargain, Ray pleaded guilty at his trial in March 1969, and was sentenced to 99 years' imprisonment. He was confined to a secure unit in Nashville Prison, from whence he tried to escape in 1971, 1977 and 1979. As a result of the 1977 escape he actually managed to remain at large for three days before being recaptured. In 1978 Ray was given permission to marry Miss Anna Sandhu.

So, why did James Earl Ray, the undistinguished petty crook from nowhere, become a figure of international notoriety? It is true that he was always known to be neurotic, and around the time of his assassination of Dr King was receiving therapy for severe depression – but he was no psychopath. He certainly did, though, display an almost desperate need for attention, but for attention of what he considered the right kind – he didn't want to be seen for the nobody that he was. In fact Ray

Ray on his way to the penitentiary at Nashville (Popperfoto)

was constantly threatening libel action against journalists and magazines who portrayed him as anything less than the heroic desperado of his own imagination. This was the secret. As one of his analysts later explained: 'He yearns to feel he is somebody. The desire for recognition in him is superior to sex, superior to money, superior to self-preservation.'

UNITED KINGDOM

The Profession of Violence

Notorious for their Gangland activities in London during the 1950s and 1960s, Ronnie and Reggie Kray were eventually arrested on 8 May 1968. The Krays had made a very lucrative business out of 'protection', which, due to their naturally psychopathic tendencies, was characterised by acts of extreme violence; but these were the minor indictments against them at their Old Bailey trial. Heading the charge sheet were the murders of George Cornell (a member of the rival Richardson gang) and Jack 'The Hat' McVitie, and the alleged murder of escaped convict Frank Mitchell, known as 'The Mad Axeman'. Police had been hampered throughout their investigation into the gang's activities by the blanket of fear which the twins had cast over London's East End. For years nobody had

dared open their mouth in accusation, but now, with the brothers and their heavies in custody, people began to come forward with information – even members of the Kray's own gang exchanged evidence for immunity from prosecution. After a trial lasting 39 days, during which the catalogue of crime and violence disclosed beggared imagination, Ronald Kray was sentenced to two life terms for murder, his brother Reginald to life for one murder and ten years as an accessory to the other; the recommendation was that they serve not less than 30 years. Other members of the Kray gang, including brother Charles, were sentenced to various terms of imprisonment. Ronald and Reginald Kray are still serving their sentences – Ronald, certified insane, serves his in Broadmoor.

1969

Charles Manson *et al*

Family Business. *Manson, professional degenerate and self-styled Messiah, in company with members of his 'Family', were responsible for a series of murders which were to become America's 'crimes of the century'. Despite his incarceration, Manson still has a huge following among young people on the fringe of today's society.*

Manson and his so-called 'Family' created shock waves throughout California, a state not unused to bizarre murders and serial killers;

Actress Sharon Tate (Popperfoto)

shock waves which spread around the world.

An ex-convict, drug addict and all-round dropout, Manson dominated his equally unattractive disciples with a mish-mash of corrupted Biblical philosophy and mistaken interpretations of the lyrics of the Beatles' songs. This, combined with his magnetic sexual attraction to the female members of his 'Family', ensured Manson's complete physical and spiritual control of the group.

The first publicised murders took place in the summer of 1969. Just after midnight on Saturday 9 August four shadowy figures crept into the grounds of a secluded mansion at 10050 Cielo Drive, Beverly Hills. Manson was not on the raid himself; tonight it was the turn of 'Tex' Watson, 'Sadie' Atkins, Linda Kasabian and Patricia 'Katie' Krenwinkel. The house on Cielo was occupied that night by actress Sharon Tate (her husband, the director Roman Polanski, was away on business) who was heavily pregnant, and four friends. In an orgy of overkill, the Family left all five victims literally butchered. Voytek Frykowski alone was stabbed more than fifty times, slashed, shot and so savagely bludgeoned with the butt of a gun that the weapon shattered. On the front door to the house the word 'Pig' was painted in blood. Not one of the murderous gang had the slightest idea whom they had killed – they were just random targets.

Only one person was not pleased with the night's activities – Charlie Manson. When news of the bloodbath came through on the television it apparently offended Charlie's sensibilities that such a messy job had been made of it. He decided to show everybody how it should be done. Two nights later, Manson led Watson, Krenwinkel, van Houten, Atkins and Kasabian to the Silver Lake home of Leno and Rosemary

The charismatic Charles Manson, surrounded by his 'family': clockwise Charles 'Tex' Wilson, Susan Atkins, Linda Kasabian, Leslie van Houten, Patricia Krenwinkel, 'Bobby' Beausoleil

LaBianca and butchered them both. Afterwards Manson and his disciples inscribed slogans in blood on the walls – 'Death to the Pigs', 'Rise', and 'Healter [*sic*] Skelter' which, according to Manson, signified the time when the blacks of America would rise and wipe out the whites – with the exception of the Family, of course, who would survive and take control. In a final act of gratuitous violence, the word 'War' was carved into Leno LaBianca's abdomen with a knife.

Following these utterly mindless killings, the Family went to ground. Susan Atkins was later arrested on a prostitution charge and while she was in custody admitted her part in the Tate murders. The Family were rounded up and charges of murder were laid against the principal members. Manson, Krenwinkel, Atkins and van Houten were tried together, and after one of the most extraordinary trials in California's history, they were convicted and sentenced to death. In view of the state's suspension of capital punishment, the sentences were subsequently reduced to life imprisonment. 'Tex' Watson was tried separately with the result that he too was sentenced to life imprisonment.

Although no further charges were brought, there is reason to believe that many other murders, including several of their own members, could be laid at the door of the Family.

And if everybody thinks that Charlie's evil – and crazy, too – then Charlie is the first to agree with them. Since he became eligible for parole a dozen years ago, Manson has insisted on his right to a regular hearing. Not that he seems to take these occasions very seriously – certainly not seriously enough to stand a hope in hell of ever being released – but it is the one time every eighteen months or so when he can guarantee that a mass media committed to keeping the cult of Manson alive will be assembled *en masse* in an adjoining room listening to the proceedings and hanging on Charlie's every word. He rarely disappoints.

In an article on Stephen Kay, the Los Angeles County deputy district attorney whose mission it has been to oppose each and every one of the Manson Family's bids for parole, Martin Kasindorf* related how at the 1981 parole hearing Manson predicted that Stephen Kay would himself be murdered in the San Quentin car park as he left the meeting. Of course, Kay suffered no such dramatic fate, and was there facing Manson across the wooden table at his next parole board. But the point was that everybody *expects* something like this from mad Charlie – so who is he to disappoint them?

Then there was the time when Stephen Kay asked Manson why it was that he spent so much of his free time making scorpions out of the thread unravelled from his socks. By way of explanation, Manson rose in his seat and intoned: 'From the world of darkness I did loose demons and devils in the power of scorpions to torment!' Needless to say this put the 'Messiah's' parole chances back by a few years.

The year 1986 found Charlie reading his twenty-page handwritten statement, described as 'bizarre and rambling', when parole was opposed by no less an authority than California's governor George Deukmejian; in 1989, Manson decided that he would not face the parole board with manacles on his wrists because: 'They'll think I'm dangerous.' They probably did anyway – but in his absence Charles Milles Manson was predictably denied the opportunity to join the world at large for a few years more.

Ironically, Manson made his latest appeal for freedom on 20 April 1992 – it was within hours of the death sentence, the first in California for decades, being carried out on Robert Alton Harris. Manson's own death sentence could not be reinstated, nor, it seemed, was he destined to win his freedom. According to the *Sun*'s correspondent in New York, Charlie surprised his new parole board by announcing: 'There's no one as bad as me. I'm everywhere – I'm down in San Diego zoo; I'm in the trees; I'm in your children. Someone has to be insane, we can't all be good guys. They've tried to kill me thirty or forty times in prison; they've poured fire over me*. They haven't found anyone badder than me because there is no one as bad as me – and that's a fact.' Charlie had blown his chance yet again.

The Independent Magazine, 12 August 1989, London.

*This was a reference to an incident that occurred in September 1984, when Manson took exception to the chanting of a fellow prisoner who had adopted the Hare Krishna faith. In retaliation the man poured paint thinners over Manson and set fire to him.

UNITED STATES

The Zodiac Killings

During a nine-month period in 1969 an unknown assassin killed five people and wounded two more in the state of California. The murders were each followed by letters to two San Francisco newspapers; they were so detailed that they could only have been written by the killer, and all of them were signed with a zodiac cross on a circle. Although there were no further killings, the San Francisco Police Department received another 'Zodiac' letter in 1974 threatening 'something nasty' and claiming a total of 37 murders. 'Zodiac' has never been heard from again, and the crimes remain unsolved.

1970

Arthur and Nizamodeen Hosein

Murder at Rooks Farm. *A classic modern example of a trial conducted without the body of the victim being found. It has been suggested that Mrs McKay's body may have been fed to the herd of pigs on the Hoseins' farm.*

In 1970, the headlines were proclaiming one of those rare, but by no means unique tragedies – the 'Case of the Missing Body'. In this instance the innocent victim was Mrs Muriel McKay, wife of the deputy chairman of the *News of the World*. Mrs McKay had been abducted from her home in Wimbledon on 2 December 1969, and ransom demands were made shortly afterwards. The whole kidnap had been bungled from the start: the intended victim had been the wife of millionaire businessman Rupert Murdoch. Then the demands were for a preposterously large amount of money: 'We are from America – Mafia M.3. We have your wife . . . You will need a million pounds by Wednesday.' It was later agreed that the amount could be paid in two instalments.

In all, eighteen telephone calls of an equally farcical nature were made to an increasingly anxious Alick McKay before, on 22 January, he received a ransom note accompanied by two letters written by his wife in which she admit-

ted that the ordeal was causing her to 'deteriorate in health and spirit'. Having followed the bewilderingly complex instructions for delivering the money, during which a police officer posed as Mrs McKay's son, the kidnappers failed to collect the suitcase. 'Mafia M.3' could hardly have failed to notice the extraordinary police presence of about 150 officers in various disguises, and some 50 unmarked cars.

A second attempt to deliver the money proved to be as burlesque; a young couple came across the suitcase full of money where it had been left on a garage forecourt. Good citizens that they were, the Abbotts called in the local force thinking that somebody had mislaid their luggage. But the police, under the experienced leadership of Detective Chief Superintendent Wilfred Smith, had laid their plans well, and when a dark blue Volvo saloon driven by two coloured men began cruising back and forth around the dropping point, they were sure they had their kidnappers.

The Hosein brothers, Arthur (left) and Nizamodeen (Syndication International)

Police search of Rooks Farm (Press Association)

The owner of the car, traced through its registration number XGO 994G, proved to be 34-year-old Trinidad-born Indian Arthur Hosein who, with his younger brother Nizamodeen, worked the ramshackle Rooks Farm at Stocking Pelham.

A painstaking search of the farmhouse provided sufficient clues for investigating officers to link the Hoseins with the kidnap, and by the time they reached the dock of the Central Criminal Court in September 1970, the scientific evidence against the brothers was overwhelming. Apart from indisputable fingerprint evidence that proved Arthur handled the ransom notes, a handwriting expert demonstrated to the court how the ransom note written in an exercise book found at the farmhouse perfectly matched the indentations on the following page.

Both the Hoseins were found guilty of murder and kidnap; on the former charge they were sentenced to life imprisonment and on the latter to additional lengthy terms of imprisonment.

Although every inch of Rooks Farm was meticulously covered by police searchers, not the smallest trace of Mrs McKay was ever found. Among the suggestions made was that the victim had been cut up and fed to the Hoseins' herd of Wessex Saddleback pigs. Whatever the truth, an undiscovered body can only deepen the sense of loss felt by family and friends deprived of even a last resting place at which to mourn.

1971

Graham Young

The Bovingdon Bug. *Having been released from Broadmoor whence he was sent for poisoning his own family, Young began work with a firm of photographic technicians where he used the readily available supplies of thallium to poison his work colleagues.*

Looking back, I can remember Graham sitting there, completely callous and totally detached, as though he were in no way connected with the suffering figure in the bed – just watching and studying him as though he were an insect or a small animal being experimented on by a scientist. Not a single sign of feeling or emotion. The word cold-blooded is rather a hackneyed one... but it is the only word to describe Graham.

The man lying in the hospital bed was Fred Young; Graham was the son who had just secretly poisoned him; the words were written by Graham's sister Winifred* – he had tried to poison her too.

Graham Young had been born in Neasden in September 1947; a few weeks later his mother fell sick with pleurisy contracted while she was pregnant. She died when Graham was only three months old, and this must certainly have been a contributing factor in Graham's development into a solitary child and, as an adolescent, a loner among his peers. He was a highly intelligent youth, though in an off-beat and rather sinister way, and a great admirer of Adolf Hitler and the Victorian poisoner William Palmer. A school-teacher recalled how Graham

had inscribed verses he had written in praise of poisons in his exercise books. He also took a precocious interest in chemistry, and at an early age was experimenting with explosives.

In 1961, when he was fourteen, Young expanded his interest to include the effects of poisons on the human body, a piece of academic research that required the administration of small doses of antimony tartrate to members of his immediate family and a school friend named Christopher John Williams. His

One of Graham Young's early heroes, the poisoner William Palmer

Graham Young as he saw himself; a photo-booth snap

sister Winifred suffered almost continual stomach upsets, vomiting frequently and occasionally publicly. In April 1962 Young's stepmother died. As he continued to lace his father's and sister's food and drink, they became increasingly ill. When Winifred began to suffer from dizzy spells after drinking some 'bitter' tea, she was diagnosed as being the victim of belladonna poisoning; his father, by this time in a very weak condition, was admitted to hospital and diagnosed as suffering from arsenic poisoning. Young's response was disdainful: 'How ridiculous not being able to tell the difference between arsenic and antimony poisoning!'

This, plus Graham's alarming obsession with toxic substances, aroused the family's suspicions and they lost no time in confiding them to the police – after all, one of them had already died, who might be next? When Graham Young arrived home from school on the afternoon of

2 May 1962 the police were already there waiting for him. His pockets were searched, but disclosed nothing more sinister than the normal contents of a schoolboy's pockets. Then Detective Inspector Coombe asked Graham to remove his shirt, and out dropped three tiny bottles.

'What is in these?' the officer asked him.

'I don't know,' lied Graham.

It was antimony. The boy was taken into custody and later made a boastful confession before being transferred to Ashford Remand Centre to await trial.

The trial opened at the Old Bailey on 6 July 1962, when Young entered a plea of guilty to the charges of poisoning his father, his sister and Chris Williams. No charge was brought in the matter of his stepmother's death because her body had been cremated and it was impossible to determine whether she had died of natural causes, as stated on the death certificate, or as the result of one of Graham's experiments.

Despite a vigorous defence by Miss Jean Southworth, in which she spoke of Young as being 'like a drug addict, to be pitied for his obsession', the most convincing evidence came from Dr Christopher Fysh, a psychiatrist and senior medical officer at Ashworth. He was supported by consultant Dr Donald Blair, who testified: 'I would say he [Young] was prepared to take the risk of killing to gratify his interest in poisons. He is obsessed by the sense of power they give him. I fear he will do it again.' It was the opinion of both specialists that Graham Young was a dangerous psychopath. Not surprisingly, he was found guilty but insane and removed to Broadmoor, where it was ordered that he be detained for at least fifteen years and then released only by order of the Home Secretary.

Nine years later, on 4 February 1971, Graham Young, now 23, walked free from Broadmoor certified as 'cured'. Presumably nobody had attached much importance to his alleged threat to 'kill one person for every year I've spent in this place'. Within a short time he found employment as a storekeeper with John Hadland's Ltd, a photographic-instruments firm

I am pleased to accept your offer, and the conditions attached thereto, and shall, therefore, report for work on Monday, May 10th. at 8.30 a.m.

May I take this opportunity to express my gratitude to you for offering me this position, notwithstanding my previous infirmity as communicated to you by the Placing Officer. I shall endeavour to justify your faith in me by performing my duties in an efficient and competent manner.

"Until Monday week, I am;"

Yours faithfully,

Graham Young.

Graham Young's letter accepting the job at Hadlands, where fellow employee Jethro Batt (above) nearly lost his life and did lose his hair

located at Bovingdon, in Hertfordshire; he started work on 10 May 1971. In June – just weeks after Young had joined the company – Hadland's head storeman, 59-year-old Bob Egle, who supervised Graham, was taken ill at work suffering from diarrhoea, nausea, extreme backache, and numbness in the tips of his fingers. On 7 July, after eight days of intense pain, Egle died in St Albans hospital; death was attributed to broncho-pneumonia and polyneuritis. Among the mourners at Bob Egle's cremation was Graham Young. Meanwhile, Ronald Hewitt, another employee of Hadland's, had also been suffering diarrhoea, vomiting and stomach cramps – symptoms which continued until he left the firm two days after Egle's death.

In September 1971 another of the Hadland's workforce, 60-year-old Fred Biggs, fell ill. The symptoms were the familiar ones shared by Bob Egle and Ronald Hewitt. Later in the same month the firm's import–export manager, Peter Buck, fell similarly ill after drinking tea with Graham Young.

During the next month David Tilson, a clerk, and Jethro Batt, a storeman, also fell victim to what was now being called 'the Bovingdon

Bug'. Both men grew worse; Tilson required hospitalisation and began to lose his hair. Mrs Diana Smart developed stomach and leg cramps, nausea, and other symptoms. On 4 November Fred Biggs was admitted to hospital with severe pains in his chest; the following day he was joined by Jethro Batt. On 19 November Biggs died. Such was the alarm that several members of Hadland's staff handed in their notice.

Eventually the management were concerned enough to hold a medical enquiry into working conditions at the plant. In an attempt to defuse the mounting panic, and to assure workers that the chemicals they had been handling were safe and in no way responsible for the 'bug', the medical team held a meeting with the entire workforce in the canteen. Dr Arthur Anderson, who had headed the investigation, made himself available to answer questions, but was quite unprepared for the barrage shot at him by one particular member of Hadland's staff, and quite taken aback when Graham Young concluded his outburst with the question: 'Do you not think, Doctor, that the symptoms of the mysterious illness are consistent with thallium poisoning?'

It was at this point that Hadland's management decided to check into the background of this young man who had continually evaded any discussion of his past. Within hours of them learning that he had only the year before been released from Broadmoor whence he had been committed for poisoning his family, Graham Young was under arrest. A search of his bedsit at Hemel Hempstead disclosed various types of poison and a diary pompously titled *A Student's and Officer's Case Book*, both of which would prove vital in convicting Young of murder – though, true to character, he finally admitted that he had poisoned six people, two of whom had died: 'I could have killed them all if I wished, as I did Bob Egle and Fred Biggs, but I allowed them to live.'

In June 1972 Graham Young was put on trial at St Albans Crown Court, charged with the murder of Egle and Biggs and several counts of attempted murder; he pleaded not guilty.

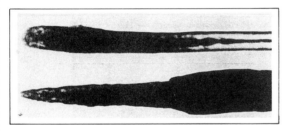

The effect of thallium poisoning on the root of a human hair; above, a healthy root 'bulb'; below, the characteristic dead root of thallium poisoning

Throughout the trial it was evident that he was having the time of his life. Incriminating extracts from his diary were read to the court: 'October 30 [1971]. I have administered a fatal dose of the special compound to F[red Biggs], and anticipate a report on his progress on Monday 1st November. I gave him three separate doses.' The court was also told that when arrested and searched, Young was found to have on his person a lethal dose of thallium – what he called his 'exit' dose; for as he had written in his diary: 'I must watch this situation very carefully. If it looks like I will be detected then I shall have to destroy myself.'

Nevertheless, Young stubbornly and arrogantly continued to protest his innocence; the diary entries, he said, were simply working notes for a novel that he was writing. And he had no idea how the body of Fred Biggs and the ashes of Bob Egle came to carry lethal amounts of thallium. The jury, however, failed to be persuaded by the cool confident manner of the prisoner; they could see through the shell to the psychopath that lurked beneath, the man who had callously poisoned his colleagues like guinea-pigs in a laboratory experiment. Graham Young was sentenced to life imprisonment.

On Wednesday, 1 August 1990, warders making a routine visit to Graham Young's cell at Parkhurst prison on the Isle of Wight found him lying crumpled on the floor. Rushed to the prison hospital, Young was found to have died from a heart attack; he was 42 years old.

NETHERLANDS

The Deadly Peanut Butter

Sjef Rijke was sentenced to life imprisonment in 1971 for the killing of three women in Utrecht – a rare example of a Dutch serial killer. The first murder was that of Rijke's fiancée, eighteen-year-old Willy Maas; the second, Mientje Manders, was also Rijke's fiancée. Three weeks after Manders' funeral Sjef Rijke married Maria Haas, who probably saved her own life by leaving him only six weeks after the wedding. However, his next lover was not so lucky, and suffered the most severe stomach pains as the result of eating the peanut butter which Rijke had liberally laced with rat poison. Sjef Rijke confessed to the killings and attempted killings, explaining that it gave him pleasure to see women suffer.

1972

The Barn Murder

An alarming case of false identification in which George Ince was identified three times as a killer. Ince was tried twice for murder and only vindicated when, by chance, the real killers were arrested.

The Barn Restaurant was what one would call a 'lively' place. And if the description 'nightspot' endowed it with perhaps too great a glamour, still it was popular enough as a place to dine and dance; and the neon sign outside reading 'Every Night Is Party Night' attracted the sort of clientele who liked to party. They were certainly partying on the night of 4 November 1972. The owner of the Barn, Bob Patience, was having a whale of a time doing what he liked best – giving his customers a good time while keeping his bank manager happy. At around 1.30 a.m. Bob's wife and faithful companion Muriel and her twenty-year-old daughter Beverley decided to call it a day and left the restaurant to walk the short distance to the family's luxury home behind the Barn. As they stepped into the house the two women came face to face with the barrel of a gun.

Shortly after 2 a.m. Bob Patience popped back and let himself into the house, pleased so far with the night's partying, and walked into the lounge to be confronted by two men, one menacing his wife and daughter with a gun. The demand was simple enough, the men wanted the key to the safe. Patience refused. 'Don't be a bloody fool Bob, give me the keys.' There was a second's silence. 'You mentioned

my husband's name,' said Muriel Patience in surprise. 'This is a family affair,' the gunman snapped back at her. Then he picked up a pink cushion from the sofa, held it in front of the gun and aimed it first at Muriel and then at Beverley: 'Your wife or your daughter? Your wife, I think.' And the room was filled with a muffled boom cut by Muriel's scream as she fell forward, a bullet in her head. 'Give me the keys.' Now Bob Patience moved; he picked the keys of the safe out of a bowl on the mantelshelf and the gunman made Beverley open the safe. Still aiming the gun directly at her, the man snatched up cash bags containing £900. When the raiders had tied up Bob and Beverley Patience, the man with the gun put a bullet into each of them before escaping in one of the family's cars.

So far an ordinary, if bloody, tale of East London gangsterdom from the period when a criminal's reliance on firearms was beginning

Bob Patience arrives for the trial of George Ince (Topham)

Identikit image of the killer of Mrs Patience

The unfortunate George Ince

John Brook, sentenced to life for the murder of Muriel Patience

to escalate. But for one man it would soon develop into a nightmare.

It was Bob Patience's son David who found the scene of carnage when he arrived home from the Barn at around 2.30 a.m. Bob had been lucky; the bullet meant to pierce his skull had just grazed him, Beverley was alive and recovered in hospital, but despite expert emergency treatment Muriel Patience died without regaining consciousness.

As soon as Beverley Patience had recovered sufficiently to give an interview the police were at her bedside taking a statement and, most important, a detailed description of the gunman. This was made into an Identikit picture and circulated. On 9 November the police had a tip-off: talk to George Ince.

Now Ince was certainly no angel; an East End gangster with a record of violence and theft, he had recently been suspected of involvement in a major silver bullion robbery. But that didn't necessarily make him a killer. Besides, Ince only fitted the descriptions given by Bob and Beverley Patience in the broadest outline. In fact when Bob Patience was shown a collection of photographs he picked out two possibles, neither of which was George Ince. Beverley, however, after careful consideration,

chose the picture of Ince on two separate occasions. George was well and truly in the frame. On 27 November 1972 two men walked into the police station at Epping; one of them was George Ince, the other was his solicitor. Ince had heard of the manhunt for him and was there to protest his innocence.

At the identity parade Bob Patience failed to pick Ince out of the line-up as he had failed to identify his photograph. David Patience, who had the merest glimpse of the assassins as they drove his car away from the house, picked out Ince but was uncertain about his choice. Beverley positively identified George Ince as the man who had shot her. Still protesting his innocence, Ince was formally charged with the murder of Muriel Patience.

On 2 May 1973 George Ince stood trial before Mr Justice Melford Stevenson at Chelmsford Crown Court. Predictably, perhaps, the trial was a noisy one, with opinions on the law and the judiciary freely and loudly expressed from the public gallery by friends and relatives of the participants; Ince himself was frequently abusive to the judge. Beverley Patience was the Crown's star witness, and she confirmed her identification of George Ince as the gunman who deprived her of a mother. On the fifth day of the trial Ince quarrelled with his attorney

246

and sacked him, declaring that he would be offering no evidence in his own defence. Whether this was 'unwise', as Mr Justice Melford Stevenson commented, or not, it certainly had the jury confused. After almost seven hours they failed even to reach a majority verdict. George Ince, for better or worse, would have to face retrial.

The second trial opened on 14 May at the same court; on this occasion the judge was Mr Justice Eveleigh. The evidence for the prosecution was much as before, but by now Ince had reinstated his counsel and was prepared to offer a defence: George Ince had spent the night of the murder in the company of a Mrs Gray at her home, and had not left until the following morning. Mrs Gray stepped into the witness box on 21 May, clearly apprehensive of the ordeal ahead, and well she might have been: in an unguarded moment Mr John Leonard for the prosecution addressed Mrs Gray by her real name. Now the whole world knew that George had spent the night of 4 November with Mrs Dolly Kray, whose husband Charles had been imprisoned three years earlier along with his brothers Ronald and Reginald. Ironically, it had been Mr Justice Eveleigh who sentenced them. This time the jury had no difficulty in reaching a verdict – George Ince was innocent.

So if George hadn't killed Muriel Patience and wounded her husband and daughter, who had?

The police did not have long to wait to find out. On 15 June a man named Peter Hanson walked into a police station in the Lake District to turn himself in for a robbery. During the course of questioning Hanson mentioned that he had been working in a hotel alongside a man who had boasted that he had a gun and had murdered somebody with it. The somebody was Muriel Patience, and her killer's name was John Brook. Although at the time it seemed a bit far-fetched, the police made inquiries in London and finally Brook was taken into custody and his room searched. Sewn into the mattress on his bed was Brook's gun – the same gun, according to ballistics experts, which had been used to kill Muriel Patience. Now the police began to round up Brook's acquaintances for questioning. They

The Man Who 'Saved California'

Herbert Mullin began to establish his credentials as a multicide on instruction from the voices which he heard in his head – voices which he later recognised as Satan's, but which nevertheless convinced him that only by shedding blood could he save California from a devastating earthquake. What was more, the voices told him that the murder victims would be inexpressibly grateful for the opportunity to help out in this way. The first sacrifice was a vagrant, in October 1972; eleven days later he butchered a young girl student. By the

Herbert Mullin (Press Association)

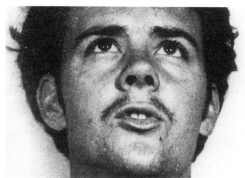

beginning of the following year Mullin had obtained a gun and was killing more randomly, and more frequently – as many as five murders during a single day in January – until he was arrested on 13 February 1973. Despite a history of in-patient treatment for paranoid schizophrenia and a long-established pattern of responding to 'voices', Herbert Mullin's plea of insanity was rejected at his trial and he was convicted and sentenced to various terms of imprisonment for eleven murders.

struck lucky with Nicholas de Clare Johnson, at the time in prison but willing enough to put the finger on John Brook and to confess his own minor role in the Barn murder.

In January 1974 the third Barn trial opened at Chelmsford Crown Court, with John Brook facing the same charges with which the unfortunate George Ince had been indicted. But if Ince thought he was off the hook then he was wrong – Brook's defence was that it was Ince and Johnson who had been at the Barn that night. But by now Beverley Patience had seen a man even more like the gunman than George Ince, and he was standing in the dock in front of her. The trial lasted four weeks, but it took the jury less than two and a half hours to find John Brook guilty of murder and attempted murder, and Johnson guilty of manslaughter. They were sentenced respectively to life and ten years.

George Ince, meanwhile, had been banged up for his part in the silver bullion job back in 1972. In September 1977, he was allowed out of prison briefly to marry Dolly, now divorced from Charles Kray; in 1980 he was released on parole.

1973

Albert DeSalvo, 'The Boston Strangler'

Between 1962 and 1964, the Strangler was responsible for the murders of thirteen women. Diagnosed schizophrenic and unfit to stand trial for murder, DeSalvo was instead sentenced to life imprisonment for sex offences and robberies committed before the crimes of the Strangler.

On 26 November 1973 one of America's most notorious serial killers was found dead in Walpole Prison hospital, Massachusetts; his body was discovered by a guard ten hours after the killing. Albert DeSalvo, the 'Boston Strangler', who had been responsible for the deaths of thirteen women, had been stabbed no fewer than sixteen times, six times through the heart. Why he was murdered we may never know; the bitter hatreds and rivalries which grow behind prison walls flare up often for no very good reason at all. But if there was a motive behind the killing of DeSalvo then the conspiracy of silence among his fellow prisoners ensured that it, and the identity of the killer, remained secret.

The first victim's body, that of 55-year-old Anna Slesers, had been found by her son naked, raped and strangled with the belt of her own blue housecoat, on 14 June 1962. Over the next almost two years the killer's method would be unvarying. After targeting his victim, the 'Strangler', as he became known, gained entry to the victims' homes by posing as a workman. All his victims were women, all were sexually assaulted and all were strangled – usually with

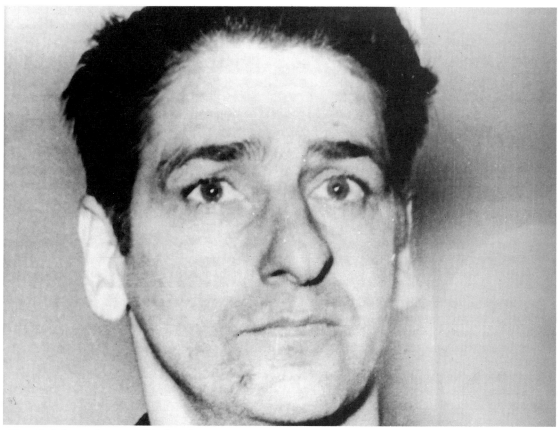

Albert DeSalvo under arrest (Topham)

an item of their own clothing, often a pair of stockings or tights which he tied with a bow under the chin. In some instances strangulation had been accompanied by biting, bludgeoning (as in the case of Mrs Slesers) and even stabbing. Despite the customary false confessions made by cranks and attention-seekers, and a blanket police response to the city's mounting panic, the Boston Strangler remained an enigmatic object of terror.

The murder of Anna Slesers was followed two weeks later by the death of 85-year-old Mary Mullen at Commonwealth Avenue. Mrs Mullen was the victim of heart failure, and it was not until DeSalvo confessed that he had been in her apartment and that she died of shock before he could rape her that she was added to the Strangler's list of victims. There

was no doubt about the events of 30 June, two days after the Mullen incident. Nina Nichols, a 68-year-old widow, was found in identical circumstances to the first victim, in an apartment on Commonwealth Avenue, the same long street where Mary Mullen had lived. That same day the Strangler struck again, killing 65-year-old Helen Blake, a retired nurse, at Newhall Street, Lynn, a few miles north of Boston. Both victims had been sexually assaulted and strangled with an item of their clothing.

Following the murder of Helen Blake, police enlisted the help of forensic psychiatrists to help profile the killer they were hunting. In the opinion of experts he was a youngish man, eighteen to 40, suffering delusions of persecution, and with a hatred of his mother (so

249

far only elderly women had been attacked). This 'portrait' was run alongside records of known sex offenders, and although a number of suspects emerged from the files and were interviewed, the Strangler remained free to kill 75-year-old Mrs Ira Irga on 19 August, and 67-year-old Jane Sullivan the next day.

On 5 December 1962, the psychological profile of a 'mother-hater' collapsed when student hospital technician Sophie Clark was murdered; she was twenty years old, just three years younger than two of the Strangler's next three victims.

Patricia Bissette, a pregnant 23-year-old from Black Bay, was found strangled on 31 December, and in March and May the following year, 1963, 69-year-old Mary Brown and 23-year-old graduate Beverley Samans were added to the grim toll of the elusive Boston Strangler.

One of the interesting psychological aspects of DeSalvo's pattern of killing, which distinguishes him from most sexually-motivated serial murderers, is that his kill-rate was decelerating. From four deaths in the month of June 1962, to two in August and two in December of the same year, it was three months until the first murder of 1963, on 9 March, and two months before the next, on 6 May. Not until 8 September did the Strangler kill again, robbing 58-year-old Evelyn Corbin of her life, followed by 23-year-old Joann Graff on 23 November.

A reign of terror that had haunted the city of Boston since June 1962, leaving thirteen women dead, and the city with a modern legend, ended on 4 January 1964. He would strike once more, ineffectually; but at least the killing had stopped.

Nineteen-year-old Mary Sullivan was found, like all the other victims of the Boston Strangler, in her own apartment. She had been stripped and bound, raped and strangled; and in a final sadistic gesture, Mary's killer had left a New Year's greeting card wedged between the toes of her left foot.

After the death of Mary Sullivan, the 'father' of American psychological profiling, Dr James

Brussell, provided a new 'psychofit' of a 30-year-old man, strongly built, of average height, clean-shaven with thick dark hair; possibly of Spanish or Italian origin – and a paranoid schizophrenic. The portrait was to prove remarkably accurate.

Meanwhile another specialist used to 'working in the dark', Dutch psychometrist and psychic detective Peter Hurkos, had entered the investigation. After some remarkable demonstrations of intuition, Hurkos revealed that the man the police were after was slightly built, weighing 130–140 pounds, five feet seven or eight, with a pointed sharp nose and a scar on his left arm. The psychic added: 'And he loves shoes.' Unbelievably, there was just such a man on the suspect list, a perfect match down to his occupation as a ladies' shoe salesman. Unfortunately, he was not the Boston Strangler.

In the end it was for the Strangler to make himself known. On 27 October 1964, posing as a detective, he entered, as he had done before, a young woman's apartment. The intruder tied his victim to the bed, sexually assaulted her, and then inexplicably left, saying as he went, 'I'm sorry.' The woman's description led to the identification of Albert DeSalvo, and the publication of his photograph led to scores of women coming forward to identify him as the man who had sexually assaulted them. But DeSalvo was still not suspected of being the Boston Strangler. It was only in 1965, while he was being held on a rape charge and confined to the Boston State Hospital, that he confessed in detail to the Strangler's crimes. His knowledge of the murders was such that no doubt could be entertained as to the truth of his confession. Nevertheless, there was not one single piece of direct evidence to support these claims, and in a remarkable piece of plea-bargaining, DeSalvo's attorney agreed that his client should stand trial only for a number of earlier crimes unconnected with the stranglings. Albert DeSalvo never stood trial for the crimes of the Boston Strangler, but was instead convicted of robbery and sexual offences and sent to prison for life.

1974

Ronald DeFeo

The Amityville Horror. *A crime which attracted considerable notoriety by being turned into a film. DeFeo shot dead his whole family, telling police afterwards: 'Once I got started I just couldn't stop.'*

Greguski was the first officer on the scene. The call had come through to the Amityville Village police department at 6.35 p.m. that evening of 13 November 1974: 'Hey, kid's just run into the bar. Says everyone in his family's been killed.' So in the autumnal gloom patrolman Kenneth Greguski was despatched to Ocean Avenue where a small crowd was beginning to assemble. The centre of attraction seemed to be the young man crouched down sobbing that 'they' had got his mom and his dad. It turned out that 'they' had got a lot more than that. When Greguski worked his way through the house he made the body count six; later identified as Ronald DeFeo Sr, a wealthy motor trader; his wife Louise; their daughters Dawn and Allison, aged eighteen and thirteen respectively; and sons Mark, twelve years old, and John, seven. Still weeping on the porch was Ronald Junior, 23 years old and the only survivor of the DeFeo family massacre.

When he was finally settled in at the Amityville police station, Ronald 'call me "Butch"' DeFeo had a strange tale to tell. As the detectives listened, 'Butch' told them that his father had been involved with the Mafia, and in particular he had crossed swords with one of the mob's hit-men, Louis Falini. A fortnight earlier

there had been an armed hold-up when money was being transported from the DeFeo car showroom to the bank, during which Ronald Junior had been obliged to part with the company's takings. According to his present narrative, Butch's father had accused him of inventing the robbery story and stealing the money for himself.

On the morning of the murders Ronald Jr had got up early and driven to the showrooms; several times during the morning he had tried to phone home but there was no reply. At noon Ronald returned to Amityville where he spent the afternoon drinking with friends. Early evening he left the bar for home, throwing over his shoulder the casual remark that he had forgotten his keys and would have to break in through a window.

While this interview was going on, other officers checked out Butch's friends, and learned that he was a gun fanatic. What's more, the DeFeos had all been shot with a Marlin .35 calibre rifle – and in Butch's wardrobe there was a cardboard box which had contained a Marlin .35.

Not surprisingly Ronald DeFeo Junior found himself spending longer in police custody than he had bargained for. He whiled away the time inventing ever more preposterous accounts of the killings until at last he was detained on a holding charge of the second-degree murder of his brother Mark.

It was nearly a year later that DeFeo stood trial. He had made good use of the time feigning insanity, and had made a pretty good job of it – at least defence psychiatrist Dr Daniel Schwartz was prepared to give expert testimony that at the time he killed his family Butch was suffering from mental disease – 'paranoid

251

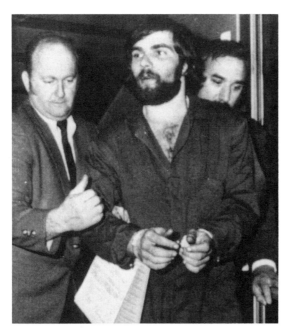

'Butch' DeFeo in the care of the police (Topham)

lying dead on her bed he claimed: 'I have never seen this person before.' But Butch didn't have it all his own way. Dr Harold Zola for the prosecution gave his opinion that the defendant was not a psychopath, but a sociopath who had so devalued human life that even his parents were expendable in his drive to assert his superiority. And the jury obviously agreed, because they found Ronald DeFeo Junior guilty on all six counts of murder. DeFeo was sentenced to 25 years to life on each count and confined to the Dannemora Correctional Facility, New York. As the six slayings are legally considered a single act, the sentences are being served concurrently.

And so a dreadful crime might have been forgotten. But that is to reckon without the power exerted when the supernatural meets Hollywood. The DeFeo home in Amityville, ironically called High Hopes, was subsequently sold to a family who, after only a year, fled following a series of disturbances by what they called 'evil forces'. This phenomenon was first re-created as a best-selling book and then not one but several films in the *Amityville Horror* sequence. It is just as well that the media cashed in when it did – the present owners of High Hopes find the place a very quiet and pleasant home.

delusions' the doctor said, a belief that if he did not kill them then they would kill him. As if to add weight to his insanity plea, when Ronald was shown a photograph of his mother

UNITED KINGDOM

The Timely Disappearance of Lucky Lucan

Richard John Bingham, Seventh Earl of Lucan – known to his friends as 'Lucky' Lucan – disappeared on 7 November 1974, leaving behind in the London home of his estranged wife Veronica the brutally bludgeoned body of the Lucan children's nanny, Sandra Rivett. At the inquest in June 1975, the coroner's jury brought in a verdict of 'murder by Lord Lucan' (the last time that a coroner's court was allowed to name a murder suspect). Although there have been reported sightings from every corner of the globe, Lord Lucan remains a fugitive – though it must be added that there has always been considerable speculation over his guilt. One recent theory is that Lucan hired an assassin to murder his wife in order to gain custody of the children, and that the killer bungled the job and killed Sandra Rivett instead. Another suggestion is that the victim disturbed a burglar who was attempting to steal Lady Lucan's jewellery, and forfeited her life.

1975

Donald Neilson, 'The Black Panther'

A thief with a habit of murdering sub-postmasters, Neilson was already an accomplished killer before he committed the crime that was to launch one of Britain's biggest manhunts: the killing of seventeen-year-old Lesley Whittle.

The first of what were to be four brutal and unnecessary murders was committed on 15 February 1974 at Harrogate. Richard, the youngest son of sub-postmaster Donald Skepper, woke with a start to find himself looking down both barrels of the shotgun held by a man demanding keys to the safe. When the intruder failed to find them where the boy had indicated, he entered the parents' bedroom with the same demand. With more courage than forethought Donald Skepper shouted 'Let's get him', and was immediately shot.

On 6 September of the same year, sub-postmaster Derek Astin tackled an intruder in his post office at Higher Baxenden, near Accrington; he was shot dead in front of his wife and two children.

Intense activity on the part of the Yorkshire constabulary forced the raider to transfer his activities to a different location, and mid-November found him in Langley, Worcestershire. Here he shot Sidney Grayland, bludgeoned his wife Margaret, fracturing her skull, and stole £800 from the cashbox.

By November 1974 the mystery man had notched up some twenty robberies in seven years, with a combined haul of over £20,000. Worse still, the elusive thief had killed three times and left several other victims seriously wounded. The *modus operandi* was almost invariable: armed with a shotgun the intruder chose the early hours of the morning to drill through windowframes and release the catches, rouse the still-sleeping occupants, mainly of sub-post offices, and demand the keys to the safe. His working uniform was always the same: black plimsolls, army camouflage suit, white gloves, and the black hood which earned him his sobriquet of 'The Black Panther'.

Less than two months later, in the first month of the New Year, the Panther committed the crime that was to move the nation and make him Britain's most wanted man.

Beech Croft was the Whittle family home situated in the village of Highley in Shropshire. George Whittle, a successful businessman who had built up a prosperous coach business, died in 1970, leaving his widow Dorothy, son Ronald, who now ran the fleet of coaches, and seventeen-year-old daughter Lesley, a student. On the morning of Tuesday, 14 January 1975, Mrs Whittle was alarmed to find her daughter missing from the house; Lesley seemed simply to have disappeared. However, it was not long before the family found three messages pressed out of red Dymo-tape in the lounge: there was now no doubt that Lesley had been kidnapped.

The first strip read: 'No police / £50,000 ransom to be ready to deliver / wait for telephone call at Swan shopping centre telephone box 6pm to 1am / if no call return following

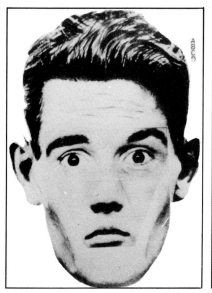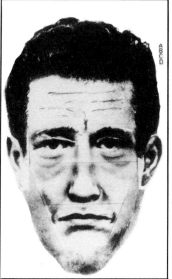

Various Identikit images of the 'Black Panther' (Syndication International)

evening / when you answer call give your name only and listen / you must follow instructions without argument / from the time you answer you are on a time limit / if police or tricks death.' The second message gave details of the drop: 'Swan shopping centre Kidderminster / deliver £50,000 in a white suitcase.' The third listed the way the money was to be made up: '£50,000 all in old notes / £25,000 in £1 notes and £25,000 in £5 notes / there will be no exchange / only after £50,000 has been cleared will victim be released.'

Despite the warnings, Ronald Whittle made immediate contact with the West Mercia police force, and although there was a quite obvious need for the police involvement to be kept secret, news of the kidnapping and of the ransom demand was leaked to a freelance journalist who, with a callous disregard for Lesley Whittle's safety that characterised the worst elements of his profession, sold this information to a Birmingham newspaper and to the BBC, which went so far as to interrupt programmes to broadcast the newsflash.

On the following night, 15 January, an incident took place which provided the first major clues for the specialist Scotland Yard kidnap team which had been called in. Gerald Smith,

a security officer at the Freightliner container depot at Dudley, was on a routine patrol when he observed a man loitering around the perimeter fence. So strange was the man's behaviour when Smith approached that he decided to call the police. Turning his back, the next thing he was aware of was the loud explosion of gunfire and a searing pain in his buttocks; the attacker then emptied the remaining five bullets into the unfortunate watchman and disappeared. Remarkably, Gerald Smith was able to crawl to a telephone and alert the police.

Subsequently, ballistics experts were able to confirm, by matching the telltale ejection marks left like 'fingerprints' on the spent cartridges, that they came from the same gun that had been used in two earlier crimes – crimes known to have been the handiwork of the Black Panther. When investigating officers traced the green Morris 1300 saloon car that had been seen parked at the Freightliner depot they were rewarded with further vital pointers to the identity of the attacker. Among the items recovered from the car were a number of Dymo-tape messages, quite clearly pieces of a ransom trail and identical to those left at the Whittle home, and a cassette recorder containing a taped message from Lesley Whittle to her mother. Soon Gerald Smith's description of his assailant had been transformed into a portrait drawing that was to become one of the best-known faces in the country and was carried by the television networks as well as by the Press and cinemas.

Just before midnight on 16 January, Ronald Whittle received a telephone call from the man claiming to be Lesley's captor. Following a trail marked by further Dymo-tape messages, Ronald arrived at Bathpool Park near the town of Kidsgrove, Staffordshire. Here the kidnapper was supposed to respond with a torch to Ronald Whittle's flashing car headlights. In the event there was no contact and Lesley's brother and his 'undercover' police escort were left once again helpless and frustrated.

For reasons best known to themselves, the police took more than a fortnight to get around to a detailed search of Bathpool Park, by which time the developments had received sufficient publicity to prompt a local headmaster to remember that one of his pupils had handed him a strip of Dymo-tape bearing the message 'Drop Suitcase into Hole' which he had found in the park a couple of days after the kidnapping. Another significant clue was a torch, found by another schoolboy, wedged in the grille of a ventilating shaft to the sewage system that runs beneath Bathpool Park.

Encouraged by these clues, police and tracker dogs began to search the underground culverts; it was during this operation that the naked body of Lesley Whittle was found at the bottom of one of the ventilating shafts. Around her neck was a noose of wire attached to the iron ladder. Still it was to be almost a year before the Black Panther was captured.

On the night of Thursday 11 December 1975, PCs Stuart Mackenzie and Tony White were on a routine Panda car patrol in the Nottinghamshire village of Mansfield Woodhouse. Seeing a small shambling man carrying a black holdall, the two officers decided to investigate; the suspect in his turn produced a sawn-off shotgun and forced White and Mackenzie back into the car. Taking the front passenger seat, and with his gun stuck in PC Mackenzie's ribs, the man issued only one instruction: 'Drive!'

With a cool professionalism, the more remarkable given the circumstances, the two officers, using a combination of verbal and visual signals (via the rear-view mirror), con-

Lesley Whittle (Popperfoto)

The 'Black Panther' as his victims saw him

The Judge Who Didn't Agree

On Christmas Eve, 1975, William Thomas Zeigler Jr telephoned the Orange County, Florida, chief of police and told him: 'I think there's trouble . . . I'm at the store. I've been shot.' The 'store' was the furniture shop which Zeigler and his father ran at Winter Garden, and when the police arrived there had certainly been 'trouble'. As well as Zeigler Jr, who was bleeding heavily from a stomach wound, four other people lay dead on the floor of the showroom. Among the victims was a man named Charlie Mays who, according to Zeigler, had robbed the store, killed old Mr Zeigler, his wife, and Zeigler Jr's wife Eunice before turning the gun on Zeigler Jr himself, who had just had time to shoot Mays before collapsing from his own wound. As the result of one of those miracles of coincidence so beloved of crime novelists, a stray bullet had

ricocheted off the walls and stopped the clock at 7.24 p.m. – more than an hour before William Zeigler called the police. This was suspicious in itself, but it took the skills of leading American forensic expert Herb MacDowell to analyse the scene of the crime and piece together indisputable proof that Zeigler had massacred his family before inflicting a gunshot wound on himself. Apparently his marriage to Eunice had taken a turn for the worse and she was about to leave him; he had responded by taking out a $520,000 insurance policy on her life and then shooting her. Convicting Zeigler Jr of two first-degree and two second-degree murders, a remarkably lenient jury recommended a sentence of life imprisonment which was overruled by the judge, who handed down the death penalty.

spired to disarm and capture the man holding them at gunpoint. Jamming his foot on the brake at a T-junction Mackenzie sufficiently surprised the gunman for White to lunge at the gun, which was now pointed away from his companion. In the struggle which followed the car became a riot of smoke and noise as the

The 'People's War'

Among the most successful and most feared revolutionary terrorists in modern political history was the left-wing group under the leadership of Berndt Andreas Baader and Ulrike Marie Meinhof, who sought to undermine the federal German government and its economy, and engaged in robbery and murder as part of the so-called 'People's War'. The leaders, including Baader and Meinhof, were put on trial in May 1975; almost one year later Ulrike Meinhof hanged herself in her prison cell. The rest of the defendants were eventually sentenced to life imprisonment.

shotgun exploded into action, and despite injuries to White's hand from pellets, and the perforation of Mackenzie's eardrums by the explosion, they hung on to their former captor. With assistance from Keith Wood, a member of the public who was queuing for fish and chips where the car had stopped and who had felled the gunman with a karate blow, the two officers were able to make an arrest. Although they did not know it yet, PCs White and Mackenzie – with a little public-spirited help from Mr Wood – had just terminated the career of the Black Panther.

The Black Panther was born at Morley, near Bradford, on 1 August 1936. Christened Donald Nappey, he subsequently changed his name to Neilson to avoid repeats of the inevitable association with babies' underwear which had tormented him at school. It was a gesture characteristic of a man who, after being conscripted for National Service with the British forces in Kenya, Aden and Cyprus, became obsessed by the techniques of 'survival' and of guerrilla warfare.

When the police searched his home at

Grangefield Avenue, Thornaby, Bradford, they found all the evidence they needed to bring four charges of murder against Neilson. For each of these he was to receive a life sentence; for kidnapping he was condemned to 61 years' imprisonment.

Gerald Smith, the nightwatchman, died in March 1976 as a result of his confrontation with Neilson. However, the laws of England allow a charge of murder to be brought only if the victim dies within a year and a day of the assault.

1976

Michael George Hart

'Give me some money...' *Hart shot bank clerk Angela Wooliscroft dead during a bank raid; although he protested that the gun had been discharged by mistake, forensic ballistics proved to the satisfaction of a court that the shooting was a deliberate act.*

On 10 November 1976, a heavily disguised man walked up to till number 3 at the Upper Ham Road branch of Barclays Bank at Richmond, Surrey. He levelled a sawn-off shotgun at the clerk behind the safety screen and, without raising his voice, simply said: 'Give me some money.'

As the terrified girl pushed money from the till across the counter the man's finger tightened on the gun's trigger, the safety glass shattered into a million fragments and Angela Wooliscroft was thrown from her stool by the impact of the burning shot ripping through her hand and chest. She died in the ambulance before reaching hospital.

An experienced team from Scotland Yard, led by Detective Chief Superintendent James Sewell, lost no time in issuing a description of the armed robber compiled from the recollections of shocked bank staff. Scene-of-crime officers painstakingly collected the glass and debris from the gun's discharge, and bagged for forensic examination a woman's yellow raincoat, in which the killer had concealed his weapon, and an empty plastic bag which had once contained chemical fertiliser. The pockets on the raincoat were found to contain two scraps of paper, one of which was to prove a vital clue in the hunt for Angela Wooliscroft's killer. Part of an entry form for a wine-making competition, it had been signed 'Grahame', and its reverse side used as a shopping list. In response to police publicity Mr Grahame James Marshall laid claim to the wine-club entry, and his sister to the shopping list. On the day of the shooting Miss Marshall had driven her car to Kingston and left it in the car-park at Bentall's department store. When she returned after shopping Miss Marshall noticed that the car was in a slightly different position and a pair of sunglasses and her yellow raincoat were missing from inside. The maroon Austin A40 had already been described by observers as the raider's escape car.

Meanwhile Home Office pathologist Professor Keith Mant had examined the body of the victim and drawn certain conclusions regarding the shooting that would prove vital in the case against the murderer. Material recovered from the body and the scene of the shooting were passed on to the ballistics team which immediately identified the weapon as a twelve-bore shotgun.

Chief Superintendent Sewell's next break came not from the police investigation, but from an informant who claimed to have seen a known criminal named Michael Hart putting a shotgun into the back of a car in Basingstoke. Although Hart initially provided a convincing alibi for his whereabouts at the time of the shooting, and a general search of his house revealed nothing incriminating, James Sewell felt that Hart's previous record was sufficient reason to keep him under supervision. It was the hunch that solved the crime, because on 22 November Hart's car, which had been involved in an accident, was picked up by the crew of a police patrol car; a search of the vehicle turned up a Hendal .22 automatic pistol with ammunition. During a more intensive search of Hart's home, a box of 'Eley' No. 7 trapshooting cartridges was found; these, together with the Hendal and its ammunition and a double-barrelled Reilly shotgun, were part of a haul stolen from a Reading gun dealer on 4 November.

But it was at this point that an alarming discrepancy began to show in relation to the ballistics evidence. The pellets removed from the body of the victim were No. 7 *gameshot*; the cartridges found in Hart's possession were No. 7 *trapshot* (which is gameshot containing more of the hardening agent antimzyne). However, when the laboratory removed the contents from Hart's trapshot cartridges they were found to be gameshot. The enigma was quickly cleared up by the manufacturers, Eley Kynock of Birmingham; it transpired that, through simple human error, the wrong label had been put on

a small batch of cartridges – the batch that was supplied to the raided gun-shop. Furthermore, the wads – the compressed board discs used to pack the shot – were both of a type unique to Eley, made from cardboard impregnated with paraffin wax and in use only since March 1976. The wads found in the victim's wound and those in Hart's cartridges were identical.

Even so, it was not until 20 January 1977 that Michael George Hart was taken into custody, and it was a further ten months before he appeared in court. In the meantime he had attempted to hang himself in his cell, and then confessed to killing Angela Wooliscroft 'by accident'. He had, so he said, tapped on the glass screen with the gun as Miss Wooliscroft had leant over to the right to fish money out of the drawer, and it had simply gone off. But it was too late for this kind of cynical deception. The scientists had done their job too well, and knew the wounds were just not consistent with such an explanation. When Michael Hart finally led police officers to the stretch of river from which they dragged the abandoned shotgun, the last piece of indelible evidence was slotted into its place.

On 3 November 1977, almost a full year after he had deliberately blasted away a young woman's life at close range, 30-year-old Michael Hart was convicted of murder and sentenced to serve not less than 25 years in prison.

UNITED STATES

Mark Gary Gilmore

'Let's do it!' *Having spent the greater part of his adult life in prison, Gilmore was sentenced to death for two separate robbery/murders in 1976. Despite every effort made to win him a reprieve, Gary Gilmore insisted on his own death, and was executed according to his wish, by firing squad.*

By the time he was paroled in 1976, Gary Gilmore had spent the greater part of his adult life in prison. In July that same year he senselessly shot and killed David Jensen, the 24-year-old attendant at a filling station in Oren, Utah. The following evening, Gilmore walked into the City Centre Motel, Provo, and murdered the young manager, Bennie Bushnel, before plundering the cashbox. Gilmore made no attempt to cover his own tracks, and was arrested that same night. He was tried, convicted and, according to Utah procedure, sentenced to death.

What elevated Gary Gilmore's case above his sordid murders was the obsessive determination with which he pursued the death penalty, despite considerable national outcry. At one point he threatened to dismiss his lawyers if they tried to win him a reprieve. It is not certain whether Gilmore was aware of the fact that his execution would be the first of a new era which would herald a renewed wave of judicial killing throughout the United States, but if he was it is unlikely that it would have made much difference.

Not noted for their sensational coverage of the minutiae of violent crime and punishment, even the *New York Times* on 17 January 1977 led with a wordy front-page headline: 'Gilmore Faces Execution at Dawn; Two Appeals to Supreme Court Fail; Ten-year Death Penalty Moratorium Due to End.' It was just six months previously, in July 1976, that the United States Supreme Court had ruled that the use of capital punishment was constitutionally permissible.

Gilmore himself, calm as ever, spent his last hours in the stark, windowless visitors' room with his aunt, uncle, cousins and his lawyers; at one point he spoke to his mother for the last time on the telephone to her home in Oregon. By all accounts Gary was relaxed and in good spirits; the only sign of tension was when somebody unwisely mentioned the word 'reprieve', at which he became very angry, began using abusive language and had to be given a sedative. At no stage in the entire proceedings had Gary Gilmore relented in his determination to die for his crimes. He had become notorious for the philosophy 'If you can get away with murder, do it; but if you get caught, don't cry about being punished'. When earlier it had looked as though he might be reprieved

Gary Gilmore under arrest at Provo, Utah (Topham)

anyway, Gilmore twice tried to take his own life.

About 7.45 a.m., in the half-light of the January morning, Gary Gilmore was transferred to the execution shed. The killing itself was to take place by firing squad in a warehouse formerly attached to the prison farm and used as a cannery; it was now a general store-room and had been specially cleared of stacks of paint cans and ladders for the occasion. Gilmore, wearing a black T-shirt and white trousers with tricolour red, white and blue tennis shoes, was escorted by guards to the leather-backed wooden armchair which had been raised about a foot off the ground on a small platform; almost like a stage set, the chair was bathed in light from above. Behind the chair was a plywood barrier half an inch thick, and between it and the concrete-block wall of the shed were piled sandbags and an old mattress – to soak up the bullets. Thirty feet away, down at the other end of the warehouse and directly in front of the chair, stood a bizarre-looking black cubicle. It had been fashioned of black muslin stretched over a wooden frame, and along the front five rectangular openings had been cut, about three by six inches. Inside, and out of sight of the condemned man, sat the firing squad. As they sat in their bunker, Gilmore sat loosely bound to the arms and legs of the chair.

When preparations were complete the score or so witnesses were ushered in and stood

The death chair viewed through one of the executioners' firing slits (Topham)

behind a line taped on the warehouse floor. The few people whom Gilmore had specifically requested to attend approached him and said their final few words – his uncle Vern Damico, Robert Moody, Ronald Stanger, and the literary agent who had bought the rights to Gary Gilmore's story, Lawrence Schiller. As the visitors walked back across the line to join the other witnesses, cotton wool was handed out to protect their ears. With the firing squad waiting anxiously, the prison governor stepped forward and asked the prisoner if he had any last message; looking first up to the roof and then straight ahead, Gilmore said, 'Let's do it!' At that a black hood was eased over his head and a black target with a white circle was pinned over his heart. At a sign from the governor a volley of shots ripped into Gary Gilmore's body, filling the void of the warehouse with a deafening crash.

Two minutes later the doctor pronounced life extinct and the body was rushed to a nearby hospital where the corneas of Gilmore's eyes were removed for transplant.

On the afternoon following the execution a short memorial service was held at Gary Gilmore's request in Spanish Fork. The ceremony was attended by his lawyers and their families, the ever-loyal uncle Vern, literary agent Lawrence Schiller and half a dozen or so others. After the cremation, Gary's ashes were taken up in a light aircraft and scattered across the landscape around Salt Lake City.

UNITED STATES

God's Executioner

Joseph Kallinger was the sort of eccentric of whom one might expect almost anything. Little surprise, then, that the man who lived in a twenty-foot-deep pit in the cellar of his house should also wear wedges in his shoes by which device he could adjust the list of his body to harmonise with his brain. It would have seemed strange if he had *not* received direct instructions from God – and from the Devil as well. Indeed it had become his conviction that God wanted him for a very special job – He wanted Joseph to annihilate mankind. For this prospective Armageddon Kallinger enlisted the help of his twelve-year-old son (the other son he had already insured for $70,000 and then drowned).

Perhaps in preparation for their higher calling, Kallinger and son spent the years 1973–75 burgling, murdering and mutilating, evading capture more through good luck than smart planning. In 1976 their luck ran out, and Kallinger – still in contact with the Lord – faced his earthly judge. By now even his defence counsel was finding it difficult not to face the fact that his client was as mad as a hatter. Foaming at the mouth and gibbering in 'tongues', Joseph the Chosen One was, incomprehensibly, judged to be able to distinguish right from wrong, enabling a jury to convict him and a judge to sentence him to a minimum of 42 years' imprisonment.

1977

David Berkowitz, 'Son of Sam'

The so-called 'Son of Sam' claimed to have been driven by the voices of what he described as 'demons', and was sentenced to 365 years' imprisonment for a total of six murders. So great was the public interest in the case, and so much in demand did Berkowitz become to journalists and TV producers, that a new law – called the 'Son of Sam Law' was introduced forbidding a criminal to make a profit from discussing his misdeeds.

At one o'clock on the morning of 29 July 1976 an eighteen-year-old medical technician named Donna Lauria and her friend, nineteen-year-old Jody Valente, a student nurse, were sitting in Jody's stationary car outside Donna's home in the Bronx. As they were about to call it a night and go home to bed a young man calmly walked out of the darkness towards the car, took a gun from a brown paper bag and started shooting; he left Donna Lauria dead and her friend wounded in the thigh.

The next shooting took place on 23 October in the middle-class Queens district. A young couple, Carl Denaro and Rosemary Keenan, were shot at as they sat in their car outside a bar at Flushing. Denaro had a small portion of his skull shattered but suffered no brain damage; his eighteen-year-old girlfriend was unharmed. Then a month later, at midnight on 27 November, Donna DeMasi and her friend Joanne Lomino were shot and wounded while sitting on the steps outside Joanne's home at 262nd Street in the same district of Queens. Donna made a complete recovery from her neck wound, but tragically the lower half of Joanne's body was paralysed by a bullet in her lower spine.

Meanwhile, ballistics experts had established that all three attacks had been carried out using the same weapon, a .44 Bulldog – giving the murderer the provisional name 'The .44 Killer'.

On 30 January 1977 another couple, John Diel and Christine Freund, were sitting in their Pontiac after a night out in Queens when suddenly

Map showing the distribution of 'Son of Sam's' attacks

July 29, 1976
One Killed,
One Wounded

NEW JERSEY

BRONX

April 17, 1977
Two Killed

June 26, 1977
Two Wounded

October 23, 1976
One Wounded

QUEENS

Nov. 27, 1976
Two Wounded

March 8, 1977
One Killed

January 30, 1977
One Killed

Upper
Bay

BROOKLYN

July 31, 1977
Two Wounded

0   4
Miles

the passenger window was shattered by bullets, one of which tore into Christine's skull; she died later in hospital but her fiancé was unharmed. A further senseless, random attack was made on 8 March, when nineteen-year-old Columbia University student Virginia Voskerichian was shot dead in the street. But things were about to take a new turn as an increasingly bold killer began to expose himself. The breakthrough came on 14 April 1977, when Valentina Suriani and Alexander Esau were both fatally shot as they sat in their car in the Bronx.

Police officers, members of the task force called 'Operation Omega', established to investigate this series of killings, found a letter, presumably left by the murderer, lying near Alex Esau's car. It was addressed to the New York

Police artist's impression of 'Son of Sam'

Police Department and read: 'Dear Captain Joseph Borelli, I am deeply hurt by your calling me a woman-hater, I am not. But I am a monster.' The killer also wrote a letter to flamboyant New York *Daily News* columnist Jimmy Breslin on 1 June: '... Not knowing what the future holds I shall say farewell and I will see you at the next job? Or should I say you will see my handiwork at the next job? Remember Ms. Lauria. In their blood and from the gutter, "Sam's Creation" .44.'

'Sam's Creation'? Now the *Daily News* had a new name for the killer: 'Son of Sam.' Breslin, through his column, replied to the letter, goading the killer into making another move; it was a dangerous game, and there were still more deaths to come.

On 26 June, in Queens, Salvatore Lupo and Judith Placido were wounded while they sat in a car. On 31 July, Stacy Moskowitz and Robert Violante became 'Son of Sam's' last victims; shot in their car, twenty-year-old Stacy died in hospital and Robert Violante was blinded.

Like many criminals before him, the mystery killer called 'Son of Sam' had just made his one fatal mistake. After the Moskowitz/Violante shooting he walked back to his yellow Ford Galaxie which had been parked blocking a fire hydrant, took a traffic violation ticket off the window and threw it in the gutter. This familiar scene was observed from her car by Mrs Cecilia Davis, who might have thought no more of it had she not seen the same young man while she was out walking her dog later that night; this time he was carrying something up his sleeve that Mrs Davis thought might be a gun. When the police were informed, they ran a check on the car that the ticket had been issued to and came up with the name David Berkowitz, resident of Pine Street in the suburb of Yonkers. When detectives found his car there was a loaded semi-automatic rifle on the seat and a letter, addressed to the head of Operation Omega and threatening another killing, in the glove box. They settled down to wait till Berkowitz came out of his apartment to claim them. No sooner had he settled himself behind the wheel, than Berkowitz was taken from the car and asked: 'Who are you?' 'I'm Sam,' he replied with a smile. David Berkowitz went quietly to the police station where he made a full confession.

David Berkowitz had been born in June 1953, a bastard whose mother introduced him early to feelings of rejection when she put him up for adoption. Despite a protective bravado, Berkowitz was always uncomfortable in female company and as his paranoia grew over the years he began to entertain the notion that' women despised him and thought him ugly. In 1974, so he later claimed, Berkowitz became aware of 'the voices' as he lay in the darkness of his squalid apartment; the voices were telling him to kill. When police searched the Yonkers flat after his arrest they found the walls covered with scribbled messages such as 'Kill for My Master'. The source of the name 'Sam's Creation' seems to have been Berkowitz's neighbour Sam Carr, whose black labrador kept Berkowitz awake at night with its barking. He began sending a series of hate letters to Carr, and in April 1977 shot and wounded the dog. With his generally peculiar behaviour and a fondness for sending anonymous letters to people he believed were intent on doing him harm, Berkowitz had already provoked complaints to the police, though such was his otherwise engaging charm that nobody seriously considered him a candidate for 'Son of Sam'.

An obvious paranoid schizophrenic, Berkowitz was nevertheless found fit to stand trial, though that process was pre-empted by his plea

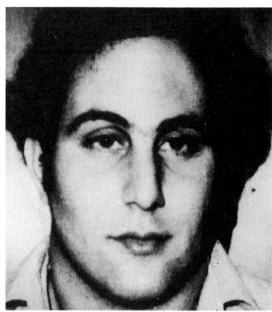

'I'm Sam', the true face of the 'Son of Sam' killer (Topham)

of guilty. On 23 August 1977 Berkowitz was sentenced to 365 years, to be served at the Attica Correctional Facility.

On 10 July 1979 Berkowitz was attacked by a fellow inmate who slashed his throat with a razor. Despite the fact that the wound was almost fatal, Berkowitz refused to name his attacker, saying only that it had some connection with his 'occult past'.

NORWAY

The Orkdale Valley Murders

Arnfinn Nesset managed the Orkdale Valley Nursing Home in Norway, and between 1977 and 1980 he murdered 22 of his elderly patients by the administration of the drug curacit (a derivative of curare, which is used by the natives of South America to tip their arrows). During a preliminary interrogation Nesset confessed to the killings, adding, 'I've killed so many I can't remember them all'; at various times he gave different reasons for the murders, including euthanasia, pleasure killing, schizo-

phrenia and a morbid need to take life. By the time he came to trial Arnfinn Nesset had retracted his confessions and pleaded not guilty. He was eventually convicted of 22 out of a final 25 counts of murder, plus charges of forgery related to the embezzlement of the deceased patients' money – not for his own use, he was quick to emphasise, but to swell the funds of missionary charities. Nesset was sentenced to 21 years' imprisonment, the maximum permitted under Norwegian law.

1978

Revd Jim Jones

Revolutionary Suicide at Jonestown. *In which the charismatic Jim Jones was able to persuade no fewer than 913 of his cult followers to commit mass suicide by drinking a deadly cocktail of Kool-Aid laced with cyanide.*

James Warren Jones was born in 1931 in Lynn, Indiana – and it may or may not be significant that the town of Lynn was most noted for making coffins. His father was an alcoholic Klansman with a taste for religion, his mother a fantasist and self-declared mystic – which may account for young Jim turning out weird. Or at least that's the way his contemporaries remember him. They recall his funeral services for dead animals particularly, and one friend is on record as saying: 'Some of the neighbours would have cats missing and we always thought he was using them for sacrifices.' Jim was also a precocious preacher of the hellfire-and-damnation type so popular in the Midwest Bible-belt where he grew up. He made his first public sermon at fourteen, and after dropping out of Indiana University he and his new wife went touting door-to-door for the Methodist Mission. In the end Jim became a tad too peculiar for the conservative tastes of the church fathers, and in 1954 he was asked to leave. With characteristic stubbornness, Jim Jones bought his own church – a crumbling former synagogue in the predominantly black district around North Delaware Street, Indianapolis.

Now the fact is, a lot of what Jim Jones believed in amounted to good Christian charity.

True, he was a communist; and true, he had strange notions – like seeing God travelling on a train – but Jim's ministry was among the poor and disadvantaged, the kind of people no other church wanted messing up their pews. His work for a multiracial community led to Jones being appointed by the mayor to the City Human Rights Commission, and he and his wife went as far as adopting eight Korean and black children. The so-called People's Temple was making its mark. Later they were to amalgamate with the Disciples of Christ, and Jones was ordained as a minister. The Reverend Jones took time out to lead a mission to Brazil, and on his return to the United States two years later he transported busloads of his congregation across country to Redwood Valley, California, buying another church in the run-down Fillmore district of San Francisco. Again the People's Temple became a refuge where the impoverished ethnic minorities could at least get food and care. Politicians were beginning to woo Jones for the enormous influence he had among the black voters, and in 1975 San Francisco's mayor George Moscone appointed him to the city housing authority.

With power came money. Soon the People's Temple had become an evangelical roadshow, and Revd Jones bought a lease on 27,000 acres of Guyana rainforest where he intended to create his Utopia. The Temple could now lay claim to more than 20,000 followers, and power was beginning to control Jim Jones when once he had controlled the power. He began to lay extravagant claims to healing powers, and started to refer to himself as God. Jones introduced an unhealthy sexual element into his meetings and was now enjoying intercourse with a considerable number of his congregation.

But something more sinister than this Bible-thumping mumbo-jumbo was afoot. The People's Temple had a hidden agenda. Some years previously Jones had elected an inner circle of his most loyal and influential supporters, called the Planning Commission. In 1976 Jones began elaborating on a curious concept which he had developed years before: the use of mass suicide as an expression of political dissidence – 'revolutionary suicide' he called it. At a meeting on New Year's Day he put his followers' loyalty to the test and suggested the congregation drink a liquid which he said was poison. Some were quite prepared to do anything for the Revd Jim, but others were less happy about their imminent self-sacrifice. The matter was resolved by an elaborate charade in which a plant in the congregation made as if to run away and was 'shot'. After everybody in the meeting had taken a draught of the liquid, Jim Jones announced that it was not really poison, but thanked them from the bottom of his big heart for their selfless gesture of loyalty. This was the first of several such meetings – called 'White Nights' – at which the ritual suicide was rehearsed. Meanwhile work was going ahead apace down in Guyana, clear-

The Revd Jim Jones (Topham)

ing the forest for the foundation of what was immodestly to be named Jonestown. An advance guard of some 300 of the faithful upped and left for Guyana to prepare the town for the expected exodus. In all about a thousand cultists invested their worldly possessions in the future Utopia, and the town began to fill out.

What most of the community hadn't realised was that this Utopia was a dictatorship, with

Murder by Proxy

The notion that money is the root of all manner of evils would have been enthusiastically supported by Mr Franklin J. Bradshaw, late of Salt Lake City, Utah. Having made a lot of money (over $60 million as a matter of fact) from his own hard work, and believing in hanging on to what he had, Bradshaw was frequently heard advising his family that if it was money they wanted then they should take a leaf out of his book. Youngest daughter Frances, however, having twice failed to marry into money and left with a family of her own to rear, was unenthusiastic about so monotonous and time-consuming a route to the riches to which she felt entitled. Fortunately her teenaged son Marc was as unscrupulous as herself, and in him Frances Schreuder Bradshaw found a willing weapon.

Although she had for some time been receiving welcome, if modest, handouts from Mrs Bradshaw, Frances had already openly declared that 'This family can't keep going much longer; not unless somebody kills father', and on 23 July 1978 Marc was dispatched with a loaded Smith and Wesson .357 magnum to take care of the job. After a protracted investigation, Marc Schreuder stood his trial in 1982, when he freely admitted killing his grandfather for the simple reason that his mother had asked him to do it as a favour. Frances Schreuder, who had never handled a gun in her life, was tried, convicted and sentenced to life imprisonment for the shooting of her father, while the worthless Marc, whose finger had been on the trigger, escaped with a token five years.

Dead bodies litter the ground in Jonestown (Topham)

Revd Jim Jones as supremo and a handful of powerful sycophants as minor lieutenants. Sex was all but forbidden to anybody but Jones and his cronies, and any follower suspected of entertaining lustful thoughts of a 'non-revolutionary' kind (that is to say, sex for pleasure) was beaten. In fact all perceived misdemeanours – such as being inattentive during one of Jim's rambling sermons – were similarly punished with public beatings and torture. With such power Jones himself was becoming more than just unbalanced; he was on his way to becoming a card-carrying psychopath. One report stated that electrodes were attached to children who failed to smile at the mention of the Leader's name. And just in case anybody felt disillusioned enough to want out, Jones fabricated a story that a group of CIA gunmen were about to attack Jonestown, giving himself the excuse to post armed guards around the perimeter, more to keep people in than to keep them out.

Despite these elaborate precautions, news of such goings-on were bound to filter out sooner or later, and in August 1977 the San Francisco *Examiner* began to print decidedly unflattering reports on the state of affairs in Jonestown. The unease forced California congressman Leo Ryan, himself a seasoned human-rights campaigner, to raise the issue with the US State Department. Ryan put together a formidable fact-finding team consisting of eight journalists and several parents of cult members, and on 14 November 1978 they flew to Jonestown.

To begin with Jones seemed amiable enough, welcoming his visitors and leading them on a guided tour of the complex. It certainly seemed impressive to the eye – even Congressman Ryan was moved to remark on how happy many of the people seemed. Then things began to fall apart. Jones almost attacked a reporter in his fury at being questioned over the heavy presence of armed guards. Several members of the cult passed messages to the team asking to return to the US with them; one lieutenant tried to stab Leo Ryan when he suggested that Jones should let those who wanted to leave go. Amid this general atmosphere of menace the fact-finding mission beat a hasty retreat in the direction of the airfield at Port Kaituma; they got as far as their waiting plane before the party was overtaken by a truck load of gun-toting cultists from Jonestown. In the massacre which followed, three of the departing journalists, one defecting cult member and Congressman Ryan were shot dead.

Meanwhile, back in Jonestown it was time for death, time to live out Jim Jones's dream of 'revolutionary suicide'. Now all the 'White Nights' were to become a reality. Some of the faithful were mobilised into preparing large vats of purple Kool-Aid drink laced with cyanide; mothers fed their babies while children and adults were given paper cups of the liquid and told to drink. Those who exhibited a lack of enthusiasm were encouraged to do the required thing by armed guards. Then, their earthly duties at an end, the guards drank. Within five minutes more than 900 men, women and children lay dead where they fell. Jim Jones, his mission accomplished, put a gun to his head and pulled the trigger.

1979

Theodore 'Ted' Bundy

'Sometimes I feel like a vampire.' *Sentenced to death for a series of kidnappings and murders of young women, Bundy spent much of his time between appeals against sentence co-operating with officers of the FBI Behavioral Science Unit in constructing psychological profiles of serial killers.*

In a classic prison interview with leading criminologists James De Burger and Ronald M. Holmes, Ted Bundy referred to a dimension of the killer's personality which he called the 'Force': an unstoppable urge that makes a person kill repeatedly and which exists secretly alongside the personality of the kindly family man, or the good neighbour – the outward personality that ensures freedom from suspicion. Perhaps the most revealing observation to emerge from Bundy's discourse on the mind of the serial killer was summed up by Holmes:

'Ted was able to talk about the classic characteristics of serial killers but not able to see the same in his own personality.'

And this was perhaps the most remarkable thing about Ted Bundy. He seemed such an unlikely killer. Most sex murderers exhibit marked emotional repression and sexual inadequacy; but this was hardly true of Bundy. A well-educated, good-looking man, Ted Bundy's charm and wit made him an attractive companion, and he experienced no difficulty in his relations with women – except the need to kill them. Bundy's academic achievements alone placed him in a separate category, having been awarded, among other distinctions, a scholarship in Chinese studies at Stanford University. In 1972 he completed his college programme by receiving a BSc in psychology, and he had been employed as, ironically, an assistant director of the local Seattle crime commission. Later Bundy was successful in gaining entrance to the University of Utah to study law; it was to be noted later that when he moved to Salt Lake the mysterious spate of killings of young women in Washington State stopped and a new wave of disappearances began in Salt Lake.

Eventually Bundy was arrested and imprisoned for kidnapping an eighteen-year-old

Some of the many faces of Ted Bundy – none looking much like the popular image of a serial killer

Ted Bundy finds something to laugh about in court (Topham)

named Carol DaRonch; which was when officers investigating the murder of Caryn Campbell began to take an interest in him, proving eventually that Bundy had been at the location of Caryn's death on the day she was killed. An extradition order was issued, and Bundy removed to Colorado to face a charge of murder. In June 1977, while awaiting trial, he escaped, but was recaptured almost immediately. Six months later he escaped again, this time climbing through the ceiling of his cell, and carried out a further series of robberies, rapes and murders in the Florida area. It was February 1978 before Bundy was finally recaptured, and then by pure luck by officers investigating a minor traffic violation. Under interrogation, Bundy admitted that the number of his killings had reached more than 100. At his subsequent trial, Ted Bundy was sentenced to death, though the American system of appeals allowed Bundy to remain – prisoner 069063 – on Death Row for a further ten years.

It was not until 24 January 1989 that he was executed.

Clearly, a man who, over a four-year period, rapes and murders no less than 40 times over five States is not normal; but nothing in Bundy's background gives any clue to the frightening Jekyll-and-Hyde personality that developed. Utah State Prison psychologist Dr Al Carlisle concluded: 'I feel that Mr Bundy is a man who has no problems, or is smart enough or clever enough to appear close to the edge of "normal".' Ted Bundy himself claimed: 'Sometimes I feel like a vampire.'

FRANCE

The Death Instinct

In November 1979 the life of Jacques Mesrine, France's 'Public Enemy Number One', came to an end when he was shot down on a Paris street by the police he had evaded for so many years. There were few crimes in which this enigmatic gangster had not engaged – kidnap, robbery, bank raids, and murder. While serving a sentence in La Sante prison, Jacques Mesrine wrote his autobiographical memoir *The Death Instinct* – in effect, his confession to murder.

The end of Jacques Mesrine – slumped where he died in a hail of police bullets (Rex Features)

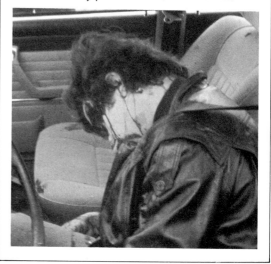

1980

David Pagett

The Case of the Human Shield. *Accidentally shot dead by an armed policeman during a siege in Birmingham, Gail Kinchin became the pivot of a unique legal battle as to whether the captor using her as a 'human shield' was guilty of murder by proxy.*

Like any other complex system, the law, and the agencies that enforce it, are subject to development if not exactly by trial and error, then by a process of learning from mistakes and closing loopholes as they are seen to appear. It is a great sadness that this gradual refinement so often results from deep personal tragedies. Such a tragedy was suffered by the Wood family of Birmingham in July 1980, but it was a decade before that the shortcomings that led to the death of seventeen-year-old Gail Kinchin resulted in improved police procedures in the matter of firearms use.

The background to this recent development was a unique siege situation which developed during the early morning of Thursday, 12 June 1980. Gail Kinchin had moved out of the home she shared with her mother Josephine and step-father Eric Wood in the Kings Heath district of Birmingham and moved in with 31-year-old David Pagett in his council flat in Rugely.

Pagett turned out to be a thoroughly nasty bit of work – at least as far as Gail was concerned – much given to the pleasures of women and drink; he was also handy with his fists. With Gail now for all practical purposes in his clutches Pagett, a man already known to be a bully, began to be driven by the blind belligerence that came with an increase in his dependence upon alcohol, and his behaviour towards Gail deteriorated into violence and paranoia.

Inevitably, Gail Kinchin became pregnant, and equally predictably, Pagett made her condition the excuse for further indignities, often forcing her to spend nights sleeping on the draughty floor. If she complained, or made to

Gail Kinchin

269

leave him, he made very believable threats to the life of Gail's mother.

If for no other reason than the safety of her unborn child, Gail Kinchin, with her mother's help, courageously made plans to flee the flat on the afternoon of 11 June 1980, travelling via her mother's home to that of a friend.

Pagett was furious, of course, and, the worse for drink, he loaded himself and a double-barrelled shotgun into his car and made for the Woods' home in Kings Heath. Here, shotgun raised, he smashed his way into the house to confront Eric Wood who, fearing for his own and his wife's life, made a life-or-death dash for the door to summon assistance. His bid for freedom was cut short by the blast of lead shot that tore into his limbs and felled him. Pagett now turned his violent attentions on Mrs Wood, who was bundled at gunpoint, screaming and terrified, into the waiting car. All Pagett wanted now was an address.

When he had similarly snatched Gail from her 'safe' house in Masefield Square, Pagett kicked and pushed her into the car to join her mother and drove off at a reckless pace towards Rugely, skilfully evading the roadblocks set up by police in the wake of Eric Wood's wounding and his wife's kidnap. It was while Pagett was negotiating one of these that Josephine Wood, thinking quickly, managed to flee the madman's clutches. Not that Pagett seemed to care, even if he noticed; he got what he had come for, and the trembling, fearful Gail was back in his power. He would teach her a lesson she would never forget.

It was only minutes after David Pagett had reached the safety of his flat, barricading himself and Gail inside, that armed police officers began to surround the block.

Detective Sergeant Thomas Sartain and Detective Constable Gerald Richards, both carrying police-issue Smith and Wessons, entered the building. Hampered by the darkness imposed by broken landing lights, the two officers positioned themselves outside Pagett's door. Before long they heard a rattling of bolts, and in the flash of unaccustomed light from the now-open front door they could see the fugitive, a shotgun in one hand and Gail Kinchin grasped with the other as a human shield.

Obviously feeling securely above the law, Pagett rejected all appeals for him to surrender his weapon and, in total defiance, forced the two officers to retreat up the stairs behind them; to their horror the policemen found themselves trapped. Behind them was a solid wall, in front of them was a madman with a shotgun and a pregnant hostage. There was a momentary scuffle in the darkness below, and then with a deafening roar the shotgun exploded in a flash of fire. Miraculously the deadly spray of lead missed the crouching officers and in what they must at the time have considered their only means of self-preservation Richards and Sartain returned fire. Pagett loosed off the other barrel of his weapon and again the detectives returned his fire. This time, Gail fell bleeding on the floor, her baby inside her killed instantly by a bullet. Despite emergency treatment in hospital Gail Kinchin died before the month was out.

To sustain a murder charge against Pagett, it

GERMANY

'The Avenging Mother'

Already a convicted child-molester, Klaus Grabowski was put on trial in March 1980 for the murder of seven-year-old Anna Bachmeier. Having sat through three days of the court hearing, the child's mother calmly rose from her seat, crossed the court, and fired seven bullets at point-blank range into Grabowski, killing him instantly. Frau Bachmeier – who became known as 'The Avenging Mother' – was convicted of manslaughter in 1983 and imprisoned; she was released on parole two years later.

had to be demonstrated at his trial that he had used the girl as a shield in the full knowledge that when he first fired the shotgun at the detectives they were likely to shoot back and could maim or kill his hostage.

It was a complex and unique prosecution which divided the jury who eventually returned a verdict of manslaughter. On the lesser charges which Pagett faced – three of attempted murder (of Mr Wood and the two police officers), and two of kidnap (Mrs Wood and Gail Kinchin – he was found guilty. Sentencing Pagett to seven concurrent-twelve year terms of imprisonment, Mr Justice Park observed: 'The use of a hostage by a desperate armed man to achieve safety for himself – and by that use to cause the death of the hostage – is a very grave offence, falling only just short of murder . . .'

Nevertheless, the victim's family have remained far from happy with the way in which the police conducted the siege, a discontentment that was not relieved by the fact that due to the conduct of the trial much evidence concerning the shooting was never heard. It has been Mr and Mrs Wood's consistent view that the police should have been prepared to shoulder a great deal more the responsibility for the outcome of the incident.

Consequently, in 1990 Josephine Wood decided to sue the West Midlands Chief Constable at the time of the shooting, Sir Philip Knights, for negligence over the death of her daughter. In October the case was heard before the High Court at Birmingham, during which the Woods' counsel, Mr Malcolm Lee, advanced the accusation that Gail Kinchin might not have died if correct police procedures had been followed. This fault in procedure, as outlined in the court, was that the two officers entrusted with the unenviable task of confronting Pagett were not senior enough to make the decisions required in such a potentially dangerous situation. Indeed, Mr Colin Greenwood, a firearms expert and former police instructor, is reported as giving his opinion that the officer whose bullets hit Gail Kinchin: 'Appears to have made command decisions he was not qualified to make. The entire command structure appears then to have failed.' It must in

Death of a Centre-Fold

Dorothy Stratton's name had been Dorothy Ruth Hoogstraten before Paul Snider clapped his eyes on her. She was a waitress then, working in Vancouver, and Snider was one of those flashy, twilight figures whose eye is always on the lookout for a way of exploiting the fast buck. In Dorothy he saw star quality: 'That girl', he said, 'could make me a lot of money.' In one sense at least Snider's instincts had been right on target – within a year Dorothy had become a celebrated centre-fold model for *Playboy* magazine. In 1978 she married Snider, and not long after won the coveted title 'Playmate of the Year'; Dorothy Stratton was well on her way to a certain kind of stardom. In a classic tale of jealousy, Paul Snider came bitterly to resent Dorothy's success, the very success which he had created. After a brief separation Snider shot his 'creation' dead at their home in Los Angeles in August 1980; then he killed himself. This modern *crime passionel* has subsequently become the subject of any number of bestselling books, magazine articles and films.

fairness be added that former Detective Constable (now Sergeant) Richards defended his position vigorously, stating in support of his self-defence claim: 'A shot was fired from the shotgun. I responded by firing four shots in all from my revolver.'

Nothing will ever compensate Mr and Mrs Wood for the loss of their daughter and unborn grandson – least of all the small sum of agreed damages paid to the family. But perhaps they can console themselves that pressure such as theirs, and incidents like the tragedy that claimed the lives of Gail Kinchin and her child, have been instrumental in a wide reappraisal of the guidelines for the police use of firearms and the strict control by senior officers over the circumstances under which they are issued.

1981

Peter Sutcliffe, 'The Yorkshire Ripper'

In November 1980, shortly after the brutal murder of Leeds student Jaqueline Hill, one national newspaper published its story under the headline 'Did one man really do all this?' It seemed incredible at the time, and no less alarming in retrospect, that one man – Peter Sutcliffe – was able, over a period of five years, to bludgeon, stab and mutilate an admitted total of twenty women, thirteen of whom died from this savage treatment. These tragic victims, aged between sixteen and 46 with occupations between student and prostitute, had only one thing in common: they had been alone on the street after dark.

The investigation of the 'Yorkshire Ripper' case was a story of determination and frustration, of a police force desperate to put a stop to one of the worst serial murderers in Britain's history, but seemingly powerless to stop the carnage. Above all, it is the story of a county in the grip of terror, its women fearful of being out of doors at night. Thirteen of them paid with their lives for that freedom.

Despite the largest manhunt ever mounted by British police, during which 250,000 people were interviewed and 32,000 statements taken, it was the very weight of all this paperwork that obscured the often obvious path through

to Sutcliffe. He had been questioned on a number of occasions during the investigation, and as the result of one of these interviews a police officer had gone as far as to voice his suspicion that Peter Sutcliffe was the Ripper; his report was overlooked. Another tragic complication of the case was the amount of time wasted by hoax letters, and by the tape recording sent to the police in June 1979, which was broadcast to the nation in the hope that the voice could be identified. Once again Sutcliffe's luck held out, and after yet another interview

Early Identikit of the 'Ripper'

he was dismissed for not having a Wearside accent like the voice on the tape.

The five-year hunt for the 'Yorkshire Ripper' ended in an anti-climax on 2 January 1981, when a routine police patrol became suspicious about a car parked in a dimly lit driveway. The owner, who gave his name as Peter Williams, was taken in for questioning; it was Peter Sutcliffe.

A multicide of the 'evangelical' type, Sutcliffe's declared mission was to rid the streets of prostitutes. As he explained to his younger brother Carl: 'I were just cleaning up streets, our kid. Just cleaning up streets.' He had, so he said, first become aware of his mission while working as a municipal gravedigger in Bingley cemetery, when he heard the voice of God coming from one of the graves. There was, though, considerable doubt as to whether Peter Sutcliffe was truly psychotic or whether his 'voices' were a clever device to support his defence of diminished responsibility. In the end, Peter Sutcliffe was put on trial and on 22 May declared guilty on thirteen counts of murder. He was sentenced to serve not less than 30 years in prison.

For the past four years a vicious killer has been at large in the North of England. There have been to date 12 horrific murders and four brutal attacks. The evidence suggests that the same man may be responsible for all of them. If so, he has struck 13 times in West Yorkshire, twice in Manchester and once in Lancashire. Large teams of police officers, including Regional Crime Squads, are working full time in West Yorkshire, Sunderland, Manchester and Lancashire to catch him. His original targets were prostitutes but innocent girls have also died. You can help to end this terror . . .

HELP US CATCH THE RIPPER

● **HAVE YOU SEEN THE HANDWRITING?** IF YOU HAVEN'T IT'S ON THE BACK PAGE

● **HAVE YOU HEARD THE TAPE?** IF YOU HAVEN'T, RING THE NEAREST OF THE FOLLOWING TELEPHONE NUMBERS:
LEEDS (0532) 464111   MANCHESTER (061) 246 8060
BRADFORD (0274) 36511   NEWCASTLE (0632) 8075

DO ANY OF THESE QUESTIONS DESCRIBE SOMEONE YOU KNOW?	IF YOU ARE AN EMPLOYER

● Has a Wearside (Geordie) accent?
● Is physically fit and reasonably strong?
● Travels between, or has connections in, the Yorkshire, Lancashire and Sunderland areas?
● Perhaps shows disgust of low moral standards?
● Is a manual worker or has access to tools?
● Possibly lives alone or with aged parents?
● Is prone to sudden outbursts of emotion?
● Owns a car of his own or has access to one?
● Sometimes strays out late at night?
	● Does your firm possibly have business connections throughout the North of England, especially in the Yorkshire, Lancashire and Sunderland areas.
	● Have you an employee who was available in Sunderland to post an envelope on the following dates:
	    March 7/8, 1978.
	    March 12/13, 1978.
	    March 21/22, 1978.
	    Shortly before June 18, 1979.
	Through his duties or being absent from work was he available to attack the 'Ripper' victims (see centre pages) on:
	July 5, 1975. February 6, 1977. December 14, 1977.
	August 15, 1975. April 24, 1977. January 21, 1978.
	October 30, 1975. June 26, 1977. January 31, 1978.
	November 20, 1975. July 10, 1977. May 17, 1978.
	January 20, 1976. October 1, 1977. April 5, 1979.
	                                                 September 2, 1979.

● BUT DON'T DISCOUNT ANY SUSPICION BECAUSE OF THE QUESTIONS, IF YOU HAVE ANY DOUBTS AT ALL, CONTACT THE POLICE AND HELP CATCH THE RIPPER.	

Wanted notice for the 'Yorkshire Ripper'

FRANCE

Issei Sagawa

An Expression of Love. *The 'Paris Cannibal' was confined to a French asylum for killing and cannibalising fellow-student Renée Hartvelt. Transferred to a mental hospital in his native Japan, Sagawa was quickly released under questionable circumstances.*

It all began in Paris in the summer of 1981 when two young women summoned the police to a spot in the Bois de Boulogne where they had seen a diminutive Oriental attempt to push two absurdly large suitcases into the Lac Inferieur. When he saw them coming the man scampered off as fast as his tiny legs would carry him, abandoning his luggage. Once they were reassembled, the contents of the plastic bags inside the suitcases were identified as 25-year-old Dutch student Renée Hartevelt. It was by way of the taxi driver who had transported the small man and his suitcases to the park that the police came to visit 10 rue Erlanger, where they found and arrested Issei Sagawa, a 32-year-old Japanese student, with his gun, his bloodstained carpet and a refrigerator full of human flesh. Sagawa, unmoved, unrepentant and under arrest, told how he had shot fellow student Renée Hartvelt after she had rejected his sexual advances and how he had then stripped the body naked and had intercourse. Then began the slow process of dismembering the corpse, pausing alternately to photograph his handiwork and to nibble on strips of raw human flesh. Finally Sagawa selected some cutlets to refrigerate for later and the rest of the body ended up in the Bois de Boulogne.

With the kind of back door chicanery that only money can buy, Issei Sagawa spent only three years in hospital in France before being returned to Japan where he was declared sane and released. It was not only the cynics who noticed how the Paris cannibal had been released from France at the same time as two large international companies – Kurita Water Industries of Japan and Elf Aquitaine of France

– had signed a very lucrative business deal. It may be no coincidence that Issei Sagawa's father was the president of Kurita Water Industries. Following his discharge in September 1985, Sagawa claimed that the eating of Renée Hartvelt's flesh had been 'an expression of love', the culmination of a lifelong desire to eat the flesh of a young woman. More disturbing still is the fact that he could not rule out the possibility that he might 'fall in love' again.

The last that this author heard of Issei Sagawa added a final touch of almost unbelievable irony to a case already bizarre in the extreme. It would appear that Issei Sagawa is currently employed on the staff of a Tokyo newspaper – as a restaurant critic!

UNITED KINGDOM

The Case of the Extra Ingredient

As eternal triangles went this one had nothing very special going for it. Susan and Michael Barber had been married long enough to have produced three children, and the relationship had long since soured. Susan had worked her way through a succession of lovers and had left home twice, only to return for the sake of the children. In May 1981 Michael Barber returned home inconveniently early from a fishing trip and found his wife and his best friend, Richard Collins, in bed together. Furious, he beat his wife and threw Collins out of the house. The following day Susan made her husband one of his favourite meals, steak and kidney pie. This time it had an extra ingredient – a dose of weedkiller containing paraquat. Now paraquat is as lethal to human beings as it is to weeds, producing fibrosis of the lungs with symptoms identical to pneumonia and kidney disorder. On 27 June 1981 Barber died in Hammersmith Hospi-

tal, London. Fortunately for justice, the obligatory post-mortem was carried out by an observant pathologist named David Evans who, suspecting poison, removed samples from the organs for analysis before releasing the body for disposal. The results from the National Poisons Unit at New Cross Hospital confirmed that Michael Barber had been poisoned with paraquat. It was not until April 1982 that Susan Barber, now in possession of her husband's £15,000 insurance, was arrested and charged with murder. At Chelmsford Crown Court in November of the same year, Mrs Barber was joined in the dock by Richard Collins; she received a life sentence for murder, he collected two years for conspiracy. But by now Susan Barber had a new lover, and in July 1983 she was briefly released from Holloway Prison in order to marry him.

1982

Charles Yukl

The Blood-Stained Casting Couch. *A typical product of a severely repressed childhood, Yukl grew up to be intensely shy in the company of women, almost fearful of them. The compensating fantasy of domination resulted in two murders.*

Emerging from a childhood characterised by rejection and punctuated by beatings from his Czech immigrant father, Charles Yukl developed into an isolated youth. Although to some extent he broke free from these early, repressive patterns by joining the United States Navy in 1952, Yukl was not long with the service, being dishonourably discharged two years later after no less than three courts martial. Thrown back into civilian life, Charles Yukl married in 1961, and after a succession of jobs began teaching music. (His father had been a musician, and an easy familiarity with music was probably the only thing he ever gave Charles.) Perhaps as a result of his childhood, he was still very shy, almost frightened of women, and knew very few.

In August 1966, an aspiring actress named Suzanne Reynolds enrolled with Yukl to take voice-training lessons. Instead, in October, he strangled her with his tie, sodomised her and slashed her body with a razor. In an attempt to divert attention from himself, Yukl dumped the body of his victim outside a vacant apartment in his own block and then called the police to report finding it.

It was his bloodstained clothing that gave the game away for Charles Yukl, though it must be said that as the result of plea-bargaining a confession to manslaughter, coupled with good behaviour while in prison, Charles was paroled after serving only five years of a seven-and-a-half-year sentence.

In 1973 Charles Yukl returned to family life; but it was not long before the psychiatric disorders which the doctors had already discovered in pre-trial examinations began to manifest themselves in his fantasies. He began to advertise in the newspapers for actresses to star in some mythical film that he was about to produce, and entertained those who answered to lavish champagne suppers. On 19 August 1979, Yukl took one of his aspiring actresses, Karin Schlegel, and starred her in a re-run of his 1966 murder of Suzanne Reynolds. When they found the body on the roof of Charles Yukl's apartment, police officers could hardly fail to notice the identical form of strangulation with a necktie, the razor slashes on the body, the sexual abuse.

Yukl confessed again, pleaded guilty at his brief trial, and was sentenced to fifteen years to life. In August 1982, he hanged himself in the prison hospital.

1983

Dennis Andrew Nilsen

'Killing for Company.' *When Nilsen was arrested on 9 February, he confessed to an unbelievable 'fifteen or sixteen' murders. Britain's worst serial killer of modern times, Nilsen lured young men to his flat, murdered and dismembered them, keeping some beneath the floorboards, some in a wardrobe.*

On 3 February 1983, residents of the flats at 23 Cranley Gardens, north London, were irritated to find that their lavatories were not flushing properly. It was not until five days later that a representative of the drain-clearage firm Dyno-Rod opened the manhole to the side of the house to check for blockages. Aiming the beam of his touch into the black hole, Mike Cattran could just make out a whitish sludge flecked with red. When he descended the twelve feet to the water line, he discovered lumps of rotting meat, some with hair attached, floating about in the slime.

Alerted by Cattran, the police made a fuller inspection of the manhole on the following morning. Although most of the flesh had been mysteriously fished out overnight, officers recovered fragments of flesh and bone later identified as being of human origin.

Among the residents of number 23, occupying the attic flat, was 37-year-old Dennis Nilsen, and when he arrived home from his job at the Soho Job Centre on the evening of 8 February it was to be met by three detectives. Nilsen expressed surprise that the police should be concerned with blocked drains, and when told of the grisly finds replied: 'Good grief, how awful.'

It was an inspired guess, something that is as vital a tool to the experienced detective as any number of computers. Detective Chief Inspector Peter Jay rounded on Nilsen and said simply: 'Don't mess around, where's the rest of the body?'

'In two plastic bags in the wardrobe. I'll show you.'

*Official police photograph of Nilsen (*Metropolitan Police)

When Nilsen had been cautioned he was driven back with the officers to Muswell Hill police station. On the journey, Detective Inspector McCusker turned to Nilsen and asked: 'Are we talking about one body or two?'

'Fifteen or sixteen since 1978: three at Cranley Gardens and about thirteen at my previous address at Melrose Avenue, Cricklewood.'

And so began the extraordinary story of Britain's most prolific serial killer. The police were at first flabbergasted by Nilsen's apparent frankness, his cold, matter-of-fact approach to the situation he found himself in, and the sheer enormity of his claims. They also found themselves in the bewildering position of having found their killer almost before the investigation had begun. Their task became one of, literally, piecing together the individuals whom Nilsen had murdered to determine when and where the crimes had occurred, and to find some answer to how such an orgy of killing could have gone completely unnoticed for so long.

However, thanks to Nilsen's uncannily clear recollection of the details, his crimes were soon a matter of record.

CHRONOLOGY OF A MASS MURDERER

23 November 1945. Dennis Nilsen was born, second of the three children of Betty Whyte and Olav Nilsen, a Norwegian soldier. The couple had been married three years earlier, but from the beginning the marriage was unhappy, with Olav frequently absent from home and usually drunk. The situation resolved itself in divorce in 1949. Mrs Nilsen and her children went to live at 47 Academy Road, Fraserburgh, Aberdeenshire, the home of Mrs Nilsen's parents, Andrew and Lily Whyte. The grandparents were the driving influence in the strict Presbyterian upbringing of the children.

31 October 1951. Nilsen's grandfather, Andrew Whyte, whom he idolized, died suddenly at sea at the age of 61. Nilsen was much affected by seeing the dead body of his grandfather laid out in the parlour.

1954. Betty Nilsen married Adam Scott, a buil-

Nilsen as a soldier (Topham)

PC Q287 Dennis Nilsen (Topham)

der, and the family moved to 73 Mid Street in nearby Strichen. Nilsen developed into a solitary child and disliked his stepfather.

August 1961. Nilsen enlisted in the Army Catering Corps at the age of fifteen to escape from home. He was trained at Aldershot for the next three years.

1964. Nilsen was posted to Osnabruck in Germany as a cook. It was at this time that he began to drink heavily and to discover his homosexuality. Over the next eight years he was relatively happy in the Army, being posted at various times to Berlin, Cyprus and Sharjah in the Persian Gulf.

October 1972. Nilsen decided to resign from the Army, partly because he was appalled by the way it was being used in Northern Ireland.

November 1972. Joined the Metropolitan Police, and was trained at Hendon before being posted to Willesden Police Station.

December 1973. He resigned from the police force, being unhappy both with the discipline and the restriction it put on his homosexual social life. He took a room at 9 Manstone Road, London NW8, and began work as a security guard protecting various government buildings in London.

METROPOLITAN POLICE
Appeal for Assistance
MISSING

Kenneth OCKENDEN, aged 26,
a visitor from Canada, vanished
from his central London hotel
in very suspicious circumstances
in December 1979.
He was looking forward to
returning to his family in Canada
for Christmas 1979.
He left most of his personal
property in his hotel room but took his camera and lenses.
These could provide a vital clue:-
Canon Single Lens Reflex Camera - Serial No:- 315448TX
Lens - Serial No:- 1210427FD50-F18
Telephoto Lens - Serial No:- 171431FD28-F28

DO YOU KNOW WHERE HE IS?
HAS HE BEEN MURDERED?
HAVE YOU SEEN OR BOUGHT THE EQUIPMENT?
Please contact the Police on
01-230 1212
or your nearest Police Station.
All information treated as strictly confidential

The only one of Nilsen's victims to receive publicity as a missing person

May 1974. After resigning his job as a security guard, Nilsen was accepted by the Manpower Services Commission as a clerical officer at the Denmark Street Job Centre, in Soho. He continued in this employment until his arrest in February 1983. A large part of his work was to interview the unemployed, the down-and-out and the young rootless who hung about in Central London. At this time he was also regularly frequenting those public houses which attracted a homosexual clientele.

1974. Nilsen was evicted from his room in Manstone Road for entertaining male visitors late at night. He found new accommodation at 80 Teignmouth Road, Willesden.

1975. A young man named David Painter claimed that he had been attacked after rejecting Nilsen's sexual advances. Nilsen had met him at the Job Centre and invited him back to the flat. It was Nilsen who actually called the police after Painter had cut his arm in the struggle. Nilsen was interrogated for some time before being allowed to leave the police station.

November 1975. Nilsen met an unemployed man named David Gallichan at The Champion public house in Bayswater Road. After being invited back by Nilsen to his home, the pair decided to share a flat and moved to 195 Melrose Avenue.

May 1977. Gallichan left Nilsen, who felt humiliated and rejected by the sudden departure.

30 December 1978. Nilsen met a young Irishman at the Cricklewood Arms. After inviting him back to his flat to continue drinking, Nilsen strangled his guest with a tie during the night. The body was carefully undressed and washed before being stored under the floorboards, a procedure that became the pattern in Nilsen's subsequent crimes.

11 August 1979. Nilsen burnt the body of the Irishman in the garden. It had, until then, been stored in pieces in two plastic bags.

October 1979. Nilsen picked up a Chinese student, Andrew Ho, in The Salisbury public house in St Martin's Lane, and took him back to his flat. Ho offered sex and agreed to be tied up. Nilsen attempted to strangle Andrew, but he broke free and ran off to inform the police. Nilsen claimed that Ho had been trying to 'rip him off' and the matter was dropped.

3 December 1979. Nilsen met a 23-year-old Canadian student, Ken Ockenden, at The Princess Louise pub in High Holborn; Ockenden was in London on holiday after graduating. This victim was also strangled in Nilsen's flat and placed under the floorboards. Nilsen tore up Ockenden's money 'because it would be stealing to take it'. Uniquely, Ockenden was missed, and his parents came to London and created considerable publicity over his disappearance, but to no effect.

May 1980. Nilsen's next victim was a 16-year-old butcher called Martyn Duffey; he took his place beside Ken Ockenden under the floorboards.

July-September 1980. 26-year-old Billy Sutherland, a Scot, went on a pub crawl with Nilsen and ended up with Duffey and Ockenden.

12 November 1980. Nilsen met Scottish barman Douglas Stewart at The Red Lion in Dean Street and took him back to Melrose Avenue. There he tried to strangle him, then threatened him with a carving knife, before deciding to let him go.

1980–1981. A succession of victims followed. A Filipino or Mexican was picked up at The Salisbury, followed by another Irishman, a building worker. There followed a half-starved down-and-out whom Nilsen had picked up in a doorway on the corner of Oxford Street and Charing Cross Road. He was burnt whole in the garden almost immediately because Nilsen was so horrified by his emaciated condition. Of the next victim Nilsen could remember nothing, except that he had cut the body into three pieces and burnt it about a year later. The ninth victim was a young Scotsman picked up in The Golden Lion in Dean Street, followed by another 'Billy Sutherland' type. The next to fall prey was a skinhead who was heavily tattooed, including a dotted line round his neck, inscribed 'Cut here'. Nilsen obliged when dissecting him.

May 1981. Nilsen had a major body-burning session in the garden at Melrose Avenue.

17 September 1981. Malcolm Barlow was sitting against a garden wall in Melrose Avenue, complaining that he couldn't use his legs, when Nilsen found him; he phoned for an ambulance and accompanied Barlow to hospital. The next day, Barlow went back to Nilsen's flat to thank him, Nilsen cooked them both a meal, and strangled his guest when he fell asleep. Barlow was the last of the Melrose Avenue victims.

October 1981. As a sitting tenant, Nilsen was offered £1,000 to leave the flat in Melrose Avenue, so that it could be renovated. After a bonfire to remove the last vestiges of his murderous activities, Nilsen moved into the top flat at 23 Cranley Gardens, Muswell Hill.

25 November 1981. Nilsen met a homosexual student, Paul Nobbs, in The Golden Lion in Soho. Nobbs woke up next morning at Cranley Gardens with a worse than usual hangover; he went to University College Hospital for a check-up and was told that someone had tried to strangle him. Nobbs did not pursue the matter.

March 1982. Nilsen met John Howlett, a young criminal known as 'John the Guardsman', in The Salisbury, and discovered that they had drunk there before, back in December 1981. Nilsen invited Howlett back to Cranley Gardens and tried to strangle him, but John put up a struggle and Nilsen had to bang his head against the bedrest before drowning him in the bath. This victim was quickly dismembered and portions of the body boiled in a pot because an old friend was expected to stay with Nilsen over the weekend.

May 1982. Nilsen picked up Carl Stotter, a homosexual revue artist known as 'Khara Le Fox' at The Black Cap in Camden High Street. Nilsen tried to strangle Stotter and then drown him in the bath, but seems to have relented halfway through. Next morning Carl Stotter went for a walk in the woods with Nilsen, who hit him violently over the head, picked him up again and continued walking. The two agreed to meet again, but Stotter wisely avoided Nilsen from then on.

Late 1982. The next victim was Graham Allen, who was picked up in Shaftesbury Avenue. He was invited to the Cranley Gardens flat, and fell asleep while eating an omelette. Allen was dissected, some parts being put in a tea chest, some in a plastic bag, and others flushed down the lavatory.

26 January 1983. Stephen Sinclair, a 20-year-old punk and drug addict, was picked up in Leicester Square and taken to Nilsen's home. Stephen's body was left, covered by a blanket, for several days and Nilsen was in the process of dismembering it at the time of his arrest.

9 February 1983. Nilsen arrested.

Dennis Nilsen returned to prison after losing his appeal
(Topham)

12 February 1983. Remanded in custody for seven days by the Highgate Magistrates' Court. This became a regular weekly routine while police were investigating the case.

26 May 1983. Nilsen committed for trial at the Old Bailey on six counts of murder (Ken Ockenden, Malcolm Barlow, Billy Sutherland, Martyn Duffey, John Howlett, Stephen Sinclair) and two counts of attempted murder (Douglas Stewart, Paul Nobbs). The remains of Graham Allen were identified from dental records too late to be included in the first indictment. Likewise, Karl Stotter was traced too late for inclusion in the second, though his harrowing experience was used as evidence at the trial.

24 October 1983. The trial of Dennis Nilsen opened in Court No. 1 at the Old Bailey, Mr Justice Croom Johnson presiding, with Mr Allen Green representing the Crown and Ivan Lawrence QC, MP, defending. That Nilsen had committed the crimes was never disputed. The main thrust of the defence case was a plea for manslaughter on the grounds of diminished responsibility.

4 November 1983. After a day and a half's retirement the jury found Nilsen guilty by a majority of ten to two on all six counts of murder and two of attempted murder. He was sentenced to imprisonment for a period of not less than 25 years and removed from the court to Wormwood Scrubs Prison, and thence to Parkhurst on the Isle of Wight after he had been slashed across the cheek with a razor by a fellow prisoner.

Dennis Nilsen is at present serving his sentence at Albany prison on the Isle of Wight, and it remains a matter of great doubt whether society will ever feel it safe to release him.

POSTSCRIPT

Such was the public fascination with this mild-mannered 'monster' that it was too much to expect the Nilsen case to rest quietly for long. As well as the periodic books and magazine articles, there has been a string of more or less literate television and theatre versions of aspects of the killings, and in January 1993 the moment arrived, it seemed, that half the nation had been waiting for. In a programme dealing with the psychological profiling of serial killers made by Mike Morley for Central Television, there, for all to see and hear, was 'Des', relaxed as you please, genially explaining his methods of dismemberment. Whether or not we feel this added significantly to our understanding of the mind of the multicide is debatable. However, the most remarkable aspect of the incident was its effect on the British Home Office and the deeply unconvincing then Home Secretary Mr Kenneth Clarke. Mr Clarke immediately sought and failed to get a High Court injunction preventing the programme from being shown. What the publicity did succeed in ensuring, however, was that the film was watched by a much vaster audience than would otherwise have bothered to stay up. The Home Secretary, smarting from defeat, then entered into burlesque threats against the programme-makers because, he contended, the words spoken by Dennis Nilsen were Home Office copyright, and that copyright had been infringed – or some such nonsense.

1984

The Hilda Murrell Case

Fraught with conspiracy theories, it may just be possible that the murder of Hilda Murrell was a simple, sordid killing quite free from political intrigue.

A disturbing case that arose out of what seemed, at first glance, to be a straightforward, if unpleasant, murder.

The body of 78-year-old Hilda Murrell was found on 24 March 1984 at Moat Copse, some half-dozen miles from her home in Shrewsbury; she had been repeatedly stabbed and then left to die.

As well as being an internationally famous grower of roses, Miss Murrell was well known as a vociferous opponent of nuclear energy, and her murder began to appear the more sinister in light of the fact that although her house had been painstakingly searched, the only item stolen was the manuscript of a paper that Miss Murrell intended to present at the public inquiry into the construction of the nuclear-power station Sizewell B. Once the suggestion of a conspiracy was in the wind, other things came to light, such as Miss Murrell's possession of certain potentially embarrassing information (via a nephew in naval intelligence) on the subject of the *General Belgrano*, an Argentinian cruiser which had been controversially sunk by the British during the Falklands war of 1982.

Although there has been no shortage either of suspects or of theories, the death of Hilda Murrell remains a mystery.

Two police artist's impressions of a man seen running from the spot where Miss Murrell was killed

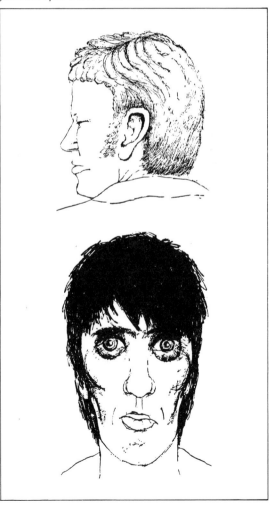

281

The Fall of the Acid King

Seventeen-year-old Ricky Kasso, known on the street as the 'Acid King', had become obsessed with black magic and Satanism to the point where fantasy and reality overlapped dangerously. At the beginning of June 1984, Kasso found himself several twists of 'angel dust' missing and repeatedly accused another youth, Gary Lauwers, of having stolen the drugs. On 16 June Kasso, Lauwers and two companions hid themselves away in Aztakea Woods in Northport to partake of some mescaline, and during the course of subsequent reveries they renewed the dispute over the allegedly pilfered drugs. The result was a vicious attack by the dope-crazed Kasso on his companion, during which Lauwers's disinclination to embrace the church of Satan resulted in Kasso gouging out his eyes and hacking him to death as an unwilling sacrifice. On 4 July, following the discovery of Gary Lauwers's mutilated corpse, the Acid King was arrested and thrown into jail, where two days later he hanged himself.

Nobody's Perfect

For the third time in a single year a prisoner on Japan's death row was freed by a court after being cleared of the charges on which he had been imprisoned. Yukio Saito had spent almost 27 years wrongfully incarcerated for the murder of a family in Matsuyama. In July 1983 Sakae Menda was released after 32 years, and in March 1984 Shigeyosh Taniguchi was released after 34 years.

1985

Jeremy Bamber

The White House Farm Murders. *In one of the most cynical crimes of the twentieth century, Bamber shot his family to death and made the murder of his sister appear like suicide in order to lead the police to the conclusion that it was she who committed the murders.*

On the vast majority of occasions the work of the police scenes-of-crime team is impeccably carried out and provides the inquiry with the support it needs to bring a case to a successful conclusion. However, nothing can be perfect as long as it contains the possibility of human error – and this includes police work; indeed, we can learn a great deal from those few cases where errors have been made.

In the early hours of an August morning in 1985, the station officer received an agitated telephone call from a young man giving his name as Jeremy Bamber and claiming to be anxious about the safety of his parents. He told the policeman that a few minutes earlier his father had telephoned to say that his daughter Sheila – Jeremy's sister – was at their Essex farmhouse home going berserk with a semi-automatic rifle, there had been the sound of a shot and the line went dead.

When an investigating team arrived at White House Farm they found the battered and shot bodies of Nevill and June Bamber, the 'insane' daughter Sheila Caffel, and her own twin children Daniel and Nicholas. From the state of the bodies and the story of his sister's mental instability enthusiastically related by Jeremy it looked like a clear case of murder followed by suicide – the young woman, a bullet through her brain, was still holding the .22 Anschutz.

This was the one insurmountable psychological disadvantage to the police inquiry: the 'killer' had already been named, and it was

Nevill and June Bamber (Anglia Press Agency)

Sheila Caffel and her sons (Anglia Press Agency)

with this misinformation at the forefront of their minds that investigating officers found themselves, in effect, looking for clues to fit the story of the young woman's mad rampage, in the process misinterpreting what did not fit the murder/suicide theory.

Information was there for the looking, and even if no other suspect came immediately to mind, then at least all the evidence indicated that Sheila Caffel *could not* have committed the murders. It was later learned that she suffered impaired hand-eye co-ordination anyway, and had no experience whatever of handling firearms. Nevertheless, she is supposed to have fired 25 accurate shots into her family, stopping twice to reload the gun. It might have seemed inconsistent, even to the untrained eye, that such extensive ballistic activity could have been carried out without the slightest damage to the 'killer's' perfectly manicured fingernails, and leaving her hands free of oil and powder deposits. What was more, the soles of her feet

284

were found to be as clean 'as though she had just stepped out of a bath' – despite having run around the house on a bloody massacre.

Nobody thought to ponder how this slim, five-foot-seven woman had bludgeoned her healthy, sturdily built, six-foot-four father with the rifle butt, which broke under the impact, without suffering injury herself. Incidentally, because of their assumption of her guilt, the real killer, Jeremy Bamber, who probably *was* bruised and marked in the struggle, was not examined by the police for four weeks.

The pathologist's report revealed that Sheila Caffel could not possibly have killed herself; either one of her wounds would have been instantly fatal, and besides, detailed examination had shown that while one of those wounds had been inflicted with a gun in its normal state, a silencer had been used during the other shot – even the most inexperienced officer might have felt that this represented an unusual extravagance for a suicide. Besides, she would have needed much longer arms to have shot herself in the head with a gun lengthened by a silencer.

Ignoring the clues offered by this victim's body was not the only area of the investigation that proved wanting. Fingerprinting procedure was, by all reports, rather lacksadaisical, and many were surprised when experienced scenes-of-crime officers moved the murder weapon with bare hands. Not all of the bodies were fingerprinted at the time, and the cremation of the victims so soon after the crime rendered the situation unsalvageable. Ironically, the police took the real killer's prints *six weeks* after the shooting. By now Jeremy had developed an almost theatrical display of filial grief. Blood was obligingly washed off the farmhouse walls, and bloodstained bedding and carpets removed and burned.

One week later the inquest on the victims opened before the deputy coroner. In evidence, a Detective Inspector outlined the scenario as seen by the police, and emphasised once again that the official view was to regard the young woman as guilty of the murders.

Rather less happy with the outcome were the surviving members of the Bamber family, in particular two of Sheila's cousins. David Boutflour and Christine Eaton were convinced that she was incapable of killing anybody, least of all the twins she adored. In more practical terms, they knew that Sheila's bad co-ordination made pouring a cup of tea without spilling it difficult enough. How could she manage to shoot her whole family? Adding a certain 'Miss Marple factor' to this already bizarre scenario, the amateur detectives visited the farmhouse and retraced the steps of the police search. They entered the study where, as the police had done before them, they found the gun cabinet. To the police it had contained nothing significant; to David Boutflour and Christine Eaton it contained a bloodstained gun silencer of a type that fitted the murder weapon. They lost no time in alerting the police to this vital piece of evidence they had missed the first time round. And vital it most certainly was, for the silencer provided indisputable evidence that their suspect could not have shot herself. The blood that had seeped into the silencer's baffles was her own – which made it rather difficult to explain how it got into the gun cupboard if she, the last to die, had killed herself.

Although the information was not revealed until the trial, the silencer, when it came into police possession, had a single grey hair adhering to it. This hair, presumably from the head of either of the elder victims, was lost by police while in transit to the forensic laboratory for testing.

The true perpetrator of this brutal and cynical act of familicide turned out to be the very young man who had so unashamedly pointed the accusing finger at his own sister. But when Jeremy Bamber stood in the dock he was not the only person to find himself on trial. Fairly or not, the whole of the initial police inquiry came under scrutiny in court. The judge himself remarked that the examination by officers at the scene of the crime 'left a lot to be desired'; and the Deputy Chief Constable of the force concerned added that 'with the benefit of that perfect science, hindsight, the judgement made at the scene of the crime . . . was misdirected'. Finally, the then Home Secretary called for an urgent report on police handling of the murder inquiry.

The strain starts to show as Jeremy Bamber is taken to jail (Syndication International)

Newspaper headlines declare Bamber's guilt (Syndication International)

UNITED STATES

The Death of Ana Mendieta

Did She Fall, Or Was She Pushed? *In September 1985 Ana Mendieta fell to her death from the 34th floor of the Greenwich Village apartment block where she lived with the famous sculptor Carl Andre. But how?*

The name of Carl Andre is more familiar in the elevated world of contemporary art criticism than in the average bar or front parlour; his one claim to notoriety in Britain – the purchase by the Tate Gallery of his sculpture 'Equivalent VIII' (the 'Bricks') in 1976 – being long forgotten by all but the most deeply cynical. That Andre finds himself in such company as Dennis Nilsen is due to a mystery that even lengthy investigation has failed to solve.

In September 1985, 35-year-old Cuban-born artist Ana Mendieta fell to her death from a window on the 34th floor of a Greenwich Village apartment block. Such was the impact that her head made a dent in the rooftop below. The case was a classic of the 'did she fall or was she pushed?' genre. Ana Mendieta was Mrs Carl Andre.

Andre and Ana had met in 1979; he was already an established artist, she was in town for the opening of her first solo exhibition in New York. Over the next five years, despite bitter quarrels and frequent separations, the couple remained emotionally close. In January 1985, in Rome, they married. By June, the familiar problems were haunting their marriage, and within three months friends were reporting that Carl and Ana were getting along as well as they ever did – which meant a lot of squabbling punctuated by periods of genuine and deep affection.

The night of Saturday, 7 September 1985 the Andres spent at home, Ana retiring to bed some time between 1 a.m. and 3.30 a.m. At 5.30 a.m. Edward Mojzis, a doorman, heard a woman's

scream followed by a huge bang. Ana Mendieta had landed on the roof of a Chinese restaurant. As to what led up to this sudden, tragic death we have only the testimony of Andre himself, though his statements to the police just after the incident are confused and contradictory. He claimed that he became anxious when he went into the bedroom at 3.30 a.m. and found his wife missing; he spent twenty minutes looking for her, and then called the police. In fact, his call was logged as being an hour and a half later. When police entered the apartment they found the bedroom in disarray. There were four empty champagne bottles in the lounge (Ana Mendieta's blood had twice the 'legal' alcohol

Carl Andre after being charged with murder (New York Post)

content), and there was one scratch on Andre's face and another on his arm – received, he maintained, while moving some furniture. Andre was also inconsistent on the subject of the state of his relationship with Ana that night; to one officer he said there had been a quarrel, to another that there had been no animosity. On the Sunday evening, Carl Andre was charged with murder. At his subsequent trial, he was acquitted of the charge, and we have no reason to doubt the court's judgement.

Why then, did Ana Mendieta die? She had been drinking heavily, and on that humid summer night all the windows in the apartment were wide open; even so, it is difficult to fall accidentally from a window the ledge of which is hip high. Suicide was a popularly entertained theory, and there was some evidence that the relationship was entering a particularly bitter phase, despite Andre's claim that they had no more problems than 'any other couple'. But suicide was not, her family emphasised, Ana's way; indeed, her sister claims that Ana had spoken of divorce only the day before she died. Furthermore, Ana Mendieta's artistic career was on an upward spiral, her ambitions were being fulfilled in the direction that was the most important in her life – would she throw that away in a drunken or desperate moment? It seemed unlikely to all who knew her well. So how did Ana Mendieta come to die?

GERMANY

Michael Wolpert

The Girls in the Woods. *Not only did the 1980s witness a huge rise in the rate of serial killers in the United States, the disease had also spread, with alarming effect, to the mainland of Europe.*

Between 8 May 1980 and 26 November 1983, eight young women were murdered within a ten-mile radius of the city of Frankfurt.

The first attack took place in Langen, and left 23-year-old Gabriele Roesner lying dead in a wood. She had been found with her underwear ripped off and according to the post-mortem report she had been raped and manually strangled. One month later, Regina Barthel, aged fourteen, was raped and stabbed to death about a mile from the site of the first murder; her jeans and underwear had also been torn off.

Twenty-eight-year-old prostitute Annedore Ligeika was found strangled at her home in Offenbach, and on 7 February 1981, another prostitute, Fatima Sonnenberg, was found strangled in her apartment in the Rodgau district of Frankfurt. Both these victims had recently engaged in sexual intercourse, presumably with a killer who was posing as a client.

Five days before Christmas 1981, sixteen-year-old Beatrix Scheible was found stabbed to death and raped in Frankfurt city park, and on 9 May the following year Regina Spielmann was stabbed and raped in the Heusenstamm Forest. The pattern of the knife-wound on her body matched those of Regina Barthel. Although they now knew they had a serial killer on the loose the German police had not at this stage associated the two prostitute murders with the series.

On 3 November 1983, Simone Newin was attacked while jogging in the Offenbach city park; she was raped and strangled with her own trousers. The next victim was Ilke Rutsch, 21, who was found raped and stabbed to death in a forest near Barbenhausen on 26 November. Again forensic tests proved the knife-wounds in this attack were consistent with those in previous cases.

Three days after the murder of Fraulein Rutsch, a 25-year-old electrician named Michael Wolpert was arrested for the attempted rape of a schoolgirl, and during questioning made oblique references to 'the girls in the woods', particularly the Heusenstamm Forest. Under further interrogation, Wolpert eventually admitted all eight murders. He had a previous record for minor sex crimes, but was unable to give any more satisfactory explanation for his actions than that he had an exceptionally high sex drive. He was sentenced to life imprisonment on 24 May 1985.

The Suzy Lamplugh Case

Who was Mr Kipper? *Although the disappearance of estate agent Suzy Lamplugh remains officially unsolved, it has been suggested – to the satisfaction of Suzy's family at least – that a man subsequently imprisoned on another charge may have been responsible for her death.*

Some homicide cases seem to transcend their inevitably sordid circumstances and by their very tragedy leave an indelible mark on society's collective consciousness. In some instances the catalyst is injustice; for example, who failed to be moved by the release of poor Stefan Kiszko after sixteen years' imprisonment for a horrific murder which he could never have committed, and to know that there was scientific evidence available at the time of his trial which would have *proved* his innocence? More recently still the frightful murder of two-year-old James Bulger created shock-waves of anger throughout the nation, not merely because of the age of the victim – child murders are sadly no rarity – but because of the age of James's alleged killers: just ten years old.

There can't be many, either, who do not remember the name of Suzy Lamplugh. Indeed the case seems so fresh in our minds that it is difficult to believe that it was as long ago as 1986 that the 25-year-old estate agent kept that fatal appointment with a bogus client. It cannot simply be the mystery of an unsolved disap-

pearance – thousands of people go missing in Britain every year; it cannot simply be because Suzy was young, attractive, intelligent and so unlikely a victim of violent crime – though she was all of those things. Perhaps what we remember most of all, however subliminally, is the way in which, in the face of such unimaginable grief and bewilderment, the Lamplugh family refused to allow Suzy's case to be confined to some dusty file lying on a long-forgotten shelf. Suzy's mother, the redoubtable Mrs Diana Lamplugh, actively perpetuated the story in order to keep the investigation fresh in the public's mind, and later used the publicity in order to launch the Suzy Lamplugh Trust, a body committed to spreading an awareness of the very dangers which robbed her of a daughter. The case will never now be just the Suzy Lamplugh story, but the Diana Lamplugh story as well.

The following chronology of the landmarks in the Suzy Lamplugh investigation has been assembled from contemporary media reports.

CHRONOLOGY OF THE SUZY LAMPLUGH CASE

1986

28 July. London estate agent Susannah Lamplugh keeps a 12.45 p.m. appointment with a prospective client calling himself 'Mr Kipper'. The arrangement to view a house at Shorrold's Road, Fulham, was made by telephone. The resident of a neighbouring house witnessed the meeting at 1.15 p.m., and is able to help a police artist create a visual impression of the enigmatic Mr Kipper. Suzy Lamplugh, a former beautician aboard the *QE2* liner, was using an office car which is found unlocked at ten o'clock that night parked in Stevenage Road on the other side of Fulham – though witnesses have suggested that it may have been there since before 5 p.m. Ms Lamplugh's purse was still in the vehicle when it was found.

29 July. Convinced that Suzy Lamplugh was abducted by Mr Kipper, police investigators, led by Detective Superintendent Nicholas Carter, issue descriptions of both the victim and the possible kidnapper: Ms Lamplugh, who lived in a flat in Disraeli Road, Putney, is 25 years old, had shoulder-length blonde hair and blue eyes. When she disappeared she was wearing a peach-coloured blouse, grey skirt and black jacket. The man police wish to interview is described as being aged between 25 and 30, about five feet seven inches tall, medium build, with neat, dark, swept-back hair, wearing a dark lounge suit. Meanwhile police frogmen search the stretch of the River Thames which runs parallel to the road in which the car was found abandoned.

4 August. Despite more than 1,000 calls from the public, and the emergence of a number of 'Mr Kippers' (one of them actually engaged in looking for property in the Fulham area), police are no nearer finding the missing woman. In the hope that it might jog the memories of possible witnesses, police stage a reconstruction of Ms Lamplugh's last known movements. Dressed in identical clothing to that worn by Suzy Lamplugh when she disappeared, Police Constable Susan Long left the Fulham Road office of estate agents Sturgis & Co at 12.40 p.m. and drove to the house in Shorrold's Road for a 1 p.m. appointment with Mr Kipper, here played by Detective Sergeant Christopher Ball. After a few moments in the house, the couple leave in Ms Lamplugh's white Ford Fiesta (registration number B396 GAN) and drive to where the car was parked in Stevenage Road. Police officers along the route of the reconstruction question residents and stop motorists who may have remembered seeing the incidents the previous week.

20 August. Scotland Yard issue a new photofit portrait of Mr Kipper based on witness accounts giving an entirely new picture of Sus-

Susannah Lamplugh (Topham)

Police artist's impression of the enigmatic Mr Kipper

annah Lamplugh's last hours. Police now think it possible that she had lunch with her client after showing him around the Shorrold's Road property. A witness claims to have seen a man holding a bottle of champagne with Ms Lamplugh outside the house. Furthermore, an acquaintance of the missing woman saw the couple driving along the Fulham Palace Road in a white Ford Fiesta at 2.45 p.m. Various other recent witnesses add to the description of Mr Kipper that he was wearing an 'immaculate' charcoal-grey suit and light-coloured shirt and tie.

September. As public interest begins to wane, the Lamplugh family – in particular Suzy's mother Diana – begins to make opportunities to keep the case in the news by talking to the press. It is a hint of things to come when Mrs Lamplugh officially launches the Suzy Lamplugh Trust.

12 November. Suzy Lamplugh's house in Disraeli Road is sold by her parents to the couple with whom Suzy was negotiating the deal before she disappeared.

14 November. Diana Lamplugh and her family take the stage at the Royal Society of Medicine seminar to announce the foundation of the Suzy Lamplugh Trust: 'I suppose it began as something just for myself, to pull something worthwhile out of the most horrendous experience. But now I've talked to so many people, I can see that even if Suzy walked back through the door tomorrow, the Trust would have to go on.'

4 December. Press conference held in London to announce the Suzy Lamplugh Trust. Its aim is to raise £450,000, and by means of videos, newsletters and courses it hopes to 'encourage women to be self-aware and to be aware of others – both to reduce their vulnerability and to increase their effectiveness at work'.

1987

15 January. Scotland Yard officers fly to Antwerp to interview a man whose car was found abandoned in north London. The blue BMW is registered in Belgium to a man named Kiper.

16 January. Police checking the clue of the car registered to Mr David Kiper were told by his family that the vehicle had been stolen the previous summer. Thirty-nine-year-old Mr Kiper himself, a diamond merchant, is on business in the Middle East. The car, which was found in Queen's Grove, St John's Wood, has been checked by forensic experts and no connection has been found with the missing Suzy Lamplugh.

26 January. Police issue a statement clearing Belgian Mr David Rosengarten of any connection with the Lamplugh case. Mr Rosengarten became implicated because his mother's maiden name is Kiper, and his uncle, to whom the car belongs, has that surname.

11 March. Following an odd clue given by a London accountant, Thames Valley Police search historic Denham Place in Buckinghamshire. Officers leading the search for Suzy Lamplugh had been told she was being held in the house.

30 March. A new theory is being tested by the police, that Ms Lamplugh was 'moonlighting' as a private beautician with a select group of clients including men, who she visited in their homes. A qualified beautician, she once worked aboard a cruise liner.

6 May. A female estate agent is lured by a bogus purchaser to a house in Margate, Kent, where he attacks her. Police on the Lamplugh case deny there is any connection between the incident and their inquiry.

July. On the first anniversary of Suzy Lamplugh's disappearance, after one of the most exhaustive police inquiries, the team is no nearer a solution to the enigma than in the first weeks of the investigation. All that seems to have been resolved is the conviction on the part of the police and the Lamplugh family that Suzy is no longer alive.

[*8 October.* Mrs Shirley Banks disappears while on a shopping trip in Bristol. The search for her abductor will throw up connections between this case and the disappearance of Suzy Lamplugh.]

[29 *October*. John Cannan arrested in Leamington Spa.]

[23 *December*. Cannan charged with murder of Mrs Shirley Banks.]

1988

[4 *April*. The body of Mrs Banks is found floating in a stream.]

23 *September*. Assistant Commissioner Paul Condon of Scotland Yard issues a statement defending the reputation of Suzy Lamplugh after a book by *Observer* newspaper journalist Andrew Stephen suggests that she had numerous lovers and was obsessed with men. The Lamplugh family had already failed in their attempt to prevent Faber & Faber publishing the book. In response the publishers emphasise that it was originally the family which wanted an independent account, and the book was based to a large extent on correspondence and taped interviews with members of the family.

14 *October*. Despite having dissociated themselves from *The Suzy Lamplugh Story*, both the family and the Trust have been unable to revoke the publishing contract under which a percentage of the book's royalties went to the Suzy Lamplugh Trust. The Trust's chairman says that under trust law they are obliged to accept the money.

1989

[6 *April* – 28 *April*. Trial of John Cannan on charges of murder, rape, abduction and assault results in him being convicted on all counts and sentenced to several terms of life imprisonment. Free from the restraints imposed by the court proceedings, the Press once again reopen the question of John Cannan's connection, if any, to the Lamplugh case. Police interviews with Cannan fail to provide any further evidence and Cannan consistently denies ever having met Ms Lamplugh.]

11 *May*. Publication of Diana Lamplugh's book *Survive the Nine to Five*, which outlines ways in which women can avoid potentially dangerous situations at work.

1990

8 *May*. Publication of the Lamplugh Trust conference report *Working With the Sex Offender*, echoing current demands for dramatic change in the way the criminal justice system treats sex offenders.

[23 *July*. John Cannan's appeal is heard and rejected.]

September. Detectives studying the Cannan—Lamplugh connection have a mass of circumstantial evidence, none of which is sufficient to bring charges. Senior officers are publicly cautious, and state that in the absence of a body, forensic evidence, eyewitnesses or a confession, John Cannan must be considered, as he himself claims, innocent. However, Suzy Lamplugh's mother has stated that she is convinced the man who killed her daughter is now in jail.

IS JOHN CANNAN MR KIPPER?

So what is this mass of circumstantial evidence which is supposed to make the connection? The main points are outlined below, though no matter how convincing, no single factor or any combination of them *proves* that Cannan is Mr Kipper.

1. The Identikit picture of Mr Kipper bears a strong resemblance to John Cannan, who was known by his fellow-prisoners in Wormwood Scrubs as 'Kipper'.
2. Cannan was released from prison on 25 July 1986, three days before Suzy Lamplugh disappeared. He had told friends he was dating a girl from Fulham.
3. John Cannan was living in a parole hostel in Fulham, just four miles from where Ms Lamplugh worked and where Mr Kipper claimed he was looking for property.
4. It is thought that Mr Kipper drove a BMW car – John Cannan did drive a BMW car.

5. One newspaper report claimed that Cannan visited two bars known to have been frequented by Suzy Lamplugh – The White Horse, and the Crocodile and Tears.

6. Cannan was fond of impressing women with champagne; there were reports of Mr Kipper carrying a beribboned bottle of champagne when he met Ms Lamplugh at Shorrold's Road.

7. Cannan had previously used the ploy of posing as a house-buyer in order to lure women.

8. Gillie Page, a girlfriend of Cannan's, recalled him discussing bodies in concrete while talking about the Lamplugh case.

9. A woman visiting Cannan in prison reported that he mentioned Suzy Lamplugh and said he knew who killed Shirley Banks, Suzy Lamplugh and another woman [Sandra Court?].

10. Suzy Lamplugh had spoken of having a boyfriend in Bristol, where John Cannan abducted Shirley Banks and which he looked upon as his 'home town'.

11. Cannan was reputed to be obsessed by numerics, and when he put false number plates on Shirley Banks's Mini he chose SLP 386S – it has been suggested that this represents a code for Suzy LamPlugh and the year of her disappearance, '86.

After interviewing John Cannan, a police spokesman for the Lamplugh investigating team said: 'He [Cannan] is a clever and convincing liar. When the dust has settled and he has had a chance to consider his future behind bars we hope he will be able to help us. We are paying close attention to the *modus operandi* of his abductions. The fact that we believe Suzy Lamplugh knew her attacker may also be important.' He confirmed that the file on Ms Lamplugh would be reopened and extra officers assigned to the investigation. Police have also said that the evidence linking Cannan with Ms Lamplugh, while circumstantial, is 'overwhelming'. It should, nevertheless, be added that through his solicitor, John Cannan still denies the connection: 'My instructions are that he has never met the lady. What the police position may be I can't say.'

The Prince of Darkness

Dr Jay Smith, Principal of Upper Merion High School, Pennsylvania, had acquired the nickname 'Prince of Darkness' on account of his eccentric behaviour. In June 1979 the body of Susan Reiner, a teacher at Upper Merion, was found naked in her car, and she was later discovered to have taken out huge life-insurance policies benefiting one of Smith's henchmen, Bill Bradfield, who was also on the staff of the school. In 1981 Bradfield was arrested and convicted of theft by deception. Two years later he was charged with the Reiner murder and found guilty. Meanwhile Jay Smith had been in prison on other indictments and when he was released in 1986 faced charges arising out of the death of Susan Reiner. He was convicted, and sent straight back to prison. Thus a man who was already known to be involved in drugs, swindling and Satanism also achieved star billing as a killer.

1987

Mahmood Hussain

Sweet Revenge Grows Harsh. *Arson is one of the most difficult crimes to hide from the skills of the forensic chemist, and when that fire itself tries to mask multiple murder, it is all but impossible to escape the hand of justice.*

Murderers frequently display a certain naivety – or at least a suspension of common sense – when it comes to covering their tracks. There is always the conviction that they can, literally, get away with murder, despite all evidence to the contrary. With the scientific techniques available today, it is an unwise killer who would seek to mask homicide with arson.

At 9 p.m. on Monday evening, 2 March 1987, a fire crew were called to fight a blaze in Christchurch Street, Preston. The routine fire was, in a very short time, to become what was later described as one of the most serious crimes Lancashire police had experienced.

When firemen entered the burning building, a Victorian terrace house broken up into single bedsits, they found the badly charred bodies of three young men, each apparently poring over his college textbooks, each stabbed to death and each doused with paraffin before being set alight. It was clear even to the most inexperienced fire officer that the fire had been a deliberate, clumsy attempt to disguise murder.

Immediately, armed police were put on standby, and scene-of-crime officers began a minute search of the area immediately around Christchurch Street in an attempt to locate the murder weapon. Meanwhile, detectives and forensic experts began to unravel the background to a sadistic multiple murder.

The victims were subsequently identified as 21-year-old Tahir Iqubal and 23-year-old Ejaz Yousaf, both students at Lancaster Polytechnic, and Peter Mosley, who was on a sandwich course at British Nuclear Fuels at Salwick. To all appearances, the attacks had been carried out with a precision that indicated an assassin possessed of a high degree of military training, and investigating officers were beginning to build up a profile of their suspect as 'an SAS-style killer', because of the stealth and speed with which the attacks would need to have been carried out without the victims having a chance to put up a struggle. As Detective Chief Superintendent Norman Finnerty, in charge of the case, stated: 'He knew the vital areas of the body to strike at, exactly what to do.' Consequently, a search was begun through Army records for any clues to disturbed or disaffected soldiers.

In fact it took the police a bare 48 hours to make their arrest, and on 5 March, Mahmood Hussain was remanded in custody by Preston magistrates on a triple murder charge.

But the 24-year-old from Birmingham who faced the bench at Preston Crown Court the following July was far from the 'highly trained SAS-style professional assassin' of the police profile; he was not even a Middle East-trained terrorist. Hussain, who fully confessed his crimes, had acted on a passion to kill that was untaught in any military academy. As prosecuting counsel Mr John Hugill explained to the

293

The Baby Farmer

Gary Heidnik was a psychotic sex killer who picked up women around Philadelphia and kept them in chains in a damp, cold cellar. The members of this 'harem' were subjected to daily beatings, were raped and forced to engage in oral sex; in an attempt to render himself inaudible to the women, Heidnik perforated their eardrums with a screwdriver. By 23 March 1987, Heidnik's sex slaves numbered five; two had already died, partly as a result of the sparse diet of oatmeal and bread. On 24 March Josefina Rivera escaped and alerted the police; on 1 July of the following year, Gary Heidnik was found guilty on two counts of murder and sentenced to death.

Gary Heidnick in the custody of Philadelphia police officers (Topham)

jury, Hussain's girlfriend, Dionne Gonga, had become friendly with Peter Mosley, and Hussain's jealousy grew into an uncontrollable monster that destroyed not only his imagined rival but two innocent lives as well.

On 2 March, Hussain hired a car, stole a knife from a Birmingham shop and bought a can of paraffin. When he arrived at the house in Preston, he repeatedly stabbed Peter Mosley in the back after a quarrel; he then called Tahir Iqubal into the room and stabbed him to death as well. Ejaz Yousaf was chased around the house before he too was stabbed to death in a frenzied attack. Hussain then set fire to the bodies.

As he serves his three life sentences he will have at least twenty years to ponder whether, as the Bard of Avon cautions, 'Sweet revenge grows harsh'.

In Suspicious Circumstances

Diana Carson, wife of the British defence attaché in the Bahamas, was found drowned in her swimming pool in October 1987. When bruising was discovered on her head, Captain Christopher Carson, her husband, immediately fell under suspicion. Carson was recalled to Britain after the Bahamas government allegedly indicated that his presence was 'no longer acceptable'. However, despite the unsubstantiated suspicions, the cause of Mrs Carson's death remains 'accidental'.

1988

John Francis Duffy 'The Railway Killer'

Known throughout the long investigation into his three murders as 'The Railway Killer', Duffy was the first criminal in English legal history to be identified by the procedure know as psychological offender profiling (POP).

A petty criminal described variously as 'weak', 'immature', 'lazy', 'lying', 'insignificant', and 'almost invisible', John Duffy nevertheless compensated for his inadequacies by throwing a blanket of fear over the activities of young women around north London and parts of the Home Counties. And far from describing him as 'insignificant', Duffy's wife told an Old Bailey jury how he had become 'a raving madman with scary, scary eyes' (he was also nicknamed by the Press 'The Man with the Laser Eyes'), who used to tie her up before sex and frequently bragged that 'Rape is a natural thing for a man to do'.

The first attack that has been linked to Duffy was a rape in 1982, during which two men attacked a 23-year-old woman in Hampstead, close to the North London Link railway line. It was the first of a four-year series of rapes, in eighteen of which Duffy worked with a so-far unnamed and uncharged accomplice. In July 1985 there were three violent attacks in a single night and the police, frustrated by lack of progress, launched 'Operation Hart', which was to develop into the most comprehensive manhunt in Britain since the search for the Yorkshire Ripper (see page 000), and which involved officers from four forces – Scotland Yard, Surrey, Hertfordshire and the British Transport Police.

In the following month, August, John Duffy was arrested and charged with offences involving violence, but quite unconnected with the 'railway rapes'. Against police recommendations, Duffy was released on bail. Nevertheless, due to the nature of the crimes, he was routinely entered on the suspect file of Operation Hart.

Shortly after his release, Duffy attacked another young woman in north London, though in her confused 'rape trauma' condition she was unable to bring herself to identify her attacker until December of the following year. By that time he had killed three times.

A remarkably accurate police artist's impression of the 'Railway Killer'

John Francis Duffy (Syndication International)

Professor David Canter

On 18 May 1986, Mrs Anne Lock, who worked for London Weekend Television, disappeared on her way home from the studios; her body was not found until July.

In the meantime, forensic scientists had been working on eliminating suspects from the Operation Hart file by matching blood samples from Maartje Tamboezer's body with those on the suspect list. The register of more than 5,000 was thus reduced to 1,999 men, of whom John Duffy was number 1505. Duffy was interviewed in July but refused (as was his right) to provide a blood sample, and after bribing a friend to 'mug' him, put himself voluntarily into a psychiatric hospital to recover from the trauma.

In 1986, psychological profiling was a relatively unknown factor, in Britain at least, in the arsenal of weapons being made available by the rapidly emerging science of forensic psychiatry. Increasingly concerned by their own lack of progress, the police enlisted the professional help of Professor David Canter, an expert in behavioural science and professor of applied psychology at Surrey University. Canter carefully built up a projectural profile of the 'Railway Killer' based on statistical analysis of police witness statements. From these reports, Professor Canter was able to make deductions such as that the killer lived in the Kilburn/Cricklewood area of northwest London, was married, childless (this turned out to be a particular source of anguish to Duffy), and surrounded by domestic disharmony. In all, Professor Canter's profile was to prove accurate in thirteen out of its seventeen points; he explained: 'A criminal leaves evidence of his personality through his actions in relation to a crime. Any person's behaviour exhibits characteristics unique to that person, as well as patterns and consistencies which are typical of the subgroup to which he or she belongs.'

While the police were awaiting David Canter's report, Duffy struck again. This time the victim was a fourteen-year-old girl who was blindfolded before her ordeal. During the struggle this mask slipped and she caught a glimpse of her attacker; why Duffy did not kill the girl is inexplicable on the basis of his former *modus operandi*. When the psychological profile

On 29 December 1985, John Duffy dragged nineteen-year-old secretary Alison Day off an east London train and took her to a squalid block of garages in Hackney where he garotted her with what is known as a 'Spanish Windlass', a kind of tourniquet favoured in the carpentry trade (which Duffy once followed) for holding wood tightly together. Seventeen days later Miss Day's body was recovered from the River Lea.

The connection with the 'Railway Rapist' was not finally made until three months later, when a fifteen-year-old schoolgirl, Maartje Tamboezer, was killed on her way to the shops in West Horsley, Surrey. Duffy had tried to remove clues by burning his victim's body, but left semen traces and a set of uncommonly small footprints (it later transpired that Duffy had always been sensitive about his diminutive five feet four inches). At this point information on the two murders was included in the computer-based files of Operation Hart, and the hunt was accelerated.

was run alongside the computer file of Operation Hart it came up with the name that officers had been waiting years for: John Francis Duffy. After a short period of intensive surveillance, Duffy was arrested at his mother's home where scene-of-crime officers recovered sufficient forensic clues to build a watertight case against him.

John Duffy's trial took place during the first two months of 1988. He offered a weak and unsuccessful defence of amnesia, and on 26 February Mr Justice Farquarson, who described him as 'little more than a predatory animal who behaved in a beastly, degrading and disgusting way', sentenced Duffy to seven life sentences, adding the recommendation that he serve at least 30 years. His Lordship added: 'You should not depend on that being the total amount of time you will serve.'

In the case of Anne Lock, Mr Justice Farquarson directed the jury to return a verdict of not guilty on account of insufficient evidence.

UNITED STATES

Jeffrey Lynn Feltner

The Man Who Had to Confess. *When Jeffrey Feltner phoned the police to confess to multiple murder, they just wouldn't believe him – in fact they locked him up for making malicious phone calls. Following his release he began to confess again . . .*

In 1988 police and local crisis centres began to receive a series of anonymous telephone calls from a man claiming to have committed multiple homicide at the New Life Nursing Home at Melrose, Florida. When questioned over the telephone he would add nothing further. The caller, later picked up and identified as Jeffrey Feltner, insisted that he had been responsible for the deaths of three women and two men at the home.

There had been one sudden death at New Life on 10 February 1988, when Mrs Sara Abrams had been found with some minor bruising around her mouth. The case was looked into, but the conclusion was that Mrs Abrams had not died in suspicious circumstances. As a result, Feltner was prosecuted for making malicious telephone calls and spent four months in prison. During this time he was diagnosed as suffering from AIDS.

Following Feltner's release from jail the telephone calls resumed; furthermore, Feltner started telling his friends that he was a multiple murderer. At the time Feltner was employed by the Clyatt Memorial Center, Daytona Beach, and after investigation by the local police force, he was arrested and charged with the murder of 83-year-old Doris Moriarty at the Clyatt Center on 11 July 1989. In custody Feltner described how he had climbed upon Mrs Moriarty's chest as she lay in bed and covered her nose and mouth with his rubber-gloved hands until she was dead. He claimed it was the same method he had used to kill Sara Abrams. In addition Feltner was laying claim to four other murders at Melrose and one at the Bowman Medical Center. He was charged with just the Abrams and Moriarty deaths.

In his defence, Feltner insisted that his motive was entirely altruistic – that he felt compassion for the elderly sick who could look forward to nothing but pain and suffering. While awaiting trial Feltner attempted suicide and this was used by his attorney as the basis for a defence of 'unfit to plead'. The judge ruled that Feltner was perfectly competent to stand trial and Jeffrey Feltner was arraigned first for the murder of Mrs Abrams at the Palatka courthouse in January 1989. The prosecution emphasised Feltner's own admission to no less than seven murders, and played the court a tape recording of his confession. Following this Feltner changed his plea to guilty and he was sentenced to life with a minimum of 25 years before parole. Feltner appeared subsequently to plead guilty to the second-degree murder of Mrs Moriarty and was given a concurrent sentence of seventeen years. Given his medical condition, it is unlikely that Jeffrey Feltner will leave prison alive.

Robert Sartin

The Man in Black. *A great admirer of the mass killer Michael Ryan, Sartin tried to copy the Hungerford massacre with his own shooting spree around the northern seaside suburb of Monkseaton. Unlike Ryan, Robert Sartin left most of his victims alive to tell the tale, and did not commit suicide.*

It seemed a relatively idyllic life, a happy contented landscape. But underneath a very dark river had flowed unsuspected for years. That river broke through and burst into terrible reality in that quiet community. What caused it we may never know.

(David Robson QC, at Robert Sartin's trial)

The date was 30 April 1989, a quiet Bank Holiday Sunday in the seaside suburb of Monkseaton, Tyne and Wear. Kenneth Mackintosh, the father of two young children and an enthusiastic member of the local St Peter's congregation, was delivering church leaflets along Windsor Road. From the opposite direction the slight figure of a young man with dark glasses and a ponytail approached, dressed entirely in black with a combat knife strapped to one thigh and a shotgun held straight out in front of him. As Mr Mackintosh looked up, the assassin fired off both barrels of the weapon, sending his victim reeling to the pavement. Reaching up his hand, begging the gunman for help, for mercy, Mackintosh heard the words 'No, it is your day to die!' before the contents of two more cartridges blasted their way into his chest from point-blank range. He was dead before the man in black had turned and walked on.

It was only later that the story of Robert James Sartin's twenty-minute rise to notoriety was fitted into the context of what became known as the Bloody Sunday Slaughter.

Early on that dry, sunny morning, Sartin had been served breakfast of sausage and egg in bed by his parents before they left their house in Wentworth Gardens to visit friends. Robert had taken his time dressing in his favourite black – the devil's colour, he liked to think – aware, as he often was, of the voices in his head and of one voice in particular, the voice of 'Michael'. Putting on the dark glasses that kept the thoughts inside, Sartin loaded his father's shotgun into the back of his beige Ford Escort and pulled slowly away from the front of the house. At 11.55 a.m. he was seen parking the car and walking along Pykerley Road. Seconds later Judith Rhodes, driving her car in the opposite direction along the street, found herself looking into the twin barrels of Robert Sartin's gun, too late to avoid it. The first shot shattered Mrs Rhodes's windscreen; as she slammed on the brakes and flung herself under the dashboard a second blast sent burning pellets into her left hand. Reloading the gun, Sartin fired a shot defiantly at the sky before turning on his heel and walking back down the street, 'Looking sharp, not nervous,' as one witness recalled. 'He was turning left and right and pointing his gun.'

William Roberts was at his garden gate exchanging Sunday chitchat with Lorraine Noble when the madman in black bore down on them. 'Oh God,' Roberts shouted, and flung himself to the ground as the shotgun's barrels levelled. There was a deafening explosion and Mrs Noble collapsed, seriously injured, to the ground.

Thirty-nine-year-old Robert Wilson, hearing

the sound of shooting and fearful for the safety of his girlfriend, who was out walking the dog, had just stepped out of his front door when the rain of shot tore into his face and left side of his body. As Wilson fled, heedless of his own injuries, in search of his girlfriend, Sartin took a pot shot at neighbour Kathleen Lynch, looking out of her bedroom window at the growing scene of carnage. The next victim was at this very moment cycling towards Sartin when he saw what he thought was an airgun in his hands; two blasts that threw him from his bike and all but robbed him of his life told Brian Thomas that this was no toy. In acute pain, and trailing blood behind him, Thomas made the effort that saved him and dragged himself to the security of a nearby house.

All the time The Voices. Michael's voice. A gunman out of control.

A car approached, the driver negotiating around Brian Thomas's bicycle abandoned in the middle of the road. The car's three occupants – Robert Burgon, his wife Jean and their daughter Nicola – drove through a hail of shot as Sartin opened fire, seriously injuring Mr Burgon and his wife, before turning his murderous weapon on to Ernest Carter and another motorist whose car careered out of control into a wall. As the windscreen shattered the sound was met by the explosion of another shot and Jean Miller was hit in the stomach as she stooped to weed her front garden.

Madness taking him over. The Voices.

'What the hell is going on?' Elderly Vera Burrows had heard the noise of shooting and was confronting Sartin for disturbing her Sunday peace.

'It's me – I am killing people. I am going to kill you.'

The gun raised like slow-motion . . . aim . . . The Voices . . . the weapon lowering again . . . 'Oh, you are old. I am not going to kill you . . .' *Turning . . . walking away . . . back to the car . . . driving off . . .*

Robert Sartin sat in a seaside car park as an unarmed police constable placed him under arrest. It was early evening already; and one person lay dead. Fourteen others were wounded.

By later that same day, with Robert out of

mischief in a police cell, his heartbroken parents Brian and Jean struggled against their disbelief: 'There was our gentle, quiet son who loves kids and animals; he loves people. He is so gentle. It must have been something inside him.'

It was The Voices that were inside him . . . one voice in particular . . .

But for every neighbour to whom 22-year-old Robert Sartin was 'everyone's favourite son', there was a schoolfriend who remembered the 'weirdo', the boy who liked to drop the 'r' from his surname so that it sounded like 'Satan', and who always wore black clothes.

Exactly one year after he had turned Monkseaton into a bloodbath, on Monday, 30 April 1990, a jury was empanelled to assess the evidence as to Robert Sartin's sanity. In the Crown Court at Newcastle upon Tyne, Mr David Robson QC, for the prosecution, instructed the jury in their duties. He emphasised that Sartin's fitness to plead went beyond whether or not he could say 'guilty' or 'not guilty', but whether his mental state permitted the defendant to understand the charge that was made against him, instruct his legal counsel and, if necessary, give evidence on his own behalf: 'You are not here to decide the issue of guilt or innocence. The whole of justice is held in the balance. On the one hand there are the victims of crime and the public interest that they should be protected; on the other that real justice is done and a man is not put on trial when he has no ability to defend himself.'

Mr Robson went on to describe the schizophrenia that had been developing over a number of years, and Sartin's conviction that his mind was being controlled by another. He recalled for the jury Sartin's statement to the police when he was taken into custody: 'I know I was arrested because I shot people, but I wasn't thinking about it . . . I don't feel anything for them now. I remember hearing people scream, I wasn't bothered if I hit them . . . I was not taking proper aim at anybody. Every time I fired I think I was shooting both barrels – the cartridges would just eject and I would put in the next ones. *It was as if it was not me inside myself.*'

Then the jury discovered who it was that

Robert Sartin arriving at court (Syndication International)

possessed Robert Sartin, the voice that made him kill. It was Michael. From childhood, Sartin had been obsessed with the macabre, with the occult, to such an extent that other children went in fear of him. In youth this unhealthy preoccupation found expression in Satanism and a morbid fascination with Moors Murderers Ian Brady and Myra Hindley, and the mad poisoner Graham Young. Eight months before his own rampage, Robert Sartin had visited the scene of Michael Ryan's Hungerford Massacre. Above all there was the influence of Michael. Michael Myers.

Home Office psychiatrist Dr Marion Swann explained to the court: 'He hears more than one voice, and one of them is Michael. Initially he didn't know who this person was, but then he watched the video of [the film] *Halloween*

and came to realise Michael's [Myers, the film's teenage psychopath who hacks his family to pieces] was the voice he had been hearing. He describes the ability to actually see Michael and many of the drawings he had were of Michael . . .' In conclusion, Dr Swann argued: 'He is so sick and mentally disturbed that he needs treatment for this condition as a matter of urgency.'

Robert Sartin was not in court to hear this most intimate evaluation of his psyche; he had been confined to Moss Side Special Hospital, near Liverpool. The jury, predictably, passed the only humane and just verdict possible – the verdict of 'unfit to plead'. Whether Robert Sartin will ever be considered well enough to stand trial is doubtful.

CANADA

The Man Who Hated Feminists

In a senseless mass shooting, Marc Lepine shot up a class of female students at the University of Montreal. In a three-page letter Lepine explained that he 'hated feminists'; it is thought that the incident, in which fourteen women were killed, may have been sparked off by Lepine's girlfriend insisting on her right to have an abortion.

1990

David Lashley

The Long Memory of the Law. *Lashley was put on trial for the murder of Janie Shepherd thirteen years before. Although he was interviewed as a suspect at the time of the killing, police eliminated him from their inquiry; it was only when Lashley boasted to a fellow prisoner that he was the killer that he was brought to trial.*

Statistically, Janie Shepherd was a very unlikely victim. She was the stepdaughter of Australian businessman John Darling, and had left the family home in Sydney in 1971. In 1977 she was living with her cousin Camilla and Camilla's husband Alistair Sampson in a luxury apartment in Clifton Hill, northwest London. Like many girls born into the wealthy middle-class, Janie was in receipt of a generous allowance from her father, and worked because she chose to rather than needed to; in her case it was at the Caelt art gallery, a specialist dealing in modern unknown artists, with premises in London's Westbourne Grove. When she left the gallery on the evening of Friday, 4 February 1977, Janie drove back to the flat in St John's Wood, changed quickly, threw a few 'essentials' into her red shoulder bag and by 8.40 p.m. was back behind the wheel of her dark-blue Mini Cooper. She had planned to spend the weekend with her boyfriend Roddy Kinkead-Weekes. He had telephoned the gallery earlier that evening and suggested they spend a quiet evening together at his flat in Lennox Gardens, Chelsea. She offered to pick a snack up on the way over and stopped in at the Europa Supermarket in Queensway.

When Janie had not arrived by 9.30 p.m. Kinkead-Weekes checked with her cousin. He rang again at 10 p.m. and at regular intervals until midnight. Then Roddy Kinkead-Weekes and Camilla and Alistair Sampson between them rang around the local hospitals to see if Janie had met with an accident. All the replies they received were comfortably negative, but with increasing alarm both the Sampsons and Kinkead-Weekes reported Janie missing to their respective local police stations.

At 3.15 a.m. on 5 February, Janie Shepherd became an 'official' missing person, and her description and that of her car were prepared and circulated.

Just four days after her disappearance Janie Shepherd's car was found spattered with mud and with a collection of parking tickets under the windscreen wiper on a yellow line in Elgin Crescent, Notting Hill. The parking tickets dated back to the morning of 7 February, but witnesses were found who would testify to seeing the car parked there as early as 1.10 a.m. on Saturday 5th – even before its owner had been reported missing.

The state of the car left police with little optimism for Janie's safety; it was clear that a fierce struggle had taken place in the vehicle resulting in two deep slashes in the soft sun-roof. The girl's boots had been left in the car, as was the red satchel bag – without its usual contents, but with two recent till receipts. One was from a petrol station where Janie had topped up the seven-gallon fuel tank of her car. Given the amount of petrol left in the tank, police scientists estimated that the car would have been driven on a roughly 75-mile round trip. The journey had been through muddy countryside, as was obvious from the state of the tyres and bodywork, but exactly where within that 45-mile radius around Notting Hill was anybody's guess.

The hunt for Janie Shepherd was relentless. Police helicopter teams made aerial searches over the area that may have been covered by the car, and for the very first time in a British murder inquiry dogs trained to sniff out dead bodies were used in the ground search. The customary 'Appeal for Assistance' posters were distributed, asking the general public for sightings of Janie or her car, while the Press carried descriptions and photographs of models in similar clothing to that worn by her when she disappeared. In addition, more than 50 officers under the direction of DCI Roger Lewis were engaged in similar intensive routine searches.

Back at Scotland Yard, Detective Chief Superintendent Henry Mooney had begun the painstaking task of searching records at the Yard and at Notting Hill police station for similar offences against women, and discovered that in July 1976 a young woman had been raped and murderously attacked in her own car less than half a mile from where Janie Shepherd's Mini had been abandoned in Elgin Crescent. The woman survived her ordeal to give a description of her assailant and to help construct an Identikit portrait of a black man with a noticeable scar on his face. Although police routinely searched their files for possible suspects, they dismissed the most likely one because his record made no mention of a scar. The man's name was David Lashley, a van driver who in 1970 had been convicted of a series of five rapes of young women in cars, and sentenced to twelve years' imprisonment. At the time of the Chesterton Street offence Lashley had recently been released on parole.

If his predecessors had overlooked the obvious connection, it did not escape Henry Mooney, and on 17 February 1977 Lashley was picked up at his current address in Southall and taken in for questioning on the Chesterton Street rape and the disappearance of Janie Shepherd. At an identity parade 'Miss A', the Chesterton Street victim, positively identified David Lashley as her attacker – he had the distinctive scar on his cheek. Mooney was

equally certain that Lashley had abducted and murdered Janie Shepherd.

It was not until 18 April, Easter Monday, that Janie Shepherd's rustic grave was discovered by ten-year-old Neil Gardner and eleven-year-old Dean James, on the common known as No-man's-land, near Wheathampstead in Hertfordshire. As soon as the body had been found and the preliminary on-site examination and photography had been carried out, the sad remains of Janie Shepherd were removed to the St Albans mortuary for forensic post-mortem. In charge of the medical examination was pathologist James Cameron, Professor of Forensic Medicine at the London Hospital Medical School.

The body of Janie Shepherd was fully clothed in her jeans and striped socks (the boots she had left home wearing were found abandoned in her car), and a black sweater with bright green cuffs and a scarlet neck. Beneath the clothing Cameron found a ligature around the left ankle and a mark on the right that indicated the feet had been bound; there were also ligatures on the upper arms. Extensive bruising on the upper part of the body suggested that Janie had put up a courageous fight for her life. Cause of death was established as asphyxia on account of congestion of the heart and lungs, and Professor Cameron gave his opinion that Janie Shepherd had died from 'compression of the neck'.

Identity was established by Bernard Sims, a forensic dentist experienced in the identification of badly mutilated human remains by means of dental features. Using a post-mortem dental chart and comparing it with that kept by Janie Shepherd's dentist, Sims was able to prove the uniqueness – almost like a fingerprint – of the victim's teeth.

At the inquest on Janie Shepherd's death, the jury returned the only verdict they could, that of murder 'by person or persons unknown'.

The case file, it seemed, was all but closed, and the officers actively pursuing the murder drastically reduced. In December 1977, David Lashley was sentenced to fifteen years' imprisonment for the attempted murder of Miss A. About Janie Shepherd he would say nothing – to the police that is. When he did decide to talk it was by way of an arrogant boast to a fellow inmate named Daniel Reece – not his real name as it turned out, but the one which he had been given, along with a new identity, after giving evidence as a 'supergrass' in an armed robbery case and had put his safety at risk. His own crimes included a thirteen-year sentence for rape and buggery.

The Shepherd inquiry was reactivated in July 1988, when Detective Superintendent Ian Whinnett of the Hertfordshire force assembled a team of seven officers to reassess the evidence and make further inquiries. It is possible that the imminent release of David Lashley in February 1989 led senior police officers to make every attempt to keep the man with an undisguised hatred of women and policemen, and who had spent the whole of his eleven-year term as a Category A (dangerous) prisoner, on the inside for as long as possible.

It is at this stage that the police are believed to have become aware of David Reece's claim that Lashley had confessed to the Shepherd murder. Both Lashley and Reece had been fanatical body-builders while in Frankland Prison, and spent much of their free time weight-lifting in the prison gymnasium. This and perhaps their mutual commitment to rape and violence, threw the two men as close together as such bizarre personalities ever can be. Lashley, according to his confidant, had boasted of grabbing a 'nice looking blonde' in her Mini car (he even recalled the 'For Sale' notice that Janie Shepherd had recently stuck on her rear window), threatening her with a knife and slashing the sun roof to show that he meant business. Then Lashley said he had driven her to a secluded part of Ladbroke Grove where the rape and murder took place. At this point Lashley began to reveal details that could only have been known to the police and the killer; Lashley demonstrated to Reece, for example, exactly how he had killed Janie, holding her neck in one hand and pressing the fist of his other into her windpipe: as Professor Cameron had observed, she died of a 'crushed throat'. Another detail that had puzzled the earlier investigation was why Janie Shepherd's body had been found dressed in her *spare* set of clothes. This Lashley obligingly explained,

saying he had slashed the clothing she was wearing with the knife, and had needed to re-dress the body in order to drive it out of town, strapped into the passenger's seat, to where it was dumped. Reece decided that Lashley was a menace to womankind and too dangerous to be released – hence his brief moment of good citizenship in reporting Lashley's conversation to the prison authorities. And without Reece's testimony in court it is very unlikely that the police, new inquiry or not, would have been able to make out a watertight case against David Lashley for the murder of Janie Shepherd.

On the morning of 7 February 1989, David Lashley was released from Frankland Prison. He was a free man for just half a minute before being placed under arrest and charged with the Shepherd murder. By the time Lashley had worked his way through the magistrates' hearings and their consequent remands in custody, others of Lashley's fellow prisoners had begun to tell tales: tales of his confessions to killing a woman in a car and dumping her body in some woods. One of them was Robert Hodgson, who had shared a cell in Wakefield Prison with Lashley; Hodgson was later to give evidence at his cellmate's trial.

Thirteen years to the month after Janie Shepherd left her home in London never to return, her killer was finally brought face to face with justice. On 7 February 1990, David Lashley stood in the dock of St Albans Crown Court; he pleaded not guilty to murder. Daniel Reece appeared as chief witness for the Crown, and as a final piece of hard fact, the prosecution was able to introduce a piece of forensic evidence impossible to imagine when Lashley first came to the notice of the Shepherd inquiry team. In the rear of Janie's abandoned car, scene-of-crime experts had found a semen stain. In 1977, technology had not been sufficiently advanced to be able to make identifications from these body fluids, but the sample had been kept. The intervening years had seen the development of DNA profiling – the genetic analysis of body secretions – and from the stored sample it was now possible to identify the source as an A-secretor. David Lashley was an A-secretor.

The jury retired to consider their verdict on

19 March. After two hours and fifteen minutes they returned with a unanimous verdict of guilty. Amid cheers of delight that the court usher had difficulty subduing, Mr Justice Alliot, the trial judge, began to address the prisoner, and in sentencing Lashley to life imprisonment, remarked: 'In my view you are such an appalling, dangerous man that the real issue is whether the authorities can ever allow you your liberty in your natural lifetime ... The decision is such that whoever is responsible must have careful regard before you are allowed your liberty again.'

David Lashley is now confined in a British prison which has not been named to ensure his personal safety.

UNITED STATES

Christian Brando

The Messenger of Misery. *When the son of America's most famous movie star commits murder, that's news! Brando, much the worse for drink, shot his sister's lover in Marlon's Hollywood home, and thanks to some skilful plea-bargaining by the best lawyer money could hire was given a controversially light sentence of ten years.*

The case began as a simple, sordid story of violent death American-style – a fatal cocktail of domestic dispute, booze and guns. As a movie script it would hardly have got past Reception, but this drama had a head start: it starred 'America's greatest living actor'.

By the time the cops drove up to Marlon Brando's rambling mansion in the Hollywood Hills it was all over. It was late on the night of 16 May 1990, and they had been summoned by the Great Man himself. There on a sofa in the TV room slumped the victim, 26-year-old Dag Drollet, a small round wound on his face where a bullet fired at almost point-blank range from a .45 had ripped through flesh and bone, leaving the skin tattooed with a peppering of

burnt powder before exiting at the base of the neck. The officers were to recall afterwards how neat it all was; there was no sign of a struggle, almost as if the dead man had simply fallen asleep. That was the weird part, because the other leading player in this family drama, Marlon's 32-year-old son Christian, had already told his father and the police that there had been a fight and he had accidentally shot Dag.

Normally only Marlon would have been found rattling around the two-acre estate, but he had invited his common-law wife Tarita Teriipia and their daughter Cheyenne to stay; Cheyenne had brought along Dag Drollet, son of a leading Tahitian politician and the father of her unborn child. Cheyenne and Christian had always been close, and on the evening of 16 May they had dined out together. It must have been during the meal that Cheyenne confided to her half-brother that things were not exactly a bed of roses with Dag, and that he had started beating her up. Now, there is no shred of evidence to support this extravagant claim, but it convinced Christian. When the pair returned to the house on Mulholland, Christian, much the worse for drink, went hunting for Dag with a .45 SIG-Sauer semi-automatic.

Later, in police custody, Christian made an incoherent statement during the course of which he recounted the story of the life-and-death struggle which followed: 'We got into a fight and the gun went off in his face. I didn't want to hurt him; I didn't want to kill him.' This maudlin whining was followed by a more aggressive claim: 'You know, we got in a struggle ... I'd been drinking ... I didn't go up to him and go *Boom!* in my dad's house. If I was going to do that I'd take him down the road and knock him off.' Later in the interview, Christian seemed to get back his old arrogance: 'If I was going to do something devious like this [murder], I would have said [to Drollet] "Hey, let's go out, you know, check out the mine shafts on the Mojave." You know, or something like that. Whoops! He fell down a hole. Couldn't help it. "See you later sucker!" You know, I mean, all delicately laid – take him out to Death Valley with no clothes on, and give him three gallons of water "Get a suntan".'

Next day a woebegone Christian stood,

handcuffed and unshaven, and wearing prison-issue grey, in the dock of the Los Angeles county court. William Kunstler, Marlon's lawyer, entered a plea of not guilty and added: 'The weapon was fired accidentally during a struggle. There was no intent to harm anyone. This was not murder by any means.' In other words, he was going for a reduced charge of manslaughter.

Predictably the Brando family closed ranks, and even Christian's ex-wife whom he had once threatened to kill was emphatic that 'He's no killer . . .' At the bail hearing five days later Marlon himself put in an appearance. This was what the media wanted – who was interested in some dipso kid with an itchy trigger-finger, who described his occupation as 'self-employed welder'? Here was the *real* news. And Marlon didn't disappoint them; standing there on the steps outside the courthouse he broadcast to the waiting cameras his belief in Christian's innocence, and as though he were back there on the set of *Julius Caesar* intoned: 'The Messenger of Misery has come to my house . . .'

Cheyenne, for her part, made only the briefest of statements to the police, but it was to the effect that Christian had 'just walked in and killed Dag'. She was prevented from making any more damaging observations by the simple expedient of flying her back to Tahiti. There, far from the clutches of the District Attorney's office, she gave birth to the late Dag Drollet's child.

Despite the court refusal to admit Christian's statement made in custody because of a legal technicality, and then its ruling that Cheyenne's statement that Christian was angry with Drollet was inadmissible, it did concede that 'there is no doubt there has been a killing; there is no doubt that the defendant pulled the trigger' – in short, Christian was going up for trial.

In the meantime moves were afoot to flush Cheyenne out of her Tahitian retreat to give evidence, though the extradition application became purely academic anyway when Cheyenne tried unsuccessfully to take her own life. When she eventually emerged from a coma, Cheyenne was judged by a French court in Tahiti to be incapable of looking after herself

and was placed in the care of her mother on the island. And so, faced with the unlikelihood of getting their star witness into court, the State of California decided to cut their losses and agree to a reduced charge of voluntary manslaughter in exchange for a plea of guilty.

When Christian Brando appeared before the sentencing hearing on 26 February 1991, his lawyer had already entered into a plea-bargain with the prosecutor's office. True to expectation, at the hearing Marlon, though clearly hating every minute of the limelight on which he had turned his back for so long, took the witness stand on his son's behalf and courageously exposed the family skeletons of Christian's unsatisfactory early life. Batted backwards and forwards like a tennis ball between his separated but still-warring parents, Christian found himself sometimes in the custody of an absentee film-star father for whom displays of affection came hard, and sometimes in the custody of his mother, Anna Kashfi, who was gradually losing herself to drink and drugs. Education was spasmodic, and after dropping out of private school at the age of eighteen, there followed for Christian a period as a California beach bum, a broken marriage, and the development of an unhealthy interest in drink, drugs and guns. In many respects, it might have been more surprising if Christian had *not* got drunk someday and shot someone.

Christian led into court to face trial (Rex Features)

After all the media ballyhoo and legal tub-thumping had died down, Christian was sentenced to ten years' imprisonment. It was, as everybody had predicted, an affair from which only the lawyers gained. For Marlon there was the unwelcome intrusion into his jealously guarded privacy; for Cheyenne a further jolt to an already unsettled mind; for the Drollet family the loss of a son; and for Dag the ultimate loss. But perhaps the most haunting figure in this script where life tried hard to imitate Hollywood is Christian Brando himself.

1991

UNITED STATES

Erik and Lyle Menendez

Life Imitates Hollywood. *The murder of super-rich parents by their offspring has become such an epidemic in the United States that it has its own special term – the 'West Coast Syndrome'.*

According to their own story, Erik and Lyle Menendez went to see the popular *Batman* film for a second time on the night of 20 August 1989. Then, again according to evidence that they gave to the police, they kept up the happy atmosphere by taking in a wine and food festival in Santa Monica before arriving for a supper appointment with a friend back in Beverly Hills.

It was approaching midnight when the brothers reached home and found their parents in the den. José Menendez had been shot eight times at point-blank range before the shotgun was forced into his mouth and a final cartridge blew the back of his head away. His wife Kitty had been shot five times. At 11.47 p.m. Beverly Hills police logged an hysterical telephone call from Lyle Menendez: 'They killed my mom and

my dad.' According to neighbours, Erik was out on the porch sobbing as though his heart would break.

The case made headlines, not just in Los Angeles, not just in California; the Menendez killings were world-wide news – from a country with more than 20,000 homicides the same year. But then, the Menendez family were not exactly ordinary. For a start they were rich, very rich. And they lived in Hollywood; in fact they lived in the reputedly $5-million mansion once the home of a succession of rock superstars such as Elton John and Michael Jackson. José Menendez himself had been big in the entertainment business. A refugee from Fidel Castro's revolution in Cuba, 45-year-old Menendez had risen to executive positions in a number of companies, and at the time of his tragic death was on the board of directors of Carolco, the company which made the blockbusting series of *Rocky* films; Sylvester Stallone was a fellow board member. José was also chief executive of Live Entertainment, a major music and video company. And now he was dead in what at first was thought to be a Mafia execution – the hit carried out quickly (there was no sign of forced entry or a struggle at the scene of the shootings) and cleanly (whoever pulled the trigger had also been meticulous in picking up the spent cartridge cases).

When, in March 1990, the Menendez brothers

Erik and Lyle were arrested and charged with parricide it was a media dream come true; real life was imitating Hollywood. And now at least four television 'docudramas' were in the making, a film or two, and the usual clutch of books about these, the latest 'celebrity' murders.

But just wait a minute! All these storylines assumed that Erik and Lyle are guilty; there wouldn't have been much of a plot otherwise. *But* the Menendez brothers have not even been put on trial yet. True, they have been held for some time without bail; true, police and prosecution have released enough tasty morsels of evidence to keep the public's interest in the boys' guilt going. *But* whatever happened to the concept of being innocent until proved guilty?

There are many, not least of the immediate family, who have been vociferous in their belief that 22-year-old Lyle and 19-year-old Erik Menendez could never have killed their own parents. One uncle is reported as believing that 'The whole situation with the kids is something the police have fallen into for lack of a better lead.'

Could it possibly be as he says?

It is true that the police did take a long time – more than six months – to press charges against the brothers for murder. It is also true that out of sympathy neither boy was checked for forensic evidence. Detectives had disposed fairly early of the 'Mafia hit-man' theory, partly because there was no evidence to suggest that José Menendez was in the grip of the Mob, or had ever had any dealings, wittingly or not, with gangsters, and partly because it is not characteristic of 'execution-type' assassins to create a bloodbath – the professional does not need to loose off a shotgun fourteen times to make his point.

Of course the Menendez brothers had been routinely questioned, and may even have been routinely considered suspects in the early weeks of the investigation. But it was not until the heartbroken youths had begun to spend, spend, spend, that they once again came under official scrutiny. By this time the brothers – sole benefactors under their father's will – had taken delivery of the first instalment of the

The Menendez brothers (Rex Features)

$400,000 insurance policy on his life. Erik's first step was to shelve plans to enter university and instead hire an expensive tennis coach in the hope that his already promising talent could be brought up to professional standard. Meanwhile Lyle was at the Porsche showrooms selecting a new car, and was soon to move into the apartment he had bought in Princeton where he attended university. For good measure he also bought a restaurant in town. But what really attracted attention was the way Lyle Menendez had taken to being chauffeured around in a hired limousine flanked by bodyguards – protection, he claimed, against those disgruntled business associates who had robbed him of his parents. Further revelations kept the media ball rolling during the latter part of 1989, when it was learned that two years previously, in collaboration with his pal Craig Cignarelli, Erik Menendez had written a screenplay. The script was called *Friends*, and told the story of an eighteen-year-old named Hamilton Cromwell who murders his parents for the $157 million inheritance. It contains this chilling passage: 'The door opens, exposing the luxurious suite of Mr and Mrs Hamilton Cromwell Sr lying in bed. Their faces are of questioning horror as Hamilton closes the door gently.' Kitty Menendez typed the manuscript for her son; we will never know what she made of such a plot.

The most significant, and the most controversial, piece of evidence gathered by the police investigators was a tape recording allegedly of the boys confessing murder to their psychologist Jerome Oziel. The existence of the recording had come to official attention in a most bizarre way. Another of Oziel's patients claimed she had been sitting in the waiting room when she heard the conversation through the wall. It was subsequently established that such a feat would be virtually impossible, but that did not prevent officers seizing a number of tapes from Mr Oziel's consulting rooms and making application for them to be accepted as evidence in court. It is normally considered that what secrets pass between a doctor and his patient are sacrosanct, but according to California state procedure, such information *may* be revealed if the psychiatrist considers the patient to be a serious threat to himself or others. The content of the tapes has not yet been made public, but at the preliminary hearing a judge ruled that the tapes could be used by the prosecution as evidence: 'Dr Oziel had reasonable cause to believe that the brothers constituted a threat, and that it was necessary to disclose those communications to prevent the threatened danger.' It was a decision strongly opposed by the Menendez defence counsel, who have referred the ruling to a higher court.

On Thursday, 8 March 1990, Lyle Menendez was arrested on suspicion of murdering his father and mother; three days later Erik returned from a tennis tournament in Israel and was taken into custody at Los Angeles airport. Both young men have pleaded not guilty to charges that could carry the death penalty.

When this entry was being prepared for publication in early 1993, it looked as though the Menendez case would never get to trial – years of pre-trial squabbling between counsel had kept it out of the courts until, in June 1993, it was announced that jury selection was about to begin. The delay had given Erik and Lyle's attorney, Ms Leslie Abramson, time to abandon the plea of not guilty and substitute one of self-defence: 'Our clients believed themselves to be in danger of death, imminent peril or great bodily injury.' Not danger in the ordinary sense of the defence, but the culmination of years of child abuse! This, of course shows the relevance of psychiatrist Dr Oziel's tapes in a new light;

they will help corroborate the fact that the killings were carried out 'out of hatred and a desire to be free from their father's domination'. Meanwhile the judge, Mr Stanley Weisberg, was wrestling with his own dilemma – whether to have one jury only, or two, so that the evidence against one brother would not sway a verdict against the other.

UNITED KINGDOM

John Tanner

The Case of the Mysterious Stranger. *The cynical murder of student Rachel McLean by her boyfriend John Tanner appeared the more awful by his televised pleas for information on her whereabouts and his enthusiastic participation in the reconstruction of her last known movements.*

In April 1991, nineteen-year-old student Rachel McLean disappeared from her lodgings in Oxford. Young, intelligent, attractive, she was destined for the same extravagant media attention as Suzy Lamplugh had been five years previously (see 1986). From Rachel's flatmates police learned that her steady boyfriend was John Tanner, like herself a student, originally from New Zealand. Over the succeeding days Tanner was interviewed by detectives and gave his account of the last time he saw Rachel. It had been on the evening of Monday 15 April.

Rachel McLean with John Tanner (Rex Features)

They had spent the weekend together at Rachel's flat in Argyle Road, and she had gone to see Tanner off at Oxford railway station. While they sat in the buffet waiting for John's train, a friend of Rachel's came up to them, chatted, and offered Rachel a lift home when she had said her goodbyes. Tanner's description of the man was later turned into an Identikit likeness – long dark brown hair, clean shaven, aged between eighteen and 22, five feet eleven inches tall, and 'scruffily dressed' in a bomber jacket, faded blue jeans and baseball boots. Nevertheless, apart from prompting some people to remark that the person it most resembled was John Tanner himself, the face staring out from every newspaper and television screen in the country jogged no memories. On 29 April a reconstruction of the farewell was enacted on Oxford station with a policewoman posing as Rachel, a student as her friend, and Tanner enthusiastically playing himself. Prior to the reconstruction, Tanner had appeared at a press conference, calm but concerned, with the hint of a sob in his voice, speaking of his conviction that Rachel was still alive somewhere: 'I would appeal to anyone who knows where she is . . . to come forward and tell us, out of consideration to her mother and father and to myself.'

Although thorough searches had already been made at the house in Argyle Road, it was not until the evening of 2 May that, with the help of architectural plans, police officers began to strip down any cavity in the building which might conceal a body. Rachel's remains were found beneath loose floorboards in a recessed ground-floor cupboard under the stairs. Within hours of the discovery, John Tanner was arrested in a public house near his home in Nottingham. It was not until the following December that Tanner appeared at Birmingham Crown Court charged with murder; he pleaded not guilty to murder but admitted manslaughter. He had, according to his own defence, become involved in a quarrel with Rachel when she confessed to being unfaithful and wanting to leave him. As the row escalated he lost all control and found himself strangling her. After concealing Rachel's body he returned home and later concocted the story of the long-

Identikit picture of Rachel's supposed 'friend', based on Tanner's description; it looks uncannily like John Tanner himself (inset) (Topham)

haired stranger at the station. As he sat alone on Oxford station that Monday, he wrote a letter to Rachel as part of his elaborate and cynical sham; he thanked her for the wonderful weekend, and signed 'your devoted John'.

After a retirement of four and a half hours, the jury returned a majority verdict 10–2 of guilty of murder. John Tanner is currently serving a life sentence.

1992

Aileen Wuornos, 'The Damsel of Death'

Highway prostitute Aileen 'Lee' Wuornos, a confirmed man-hater and recent lesbian, killed and robbed seven of her clients. According to the FBI Lee Wuornos is the first of a new breed of female serial killer.

Since the end of 1989, the Florida State Police had been taxed by a series of unsolved murders around Marion County which looked as though they followed a pattern. All the victims had been white males, middle-aged or older, and all had been shot dead with a .22-calibre handgun; some of them were found naked. When the victims had been identified it was further learned that they had all been travelling alone by road along one or other of Florida's Interstates, and the stolen cars had later been found abandoned. Twelve months later, the Marion County Sheriff's Office task-force investigating the deaths were convinced that a serial killer was stalking the highways – not difficult to believe in view of the fact that an estimated 100 serial killers are at large in the United States at any given time. What was unusual in this case was that it was beginning to look as

though the murderer was a woman. This was consistent with the fact that some of the victims were naked, and that their cars were found with condoms on the floor and long blonde hairs on the upholstery. It would also account for how the killer could get so close to the victim without arousing suspicion. The most probable explanation was that their suspect was a prostitute working from the roadside.

The first victim grouped with the series was 51-year-old Richard Mallory. His badly decomposed body was found in some woods in December 1989; he had been repeatedly shot with a small-calibre gun. Over the first few months of the new year five more bodies were found in similar circumstances. Finally, in June 1990, a 65-year-old missionary named Peter Siems left his home in Jupiter, Florida, bound for Arkansas along the Interstate 95 coast road through Daytona Beach; he never saw either his home or Arkansas again. Indeed, Siems's bodily remains have never been located. However, on 4 July his grey Pontiac Sunbird was involved in an accident at Orange Springs. Witnesses running to the scene were just in time to see the two female occupants of the car flee from the wreck and disappear over the fields; from their descriptions police artists were able to compile a pair of likenesses which were broadcast nationwide. It was not long before detectives came up with the names of Tyria J. Moore, a 27-year-old sometime hotel maid, and her lesbian lover Aileen 'Lee' Wuornos (alias Camie Greene, Lori Grody and Susan Blahovec). With co-operation from Ty Moore, who was to turn state's evidence, undercover officers were able to stake out the bars and clubs around the Daytona Beach area, hoping to get a sighting of Aileen Wuornos. At a seedy, single-storey brick shack which called itself the Last Resort, they got lucky.

Aileen Wuornos had been born in Detroit, Michigan, in 1956; when she was six weeks old her teenage mother deserted Aileen, her brother and a psychopathically violent father who regularly beat his wife and anybody else who happened to be in his way. Aileen and Keith found themselves abandoned to the care of an elderly, well-meaning grandmother and a brutal, alcholic grandfather, whose ill-treatment of the children, according to Aileen, made their every day a living nightmare. By the age of twelve, Aileen had already succumbed to the family weakness for alcohol; at thirteen she was pregnant, and supplementing the booze with drugs. After her baby had been given away for adoption, Aileen dropped out of school in tenth grade and began to sell her favours on the streets in order to finance a growing habit. Over the coming years, she would work her way through a succession of dead-end jobs. As she hitched around America, Aileen claims to have been raped more than a dozen times, and beaten more often than she can remember. It was in 1976, when she was twenty, that Aileen arrived at Daytona Beach, Florida. She formed a succession of unsatisfactory relationships with men and after one particularly acrimonious separation she tried to commit suicide by shooting herself in the stomach. It was just the first of several unsuccessful attempts over the years.

Aileen met Tyria Moore in 1986, in a bar called the Zodiac. In the beginning, at least, a close and intense affection existed between the two women – though by all accounts heavy drinking resulted in frequent bitter arguments. If we can believe Aileen's subsequent stories, she was utterly devastated by Ty's desertion, and for her it marked the end of her world. Throughout their love affair Aileen continued as a highway hooker – but the strain was beginning to unhinge her already unstable mind. Although Aileen claimed to have up to a dozen clients a day, there were some who wouldn't pay, and some who would beat her up, just for the heck of it. If she hadn't already hated the

whole of the male gender, she certainly did now. In 1989 she picked up a .22 revolver – an equaliser. Shortly after this the killing spree began.

The trial of Aileen Wuornos, by now dubbed the 'Damsel of Death', opened at Deland, Florida, on 12 January 1992. Although she had made a videotape confession to seven killings, there was only one charge on the indictment – the first-degree murder of Richard Mallory, her first victim. According to State Prosecutor John Tanner, Aileen had been plying her trade when she was picked up by Mallory at an overpass near Tampa. They drove along Interstate 4 to Daytona Beach, where Mallory pulled the car off the road into some woodland where they had sex before Aileen shot Mallory dead and hid his body. This much she was prepared to admit. But she insisted that the killing was self-defence. In Aileen's version of things, Mallory had tied her to the steering wheel of the car, raped and sodomised her, and threatened to kill her if she kept struggling. She just managed to pull her gun from her purse as Mallory, so she said, lunged forward at her. Through her attorney Aileen protested that Mallory was drunk and had been smoking marijuana. 'What happened was bondage, rape, sodomy and degradation.' What's more, she was convinced that Mallory wasn't going to pay her.

It was a defence that attracted ridicule from the prosecution: 'She was a predatory prostitute,' John Tanner told the court. 'She killed out of greed – no longer satisfied with the ten, twenty, thirty dollars, she wanted it all. It wasn't enough to control his body, she wanted the ultimate – his car, his property, his life.'

Giving evidence against her former lover, Tyria Moore said that on the evening of 30 November, Aileen had come home a little the worse for drink, driving a new car. Later Aileen announced she had just killed a man. Moore said: 'I didn't believe her.' Cross-examined, Ty Moore was adamant that her partner made no mention of being raped or beaten, nor seemed particularly upset about anything. Tanner's implication was clear: here was a cold-blooded, emotionless killer who, far from suffering the trauma of 'rape, sodomy and degradation', had simply shot one of her clients for his car and the contents of his wallet.

It was clearly the explanation favoured by the jury who, on 27 January after a 95-minute retirement, found Aileen Wuornos guilty as charged. As she was led from the dock, Wuornos turned on the jury, screaming 'Scumbags of America!' before being hustled out. Two days later, acting on the jury's recommendation, Judge Blount sentenced Aileen Wuornos to death. In May 1992, Wuornos was tried and convicted of three more of her seven admitted killings. After Judge Thomas Sawaya sentenced Wuornos to death she yelled: 'Thank you, I'll go to heaven now, and you will rot in hell.'

RUSSIA

Andrei Chikatilo, 'The Rostov Ripper'

In April 1992, news reached the West via the news agencies that in the southern Russian port of Rostov a 56-year-old grandfather and former schoolteacher was about to stand trial accused of torturing, butchering and cannibalising no fewer than 53 victims, many of them children, and some, it was said, his own pupils. Andrei Chikatilo insists he has claimed at least two more victims, though so far no tangible evidence had been found to support legal charges. One fact is certain: Chikatilo has earned his place as one of the most brutal and prolific multiple killers in the criminal history of the world.

Andrei Romanovich Chikatilo was born in 1936, in the shadow of the Stalinist purges, in the town of Novocherkassk, north of Rostov on the southeastern corner of what was the USSR. Although his youth was reportedly disturbed by feelings of inadequacy, particularly in the company of women, Chikatilo was bright enough to earn a good degree in Russian litera-

ture from the University at Rostov. He remained a studious and rather serious young man throughout his military service, usually preferring books to bars. In 1966, when he was 28 years old, Andrei Chikatilo married, and shortly afterwards fathered a son and, in quick succession, a daughter. The marriage was to all recollection a happy one, and in his spare time Andrei became not only an active member of the Communist Party, but was elevated to chairman of his regional sports committee.

It was probably around 1975, during the early months of Chikatilo's post as lecturer in Russian literature at the nearby school of Novo Shatinsk, that his sexual envy and frustration became uncontrollable; perhaps it was, as one journalist suggested, being surrounded by eager young women experimenting for the first time with new adolescent emotions, but for whom he could never be more than a schoolmaster. Shortly afterwards, Rostov would be thrown into a twelve-year reign of terror by an unknown assassin whose young victims had been subjected to unspeakable torture and mutilation before death, and against whom the police seemed utterly powerless.

The first victim, a teenaged girl, was found dead in a wood in 1978. The horror of the crime was avenged with swiftness and finality when a known child molester was successively arrested, tried, convicted and executed for the killing. The police were still slapping each other on the back when the next bodies were found. The wrong man had faced the firing squad.

Over the succeeding years the list of those who disappeared grew longer, the discovery of mutilated remains punctuated the normally quiet life around the port with increasing regularity; in one year alone there were eight deaths in a single month. The killer's approach was always the same. With the uncanny sixth sense of the natural predator, he could pick out the weak and vulnerable on the edges of society's groups. Trawling the streets and railway stations for the homeless drifters who were unlikely to be missed, he singled out the solitary child on his way to school. Years later the monster who had become known as the 'Rostov Ripper' would himself explain: 'As soon as I saw a lonely person I felt I had to drag them off to the woods. I paid no attention to age or sex. We would walk for a couple of miles or so, then I would be possessed by an awful shaking sensation.' The savagery of the attacks have rarely been matched in the history of violent crime. First the killer cut out the victims' tongues to ensure they did not cry out; then he gouged out the eyes and spiked through the eardrums. While the mute and struggling bodies were still alive, the 'Ripper' carried out his surgical operations, sometimes raping, always hacking at the genitals with his knife and cannibalising the flesh. The awful remains were buried where they lay, in the woods alongside the railroad tracks, a characteristic that earned the monster his second nickname, 'The Forest Strip Killer'.

Despite an extensive manhunt that stretched from Rostov to Siberia and was led by experienced detectives seconded from Moscow, the police still seemed helpless in the face of a catalogue of carnage. It had spread to the neighbouring states of Ukraine and Uzbekistan when schoolmaster Chikatilo changed his job to become head of supplies at the Rostov locomotive repair shop, a post which enabled him to travel all over the south of the USSR. But if anybody had even hinted that the quiet, kindly ex-teacher with his white hair and thick spectacles was the Rostov Ripper the whole of Novocherkassk would have laughed out loud – the very thought was absurd.

On one occasion the police did arrest a suspect; he committed suicide while in prison awaiting his trial. And still the death toll rose.

In 1979 another man had been picked up in an isolated wooded area, but persuaded the police that he was simply an innocent hiker; after taking his name and particulars he was allowed to wander on his way. Five years later the same man was picked up close to the scene of one of the murders and this time was found to be carrying a length of rope and a knife in his briefcase. When he was subjected to a blood test and it was proved by the laboratory that the man's blood group differed from that of the semen samples recovered from the bodies of some of the victims, the suspect was immediately released. His name was Andrei Romanovich Chikatilo.

What the Russian police, with their rather primitive grasp of forensic procedures, did not learn until many years and many murders later is that in extremely rare cases secretions from different sources in the body can have different serological groupings. Andrei Chikatilo is one of those rare cases.

Early in 1990 the police investigation team, still no nearer to stopping the Ripper's reign of terror, co-opted the expertise of psychiatrist Alexander Bukhanovsky who, using relevant data contained in the case files on each of the murders, and relating it to his experience of human behaviour patterns and predictability, built a psychological profile of the Rostov Ripper which proved to be remarkably accurate. The fact that initially so many murders had been committed in such a restricted geographical location indicated a fundamental requirement of the home-based serial killer – social respectability. The killer needed to be known as a loving family man, a trusted employee, co-operative neighbour, loyal friend, and so on: the kind of man of whom nobody could believe ill.

The killer had been able to approach and lure children, many of whom might have been expected to view an elderly stranger with mistrust, even fear, into the woods. The fact that there were never any consistent reports of misconduct against an individual suggested to Bukhanovsky that his suspect might be a schoolteacher, a person used to putting children at their ease and feeling at ease with them, a person capable of generating trust. The savage nature of the mutilation and the areas of the body chosen for it were consistent with a violent repressed sexuality and a resentment of other people's physical sexuality.

It was in November 1990 that the net began to close around the Rostov Ripper, the Forest Strip Killer. On 6 November a police officer routinely stopped Andrei Chikatilo in the street, reportedly after spotting a bloodstain on his face. When shortly afterwards another body was found in the woods the officer reported the incident of the bloodstain to his superiors, and Chikatilo was put under heavy surveillance. On 20 November police saw Chikatilo approach a young boy at a railway station; he was immediately taken into custody, where under questioning he readily confessed to an unbelievable 55 brutal murders, though, as Chikatilo is the first to admit, 'there may be more'.

To sophisticated Western eyes, the trial of Andrei Chikatilo presented a spectacle almost as bizarre as his crimes were dreadful. The process took place in Rostov's own very unceremonial court. Chikatilo was tried by a chairman – a professional judge named Leonid Akubzhanov – and two 'people's representatives', who have no legal qualification at all; there was no jury.

In the centre of the threadbare court a huge iron-barred cage had been built around the dock. Inside sat the prisoner, chained liked a wild beast. Around the cage were the baying crowds of his victims' families, screaming for his blood, demanding that the Ripper be handed over to the mob for the dispensation of instant 'justice'. There were to be many occasions during the trial when the first-aid team on duty were called upon to revive spectators faint from overtaxed emotions.

As the trial opened on 14 April 1992, it took two hours to quieten the crowd sufficiently to read the two-volume document listing the charges against Chikatilo; they consisted of 35 child victims – eleven of them boys – and eighteen young women. In all it was anticipated that scores of witnesses and upwards of 200 documents would be brought as evidence to support the charges. Although he had previously been described as a quiet, retiring family man, Andrei Chikatilo sat in the cage now with his shaven head lolling rhythmically from side to side, and with wild, rolling eyes. He inflamed the court into further outrage by holding up pages of photographs of naked women torn from pornographic magazines and jeering back at the crowd. If he was not mad before, he was certainly giving an impressive performance as a madman now.

Not surprisingly, Andrei Chikatilo has been subjected to extensive psychiatric evaluation since his eventual arrest late in 1990. Although it is clear that he falls broadly into the category of serial 'lust' killers – that is, his motivation to kill is determined by his need for sexual gratification – his basic requirement for sex has been interwoven with other, far deeper fantasies. According to the published theories of psychiatrist Alexander Bukhanovsky, it is likely that his patient's deep sense of his own worthlessness originated in the arrest of his father on political charges during the Stalinist regime. The grievance that he nurtured against the world for this injustice triggered his self-protective delusions of grandeur, the pivot of which was his fantasy of being able to dominate women. In reality Chikatilo's sexual inadequacies soon gave lie to the delusions, and it became clear that he could only ever exert domination by exercising the power of life and death over his victims. As to the cannibalism, Dr Bukhanovsky says Chikatilo refers constantly to an episode during a famine in the 1930s – as yet unconfirmed – when a group of starving peasants killed and ate his brother.

Towards the end of the first week of his trial, Andrei Chikatilo insisted on addressing the court, and in addition to confirming once again his guilt, he gave the court a self-pitying account of the early privations of his home life and of his 'dreadful' childhood. He also referred again to the eating of his brother by hungry Ukrainian peasants who, he claimed, had been deprived of food as a result of Stalin's collectivisation of private farmland. Chikatilo concluded his speech: 'I am a freak of nature, a mad beast.'

There was never any likelihood of Andrei Chikatilo being found not guilty of the crimes with which he was charged – after all, he not only confessed in detail, but he led police searchers to forest locations where many of his victims still lay buried. What is in dispute is his sanity, and therefore his culpability. If, as the prosecutor claims, Chikatilo was sane at the time of his killings, then he faces death in front of a firing squad. On 15 October 1992, the three judges decided: 'The court cannot but sentence this man to what he deserves for his terrible crimes – that is, to death.'

At present, Audrei Chikatilo awaits execution in the squalid surroundings of Cell 33 in Novocherkassk Prison.

Alphabetical Index of Cases